PICTURES

FROM

THE HEART

✳

PICTURES
FROM
THE HEART

A TAROT DICTIONARY

✳

Sandra A. Thomson

ST. MARTIN'S GRIFFIN
NEW YORK

www.stmartins.com

Design by Kathryn Parise

LIBRARY OF CONGRESS CATALOGING-IN-PUBLICATION DATA
Thomson, Sandra A.
    Pictures from the heart : a tarot dictionary / Sandra A. Thomson.
      p.   cm.
    Includes Bibliographical references (pp. 459–466).
    ISBN 0-312-29128-0
    1. Tarot.   2. Tarot—Dictionaries.   I. Title.

BF1879.T2T52   2003
133.3'2424—dc21

2003041412

10 9 8 7 6 5 4 3

To Robert, my life partner,
who first set my feet on the tarot path.

To Mary K. Greer, my beloved teacher,
whose innovative approaches keep me
skipping with joy along that path.

To Arielle Smith, my blessed mentor and "shadow sis."
Her influence sends me down more meaningful
detours than I ever imagined.

CONTENTS

✳

ACKNOWLEDGMENTS

✳

The tarot field is filled with wonderful people, eager to offer their assistance to each other, and to share their knowledge. I'm certain that each of us contributes to another's work by our own working and writing; however, some people deserve special mention for making the extra effort on my behalf.

Endless thanks to Mary K. Greer, for reading and correcting far more entries than she likely ever expected.

Thanks to James Revak and his careful historical efforts on behalf of us all, and for reading and correcting the historical entries here. Appreciation to Art Rosengarten, for allowing me to present, pretty much intact, his material on the five-card "future direction" spread.

Eternal gratitude to Elizabeth M. Hazel, the talented astrological tarotist who untiringly wrote, and rewrote, the astrological entries.

Valerie Sim-Behi, always delightful, interrupted her limited time to offer insights on all entries referring to comparative tarot. Her Internet list put me in touch with a number of helpful experts I would not otherwise have found, and inspired me to expand my thinking about the cards.

John Gilbert, former executive director of the American Tarot Association, graciously gave me permission to use information from many of the association's materials, and did his own share of updating entries.

Lynne Luerding struggled with me to correct my understanding of her unique way of reading the directions in which court cards faced.

My apologies to all for the ruthless editing required to remain within my word count. All errors that occurred as a result are mine.

Special thanks to Barbara Rapp, co-owner of the Crystal Cave bookstore in Costa Mesa and founder of Los Angeles Tarot Symposium, for bringing the Southern California tarot community together and for giving me a forum in which to express my ideas.

My appreciation to the Philosophical Research Society, especially Jeannie Harris and Steven Konstantine, ever helpful in encouraging Robert and me to hone and teach our ideas in classes for them.

Love to my wonderful agent, Bob Silverstein, who makes all things tarot possible. Thanks to my editor at St. Martin's, Keith Kahla, who liked what he saw and kept my ideas pretty much intact.

PART ONE

Power Tarot

1

＊

Flashcards of the Self

You've seen it happen in movies or read it in mystery novels. The hero, seldom the villain, happens upon a tarot reader who draws a card and it is—what else—the Death card. Gasp, sigh. You, yourself, might have easily predicted that would be the single tarot card to turn up, especially in a mystery. And, until recent television advertisements, that one card-turning action was likely the only thing that many people knew about tarot readings— turn over a card and its name or title tells you all you need to know to foresee the future. That cliché of a plot twist has misled millions of viewers and readers into thinking they've experienced the essence of the tarot.

Recently, television commercials promoting tarot readers assure gullible listeners there is another "essence" to tarot, namely that the cards can tell them whether or not they are pregnant, who is the father of their child, and the answer to many other of life's mysteries. In Los Angeles, where I live, little shops located every few miles along major boulevards light their otherwise unimaginative decor with brilliant purple neon signs declaring "Fortune Telling. Tarot. Palm Reading."

So, it's little wonder that if you tell people you read tarot cards, they may indicate either that they've never heard of them or, with a knowing nod or wink, will ask you to predict their future. After all, they've seen how it's done on television.

Even publishers of decks subtly promote the fortune-telling idea with the little white booklets (LWBs) that accompany their decks, that list a string of words or phrases ("misery," "voyage," "contentment") for each card. One well-known California tarot expert demonstrates the insignificance of these booklets by opening a brand-new deck at each of her presentations and throwing the LWB over her shoulder. As newcomers gasp, long-time tarot readers nod knowingly.

The American Tarot Association runs a Free Tarot Network where readers can get a free one-card reading and a Free Reading Network, providing three-card readings. What are the two most popular questions? Those that have something to do with romance (Does Mikey love me? Will Mikey marry me? Is Sharon my true love?), and those that either request winning Lotto numbers or want to know whether or not the questioner will win the Lotto and, if you please, when.

If you are an experienced tarot reader, you already know that these are not questions the tarot answers well and, if you are a beginning reader, now is the time to learn. One of the major jobs those of us who read for the networks have is to educate people about the kinds of information the tarot can give.

For the last decade there has been a movement afoot—or should I say, at hand?—which well-known tarot authorities Mary K. Greer and Rachel Pollack call the Tarot Renaissance.[1] It incorporates the idea that tarot readings can form a new basis for stimulating self-awareness, personal growth, and inner transformation. This approach has become so popular among tarot devotees that it is rapidly replacing the idea of the tarot as a fortune-telling device, except in those ubiquitous novels, television commercials, and desolate storefront tarot parlors bereft of any capacity to kindle an inner flame.

Contemporary users of the cards (called "readers") realize that tarot readings correspond to, and express, the ongoing progress and needs of our own daily lives. They act as a map of our personal lives, both exterior (the mask) and interior (the psyche).

Someone—I think it was the famed American journalist, columnist, and sociologist Walter Lippmann—wrote that the greatness of Charles de Gaulle was not that he was in France, but that France was within him. Paraphrasing Lippmann, it's not so much that we can find ourselves in the tarot—and certainly we can easily enough—no, the greatness of the tarot lies in the fact that the tarot is within us, card by card, stimulating and expressing aspects of our life journeys if we care to access them.

To understand how that can be, we need to look at both the basics of the tarot and its relationship to archetypes.

The Mysteries

The tarot deck consists of seventy-eight cards, divided into a group of twenty-two cards called the Major Arcana (arcana means mysterious knowledge) and fifty-six cards called the Minor Arcana. The Major Arcana is further subdivided into sequentially numbered cards, starting with a card numbered zero—usually placed at the beginning, sometimes at the end, of the other Major Arcana cards and typically called The Fool—plus twenty-one additional cards called Trumps.

The fifty-six Minor Arcana cards—called simply suit cards in older decks—are divided into four suits: wands (also called batons, rods, scepters, staffs, or staves), swords, cups (chalices), and pentacles (coins, disks). Each suit has fourteen cards numbered from aces (ones) to tens, plus four court cards, often called the page (sometimes princess), knight (sometimes prince), queen, and king.

Contemporary-themed decks may contain additional cards or attach different names to cards to more fully carry out their theme. Caitlín and John Matthews's Arthurian Tarot identifies the zero fool card as "The Seeker" and the first Major Arcana card (The Magician) as "Merlin." Subsequent Major Arcana cards are also renamed to fit the Arthurian legend.

Until the twentieth century, Minor Arcana cards showed only designs (called "pips") for the ace to ten cards, that is, the Ten of Coins simply showed ten coins on the card. Cards designed for use by members of the Hermetic Order of the Golden Dawn, a nineteenth-century occult order, added a divinatory name to each of the Minor Arcana cards, such as Lord of Great Strength (Nine of Wands) or Lord of Abundance (Three of Cups). Then, in 1909, Arthur E. Waite, a Golden Dawn member, created a deck and commissioned the visionary artist Pamela Colman Smith, also a Golden Dawn member, to paint it. Her innovative inspiration was to fully illustrate scenes for each of the Minor Arcana cards. A new model for the construction of future decks was born, and it became a fantastically popular idea.

THE COLLISION OF MYTH AND REALITY

Imagine yourself sitting around the campfire at tarot camp, listening to your tarot counselor tell stories. She begins, "Once upon a time there were a group of people known as Gypsies." Here she smiles knowingly and adds, "because they came from ancient Egypt.

"When they did," she continues, "they brought with them ancient mysterious knowledge printed as tarot cards, yet disguised as fortune-telling cards. These were later transformed into bridge or gaming cards."

You've heard this story from other counselors in other years. You and the story are good friends. You smile and nod as you listen because its familiarity makes you feel so comfortable that you are certain it is true. Unfortunately, nothing could be further from the truth, and the next day your tarot counselor is fired.

The group of people commonly called Gypsies have never used that name for themselves—they call themselves the Romany, or Roma—and they and their culture did not originate in Egypt. Further, thanks to a dedicated group of tarot historians who operate as an Internet group known as TarotL, we know that tarot decks were first used regularly throughout Europe in the early fifteenth century and then only as gaming cards, seldom as fortune-telling devices, and never as personal empowerment tools.[2]

Playing cards, used in the late fourteenth century, preceded tarot cards. At that time the ruling family of Milan, the Visconti family, commissioned two decks of lavish hand-painted cards. The first, known today as the Cary-Yale tarocchi deck, had a background of gold leaf and featured twenty-two images known as the triumphs, *trionfi*. Later, the family commissioned a second deck, known today as the Visconti-Sforza deck, likely to commemorate the marriage of Bianca, illegitimate daughter of Duke Filippo Visconti, and Francesco Sforza. Both the cards and the game they inspired were called *tarocchi*.[3]

In the eighteenth century, Court de Gébelin and le Comte de Mellet introduced the tarot to the public as the work of the Egyptians (see their entries in the dictionary section). Counteracting that myth has been an uphill battle ever since. It was furthered by nineteenth-century French occultists and members of the aforementioned English organization, the Hermetic Order of the Golden Dawn. At this time, members of the French and British groups alike began creating their own decks, and associating the meanings and origins of the cards with secret ideas and artistic symbolism, Hebrew letters, Kabbalistic concepts, astrological connections, and other "divinatory" systems (see various entries in the dictionary section).

The "myth" of tarot is heavily intertwined with fanciful ideas, some quite erroneous. No matter how compelling or inaccurate they are, they have also led us to understand that attending to various symbolic expressions associated with tarot cards, whatever the deck, can stimulate us to delve deeper into understanding ourselves, as symbolism has always been meant to do.

THE SYMBOLIC QUEST

Dictionaries tell us that symbolism is a way of expressing the invisible. It is an artistic method for revealing or suggesting otherwise intangible truths or states, and a way of representing divine beings and spirits. The artistic or storytelling expression of symbols serves to evoke emotions within and, thereby, to provoke us to more fully consider who we are.

The well-known Swiss analyst C. G. Jung spent a lifetime studying our human ability to understand certain emotions, ideas, and motifs (storylines) through symbols. He borrowed a medieval term for "idea" and called those symbolic ideas "archetypes" (first patterns). Jung believed they were "memory deposits"—innate predispositions—derived by condensing innumerable similar, natural tendencies of the human race. He called this totality the "collective unconscious." By this he meant that at the most basic level, humans everywhere share certain instinctual patterns—often referred to as psychic energy, primal forms, myth-building structures—which we transform into images and symbolic models. When these come into individual consciousness, they always are expressed as *images*, since archetypes themselves are formless.

Psychologist Jean Houston calls archetypes the "organs of Essence," the "gossamer bridge" that joins spirit with nature and "self with the metabody of the universe."[4] Archetypal images, as images always have done, serve to help us confront the unknown, without and within. They give our lives a sense of meaning and authenticity.[5]

Archetypes and their images are the primary life-motivating agents in our individual psyches, and the overall psychological patterns shared by all cultures. And we have twenty-two of them in the Major Arcana of the tarot deck.

For Jung, the value of an archetype was not that we could, or should, identify each one as a specific image acting within, but rather that we could use it as a springboard for a process he called amplification. If we use an image as the stimulus to connect associated images, thereby touching its multiplicity within our own being, we expand our knowledge of the many facets of our character. Archetypes prevent us from having too limited and literal a notion of ourselves. Attending to archetypal images and associations helps us to enhance our inner perspective, and especially to awaken to unrealized possibilities.[6]

In addition to artistic renderings, another of the most prevalent symbolic ways that archetypal concepts are presented is through myths and fairy tales. Although we have a tendency to think of myths as depicting "ancient" fantasies, their characters were, in fact, expressions of archetypal human situations, themes, and concerns that still exist today in our psyches.

Clothed in different costumes, those concepts continue to shape current movies and television shows. Consider, for example, the "redeemer-hero" archetype, who typically appears modest at some level yet by his struggles or battles with various types of "monsters" or villains saves a maiden in distress or, better yet, an entire kingdom. Ever heard the story or seen it dramatized? Think Jack of beanstalk fame, who saves his poor, starving mother and redeems himself from his earlier silly mistake of using all their food money to buy "useless" beans.

Think Superman or Batman. We all know how well they save maidens in distress and their respective cities from evil exploiters. Would poor Gotham City still exist without the constant efforts

9

of Batman? Thanks to James Bond, both women and England—and sometimes the world—remain safe. As for Luke Skywalker from the *Star Wars* sagas, who can do better than rescuing the princess and saving the entire universe at the same time?

The popular 1999 movie *The Sixth Sense* even presented the story of a child hero who bravely undertakes to face the demons that haunt him.[7] No matter whether it is the hero of the latest movie, legal thriller, or detective novel, the "redeemer-hero" still actively exists in our consciousness.

This archetypal story is not likely to ever disappear since rescues and the righting of wrongs reassure us that we are not doomed. It reflects the notion that there is hope, that we "lesser heroes"—Joseph Campbell referred to us collectively as *The Hero with a Thousand Faces*—can find our way in our individual journeys through our own complicated, convoluted world.

The point of all this is that like those heroes, all of the cards of the tarot deck represent expressions of ourselves, or experiences along our own heroic archetypal journeys.

If we choose to understand them that way, tarot cards are like signposts of interior messages, "flashcards of the Self." The late Jungian analyst Marie-Louise von Franz wrote that when we use a "divination" device, such as the tarot, we are really attempting to contact, at that given moment, the rhythm of the Self, our core regulating archetype, sometimes perceived as the soul.[8] If we fail to relate to, or connect with, our archetypal dimension, says Jungian analyst Edward Whitmont, the result is spiritual impoverishment and a sense of meaninglessness in life.[9]

Tarot cards, especially the Major Arcana cards, represent active archetypal forces and principles in the universe and in the lives of each of us. Rachel Pollack calls them seventy-eight images that are gateways to the imageless.[10] Our work with them, if done properly, constitutes an attempt to contact what Canadian analyst and author Marion Woodman regards as "the God within."

Tarot cards and layouts are, indeed, gateways into the rhythm of that higher dimension—certainly not because they predict the future, but because when understood in depth, they offer a new opportunity to review aspects of our past and present lives and to make subsequent decisions with meaningful new awareness. They can open us to the hidden or deeper spirituality of our psyches.

The information in this book allows you, the reader, to have a more complete understanding of the symbols on the cards and of each card itself. It allows you to partake of your own inner adventure, to live your life through an awareness lens. Studying the cards "nudges" you to be open to the variety of possibilities that exist for understanding any one tarot card with respect to your own life. In that understanding, the cards empower you to consider new ideas and possibilities. By giving in-depth credence to the "inner world" of tarot symbols, you have the chance to affect your own inner and outer worlds, to bring about growth and change, to enhance your creativity. This is the difference between using the cards to "tell" the future and using them to stimulate and assimilate future choices and experiences.

We are not called "human stagnates." We are called human *beings*, persons in process, persons involved in the act and art of actually shaping or reshaping ourselves, or working to understand what Frank Barron calls the "patterns within diversity."[11] At whatever age, but especially as we grow older, it may be that one of the most important tasks we can undertake is what psychotherapist Mary Baird Carlsen calls "meaning-making"— taking what we have experienced and arranging the symbols to make sense of who and what we are.[12] Marie-Louise von Franz said, "The only worthwhile adventure for the people of today is the adventure within."[13] Little can provoke our sense of that adventure more than an understanding of how the tarot cards apply to each of our lives.

2

*

Delving the Depths
of the Tarot

A tarot reading acts as a threshold into understanding life processes. It offers new opportunities to review aspects of our life story and to make subsequent decisions. Our response to a reading can act as a tool to help us attain closure on unpleasant past or present situations. It can help us sort out confused ideas, honor and maintain past memories, or spur us on to create new ones. If we respond to the cards not as visions of the future but as springboards into our greater story—as portals to understanding how we make sense of ourselves—we may begin to ascertain how we weave the fabric of our lives.

"Reading" the cards is an active process that draws us ever deeper into personal understanding. Archetypal psychologists sometimes speak of images as a "telling of the soul"[1] and learning to listen to the voice of the tarot cards is one way to listen to that "telling."

In addition to understanding basic meanings of tarot cards, moving into the depth of their messages involves recognizing and connecting with—decoding—the various kinds of symbols associated with each card. Symbolism is one of the most ancient and fundamental methods of artistic expression. It can be specific to a given culture, or its many subgroups. It can be timeless, in that certain symbols have suggested the same thing for centuries. Typically, symbols simultaneously embody more than one level of meaning. The emblems of a divinity may represent that particular divinity, the greater cosmos, and some part of cosmic laws and functions.

Combining certain parts of a representation into the whole can symbolize an ongoing process, or active principle. A tree can symbolize a person, and its roots reflect that person's grounding and depth (or lack of it with shallow roots), or a family connection. The trunk can symbolize growth, the person's backbone, and stability (or a twisted life). Leaves can represent fruitfulness, budding creation, spreading one's influence, or cycles (if a deciduous tree). At the same time, the tree can also represent all of humankind or, depending on what is happening around the tree, celestial or other influences.

LEARNING TO LISTEN TO THE TELLING

The most basic and limited understanding of a card occurs in the meaning given for it in the pamphlet that comes with the deck. Often derisively called the "little white book" (LWB) or "little white pamphlet" (LWP). It is usually brief, giving five or six meanings for each card upright and about the same number for the reversed card. Unfortunately, most of these terms have to do with prediction since the publishers know that this is frequently the reason many people buy their first tarot deck. LWBs are of little or no use for more intense "listening." Soon, serious readers find that they need more information and seek books written about their particular deck, especially if they offer some insight into the symbology of the cards' designs.

I Am Everyone and Everything

Another way to deepen our *personal* understanding of a card is to speak as the card by changing its description into "I" statements. Using a technique for dream interpretation, assume you are every person and object in the card and have each of them speak to you in dialogue. This technique works best when trying to discern the personal meanings of a card at work in your own life.

I am indebted to Mary K. Greer for teaching me that a quicker way to get at a personal understanding of a card, especially when reading for someone else, is simply to have the person describe what's happening. For instance, two different people looking at the Strength card might say:

PERSON A: Here is a woman so close to nature and so innocent that she easily interacts with the lion, which is licking her wrist. I read somewhere that the lion Aslan in C. S. Lewis's *The Chronicles of Narnia* represented God. The girl is dressed in white for purity, so we have the eternal interaction between the male and female aspects of the God nature. Well, the card is titled Strength, so I guess it represents Universal Strength.

PERSON B: This woman looks innocent enough—look at those flowers in her hair—and the lion has fallen for it. She will subdue him—look how her hands are closing his jaws—and then she will render him powerless. He will be subservient to her forever, as the eternity sign above her head shows. She's like my wife, sweet and innocent on the surface, but watch out or you're a goner.

Obviously this card represents quite different things to these two people, which certainly will influence the meanings of the cards near it in the layout and, likely, the understanding of the entire layout.

READ MY NUMBERS

Many tarotists attach symbolic importance to a card's number. Numbers past nine in the tarot deck can be reduced to their lowest number ($19 = 1 + 9 = 10 = 1 + 0 = 1$) and connected to other numbers in the deck possessing the same value. Numbers express archetypal symbology and also have personal meanings, depending on whether you feel positive or negative about them ("I hate four because when I was four . . ."), and what your culture and its subgroups teach.

COLOR ME TAROT

Colors, too, have their own symbolism, both general (derived from historical repetition) and personal (through our own reactions to them). The violet robe of the angel on the Rider-Waite-Smith Lovers card refers to truth and healing. Its red wings and flaming hair, and the flames on the Tree of Life behind the male figure, refer to the fire element and all that it stands for (strength, will, courage, and also sensuality, desire, passion). Yet, someone looking at the card may have a strong aversion to either violet or red because of its association with past negative experiences. Naturally this will "color" the reaction to both the card and the objects in the card. It is just as likely, however, that a favorite violet blouse or shirt may foster the conclusion that the angel is really feeling good and benevolent.

It's in the Stars

Many tarotists connect astrological signs and their meanings or attributes to the cards and these differ considerably.

Early tarot developers related the twenty-two keys of the Major Arcana to well-known astrological images and meanings and thus connected some of the meanings and techniques of astrology into use with the tarot. The earliest system of astrological attributions was documented by Etteilla in the 1780s. Subsequent zodiac attribution sets were created for the Falconnier Tarot and others. A popular European or "continental" set of attributions was developed for the Tarot de Marseilles, and it is commonly found in European decks. The system associated with the *Sephir Yetzirah* assigns the signs of the zodiac to the letters of the Hebrew alphabet. Depending on how the letters are assigned, Major Arcana cards acquire each letter's zodiacal attribution as a secondary correspondence.

The Golden Dawn's system is likely more familiar to British and American tarotists. In their system, Minor Arcana cards were not grouped consecutively in suits. They were presented to the initiate in the astrological sequence of the year to which they were related. This represented their "true" occult meaning, and required members to possess a basic knowledge of astrology.[2]

If zodiacal symbolism appeals to you, choose a system of attributions that satisfies you, and stick with it for as long as it works for you. As you become a more experienced reader, other zodiacal ideas or viewpoints may come to make more sense to you.

Many varieties of religious symbolisms have been attached to the cards. In the late eighteenth century, Court de Gébelin connected the twenty-two letters of the Hebrew alphabet with the twenty-two cards of the Major Arcana. Then, in the nineteenth century, Eliphas Lévi aligned the Major Arcana cards to Tree of Life pathways of the Hebrew Kabbalah, each path on the tree being assigned a letter of the Hebrew alphabet.[3] Subsequently, others have used completely different pathway assignments.[4]

Lévi's association of the Hebrew alphabet to the Major Arcana cards differed considerably from that of the Hermetic Order of the Golden Dawn. That version had most likely been created by MacGregor Mathers, one of the Order's co-founders, although its actual origin has been somewhat obscured. Lévi may have deliberately made the change to divert attention from the Golden Dawn secret sequence.[5] Then again, it may have been Mathers who first changed Lévi's associations and then claimed that Lévi had purposely given the cards incorrect attributions.[6]

Whatever is the truth, the work of successive authors who assign Hebrew letters to the cards differs depending on whom they use as an authority. Lévi, Papus, and Oswald Wirth used one system of Hebrew letter attribution for the Major Arcana, while Paul Foster Case's assignment closely follows A. E. Waite's arrangement, which has been called "blatantly inaccurate" for esoteric work.[7]

A tarot reader can gain a lot of mileage, symbolically speaking, out of the Hebrew letters associated with the cards, since each letter represents a microcosmic universe. Together they are capable of "resolving the problems of the soul."[8]

A good book to help you begin connecting Lévi's Hebrew letter associations with the cards is *Tarot and Individuation*, which employs sketches and illustrations from several decks.[9] One of the best tarot books for understanding associations based on

Waite's arrangement is that by Paul Foster Case, related specifically to his own B.O.T.A. (Builders of the Adytum) deck.[10]

Several books have also been written relating Christian symbolism to the tarot. Those by Harriette A. and F. Homer Curtiss, founders of the Order of Christian Mystics, connect occult Christianity and the tarot. Their books also connect the tarot with Hebrew letters, numerical symbolism, and the ten commandments, and tie an understanding of the tarot to biblical references.[11]

ALCHEMY AND THE TAROT

Thanks largely to C. G. Jung, a modern understanding of the work of the alchemist redefines it as the act of projecting inner perceptions or fantasies into, or onto, outer matter as a way of communicating an understanding of the soul's workings. The emerging knowledge and self-awareness results in revitalization of the inner spirit and eventually the union of the conscious mind with the unconscious to form a "new being" who understands himself or herself in a different way—who constantly moves closer to the unknown potential within—and acts accordingly. Several books and at least one deck connect tarot cards with alchemical principles and symbolism.[12]

THE CARDS AND MYTHS

Recently it has become popular to pay attention to ancient myths and to associate them with tarot cards, not because we are once again resorting to pagan beliefs but rather because myths are now recognized as excellent examples of "repetition[s] of patterns of becoming."[13] And the tarot is all about becoming.

Think you have outgrown directing attention to Greek or

Roman gods, or believing that they are real? Check out your favorite movies. Mars, god of war, frequently appears in a war-hero disguise. Venus, goddess of love, will never stop appearing as a beautiful, seductive (sometimes deadly) female.

All mythical figures correspond to inner psychic experiences and originally sprang from them.[14] They are the "great untapped resource[s] that we all bear as part of our natural equipment."[15] As stories of life patterns, myths serve as symbolic codes to illuminate another level of meaning of a tarot card. When we lose our myths, we lose our way, our sense of being a harmonious part of the life-giving cosmos.[16]

While myths from many cultures will be presented in Part Two as they refer to specific cards, if they do not correspond to your familial and ethnic culture, please make a serious attempt to connect the stories to similar ones from your own historical background so the cards may have more personal significance for you.

When Court de Gébelin found tarot cards, he sensed that they had a mythic background and used the mythology he knew best, that of ancient Egypt.[17] Likewise, MacGregor Mathers updated the tarot by integrating it into the mythology he knew best, that of the Renaissance.

Today, because of our familiarity with the myths of many cultures and countries, we can link the cards to a cornucopia of mythologies. Yet the important notion to realize is that we are coming to recognize the bond "between tarot and the nature of myth itself, between tarot and the cultural imagination."[18]

There are often several mythological themes that can be related to the story of each tarot card. It remains for the tarot reader, or the client, to decide how any of these pertains to his or her present situation. It's true that many myths are interesting or highly entertaining, yet when considering the application of mythological themes to the tarot, the major question must always be, "Does an analogy exist between the stories attached to this card and my present situation?"

The Gifts and Challenges

It is always tempting to engage in the simplistic thinking that some cards or suits are "good" and some are "bad," e.g., The Devil card, or the suit of Swords.

If, however, you consider a gauge or scale from left to right (1–10, best to worst) for each card, you can see that each card has, in fact, an entire range of attributes. Mary K. Greer, one of the most innovative tarot authors today, defines the ranges on this meter as extending from the *beneficial* aspects of a card to its *problematic* aspects. Recognizing the problematic aspects of a tarot card often makes reading reversals unnecessary.

Greer's conception of an entire range of attributes matches what psychologist Al Siebert found when he identified the "survivor personality." The most prominent characteristic of people possessing this personality is that they do not think in all or nothing dichotomies. They are able to combine personality opposites that seem paradoxical (playful and serious) with no conflict, which enables them to adapt to a wide range of crises and other situations with equanimity.[19] They would never look at a tarot card and see only one aspect. They also would not be confused by paradoxes in the cards.

Clowns and comedians often play this part in present-day life, pointing out the "other side" of what we think most valued or holy. They keep us alert to the realization that beneath our most cherished notions and ideals is a "seamy underside."[20]

By determining for yourself what you think are the beneficial, and problematic aspects—the gifts and the challenges—of each card, you can develop some ideas about what the benefits and problems could be when each card is drawn in a spread.

It may seem to you at this point that you could spend hours on each card, when in reality you have fifteen, thirty, or sixty minutes for a reading. Naturally, you will not bring everything included in this chapter into your interpretation of the card. If you have worked behind the scenes to develop your own understanding of each card, however, when you sit down to do a reading you will bring the important aspects of this knowledge into awareness—depending on the person and the reason for the reading—without deliberately thinking about it. Then you will have become a resource for the symbolic.

3

✳

Decks:
Twenty-Five Top Gateways

Hundreds of tarot decks exist, some now out of print, but at least two hundred are still available. Almost weekly, and certainly monthly, new decks are published, and many more will be designed and printed in the ensuing years.

Many decks have one or even several books written to explain, and expand on, card meanings. A recent count of current tarot books at the Bodhi Tree, a Los Angeles metaphysical bookstore, showed 120 different books on the shelf, while Amazon.com has more than 1,100 tarot entries, some of which are decks, but most are books.

Clearly what this proliferation of publications shows is that there is a personal need and demand for more than one deck, or more than one way of understanding the cards. Each deck addresses or shapes a specific focus of learning. It expresses tarot concepts in its own unique "voice" via the scenes, symbols, and colors employed.

CHOOSING YOUR DECK

To begin your tarot work, you will likely only want to work with one deck. This chapter reviews twenty-five of today's most popular decks. Other decks can be reviewed from the Web sites listed on the Internet Resources page.

It is important to view several decks to find those where the concept and the power of each card opens your own gateways to self-understanding. Any and everything on a card can be a catalyst for deeper self-understanding. Compare not only decks but several of the same cards in different decks. Consider how they "speak" to you, what feelings they evoke.

Does the deck adhere to a certain mythology or motif that you think might be symbolically active in your own life or that you would like to explore? Or does the motif completely turn you off? Do you enjoy the deck's illustrations (the landscapes and the people), or are you turned off by them? Are the colors too bright, too garish, or too subdued for you? The Rider-Waite-Smith deck (referred to hereafter as RWS) comes in several different types of coloring to because, obviously, styles of coloring are important to people who are going to be using a deck for some time. Some black-and-white decks exist for self-coloring.

On the more practical side, for a deck you are going to use with some regularity, select one that fits your hand so you can easily shuffle and arrange the cards. As you will see from the descriptions in this chapter, decks come in all sizes. You need not be deterred, however, by a deck that comes in a size difficult for you to shuffle, or a round deck (almost impossible to shuffle), because cards can be "mushed" and stirred around and individual cards selected from the mixed-up pile, or they can be restacked and turned over one by one.

Choose a deck that intuitively "feels right" and then use it for awhile, allowing its symbolism to work deep within. If it doesn't seem to work well for you, put it aside, or give it away, and continue the process until you find the "right" deck. Eventually, you also may find that your first deck no longer appeals the way it once did—a signal that it's time to adopt another deck, or to do different kinds of readings with alternative decks.

Some tarot readers have certain decks they use to read for others and one (or more) deck(s) that they reserve only to read for themselves. One tarotist keeps several decks decoratively wrapped up in men's handkerchiefs. Her clients intuitively choose which wrapped package they want, and she reads from that deck.[1] Of course, that takes a lot of experience with a number of decks.

The RWS and the Thoth/Crowley deck are the two most popular decks sold, according to Los Angeles booksellers. Both decks have spawned a number of "relatives" that retain the principal idea of each card but express it differently. It is appropriate, then, that we look at these two groupings first.

THE RIDER-WAITE TAROT DECK AND RIDER-WAITE-INFLUENCED DECKS

1. The Rider-Waite Tarot Deck (U.S. Games)

The first deck to use allegorical drawings for all seventy-eight cards, the deck has been a major influence on the production of subsequent decks. Now unofficially called the Rider-Waite-Smith deck to acknowledge its artist, Pamela Colman Smith, it was first published in 1909 by Rider & Son. Both Smith and Arthur E. Waite, who guided Smith's efforts, were members of the Hermetic Order of the Golden Dawn and many have presumed, although it was never actually proven, that they employed their Golden Dawn knowledge in designing the deck. Others have suggested that the deck's designs drew heavily on secret Masonic symbology (Waite was a Mason). Several recolored versions of the deck exist, which will, of course, change not only personal reactions to the cards, but symbolism as well. The Universal Waite deck, for instance, uses softer tones and adds some three-dimensional elements, while the Albano-Waite deck employs psychedelic-like colors.

The deck comes in many useful sizes ranging from a tiny deck (1 ½" × ¾") to a small deck measuring 2 ⅞" × 1 ⅞" (good for carrying in pockets or purses), to a large deck measuring 6 ⅞" × 3 ⅞" (usually used for display and teaching purposes). In between is a 3 ½" × 2 ¼" size, good for smaller hands, and the more commonly used 4 ¾" × 2 ¾" deck.

2. *The Robin Wood Tarot* (Llewellyn)

Robin Wood's vibrant drawings combine traditional RWS card designs, and some of its symbolism, with a more feminine, pagan, Celtic, and nature-oriented approach. Since real models were used for many of the illustrations, its people are more realistic. Some of the key names for the Minor Arcana cards help fix the meaning of the card. The key to the Knight of Pentacles is "dependable help," while that for the Nine of Cups is "party hearty." To fully understand the symbolism and the rationale for each item on each card, it is essential to own Robin Wood's book.[2] Size: 4 ⅝" × 2 ¾".

3. *The Spiral Tarot* (U.S. Games)

Although the advertising on the box for this beautifully illustrated deck, published in 1977, describes it as employing ancient Celtic wisdom, the myths that artist/author Kay Steventon uses are largely those associated with Greek, Egyptian, and Arthurian mythology. Some of her associations are not so different from those used by other authors, e.g., Hermes associated with The Magician, and the Great Mother Goddess for The Empress. Some are quite different, as associating the centaur Chiron with The Hierophant, Hercules with The Chariot, and Dionysus with The Hanged Man. The deck emphasizes the cycles of life.

To more fully understand Steventon's thinking, use her 1998 book. There she goes into detail for each myth, refreshing our memories of why this particular card represents a particular archetypal experience. She explains the Hebrew letters, Kabbalistic relationship, and associated astrological symbols (Steventon is an Australian astrologer) printed on each Major Arcana card. Unfortunately you may need a magnifying glass to decipher some of these details, as they were largely lost when the beautiful originals were reduced to the card size of 4 ⅛" × 2 ¾".

4. The Morgan-Greer Tarot (U.S. Games)

Created in 1979 by Bill F. Greer under the direction of Lloyd Morgan, the Morgan-Greer cards are unique in not having a border. The brightly colored illustrations extend all the way to the edge of the card. Paul Foster Case's ideas were used to get the proper symbolic color scheme (see his dictionary entry). Images are clear and relatively easy to understand.

The Minor Arcana suit of Wands has become Rods and, as in the RWS deck, they are budding—this time with oak leaves. Court card figures are shown from the waist up only, but there are plenty of other items in each card to enhance their meanings. Size: 4 ¾" × 2 ¾".

5. The Aquarian Tarot (U.S. Games)

Taken on as a commission for the Morgan Press, David Palladini, then an art student, created a classic deck of the early 1970s, painted in art-deco style and designed to bring ancient ideas into the Aquarian Age. Most of the figures in the Major Arcana cards wear ornate crowns and headgear. Oranges, reds, pinks, and browns dominate the cards with, fortunately, lots of white space to give the eye a rest. Elaborate use is made of triangles, circles, and zigzag lines, and their symbolism enhances the meaning of the cards. The designs on several of the Major Arcana cards—notably, The World, Strength, The Moon, The Star, and The Sun—differ considerably from traditional designs and their symbolism changes the meaning of the cards. Carl Japikse has written an excellent book, exploring the tarot for spiritual development and insight using this deck.[3] Size: 4 ⅝" × 3".

6. *The New Palladini Tarot (U.S. Games)*

Originally rendered in ink, magic marker, and pencil on rag paper, the rich illustrations on this deck combine elements of medieval, Egyptian, and modern art. David Palladini has created a deck quite different from his earlier Aquarian deck. Human figures are more personalized, and the costumes they wear are gorgeous, although some people find them so vivid they're distracting. Wands have become flowering Rods, and the figures in this suit are clothed mostly in rich greens. While Palladini says that he tried to depict all races, that is sometimes difficult to ascertain, and there are decks that are more obviously multiracial than this one. Comes as a deck or a deck-book set with a guide by Susan Hansson. Size: 4 ⅝" × 3".

7. *Light and Shadow Tarot* (Destiny Books)

Illustrations for the oversized cards of this striking deck by the late Michael Goepferd are created from carved linoleum blocks. Their dramatic black-and-white designs pulsate with energy and are filled with symbols so carefully worked into the design that it is easy at first glance to miss their significance.

Influenced by both the RWS and Thoth decks, many of the cards are quite original. The Eight of Wands, typically shown as wands in flight or in the air, is here portrayed as eight wands rising from rippling waters. They cross and recross each other in a trellis-like design to form triangle after triangle and a central jewel. The accompanying book of the deck-book set by Goepferd and Brian Williams describes the action as one of chaotic growth weaving itself into a pattern of order.

In the Four of Cups, traditionally shown as a young man sitting under a tree and being offered a fourth cup, a crab rises from the water, in which four cups sit, to reach toward a glowing moon. With one leg anchored in a cup bearing the sign or sigil of the "moon" and a second in a cup bearing the astrological sign of "cancer," the card represents lunar influences and the "overwhelming fertility of watery forces."[4]

By the time Goepferd was ready to carve the queens, they came to him in his dreams to "announce" how they should be portrayed. Each appears with her totem animal—not always what you would expect. The wonderful Queen of Pentacles is crowned by broad antlers, while the Queen of Cups sits on a lotus throne and is crowned with an enormous rosebud. You could spend days getting lost in the designs of these cards. Size: 5 ½" × 4 ¼".

THE THOTH DECK AND THOTH-INFLUENCED DECKS

8. Aleister Crowley's Thoth Tarot Deck (U.S. Games)

Designed by Aleister Crowley and painted by Lady Frieda Harris, the deck was first published in 1944 as "The Book of Thoth." In 1986 a new eighty-card set of the deck was issued. It included three versions of The Magus or magician not included in the first publication of the deck. If you are fortunate to own one of these decks, the choice of which Magus card to use is left up to the purchaser. Subsequently, it was decided that since two of these paintings had been rejected by Crowley, they should not be included in future printings, and are not.

The symbolism of the Thoth deck is extremely beautiful, but its complex and abstract designs are often difficult for the beginner to understand and the original book by Crowley is not a lot of help. At least two additional guidebooks, quite different in their approaches, have been written.[5]

Only the Major Arcana cards have pictures and some of their names differ from the RWS: Justice (the eighth Trump in the sequence) becomes "Adjustment"; The Wheel of Fortune is now simply Fortune; Strength (the eleventh card) becomes "Lust"; Temperance (the fourteenth card) is "Art"; Judgement is now "The Aeon"; and The World card becomes "The Universe". Minor Arcana cards are illustrated with "pips" in decorative patterns and have titles (seed ideas) printed at the bottom of the card, e.g., the Six of Swords is "Science", the Three of Wands, "Virtue." Although court cards do have figures in them, they are typically caught up in dark and swirling designs. The deck comes in two sizes: 5 ½" × 3 ⅞" and a smaller 4 ½" × 2 ⅞".

9. *The Haindl Tarot* (U.S. Games)

German artist Hermann Haindl, who consulted Crowley's writings as one of his sources, juxtaposes Hebrew letters, runes, and astrological symbols over his Major Arcana artwork. Haindl believed that he was healing some of the wounds of the Holocaust by doing this, and his deck has been defined as a spiritual work, "dealing with the joys and problems of sacred reality."[6] Haindl also places *I Ching* hexagrams on the Minor Arcana cards, except for the aces. Pentacles are renamed the Suit of Stones; all others remain the same. Titles for each of the Minor Arcana cards are also included, e.g., "Dominion" for the Two of Cups, "Mixed Happiness" for the Four. Court cards are renamed Son, Daughter, Mother, Father, and are associated with a different direction and ethnic group: Native Americans (Pentacles and north), Eastern Indians (Wands/east), Northern Celts (Cups/north), and Egyptians (Swords/south).

Although the reserved colors of the artwork may at first seem dim and dark compared to other decks, the longer you work with the deck, the lighter they appear (reflecting enhanced understanding or, perhaps, merely comfort with the complicated artwork?). Anyone working with this highly complicated, extremely symbolic deck, needs Rachel Pollack's two-volume set.[7] Size: 5" × 2 ¾".

10. *Tarot of the Spirit* (Samuel Weiser, Inc.)

With tributes to the RWS and Thoth decks, and the Kabbalistic Tree of Life, designer Pamela Eakins and artist Joyce Eakins produced a deck that contains the "traditional" seventy-eight cards, plus an additional "mystery card." Untitled, it is presented as the master or "overarching card" of spiritual realization. Minor Arcana suits are renamed after their elements: Fire, Water, Wind, Earth, and each one has its own title (Seven of Fire, "Courage"; Seven of Wind, "Many Tongues"; Seven of Water, "Insight"; Seven of Earth, the "Garden"). Court cards become Sister, Brother, Mother, Father. In the Major Arcana, Justice is renamed "Karma", Judgement becomes "Resurrection", and The World is called "The Universe". Many of the cards are filled with swirling colors that give the sense of inner movement and stir the imagination. An appendix in the 424-page book—needed to understand the deck's rich symbology—ties the cards to astrology and the *I Ching*. Size: 4 ¾" × 2 ¾".

11. *The Nigel Jackson Tarot* (Llewellyn)

Nigel Jackson says the earliest extant examples of tarot decks were illuminated with precious pigments on vellum, and each of his tarot cards has exactly that look. Bright and vivid, yet at the same time making use of watercolor-like pastel tones, each card has the capacity to draw us into a beautiful and imaginative landscape that can provoke an impromptu or deliberate meditative experience. Jackson, an English artist of the esoteric, calls his trumps "stations of the psyche." He has renamed some of the Trump cards with their earlier names: The Magician becomes "The Juggler", "The Popess" replaces The High Priestess, and The Hierophant is now "The Pope". Also following earlier traditions, Jackson reverses the positions of Justice to eighth and Strength, renamed "Fortitude", to eleven.

Swords represent the element of fire, while Staves (air element), look more like arrows than staffs or wands to reflect the fact that some of the earliest decks did use arrows rather than clubs or wands. The designs of the minor cards show the suit's emblem (cups, swords, staves, and pentacles) arranged as pips at the top of the card, with a unique scene below them.

Although Jackson's descriptions of the trumps involve us in ancient mysteries, legends, and mythologies, many of his divinatory meanings for both Major and Minor Arcana cards are not so different from other decks or authors. Some do differ considerably, however. The Nine of Staves (shown in the RWS deck as a wounded figure holding a staff and standing in front of eight additional wands), shows nine crisscrossed staves in the orange sky above an elaborate castle or castle-compound. At the base of the card, we see the tops of green trees and, extending above them, brightly colored tents topped with banners. Jackson defines this card as "unassailable security; strength; safety and integrity."[8] Size: 5 ⅛" × 3 ⅜".

MYTHIC-THEMED DECKS

12. *Legend: The Arthurian Tarot* (Llewellyn)

Traditional card titles appear at the top of each card; Arthurian titles appear at the bottom. In the Minor Arcana, Wands become Spears and Pentacles become Shields. Although it is not always clear just why they have been selected, certain totem animals substitute for the Page in each suit: badger (Shields), hare (Spears), salmon (Cups), and an adder (Swords).

The accompanying book by deck designer Anne-Marie Ferguson gives both a traditional meaning for each card as well as describing its place in Arthurian lore. Because there are other Arthurian-themed decks (see below), in the dictionary section of this book, Ferguson's deck will be referred to as the Legend Arthurian Tarot. Size: 4 ⅝" × 2 ¾".

✳

Other decks related to the Arthurian tales include the *Avalon Tarot* (Joseph Viglioglia) and the *Arthurian/Hallowquest* (Caitlín and John Matthews). The brightly colored Avalon Tarot is produced by Lo Scarabeo in Italy and redistributed in the U.S. by Llewellyn. The style is almost comic-strip and some of the Minor Arcana have names like Foolish Images (Three of Pentacles), Meeting of the Knights (Eight of Wands), and Abstinence of Perceval (Nine of Swords).

The Matthews' Arthurian deck (The Aquarian Press), commonly referred to as the Hallowquest pack, is a much more complicated deck. The 1990 handbook that accompanies the deck provides Celto-Arthurian background for the cards. It is expanded on by the year-long Arthurian Tarot Course, produced in 1993 and designed to enhance the reader's relationship to the legend through study tasks, meditation and ritual enactments.

13. *Mythic Tarot* (Simon & Schuster)

Designed by Juliet Sharman-Burke and Liz Greene, the cards, drawn by Tricia Newell, portray the images of Greek gods. The Fool is Dionysus. Hermes is portrayed on both The Magician and Judgement cards. The Star card tells the story of Pandora, The Sun card portrays Apollo, and The Moon speaks of Hecate.

Court cards tell their own myths, while the numbered cards tell a sequential mythological story. In the suit of Cups they tell the story of the relationship of Psyche and Eros, while the suit of Wands tells of Jason and the Argonauts. Pentacles involves Daedalus, the Athenian craftsman who built the Labyrinth for King Minos of Crete. The story of Orestes and the curse of the House of Atreus plays itself throughout the suit of Swords. Size: 5" × 3".

Another well-done deck that falls in the mythic-based category is the *Kalevala Tarot*, based on the Finnish national epic. Although characters from the myth are integrated with traditional tarot images, this may still be a difficult deck for a beginner to use. The *Goddess Tarot* (U.S. Games) illustrates the Major Arcana cards with goddesses from traditions around the world. Although each Minor Arcana suit is associated with a particular goddess (Cups/Venus/Greek; Staves/Freyja/Norse; Swords/Isis/Egyptian; Pentacles/Lakshmi/Hindu), the Minor Arcana do not carry the goddesses' stories through.

CLASSIC AND NEO-CLASSIC DECKS

14. *The Tarot de Marseilles* (B. P. Grimaud)

First published in the eighteenth century, it is now a historical classic, partly because of its age and partly because many of its cards are closely related to even earlier card motifs. It is still influential in the style of subsequent decks, and several modern modifications of it also exist. Only the Major Arcana and court cards have images on them, while the Minor Arcana simply display pips, sometimes with elaborate flourishes added.

The Marseilles was the most popular and readily available deck before the publication of the RWS. The deck and its several modifications come in various sizes, but the original Grimaud deck measures 4 ⅞" × 2 ½". Other publishers have created different "Marseilles"-inspired decks in differing colors and sizes.

15. *Renaissance Tarot* (U.S. Games)

The Major Arcana cards of this deck are associated with classical Greco-Roman deities, demi-gods, or other legendary personages, each of whom stands beneath a golden arch that becomes part of the border of the card. The late Brian Williams, artist and author, goes into great detail in the accompanying book regarding the mythology related to each Major Arcana card, and provides historical sketches of earlier versions. It is impossible to fully appreciate this deck without the book, which can be purchased separately.[9] Worth owning in its own right, the book will help you more fully understand some of the history behind the Major Arcana cards. The numbered cards of the Minor Arcana play out four stories from classical mythology: that of Achilles (for Swords), Herakles (Staves), Psyche (Cups), and Persephone (Coins). Size: 5" × 2 ⅜". Note: there are several decks using the name "Renaissance Tarot."

COLLAGE-TYPE DECKS

16. *Voyager Tarot* (Merrill West Publishing)

When it was first published, this deck, a collage of photographs selected and arranged by James Wanless and Ken Knutson, was considered an astonishing revolution in tarot decks. The creativity of its design is relished by some and considered too busy by others. One of the most beautiful aspects of the deck is the back of the cards, which shows an elegant cross-section of a DNA molecule, which Wanless calls "nature's mandala."

Although many Major Arcana cards bear the same names as neo-Rider decks, they are considered to represent universal personality types, archetypes. Justice, the eighth card in the sequence (with Strength as the eleventh), is renamed "Balance"; the Wheel of Fortune is simply Fortune; and Temperance (XIV) is "Art". The Devil becomes "Devil's Play"; Judgement becomes "Time-Space", and The World is renamed "Universe".

Minor Arcana cards have key words on them, e.g., Reflection for the Two of Worlds, Anger for the Four of Cups. Court cards, depicting stages in a person's life, have become Child, Woman, Man, and Sage. Swords are now the Suit of Crystals and Pentacles have become the Suit of Worlds.

It is not possible to comprehend all the symbols on any given card at once, so what usually happens is that the reader focuses on the symbol that stands out at the moment, and works with that, plus the idea of archetype.

Wanless has written a number of informative guidebooks and

created correspondence and certification courses for those who want to become more competent in using the deck.[10] Size: 5 ½" × 3 ¾".

Two other popular collage decks are the Hudes Tarot, which blends watercolor drawings with antique maps and marbled papers, and the Victoria Regina, which combines black-and-white nineteenth-century illustrations.

MULTICULTURAL DECKS

17. *Shining Tribe* (Llewellyn)

A revision of Rachel Pollack's Shining Woman deck, the cards are based on tribal and prehistoric art from around the world, sacred traditions, and multicultural mythologies. The names of four Major Arcana cards have been changed: the Hierophant becomes "Tradition", the Wheel of Fortune becomes the "Spiral of Fortune", Judgement is changed to "Awakening", and The World has become the "World-Shining Woman". Minor Arcana suits are Trees, Rivers, Birds, and Stones. Court cards have become the Vision Cards, with four cards titled Place, Knower, Gift, and Speaker. Rather than representing persons, as in many decks, their function is to develop deeper and progressive understanding of the power of each suit element. Size: 4 ½" × 2 ¾".

18. *The Ancestral Path Tarot* (U.S. Games)

Designed by artist Julie Cuccia-Watts, the almost photographic-like cards of this deck rely on myths from four cultures to jolt us out of the impact of our own cultural experience and to prompt us to connect with the greater human experience. Swords represent the time of feudal Japan, while Staves (Wands) represent ancient Egypt. Cards in the Sacred Circles suit (Pentacles) derive from the Native American tradition, and Cups represent the time of King Arthur. Only the court cards, however, bear names from each of these cultures, and these are identified only in the LWB that accompanies the deck, and the more expansive, separate book by Tracey Hoover. Major Arcana cards carry the usual titles, except that The Hanged Man is now called The Hanged One, but the pictures are quite different and multi-ethnic. Size: 4 ⅛" × 3 ⅛".

FEMINIST AND ECO-FEMINIST DECKS

19. *Daughters of the Moon* (D.O.M.)

This oversized round, multi-ethnic deck is designed by Ffiona Morgan and illustrated by a number of people. Its images are brightly colored and thought provoking.

Major Arcana cards are not numbered and some concepts are similar to RWS cards with different names, as "The Amazon" for the Chariot. Some are not so obvious, e.g., Kali, "The Awakener" for The Tower. There are a "Witch" (magician) and a Priestess card, no emperor. Two lovers cards are provided so one can choose one's sexual preferences, and two fool cards (Pan and Coyotewoman, the Trickster).

Minor Arcana suits are Flames, Blades, Pentacles, and Cups. Suit names and numbers appear at the top of the card, while a key word or name appears at the bottom. As befits a feminist deck, the three court cards represent the three phases of the goddess: maiden, mother, and crone; hence only seventy-four cards in the deck. Beautifully colored borders surround each vividly colored card, but those colors offer no clues as to which suit they belong and whether or not they are Major or Minor cards.

Whether showing glory or destruction, all the cards are dramatically illustrated. The crises of the fives is quite clear. Five cups bounce on stormy, windblown waves (The Storm), while five knives/blades circle the air in the wake of a Hurricane. Five pentacles fall into a rift that opens along a red landscape (Earthquake), and the Hawaiian volcano goddess Pele is alive and active in the Five of Flames. This is a good deck for dealing with the personal development of women and their issues. An accompanying book, sometimes hard to find, has been written by Ffiona Morgan.[11] Size: 5 ¼" diameter.

20. *Wheel of Change Tarot* (Destiny Books)

This deck, with its accompanying 383-page book, took medieval scholar Alexandra Genetti some ten years to create. The Major Arcana cards do not have numbers, so they can be "interwoven" in ways that don't follow a traditional order, thereby permitting them to cover broader variations in our archetypal journeys. If you need some guidance, however, Genetti presents a Tarot Tree pattern (tableau) for the Majors, which aligns them in a triangular pattern and offers another way to understand various combinations of cards.

In truth, however, it is the art itself that will set your mind swirling into new archetypal depths and variations. The green-clad Fool stands with one foot on either side of a canyon while a band of stars twine about him and spill off into the universe. Around him, roses and rose petals fall from the lavender sky. He tells us that there truly is glory to be expressed here.

The brightly colored cards and multiracial scenes have borders that give you a clue as to what they are. Gray borders represent the Major Arcana. Orange is used for Cups, green for Disks, yellow for Wands, and blue for Swords. Although the cards have traditional names, their paintings challenge you to expand your definitions and ideas of what a card can mean. In The Chariot, a stone circle connected by "energy lines" mirrors and connects itself with cosmic wheels that originate from, and align with, a silhouetted female. This is travel within cosmic cycles and addresses our relationship to the life-giving nature of the ancient Great Goddess and to the entire universe, spiritual ecology at its finest. The complex symbolism of this deck cannot be fully appreciated without the accompanying book. Size: 5" × 3".

21. Songs for the Journey Home
(Alchemists and Artists)

The colored-pencil drawings for this expensive (self-published, hand-assembled) round deck, created by Catherine Cook and Dwariko von Sommaruga, are somewhat primitive yet direct our attention to many modern world dilemmas, especially those of protecting local and greater environments inner and outer. Major Arcana cards are renamed Life Songs, and most carry the same names as the RWS deck, although The Hierophant has now become "The Luminary", and The World is now "Homecoming". Some of the pictures are riotously whimsical. The bungee-jumping Hanged One represents the thrill-seeking escapades we engage in that have unexpected effects on our perceptions. This relates him more to the trickster archetype than some other decks have. The Devil card, combining artistic elements of early Picasso, shows a green witch surrounded by strange "monsters," representing our unresolved feelings.

As a group, the Minor Arcana are called Hearth Songs. Pentacles become Earth Songs; Wands are Flame Songs. Wave Songs represent Cups, and Wind Songs are exchanged for Swords. Court cards fall into the category of Shell Songs to represent the "shells" we put around us, the masks we wear. They are renamed Innocence (Pages), Awakening (Knights), Creating (Queens), and Resolving (Kings) for the processes that may be occurring in our lives.

It is often not easy to understand the Minor cards without the book, and even then some of the drawings will keep you guessing. The Seventh Flame Song (in no way equivalent to the Seven of Wands) shows a trickster-like fellow, clad in a rainbow shirt. With a pair of giant scissors, he has cut the central string controlling a group of unhappy stick-figure marionettes. Or has he? They are still being held upright by a giant hand. Was he once one of those marionettes and, having cut his own string, is now blossoming? One experienced reader says she sometimes perceives the card as one of cutting herself free from all the things that tie her down, as she separates herself from dark, empty (stick figure) spirits.[12] The authors' accompanying book describes the card as reflecting a "pregnant pause" in which you are in harmony with your own and seasonal cycles, yet also a card of alert readiness. Clearly this is a deck that will speak to the reader in many different ways many different times. Size: 4 ⅛" diameter.

ESOTERIC DECKS

22. *Osho Zen* (St. Martin's Press)

Although this evolution of two earlier decks purports to be a deck based on Zen principles, there is no direct lineage transmission here and, indeed, that is apparently just the way the Osho International Foundation, which is behind this newly revised deck and its accompanying book, wishes it to be. Still the deck is rapidly becoming a favorite among experienced tarot readers. It is, however, definitely not a deck for beginners, and will require that even experienced readers develop a new sense of symbolism for the cards.

Both the Major and Minor Arcana have titles at the bottom. While some match the understanding of the cards in other decks, many do not, offering a new viewpoint. The seventh Major Arcana card—The Chariot in most decks—becomes "Awareness," and depicts a burning veil through which can be seen a young Buddha-like face. Justice, now called "Courage," is illustrated with a brightly glowing daisy growing from a stone wall. An unnumbered, additional card titled "The Master" has been added to the Major Arcana and symbolizes "transcendence," the main theme of this deck. It portrays Osho, known in the United States as Bhagwan Shree Rajneesh.

The four Minor Arcana suits are renamed and marked with a color-coded diamond for the predominant color of the suit: Fire (Wands/red), Water (Cups/blue), Clouds (Swords/gray), and Rainbows (Pentacles/rainbow). This deck is full of challenging ideas, and the accompanying book by Ma Deva Padma (Susan Morgan) is definitely a must. It is a good deck to inspire meditation and daily guidance. Size: 4 ¼" × 2 ⅞".

23. *Alchemical Tarot* (HarperCollins)

Sculptor and artist Robert Place has created a deck that draws on the symbolism of alchemy and invites you to embark on your own symbolic alchemical journey of spiritual transformation. The accompanying book by Rosemary Ellen Guiley briefly describes the basics of alchemy and relates the alchemical symbolism behind each Major Arcana card, and some of the minor cards. Where appropriate, she also connects each of the Major Arcana cards to an appropriate mythological person.

Delicately illustrated and colored in the style of Renaissance alchemical art, many of the drawings, though based largely on RWS concepts, are quite unique in all or part of their design, especially those in the Minor Arcana. Pentacles are renamed Coins; Cups become Vessels; and Wands burn brightly as firetipped Staffs. There are many nude figures in the Major Arcana, including The Magician, The Empress, The Emperor, The Lovers, the two-headed Devil, The Sun, Judgement, and The World. Size: 4 ¾" × 3 ⅛".

24. *World Spirit Tarot* (Llewellyn)

People of every shape and color populate this colorful deck illustrated by Lauren O'Leary from her hand-colored linoleum block prints. Inspired by both the RWS and Thoth decks, this globally oriented deck has some entirely new scenarios, many involving tropical or exotic landscapes. The glorious wings of the bright blue Temperance angel make him one of the most beautiful angels ever created. Blue, with vivid rainbow-colored feathered wings that drape to the ground, he pours an orange-yellow-pink spiraling liquid between two chalices.

Although shorthand names or titles for the numbered Minor

Arcana cards are given in the mini-book, these are not included on the cards, leaving the reader free to use them or not. Court cards are renamed the Seer (page), Seeker (knight), Sibyl (queen), and Sage (king). Nothing is written about the symbolism of the individual items on each card, and part of exploring the deck more deeply will be the fun of developing your own understanding. Size: 4 ¾" × 3 ¼".

25. *Shapeshifter Tarot* (Llewellyn)

Rooted in Celtic shamanism, the pastel, ethereal, half-human and half-animal images created by artist Lisa Hunt draw you into ancient Celtic shapeshifting lore. The accompanying book by D. J. Conway and Sirona Knight not only explains shapeshifting but also explains each card's symbolism or artistic presentation. Three new Major Arcana cards have been added to the deck: "The Double," "The Journey," and "The Dreamer." Altogether the eighty-one cards honor the legend of the eighty-one knights of the Nine Rings of the Cordemanons of the Celtic Gywddonic Druid tradition, of which Sirona Knight is a High Priestess and Third Degree Craftmaster.

The names of so many of the Major Arcana cards have been changed that they have little in common with the usual concepts or archetypes of the Major Arcana of other decks, although a few do. The Fool becomes "Initiation," "The Hermit" is "The Seer," and Temperance becomes "Balance"—all acceptable understandings of the cards from other decks. Yet, The Devil is renamed "Choice," The Tower becomes "The Serpent," Judgement is renamed "Transcendence," and The World is "Oneness." Experienced readers will likely understand these changes, but beginning readers may not.

The four Minor Arcana suits bear their elemental names: Earth (Pentacles), Air (Wands), Fire (Swords), and Water (Cups), and each card also bears a defining title. Additional key words for all cards are included in an appendix to the book. The deck shifts the element of air from Swords to Wands and attributes the element of fire to Swords. Like the Major Arcana, while the ultimate meaning of the Minor Arcana cards are often not so very different from other decks, the images certainly are, and serve to draw you into deeper consideration of the title of the card. In the Seven of Air (Wands), retitled Valor, a part-lion, part-griffin woman flies over a wolfhound surrounded by fruit-bearing grapevines. The card represents the action of moving toward fulfilling your desires. The Three of Water (Cups) shows the faces of two women, one named Waterfall-Woman, and one man, who make their home in the pool. The card represents riches of the body, mind, and spirit and a healing to come. Court cards are the Seeker (Page), Warrior (Knight), God (King), and Goddess (Queen), with the Goddess card acting as the highest card in the sequence.

In addition to using the deck for readings, the authors suggest using it to interpret or clarify dreams, replace negative dreams, and in meditation to become more aware of the animal energy within yourself and another. One of the purposes of this deck is to make you aware of your oneness with everything in the cosmos. Size: 4 ⅝" × 2 ¾".

FANTASY-BASED DECKS

I have not included any fantasy or magical decks in this review of basic decks, although there are many out there. They are sometimes difficult for beginners to use. If imaginative or fantasy decks are of interest, you may care to take a look at the *Tarot of the Cat People*, the *Dragon*, *Unicorn*, *Masquerade*, *Halloween*, *Whimsical*, *Phantasmagorical*, and *Terrestrial* decks, among others.

4

✳

Spreads:
Destiny Narrations

Spreads (also called layouts) form the structure of a reading. They create or provide order to information received from the cards. Otherwise, you might as well throw the tarot deck into the air and read "meanings" into how and where the cards fall in the room. It if weren't so complicated, that in itself wouldn't be a bad idea, but since it might take a lot of bending over and stretching upward (to reach those cards dangling from the light fixture), a spread becomes one way of simplifying and clarifying the reading process.

Cynthia Giles calls spreads "destiny narrations."[1] They help us tell our story, or mirror that story back to us in a new or different way that inspires insight and offers a broader perspective. They help us analyze a particular moment in time.[2]

Psychologist Arthur Rosengarten describes a spread as a "symbolic map of dynamic interrelationship" offering a "cohesive picture of a situation" or a "compelling new possibility." Spreads offer a unique combination of themes related to our own particular life experience.[3]

At a tarot conference on spreads in Irvine, California, in October 2001, participants came up with some of the following purposes of a spread:

- Allows us to recognize and consider available possibilities
- Presents us with a map of our life/situation/issue
- Allows us to discover information we might not otherwise consider
- Creates a picture of an ongoing process
- Helps awaken us to the influence of past experiences, a narrow focus, or restricting life patterns, thereby stimulating new action/creativity
- Can serve as a healing experience as we recognize and move toward resolving old fears and pains

One participant poetically extended the idea of a "spread" to the analogy of butter melting into an English muffin. It creates a way for us to extend ourselves, melt in, and discover the nooks and crannies we might not otherwise find.

Components of a Narration

In order to accomplish our purpose, we need to enter into a reading with a specific and well-formulated question that addresses our own personal purpose or intent—something specific we want to know more about. We may be reading for ourselves or for another; hence, people are an important component of a reading. Once we have determined these aspects of the reading, we need a deck of tarot cards and a specific spread or format in which to arrange the cards.

Spread Formats

Spreads typically are laid out in patterns or spatial arrangements, e.g., straight lines, stars, spirals, V or inverted V-shapes, X-shapes, arches or fans, pyramids, squares, circles, diamonds—almost any shape you can think of. Some spreads are based on metaphors and motifs, e.g., a door spread or a chakra spread. Some rely on religious concepts: the cross and the tree of life formats.

Each spread can have any number of positions, and each of the positions in the pattern is named or carries a special identity. Typical positions might be named "what inspires me," "what supports me," "what drives me," "my strengths," "my weaknesses." The list of possible positions is endless and is limited only by the creator's imagination or by the design or pattern within which he or she has chosen to work.

Spreads can provide a general time continuum, as in past, present, future. They can provide "next step" answers (What do I do next? What are three things I need to do to . . . ?) Cause-and-effect spreads deal with options (If I do x, what will be the result?). Need information to help make a decision? Choose a thread with three positions: "in favor of," "against," "aid in deciding." Astrological spreads can provide information with regard to months, quarters, or yearly cycles, as well as being organized by houses.

Whatever the original number of positions, any spread can be expanded by adding cards for clarification that are not part of the original spread ("What is the obstacle?"; "What enhances this situation?"; "What are the next three things that need to be done?"; What are three things that more fully explain the card's meaning?").

Often a spread is tailored to the question being asked, although some spreads can be used for any type of question. Some of the best spreads are made up on the spot to fit the question, so don't be afraid to create your own spreads.

Because the typical ten-card Celtic Cross spread didn't seem to answer questions suitably for her, one of my students created a multilayered Celtic Cross reading that satisfies her immensely. It is a beautiful thing to see her work the forty-card spread, although it's quite daunting for unprepared observers.

For those who would like guiding spreads, almost every tarot book contains some unique spreads created by the author. Try these and keep or change those you enjoy. Sylvia Abraham has created a book filled with thirty-six of her spreads, ranging from six to fifteen cards, and based on such categories as home and family issues, love and romance, finances, spiritual aspirations, among many others.[4] Evelin Burger's and Johannes Fiebig's book on spreads, originally published in German in 1995, has been translated and is now published in English.[5] The American Tarot Association offers a series of instructional tapes for members outlining various levels of working with spreads.[6] In addition, consider some of the types of spreads that follow.

ONE-CARD READINGS

Many tarot users have developed the habit of drawing a daily card as a guide for their awareness, to act as an inspiration, or to provide an orientation theme or intentional focus, for the day. It's also fun to draw only from the court cards and ask, "Who do I need to be today?"

Your response to the card may range from a couple of words to a couple of sentences and that may be all the information you desire first thing in the morning. However, if you choose to consider the card in detail, your reading can take almost as much time as you want by exploring the multilevels of the card's symbology (*see* Chapter 2).

One tarotist suggests that when doing a one-card reading, define the card itself as the main reason or answer to the question. An upright card then represents outside influences, a reversed card, internal issues.[7]

Other possibilities for questions to consider with a one-card reading include asking:

- What do I need to be aware of about my relationship with . . . [a specific person or situation]?
- What is the best way to approach . . . [a specific person or situation]?
- What does god/goddess/higher energy want from me today?

Two-Card Layouts

Two-card spreads are often based on polarities, as in questions that ask for yes/no, against/in favor of, this/that answers. The problem with these types of readings is that you may not get a clearly defined answer. Many tarotists believe that questions phrased to require a dichotomous answer don't make the best use of tarot cards, border on fortune-telling, and seldom lead to exploring self-growth issues. For these reasons they, and I, will change the question rather than answer it.

To get around, or expand on, dichotomies, one tarot reader

poetically thinks of two-card readings as "the hype and the scoop," i.e., what the querent thinks about the situation and what it's really about.

Another way to expand on dualities might include naming the positions:

- What you need to look at; how you approach it
- What you want; what you need
- What's known about a situation; what's not known
- Situation; greatest potential for problems

My favorite two-card reading is still the Challenges layout presented in *The Heart of the Tarot*.[8] It makes use of the mini-cross from the classic Celtic Cross reading which, in that spread, deals specifically with the tension currently existing between you and the situation or issue being asked about. In the mini-cross, the first card drawn is placed upright and the second card is placed horizontally across it.

The Challenges layout renames and redefines the first position as The Situation. The card in this position expands on the perception, or understanding, of information being brought into or awakened with regard to the issue or question. It may suggest the strengths or weaknesses a client brings to the situation, or ones that may be inherent in the situation itself.

The Challenge card offers a growth opportunity. It may offer information the client needs to consider, conflicts needing to be recognized, or actions needed to change the situation or increase its effectiveness.

The advantage of the Challenges Spread is that it does not fall into the either/or category. It provides a quick, timely reading for when you want a quality reading yet don't have, or want to take, the time to use more cards.

THREE-CARD SPREADS

One of the advantages of three-card spreads is that you can come up with an almost endless number of positions of three. Some common positions or ideas for three-card spreads include:

- *past* influence, *present* issue, *future possibility* (what might occur if you do not address the issue in question)
- emotional, physical and intellectual issues
- body, mind, spirit
- physical, mental, spiritual
- health, career, relationships
- issue, action, outcome
- inner mother, ego/persona, inner father (These positions might be used for general clarification of what is trying to be expressed, or for information on how those aspects of oneself are enhancing or interfering with a given situation.)
- financial, intellectual, and emotional issues (as themes/issues playing an active role in a given situation or as issues needing to be recognized and taken care of in a relationship)

One of my students, Jayne Speich, has converted what was originally a two-card daily spread with the positions "What the Universe Wants Me to Focus On" and "What Specific Thing I Can Do in the Context of That Theme" to a three-card spread. She adds the sum of the first two cards to arrive at the number of a Major Arcana card (*see* **quintessential card** in Pt. 2), which gives her a summary of the reading or a clarification.[9]

By now you likely have discerned that for any basic two-, three-, or four-card spread, you can be as creative as you like in naming the positions and in deciding how you can increase the amount of information you get from the reading by adding additional positions, such as "help," "hinder," "outcome." The writings of Gail Fairfield and Donald Michael Kraig offer additional suggestions for naming positions.[10]

FOUR-CARD READINGS

Take any three-card spread that you like and add a fourth position. Although that fourth card position might be defined as one that sets you on a new journey or path, the most common tendency is to use it to establish some kind of stability or ending, such as "outcome" or "possible outcome."

More helpful fourth-position titles might include:

- Strength Available
- What Hinders This Issue
- What I Need to Know
- What I Don't Know
- What the Situation/Issue Is Really About
- Complications/Interferences
- Available Help/Support
- Recurring Patterns
- Potential Problem

Be as creative as you like in naming the positions to fit your particular question and readings.

FIVE-CARD READINGS

For a good five-card spread to help groups or individuals clarify their future direction, Arthur Rosengarten uses five Major Arcana cards.[11] The first four are drawn by the person (or someone from the group), while the fifth card is determined by the numeric total and reduction (if the total is more than twenty-one) of the first four cards. The positions are:

1. What is working for me/us
2. What is working against me/us
3. What I/we know

4. What I/we don't know
5. What is needed

Example: If the first card is the Wheel of Fortune (#10), the second is The Emperor (#4), the third is The Sun (#19), and the fourth card is Temperance (#14), their total equals 47. This is reduced to $4 + 7 = 11$, so the fifth card chosen to complete the reading would be Justice (#11) for "what is needed."

Five-pointed star-shaped spreads also are common for five-card readings.

BEYOND FIVE CARDS

Larger spreads typically become variations of the one-, two-, three-, and four-card layouts, simply adding more positions that seek additional information to clarify the situation, although many are unique in themselves.

Six-card readings are often laid out in the shape of a hexagram. Many ideas for working with this type of spread can be found in Mary K. Greer's *Tarot Mirrors*. A common seven-card reading is based on the seven chakras and the cards are laid out vertically to represent them.

Probably the most well-known ten-card spread is the Celtic Cross. First featured in Arthur Waite's book accompanying his deck, it was derived and modified from a spread used by members of the Hermetic Order of the Golden Dawn. Some version of it (there are different ways to lay out the cards) is typically included in the LWB that accompanies almost every new deck, and in most tarot books. Beginners often find it a difficult spread to use and, fortunately, as you can see from this chapter, need not be restricted to its use.

Another rather popular ten-card spread is that based on the positions on the Kabbalistic Tree of Life and laid out in the pattern of the Tree.[12]

Mary K. Greer has developed a unique ten-card chakra spread where the two cards for the third (solar plexus chakra) represent will/ego and emotional connections. The two cards for the fifth (throat) chakra represent inner and outer communication. The two cards for the sixth (third-eye) chakra refer to right and left brain orientations.[13]

ALTERNATIVE TO YES/NO QUESTIONS

Instead of sticking with a yes/no option, if you can rephrase the question to consider looking at two choices, then you can draw as many cards as you need to acquire more specific information regarding each choice, naming the positions using titles suggested previously. I like to define the final card in each of these two sets as offering information about the most important factor to take into consideration in making "this" choice or "that" choice.

CREATING YOUR OWN SPREADS

The number of positions in self-created spreads can be deliberately limited by the design you select, or decided intuitively. One tarotist utilizes "a new paradigm spread," where not only are the cards drawn but also the names of the positions.[14]

Possible position names are written on blank cards and shuffled. They are laid out first and the tarot cards placed on top of them. Some possible position names include Outside Influences, Inner Motivations, Block to Success, Next Week, Next Month, Working with Others. Experiment. Create position titles that you like or that work for you.

You may want to design a spread based on the question being asked. James Ricklef, writing as KnightHawk, is excellent at creating three-card spreads with appropriate position names that match the situation or question of various characters from fairy tales, mythology, and history.[15] When Mrs. Claus wrote about her husband being a workaholic, and wondered if he really loves her, KnightHawk created the positions (1) the foundation of your relationship, (2) the challenges/problems of the relationship and, (3) what you need to know or do about them. When Galileo wanted to know the result of his heresy trial, he consulted KnightHawk whose positions for the spread were (1) the current situation, (2) a recommended course of action, (3) a likely outcome.

Self-created spreads can help clarify goals, a developmental or life process, or simply supply more information about a characteristic such as self-esteem or spiritual development. You can derive the inspiration from, and create your own spreads, by looking at a specific image (a body, an animal, a lantern) and creating positions metaphorically related to the various parts of the image.

Consider the theme of a story or fairy tale and create spread positions from the phases or actions delineated in the story. Allow a birthday, a holiday, or other special occasion to stimulate a spread design. Ponder the qualities of a mythological character, and name a series of spread positions according to those qualities, the purpose being to find out how those qualities apply to you. Delve into a piece of inspirational reading you have enjoyed and create positions around that.

WHEN ALL ELSE FAILS

There are times when I want information from the tarot but don't have a particular question in mind regarding the situation, or no spread seems to be just right. Things are still too amorphous. It's then that I rely on my "What's-the-story-here?" reading.

Begin laying out cards, interpreting them one-by-one, until you intuitively feel you have the "story" of what's going on in your specific situation and can tell that story. Add the total numbers of those cards and break it down to the highest number between one and twenty-two (*see* **reduction**, Part 2), for the final, quintessential Major Arcana card, i.e., where the story/situation ultimately is leading.

By now you have likely discerned that stories about your life journey or destiny are fulfilled through your own rich imagination, curiosity, and exploration. What else is there left to say, except *bon voyage*?

PART TWO

The Tarot Dictionary

How to Use This Dictionary

At the outset, attempts to explain symbols present a problem, namely, something that is symbolized is meant to express the inexpressible. That is the first "truth" about symbols.

A second truth is that they never mean simply one thing, and they can mean something different each time they appear in a reading or on different cards. Any card in proximity to another card in a reading can change the meaning of the symbol somewhat. The fact that a representation appears on a certain card with all that card's other symbolism, as well as on a particular portion of a card, e.g., alone or overlying something else, can well change the meaning of the symbol.

While it is apparent that over time common meanings have developed for many symbols on a tarot card, remember that a particular item may also have personal meanings for the client and/or the reader. A star may not mean the same thing to the reader as it does to an amateur astrologer, to someone whose family spent summer nights making up star stories, or to someone who aspires to be a "star."

One way to deepen your symbolic understanding is to explore the images of one item, say, bridges or the moon, in the various cards of your deck and determine how their meaning may change in the context of the other images in each card.

Many tarot card readers believe that the best way to interpret a card is to pay attention to the image that stands out for you on a particular card during a particular reading. It may be a different image for another reading.

Rather than limit the meanings of tarot symbols and images, consider these entries as suggestions pointing to ideas you may not have considered. Allow them to trigger and amplify your own ideas and reactions. Remember that no matter how well you are able to interpret an individual card, its meaning may alter in a spread where it is in juxtaposition or relationship with other cards. Then, all cards may need to be understood as presenting a unified, complex message.

Where an image is also a symbol or attribute of a god or goddess, you may want to review that deity's story in order to check whether it pertains to an ongoing life process recognizably active, or to one attempting to make itself known in your awareness. All myths express archetypal processes or motifs. By catching us up in the story, they remind us of the complexities and paradoxes of human nature with its many illusions and entanglements, limitations and conflicts. They are stories of the interactions between humans and the divine, and of soul development and the search for wholeness; hence, you will find in the dictionary many references to myths as they relate to the tarot cards. Their purpose is to *catch you up* in a deeper sense of archetypal resonance, to connect you with the gods within.

Please regard the dictionary entries as openings to allow the symbols and the myths contained therein to spark the next step in your own search for awareness, rather than as the final word on what a card, or some portion of it, means. Because of space and publication constraints not every symbol on every card could be mentioned. Let those that are included spur you to ponder the symbols on your own decks more deeply.

NOTE: The acronym RWS in dictionary entries refers to the Rider-Waite-Smith deck. The term Renaissance card or deck refers *only* to the Renaissance Tarot designed by Brian Williams and to no other decks of the same name.

abyss

A canyon, often called an abyss, is seen in The Fool card of the RWS deck, as well as The Fool cards of many other decks. It symbolizes the unknown and the depths awaiting The Fool in his discoveries. Standing above it suggests the superficiality of his personality at the beginning of his journey. There is an UnderWorld tradition called The Secret Way Across the Abyss, which involves a series of related experiences that ultimately provide a radically altered awareness,[1] not unlike The Fool's journey.

In mythology, the Great Abyss represents both the underworld (psychologically, the unconscious) and the Great Mother, especially if water is seen below. As a female symbol, the abyss represents fertile, creative ideas. Mythologies that describe the world as emerging from a great abyss (the Great Mother, the Great

Mother's vagina) also suggest the new life and potential awaiting The Fool on his journeys. An abyss can also symbolize ambivalence in making a choice, depending on where The Fool is in relation to the canyon.

In The Star card of the Tarot of the Spirit, the abyss of the unconscious or "great unknown" is blackness, from which the "scene" emerges. On the Renaissance Tarot's Wheel of Fortune card, "Dame Fortune" points to an abyss, indicating the "fall" destined for some, while a third figure in the Morgan-Greer Wheel card clearly falls off the wheel into the abyss below.

See **mountain(s)**.

aces

Minor Arcana aces represent the gift, the impetus, and the consciousness to begin new work on the tasks, or energy pathway, of their particular suit. New potential stirs within, striving to become conscious. We are filled with a new urge. It's time to consider how we want to express this focused, building energy.

Aces show that suit-related spiritual emanations, transmissions, or opportunities are entering our personal universe. We are not in the picture because we have to be open and receptive to this energy. Aces are associated with Kether, the crown sephira in the Kabbalistic Tree of Life.

Subsequent cards of the suit show scenes or teachings of our search to link with, and comprehend, this spirit/energy impulse and bring it to fruition.

See **ones**; Minor Arcana suit aces.

acorn(s)

Symbols of fertility and fecundity, and spiritual growth. Some describe the design at the top of the RWS Hierophant pillars as an acorn and oak leaves.

See **tree, oak**.

affirmations

Positive statements couched in the present tense (as if something already is in existence rather than "will be" in the future) help reprogram the unconscious mind. They remind us to consciously act and think in more positive or healing ways. Affirmations created with tarot cards can inspire us to develop the characteristics related to specific cards.

Creating an affirmation from a card that best reflects a quality one would most like to develop is one of the activities in Mary K. Greer's "breakthrough process" for Celtic Cross readings.[2] Many tarotists have created and published affirmations for the cards, and in 2001 U.S. Games published Sally Hill's Tarot Affirmations deck.

air (element)

Air is often considered the primary element as it is related to creativity in several ways: the breath of life (first breath at birth), the breath of the cosmos (spirit), and speech. Hermes, originally a wind god, and Thoth, who makes it possible for souls to breathe, are mythologically connected to the element of air[3] and, therefore, to the suit of Swords (in most decks).

See **elements**.

alchemy

Originally put forth as a process for turning lead into gold, it was later realized that it symbolized the process of becoming personally enlightened or spiritually awake. Substances *and* personalities could become "ennobled" or transformed to more valuable states.

Alchemical theory held that there was a first, base, or primary matter, *prima materia*, from which the world originated. It was divided into four elements, earth, air, fire, and water—the same four elements later attributed to the four suits of the tarot's Minor Arcana. These four elements could be recombined by using the philosophical elements, or spiritual forces, of salt, sulphur, and mercury. Their symbols appear on the RWS Wheel of Fortune card, suggesting that Waite may have incorporated alchemical principles into his deck.

It was the alchemist's job to separate *prima materia* into two or more of the elements, to alter and cleanse them through various alchemical processes in order to release their divine "spirit" and, finally, to transform the base matter into an entirely new transcendent substance—the philosopher's stone, the *lapis philosophorum*. This is akin to the Jungian process of individuation.

The number of phases and the processes differed within various alchemical systems. Eventually they were simplified into four phases—blackening, whitening, yellowing, and reddening—and finally into three: *nigredo* or blackening (*see* **Devil, The (XV)**), *albedo* (whitening), and *rubedo* (reddening). Within those phases, there were a number of stages, sometimes twelve (each aligned with an astrological house) but, most frequently, seven. All the stages were associated with planets, metals, and sometimes animals.

In the *nigredo* phase, the *prima materia* was separated into its respective elements, grouped according to various kinds of opposites (masculine/feminine, sun/moon, sulphur/mercury, etc.), then eventually brought together in a union or integration (the *coniunctio*) that resulted in their individual deaths (blackening). The union was often depicted as taking place in a vessel with the help of a mediator, Mercurius—The Fool or The Magician in the tarot deck.

In the second phase, the blackness was overlaid with rainbow colors, often represented by a pearl or a peacock tail, which were, in turn, overlaid by white, the feminine light of the unconscious. This symbolized the first transformation process (*albedo*), the results of which had to be assimilated or understood before proceeding to the red (*rubedo*) phase. Here the red king (sulphur of the wise) and the white queen (mercury/white rose) were united in the fire of love—sometimes depicted as a marriage—producing perfection: the philosopher's stone, which was capable of transmuting base metals into gold. The androgynous or hermaphroditic figure often portrayed as resulting from this union is also related to the tarot's World card, frequently described as the union of opposites and as a hermaphrodite.

Several authors have combined the concepts of the tarot with the alchemical process.[4]

See **individuation; mercury** (alchemical); **philosopher's stone; salt** (alchemical); **Self; sulphur** (alchemical).

amplifying

To amplify a card is to enhance its personal meaning and to delve into it more deeply for personal insight and growth. One of the easiest ways to amplify a card is to assume the posture of the central (or other) figure(s) on the card and become aware of how you feel, what you're thinking, and what you would like to do next.

A second way is to tell the "story" of the card (what's happening) from your point of view. Tying your present understanding of the card to any associated images from other tarot decks, as well as reviewing myths, archetypes, or motifs typically associated with the card can also deepen your personal understanding of that card.

Looking at an image contained on a card (flame, fire) and describing its intrinsic characteristics (hot, dangerous, flickering) may deepen your understanding of the card, especially if you also consider any puns or wordplay based on those characteristics that might apply to you and your life.

androgyny

In the RWS Sun and World cards, the sex of the main figure is indeterminate and, especially the world figure, often described as androgynous. Symbolically, "being androgynous" refers to the union of the strongest and most striking opposites, as well as the primitive state of mind in which the child enters this world.[5] On the Thoth "Art" (Temperance) card, an androgynous figure blends the elements in a golden cauldron, representing the Solar (Father of All Life) principle. The action represents the alchemical marriage of sulphur and mercury, the uniting of opposites.

See **World, The (XXI)**.

angel(s)

Angels are considered messengers or intermediaries from the divine or the "higher" realm; therefore, also messages from one's higher self or inner God. In alchemy they represented the ascension of humanity's volatile or passionate nature, i.e., sublimation. Angels, with their messages, appear on a number of tarot cards, notably in the RWS deck on The Lovers, Temperance, and Judgement.

anima

Originally Jung considered this archetypal concept to express the ultimate feminine life principle of the collective unconscious, and also that within the male personality; hence, it is commonly simplified to refer to the feminine aspect of the male. Believed to develop out of a man's relationship with his own mother, and his cultural mores regarding what constitutes "feminine," the *anima* is somewhat shaped by the patriarchal values or sexism of a given culture. Some modern Jungians, therefore, consider the *anima* as that process that brings to conscious awareness messages from the unconscious (the Self) about the self-growth process. One Jungian tarotist identifies the head in the upper left row of the RWS Seven of Cups as the *anima* and *animus*.[6]

See ***animus*** for the *anima*'s related role in The Lovers card.

animal(s)

Although animals typically represent the instinctual life, their meaning in tarot cards differs depending on the type of animal portrayed and whether it is shown in combination with other animals or persons. When shown with a person, it often represents the person's instincts and/or the higher spirit guide of the person.

The behavior (sitting, jumping, howling, running) of the animal needs to be considered. In many Fool cards, a dog—sometimes black, sometimes white—accompanies the fool. Sometimes it jumps; sometimes it nips at him. It is usually considered to be helping or warning him regarding his quest, or even to be hastening the insentient fool toward his destiny.[7]

See **bird(s);** and specific animals.

animus

Originally Jung considered this archetypal concept to express the ultimate masculine life principle of the collective unconscious, and also that within the female personality; hence, it is commonly simplified to refer to the masculine aspect of the female. Believed to develop out of a woman's relationship with her own father, and her cultural mores regarding what constitutes "masculine," it is somewhat shaped by the patriarchal values or sexism of a given culture. Some modern Jungians, therefore, consider the *animus* as that process that helps a woman act on, or express, her inner thoughts, ideas, and impulses.[8]

The two figures in The Lovers card represent the *anima* and *animus*,[9] and our task of uniting or recognizing, and being able to express, these two components in our personalities.

See *anima*; **personality** (Jungian theory).

ankh

A tau or T-cross topped with a loop, it is the Egyptian symbol of life, the universe, and immortality. Formed from the combined male (Osiris) and female (Isis) symbols, it symbolizes the reconciliation, or union, of opposites and of the two generative principles. Its shape links it to the symbolism of a key (for unlocking the mysteries of life and death). The RWS Emperor holds an ankh in his right hand. An oversized ankh dominates the Tarot of the Spirit, Three of Water. Both the Thoth and Light and

Shadow hanged men are bound to an ankh. All suggest higher spirit and personal integrative processes at work.

antlers

An attribute of the Celtic Horned God, antlers denote fertility and fecundity. The Robin Wood Magician wears a hood made of a deer head with ten antlers, the mark of a shaman.

Aphrodite/Venus (Greek/Roman goddess)

There are two versions of the birth of the goddess of love. One says she was the daughter of Zeus and the sea nymph Dione. The second says she was born fully grown from the white foam that spread around the severed genitals of Uranus, thrown into the ocean by Cronos. The wife of Hephaestus/Vulcan, she, nevertheless, conducted affairs with numerous gods and mortals.

Aphrodite/Venus owned a belt (girdle) that made the wearer irresistible; hence, herbs and foods that stimulate lust are called aphrodisiacs, and the Aphrodite archetype is one involved in sensual or sensory experiences. The Aphrodite archetype is active when a person's desire drives him/her to attain and achieve, and when desires overwhelm common sense. A mighty force for change, Aphrodite patterns emphasize the role of love and creativity, as they inspire the imagination, and the magnetic attraction(s) between lovers. When "desire nature" is guided by intelligence and practicality, it can produce great beauty and satisfying relationships. When rampant, it can result in the need for vengeance for betrayed love, an overemphasis on the material, and the acquisition of desires at all costs.[10]

Her mythology is evoked and associated with cards ruled by the planet Venus, especially the RWS Empress card, where her symbols are prominent.

See apple; Venus (planet).

Apollo

The son of Zeus by Leto, and the most brilliant of the Olympians, it is little wonder that he came to be associated with the sun. In that aspect, he is called Phoebus Apollo, "Phoebus" signifying the radiant nature of sunlight.[11] As such, he stands on The Sun card in the Mythic Tarot.

Gifted with many talents, Apollo was seen as the perfect model of manhood, the winner of competitions with mastery of all good, manly skills.[12] Occasionally, however, he overwhelmed his competitive opponents through underhanded tactics.

Noted for his generosity to mankind, Apollo encouraged the development of culture and civilization through his patronage of heroes and leaders. He carried a bow that could inflict either a cure or an affliction and he used it to kill the serpent monster Python—his mother's enemy—when he was only a few days old.

Apollo once changed himself into a dolphin and swam after a ship. He sprang onto its deck and, back in his original form, he commanded the crew to travel to Mount Parnassus, where he had previously seized the Oracle of Mother Earth (Delphi) for his own.

See **dolphin(s); Sun, The (XIX)**.

apple

One of the sacred fruits of Aphrodite/Venus, the apple symbolizes sexual desire and fertility. Its roundness suggests wholeness. When sliced, its seeds resemble a five-pointed pentacle, symbol of humans, as well as the five phases of feminine life (birth, menarche, motherhood, menopause, and death).[13]

Slices of apple become the Wheel of Change's Four of Disks. The initiate in the Shapeshifter equivalent of The Fool card holds an apple in his right hand, symbol of rebirth and reincarnation. In the Mythic Tarot's Lovers card, Paris holds an apple in his left hand as he considers the choices of power, love, and victory, which the goddesses Hera, Athena, and Aphrodite offer him to name one of them as the fairest of all.

See **Lovers, The (VI); tree, apple**.

arcana

The plural of *arkanum*, Latin for secret. There are twenty-two Major Arcana in the tarot deck and fifty-six minor "secrets." Without the presence of The Fool, the Major Arcana were called Trumps in older decks.

Aquarius (astrological sign)

Eleventh sign of the zodiac: January 21–February 19.

Element: Air
Modality: Fixed
Polarity: Yang
Ruled by Saturn, co-ruled by Uranus

Cards that are attributed to Aquarius reflect the humanistic qualities of the sign. The constellation depicts a man carrying a jug containing the waters of knowledge that are pouring from the heavens onto humanity. This sign represents efforts for social welfare, just as Prometheus risked the wrath of the gods to give fire to mankind. Aquarius is connected with societal and cultural development, and the different groups that compose a society or a collective. This sign is noted for controlled yet inspired intellect. A well-dignified Aquarius card's meanings include: vast intellect and problem-solving skills; curiosity about all aspects of life, both mechanical and organic; concern for the welfare of the community; friendliness; patience in developing ideas; farsightedness and intuition, technical skills and broadmindedness; behavioral eccentricities; the intellectual vanguard. An ill-dignified or reversed Aquarius card may be interpreted as: emotional coldness, detachment from others, abandoning society for solitude, nervous afflictions, panic attacks, neurotic compulsions, fanatic adherence to extreme political movements, tunnel vision or prejudice, scorn, and ideas that are too far ahead of their time.[14]

See **Ouranos/Uranus; Saturn** (planet); **Uranus** (planet).

arch/archway

As a portal, its presence in a card may represent an initiation and/or the concept of being born again, new life, a new beginning with fresh insights. The archway behind the Thoth Empress symbolizes her as a birth portal.[15]

In ancient times passing through an arch could herald and celebrate a military victory or triumph. In Greek mythology it was one of the symbols of Zeus/Jupiter, the allfather sky god. In the RWS and Morgan-Greer decks, arches appear as the rainbow of the Ten of Cups (emotional victory), the Ace (potential success), and Ten of Pentacles (financial/material success). They are implied when flowers cover the top of the card, as in the RWS Magician and Queen of Pentacles cards. Arches as part of church windows (the religious or spiritual portal) appear in the Morgan-Greer Three of Pentacles and Four of Swords, and a tiny archway/doorway is connected to the castle seen in the distance on the Morgan-Greer Five of Cups (hope, potentiality). Arches figure prominently in the Light and Shadow Tarot's Chariot card where they represent divine geometry: the structures of life and all life's great questions.[16] The legs of the dancing skeleton on the Thoth Death card form an archway through which a dancing blue figure is seen, suggesting movement into a new, lighter way of being.

archetypes

As used by Jungian analysts, the concept refers to the notion that humans everywhere share certain basic, timeless (primordial) ideas or blueprints (psychic patterns)—deduced from observable behavior, even though their specific presentation differs between races and cultures. Basic archetypal experiences are colored by personal experience. For instance, the overall archetypal experience of mother/mothering is common to most cultures, while our personal understanding of it comes from our experiences with our own mothers.

Archetypes are not literal or solid things, but rather "operative agents"[17] or processes, which can only be deduced from their manifestations or expressions in literature (stories, myths, fairy tales), artistic images, and in dreams and fantasies. Archetypal psychologists consider the numinous value assumed to be inherent in every image as a direct expression of the Self.[18]

Tarot cards are one artistic, systematic form for organizing certain archetypes into comprehensible patterns. Using the tarot cards, especially the Major Arcana, brings these archetypes into consciousness.

Ultimately all archetypes are linked, or overlap in meaning, and their relationship is arranged or regulated by the most powerful archetype of all, the Self. Therefore, all the tarot cards are also ultimately linked. They are like neighbors or relatives. All archetypes, and all tarot cards, have shadow or dark aspects.

See **collective unconscious; numbers; reversals; Self; shadow**, and "The Symbolic Quest," Chapter 1, Part 1.

Ares/Mars (Greek/Roman god)

Ares, who began his history as a fertility god, became the Greek (and Roman) god of war. One of the sons of Zeus/Jupiter and his sister-wife Hera/Juno, Ares was an extremely masculine god, an insatiable warrior, and was often honored on earth with martial arts exhibitions. Powerful and unwearied, he was the "foe of wisdom."[19]

The Ares/Mars archetype is reflected in character that is driven by unbounded passions, intense reactions, and immediate physical action. If provoked, the Ares personality acts first and thinks later, frequently with detrimental consequences to himself or others. This characteristic can also mean expending energy without planning, possibly on lost causes or imaginary battles. In the long run, he may never develop the ability to reflect on, and understand, his behavior. When his energy is coupled with the skills of logic and strategic thinking, however, the Ares personality displays the kind of warrior energy that allows him to boldly attain goals and overcome challenges and obstacles.[20]

See **Aries**; **Mars** (planet); **Scorpio**.

Aries (astrological sign)

First sign of the zodiac (March 21—Spring Equinox—to April 20).

Element: Fire
Modality: Cardinal
Polarity: Yang
Ruled by the planet Mars.

A card attributed to Aries partakes of its dynamic, pioneering energy, as this sign is filled with the awakening life of spring. Aries initiates action, and charges forward to attain goals. It is fearless, vigorous, hasty, and loyal. The Aries type is considered much like the character Parsifal, charging forward into the unknown to rescue the distressed. In addition to given meanings of a card, a well-dignified card attributed to Aries will include qualities of: leadership skills, high-minded ethics and idealism, keen sense of adventure and drama, and accomplishment. An ill-dignified or reversed Aries card may include such meanings as: bossy, inconsiderate and selfish, and accident-prone; failure to consider potential obstacles before starting a quest; underestimating an enemy.[21]

See **Mars** (planet).

armor

Represents protection, defensiveness (not totally open and revealing), the willingness to defend one's ideals/principles. Steel armor is the symbol of Mars. Armor appears on many of the knight cards (especially RWS), and The Emperor, where it protects inner lushness.[22]

See **knights.**

Artemis/Diana (Greek/Roman goddess)

Before she became the Greek goddess of the hunt, Artemis was an Anatolian goddess of the moon, and later came to be known as Kybele, one of the great mother goddesses. In Greek mythology, she was the twin sister of Apollo, the sun god. The slender arc of the moon is her bow and its beams are her arrows. As a moon goddess she was frequently identified with Selene, a more ancient Greek divinity of the moon, whose attributes and adventures eventually were merged with those of the more modern Diana. Although Artemis/Diana was a consummate hunter, she was also the guardian of wild beasts. She favored marsh and mountain, springs and woodland brooks.[23] Her mythology is evoked and associated with any tarot card in which a moon appears and particularly The Moon card.

See **Moon, The (XVIII).**

Astraea

When the world was "wet with slaughter,"[24] in the battle of the Titans against Zeus, Astraea (As-TRAY-uh), daughter of Zeus, and Themis, the starry virgin of justice, came down to dwell on earth rather than unite with the Titans. She took upon herself the task of spreading blessings, peace, and joy throughout the human world. However, in the Bronze Age, "when man's wickedness was apparent,"[25] she finally abandoned her mountaintop home and traveled into the heavens, becoming the last goddess to linger on earth. Because she was the goddess of innocence and purity, Zeus transformed her into the constellation Virgo, and because her mother was Themis (Justice), she holds aloft a pair of scales. Her myth is one of those associated with The Star card in tarot decks.

See **Star, The (XVII)**.

astrological signs

When astrological signs appear in the art of a card in a group, rather than as one specific sign, they may represent cycles, the passage of time, a map of consciousness, or the combination of personality traits in general. Typical groupings occur in the canopy and on the garments of the charioteer in the RWS Chariot card, and on the blanket of the RWS Nine of Swords. They are engraved on coins on the Thoth Fool card, where they symbolize the materialization of archetypal principles.[26]

See **zodiac; zodiacal attributions**; and specific astrological signs.

Athena/Minerva (Greek/Roman goddess)

Athena, or Athene, the protectress of heroes, represents a psychologically positive force against the masculine psyche being overcome or overwhelmed by the feminine *anima*. Born from the head of her father Zeus, she is definitely a mindful or intellectual force, the virgin goddess of wisdom and truth. It is in that sense that she is associated with the Justice card. Born in a blinding flash, she also represents sudden insight. The olive and the owl are sacred to her, as well as the serpent and the bird.

See **owl(s); tree, olive**.

aureole

See **nimbus**.

axis mundi

See **world axis**.

B

Bacchus
See **Dionysus/Bacchus**.

background

Items in a card's background may be what "backs up" or supports the figure, or what the figure is ignoring or leaving behind. They can, therefore, symbolize personal, psychic, and sometimes cultural ideas, or concepts from the reader's or querent's "background." In the Haindl deck, card designs and figures are presented in layers, with the major idea being in the foreground, what's behind it being placed farther back behind the major figure, and then a more cosmic or other connection pictured even farther back. One moves through this "economy of symbolism"[1] to a deeper understanding of the card.

For a different understanding of some RWS backgrounds, *see* **stage cards.**

beard

While a beard is generally a symbol of masculinity and strength, a white beard represents age and wisdom. It associates a figure with the archetype of the Wise Old Man, as do the long white beards of the RWS Emperor and Hermit.

See **Wise Old Man/Woman** (archetype).

bee(s)

Bees represent industriousness, organization, and life "buzzing" with activity. Bees' ability to transform nectar into honey ("sweet effort")—the basis of many a divine and initiatory food and drink (as in mead)—elevates them to the realm of the alchemical transformative process, doubly so when you consider that bees are also seen as a symbol of the soul. Bees dancing in a circle, and otherwise, form the pattern for the Thoth Empress's gown, where they symbolize the "queen in the beehive." The golden bees on the Thoth Emperor's coat represent the structure and order of the hive.[2] Together they participate in the alchemical marriage of the feminine and masculine principles represented by the cards.

Some tarotists say there are tiny bees flying about the head of the maiden in the RWS Strength card, which represent purposeful consciousness connected with the higher realm. Bees and their symbolism are implied in the bee skep (hive) that appears in the Robin Wood Empress card. Bees fly over the head of the Seer (Page) of Pentacles (World Spirit Tarot), representing her steadfastness and goal-oriented behavior.

beggar(s)

Traditionally, beggars symbolize the lowest level of a culture's social or economic status. They may remind us of the possibility of return to a dependent financial or economic position. As with

Asian monks who must still beg part of their food, a beggar can signal a deliberate choice for humbling oneself, or getting out of the ego's pompous ways and the need for worldly possessions. One ancient sign of a beggar was the white staff or stick he carried, symbolizing a person forced to abandon his land, or surrender his property,[3] and in the Tarot de Marseilles, The Fool does, indeed, carry his bundle bound on a white stick, although his staff is gold.

Two beggars—or certainly tattered, wounded persons—appear in the RWS Five and Six of Pentacles. One of the myths connected with these cards concerns the visit to earth of Jupiter and Mercury, disguised as weary travelers. All doors were closed to them except that of Philemon and his wife Baucis. Beggar figures can also represent an impoverishment of the soul, so the motif of two gods who come to men in disguised form occurs at a time when our individual relationship to the divine has become a necessity,[4] one of the possible messages of the RWS Five and Six of Pentacles. A bearded beggar also appears in the Spiral Tarot's Six of Pentacles.

bells

In ancient times bells symbolized the connection between heaven and earth. They were thought to reflect cosmic harmonies. In the Middle Ages they were believed to ward off misfortune and to conjure up good spirits.[5] The Fool in the Haindl deck wears six bells, which connect him to the six planets in the card's background and ultimately with the Greek myth of the music of the spheres (the harmony of existence).[6]

See music (inner).

belt/sash

Called a girdle in earlier times, it referred to "girding the loins"[7] in preparation to perform a task or to journey into danger. It simultaneously symbolized energy and power, protection, and a choice.[8] Belts and sashes can symbolize a vow undertaken, or a certain level of achievement or initiation (as in the martial arts' black belt) with its accompanying responsibility.

As a garment or decoration that wraps around the middle of the torso, it separates the upper body from the lower, and can be said to psychologically symbolize the separation of the mind and heart from instinct or sexuality, higher ideals from the more base instincts. "Girdles" are often artistically depicted as hanging looser or lower than belts or sashes.

Many symbolic belts and sashes are shown on figures in tarot cards, especially on the Marseilles deck. Their color and decoration may suggest additional symbolism. In the RWS deck, The Fool wears a belt that some have suggested symbolizes the seven planets and possibly the entire zodiac (if the unseen portions of the belt are included), while The Magician wears the ouroboros belt (*see* **ouroboros**). The RWS charioteer's belt displays planetary and alchemical symbols. He has prepared himself for a journey of enhanced consciousness and personal development. The female in the RWS Strength card wears a belt of flowers that connects her to the lion (her natural and instinctual life). The RWS Hanged Man and the Two of Pentacles figure wear red belts, suggesting instinctual vitality that either creates a temporary separation so other interests may be pursued or that attempts to combine the upper and lower. All of the Robin Wood pages wear a belt from which a mnemonic device hangs to succinctly express one of the major meanings of each card.

bird(s)

The elemental spirit of the suit of Swords, birds are mythologically associated with the golden-haired, blue-eyed Norse goddess Freya, who sometimes traveled in the guise of a bird. Because of their ability to fly, birds have long been considered messengers or mediators between heaven and earth, and to also symbolize higher consciousness, and spirit itself. They can represent freedom from restriction or the wish for such freedom. As such, and as spiritual guides during such freedom, exotic toucans, parrots, and an owl appear on the "Fool-Child" card of the Voyager deck. The entire suit of Swords has been transformed into the suit of Birds in the Shining Tribe deck, and their symbology varies depending on the card. In the Robin Wood Two of Pentacles, bird-shaped ships fly in the air behind the juggler, representing the heights to which her imagination can soar because she is so balanced. Unidentifiable birds appear on many tarot cards, especially Swords cards, but in some cards the birds are very specific and take on a more definite meaning.

See **dove; eagle; falcon; ibis; Pentacles, Nine of; swan.**

black

The color of the primordial void before there was light, black is also a color of the underworld, the night, and a symbol of the hidden knowledge and workings of the unconscious, especially its shadow aspects. In Egypt black represented the "mothering darkness of germination."[9] It can symbolize the absence of light or insight, emptiness, and ignorance, but also the possibility of receptivity and inner protection. Saturn is the ruling planet of black.

See **checkerboard pattern; colors; shadow.**

black-and-white pattern

See **checkerboard pattern.**

blindfold

As something that prevents sight, it refers to the inability to see or find one's way, as in the blindfolded figure on the RWS and Robin Wood Eight of Swords. The card calls upon us to open our eyes. Still, it also can represent turning inward to listen to one's self (the blindfolded RWS Two of Swords figure). An old term for being blindfolded was "hoodwinked," so sometimes a blindfold may suggest that we have been fooled by our beliefs or illusions. The blindfolded fool in the Alchemical deck suggests that as he begins his journey, he is ignorant of alchemical principles.

blue

Shades of blue appear as the sky in many tarot cards (other popular sky colors being gray and yellow, and in older RWS cards green and orange). Blue sky can refer to overseeing spirit, or heaven (often modified by whatever appears in the sky), the inner spiritual process, and cosmic consciousness. It represents a two-way connection with the divine, and is the color of the fifth (throat) chakra. Its darker version, indigo, is associated with the third eye (seeing with the eye that sees truth).

As a garment color, it often gives a clue as to the possible emotions of the figure in the card. In ancient Egypt, blue—and especially a starry blue cloak similar to the canopy found on the RWS Chariot card—symbolized Nut, the sky goddess. In Greece, it reflected Zeus/Jupiter and Hera/Juno, god and goddess of heaven. More generally, it has become a color for the feminine divine or goddess, although it was also the color attribute of masculine sky gods in several ancient cultures.

As the color of water, blue can symbolize unconscious processes at work, emotions, ideas flowing from the unconscious, intuition, and the process of reflection. Because it can represent both sky and water, blue can symbolize vertical alignment (height/depth; above/below) or alignment of the personal soul, or spirit, with higher spirit, depending on the scene shown.

In fairy tales, blue flowers often refer to spiritual aspirations (making the unconscious known), and to greater, or higher, mysteries. A catalyst color in alchemical symbolism, some alchemical artistry shows the blue rose of wisdom, a modification of saturnine black and "the sign of high spirituality and arcana knowledge."[10] Blue's ruling planet is Jupiter.

See **background; chakra(s); color(s); water.**

blueprint/plans

As devices to help us build physical structures, blueprints represent creation plans, creative processes about to be accomplished, and the structure to build, discover, or move on to something new and greater.[11] Such a sketch appears at the base of the Thoth Universe card. Blueprints can also call upon us to compare our dreams with the reality we create. Schematic drawings are held by one of the figures in the RWS Three of Pentacles, calling for a time of evaluation and possible reordering of priorities.

boat(s)

Boats appear in many tarot cards, and the overall card meaning, and the shape and size of the boat all contribute to their symbolism. Boats may symbolize the transition from the realm of life into death (*see* **rivers/streams**) and are seen in the RWS Death card. A small boat is prominent in many Six of Swords cards, representing the personal journey or progress through life. In the Morgan-Greer Six of Swords, the boatman represents Fate.[12] Since boats travel on water, they can represent the relationship of the conscious to the unconscious, the known to the unknown.

See **ship(s)**; the reference to bird-shaped boats in **bird(s)**.

book(s)

Books symbolize learning, knowledge, scholarship, and wisdom. They relate to life and its cycles (the book of life), and to the revelations and manifestations of the universe or cosmos. The four evangelical figures on the RWS Wheel of Fortune, and some other decks, read cosmic and cyclical books. La Papesse (High Priestess) of the Marseilles deck holds a book representing esoteric wisdom and teachings, although in many decks, the book is replaced by a scroll (sometimes thought to be the Torah because the letters TORA can be read on it).

branches

Branches usually take on the symbolism of their trees, so see entries regarding various trees.

See **Swords, Ace of**.

bridges

Like rainbows, bridges mark the threshold between two realms, e.g., between divine and earthly, between one psychological or emotional state and another. They are related to the mythological ferryman who escorts or transports souls into the afterlife.[13] Bridges not only join, but have the capacity to overcome what is in the gap.[14] A bridge appears in the RWS and Alchemical Tarot's Four of Wands and the RWS Five of Cups (a transition to be made in the future). One is possibly implied in the RWS Chariot, where the transition from the safety of the community into the outer world has been made.

See **rainbow**.

bridging

See **linking themes**.

brown

Associated with the earth, brown most commonly represents the potential for growth, and groundedness, particularly if it depicts a plowed field as in the RWS Page of Pentacles. If, however, a patch of earth is brown while all around it green things grow, as in the Robin Wood Four of Cups, it can be considered a color of barrenness, lack of creativity, and stagnation; energies being held in check or restricted. Saturn is its ruling planet.

See **colors**.

bull

In early cultures the bull often represented the heavenly sperm that fertilized the world.[15] Later it came to also represent vitality, masculine strength and potency, and untamed energy or nature (often with the accompanying idea of its needing to be overcome). The sacrifice of the bull represents the triumph of human spiritual nature over animal instinct, the developing personality's influence over instinctual desires,[16] and carries a similar message as the RWS Strength card.

Because of their curved horns, ancient cultures linked bulls, and cows, to lunar symbology and the lunar crescent. As such, bulls are considered either the consorts of a culture's earth goddess or its moon goddess. The Egyptian moon god Osiris, often depicted as a bull, was paired with his wife, the mother moon goddess Isis. Greek mythology links the bull with the Minotaur (half man, half bull), which guarded the Cretan labyrinth.

The first letter of the Hebrew alphabet, *aleph*, means "bull" (or ox) and, for those readers who attribute Hebrew letters to the cards, *aleph*/bull is associated with The Fool card. Bulls' heads are carved on the throne of the RWS King of Pentacles, suggesting his achievements and prowess and the Golden Dawn's astrological association of the card with Taurus. A bull also is shown on the RWS Wheel of Fortune and World cards, where it simultaneously represents the fixed zodiacal sign of Taurus, the archangel Auriel (Uriel), the element of earth, and the suit of Pentacles.

See also cow; horn(s); Taurus.

butterfly

Because of their ability to awaken from an apparently lifeless cocoon (metamorphosis), butterflies have long symbolized transformation—a major change in the life cycle—as they do in the tarot. They also can represent the psyche or the soul; and since they have two well-developed wings and two lesser developed ones, in Jungian psychology they represent the two more- and the two less-developed four functions (thinking, sensing, feeling, intuiting).

Butterflies often appear with other heavenly creatures who

possess "flighty" energy (cherubs), as on the throne and crown of the RWS Queen of Swords. The roots of the lotus plants in the Thoth Five of Cups form a butterfly, suggesting that "disappointment," the name of the card, can be a transformative agent, while the butterfly in the deck's Fool card suggests the need for, and possibilities of, future development.

A butterfly flies before the Nigel Jackson and Light and Shadow fools, indicating the transformative soul journey about to begin.

C

✳

caduceus

A staff entwined with two serpents and topped with wings was traditionally carried by the messenger god Hermes, and also associated with Asclepias, the healer, although his staff only had one snake twined around it and no wings. It symbolizes fertility and the rising of kundalini energy, as well as the rhythm of balance. Probably an image imported from Middle Eastern cultures, it also represents the combination of the monster and the great goddess serpents renovating the world.[1] Likewise, in alchemy it represented the union of opposites. Several of these meanings may apply in the caduceus seen above the couple on the RWS Two of Cups. The winged caduceus of Hermes is held in the hand of The World figure in the Alchemical deck, and is embodied in a spiral around the Thoth Fool, where it hints at the awakening into which the fool will progress.

See chakra(s); snake(s).

camel

The camel carries a variety of meanings: moderation, arrogance, laziness, awkwardness. Most important for the tarot, however, it also represents discernment because it will only allow itself to be loaded with burdens that it can actually carry.[2] Because it could take a traveler across the mysterious desert, the camel also symbolizes the ability to reach the "hidden center of divine essence."[3] An ethereal-appearing camel sits below the High Priestess's root chakra in the Haindl card, and represents "crouching energy" waiting to be uncoiled. Simultaneously it represents the seeming "stillness" of the card, as well as the source of cosmic energy that lights the scene.[4]

Cancer:

Fourth sign of the zodiac: June 22–July 23.

Element: Water
Modality: Cardinal
Polarity: Yin
Ruled by the Moon

A card attributed to Cancer partakes of its nurturing, maternal qualities, the powerful cycles of birth, growth, and death. Cancer represents the necessary return to origins after the first three signs of the zodiac; the need to secure and protect all that those signs have accomplished in turn; the pause for reflection on the inner, domestic side of life. The crab is a symbol of tenacity, protection, and regeneration; the connection between sea and shore. The meanings of a well-dignified Cancer-attributed card include: cyclic fluctuations and trends, emotions, family traditions and domestic life, genetic inheritance, multi-generational family traits, maternal qualities; wanderlust and adventures far from home—particularly journeys by sea; and a desire for acquisitions, like money or property, that enhance security through ownership. Ill-dignified or reversed Cancer card meanings include: clinging, insularity, xenophobia, emotional cruelty or instability, a myopic intellect, abuse or neglect of parental authority.

See **Moon** (planet).

candle(s)

As a source of light, candles carry the association of enlightenment, illumination of the dark (unconscious), and aspirations to achieve higher insight. They can represent the living, or burning out, of a person's life. The candleholder or color may add to the significance of the symbolism. For all of these reasons, candles have long been associated with ritual.

Candles in the colors of the four directions and elements burn on the Wheel of Change Five of Wands. Burning candles light the magician's room in the Ancestral Path's Six of Cups. They are held in containers made of antlers, symbol of the stag and of the horned god (*see* **antlers**).

Capricorn (astrological sign)

Tenth sign of the zodiac (December 22—Winter Solstice—January 20).

Element: Earth
Modality: Cardinal
Polarity: Yin
Ruled by Saturn

Cards attributed to the sign Capricorn partake of its organizing, structuring, disciplined, hierarchical and form-building qualities. The Sun is in Capricorn when the dark of winter is in full sway, resulting in a dark and pessimistic view of the sign.

Capricorn tests the practicality of the ideas and concepts of Sagittarius, and builds on them once proven. It represents the power of parental and authority figures, governmental structure, and the realities of life. This sign also has mystical qualities, particularly regarding spiritual discipline and mastery of occult techniques and knowledge, and understanding the cycles of time and the limits of human nature. A well-dignified Capricorn card will mean: tenacity, self discipline, productivity, organization, a capacity for management and leadership, high authority and reputation. A badly dignified or reversed Capricorn card's meanings include: excessive control, abuse of force and power, corruption, bad reputation, oppression by authority, burdensome family matters, sorrows, losses, difficult tests of character that may be karmic in nature.[5]

See **Saturn** (planet).

card meditation

There are several ways to meditate on a card to deepen one's understanding of it. One way is to look at the card until it is fixed in your memory, then, with eyes closed, imagine the card becoming life-size. Step into the card and look around, speak to the figure(s), and allow all your senses to further add to the visual information on the card. When finished, step out of the card, reduce it to its normal size, and open your eyes. Additional information may be obtained if, when you step into the card, as an alternative to regarding yourself as a visitor, you imagine yourself becoming the figure(s) on the card and surveying the landscape from that perspective.

See **moving meditation**.

Case, Paul Foster (1884–1954)

Believing that the tarot serves to transmit esoteric teachings and to evoke creative and expanded states of consciousness, Case created a black-and-white deck, drawn by Jessie Burns Park. It is still distributed—along with lessons for using the cards—by the acolytes of his Builders of the Adytum (B.O.T.A.), based in Los Angeles. They offer specific instructions for coloring the trump cards, which are believed to be artistically corrected drawings of the RWS deck. Case's face appears on The Hierophant card. Minor Arcana cards do not contain scenes.

Case is the author of two important books on the tarot (*see* Bibliography), one expounding on the symbolism of the Major Arcana cards of his deck and the other offering a series of meditations for them. His scholarship notwithstanding, Case purported in his first book that according to occult tradition the tarot had been invented in 1200 A.D. by a group of adepts who met at various intervals in Fez, Morocco. Being of different nationalities, and speaking different languages, they embodied their important doctrines in a book of pictures, "whose combinations should depend on the occult harmonies of numbers."[6]

castle

When a castle appears in a card, consider whether it is large or small, where it is located on the card, whether or not it dominates the background or the foreground, and on what it is situated (green hills, rocky promontories). As a man-made structure, a castle can suggest future fruition or manifestation, a place of refuge and safety, and the source of, or protection for, a hidden treasure (note how they are often set apart).

Castles are symbols of security and protection. Situated on the left side of the card, the castle may suggest that the message of the card is influenced by one's past family of origin. Castles may also represent fantasies that can protect or nourish, but that ultimately must be transformed into a new image,[7] as on the RWS Eight of Cups. In fairy tales the castle is often a feminine symbol, sometimes of the *anima*, sometimes representing the collective maternal image.[8]

cat(s)

Depending on the culture, cats are either inherently good or thoroughly evil. In Kabbalistic lore as well as Buddhism, cats are associated with snakes or serpents. For the Egyptians, the cat was associated with the moon and was sacred to the goddess Isis. The Egyptian lion or cat-headed goddess Bast/Bastet was the great protectress of homes and marriages, mothers and children, and associated with fruitfulness and the vitality of life. Her solar form was the lion-headed goddess Sekhmet, a goddess of war and bringer of epidemics and, incongruently, of healing. The Greeks and Romans identified Bastet with Artemis/Diana. In Norse tradition the beautiful, blue-eyed Freya drove a cat-drawn chariot. As the goddess of love, beauty, and fecundity, she inspired all sacred poetry.[9] When thus associated with goddesses, cats symbolize divine feminine wisdom.

Because of their ability to hunt in the night, cats became associated with the forces of darkness and the underworld; hence, a black cat was considered the quintessential familiar of medieval witches. Although Siamese, such a cat sits inside the magic circle of The Witch (Magician) card in the Daughters of the Moon deck.

Because it can see in the dark, the cat sometimes symbolizes a "seer." Black cats are often considered symbols of death and darkness and, therefore, associated with the moon and all that is "dark" (shadow) about the feminine, including feminine calculation, mystery, and hidden wisdom. The nature of cats is such that they often symbolize liberty, independence, cunningness, patience, agility. Cats may also symbolize instinctual energy that has been tamed and still relatively close to conscious awareness. Before the patriarchs of Christianity banished the feminine shadow (to be replaced with the virgin mother), cats, and especially black cats, were not regarded as scary, evil, or associated with witchcraft.[10]

A cat appears on the Nigel Jackson Fool card (where it stands in for Dionysus's panther) and Nine of Coins; at the foot of the RWS Queen of Wands, where it likely represents her intuitive skills; and in the border of the Renaissance Priestess card, where it represents Demeter's cat. Cats, symbolizing independence, resourcefulness, and wisdom, accompany the initiate on the Shapeshifter Journey (22) card. The one accompanying the Welsh Goddess of Air, Arianrhod (King of Wands), represents magic and wisdom hidden from the uninitiated.[11]

Cats, hunted by bats, are the topic of the Haindl Ten of Wands, reflecting what happens when the reverse of power occurs and the hunter becomes the hunted.

See **lion(s).**

cauldron

A vessel traditionally used by practitioners of magic to cause transformation, either by the act of magic or by employing the contents of the cauldron as a compress or drinkable potion. As a vessel used in ritual, the cauldron symbolizes renewal and regeneration. When its contents bubble, it may refer to fullness and abundance or wicked energy, depending on the contents. An alchemical cauldron appears on the Thoth Art (Temperance) card.

In mythology and fairy tales there are many famous, magical cauldrons. The Celtic Cauldron of Annwn produced food for anyone but cowards and revived the life, but not the speech, of fallen soldiers placed within it. In the Legend Arthurian Tarot's Temperance card, a sisterhood of nine priestesses, attendants of the Triple Goddess, attend the huge, blue, overflowing Cauldron of Annwn.

In Babylonia the fate-goddess Siris had a cauldron made of lapis lazuli, which was later sometimes considered the Philosopher's Stone. The many myths associated with cauldrons of regeneration or inspiration entered Christian tradition as the Holy Grail,[12] topic of many tarot cards.

A golden woman is released from the cauldron of alchemical

fires in the Robin Wood Judgement card. She represents the world soul, the *anima mundi*.

cave/cavern

Caves have long been a symbol of the womb, and specifically that of Mother Earth. They also represent "going down" into the earth and, therefore, entering the unconscious and making contact with the hidden, the dark world. As a dark place where one has to go to face demons and survive, the cave is associated with the archetypal theme of death/rebirth and initiation into life's greater mysteries. The space within the cave can also symbolize the "world egg." It is a passageway into something more universal and cosmic.

Insofar as the unconscious is seen to carry a negative meaning, however, then the cave also may be seen as carrying negative symbolism. Hence, the many stories of monsters in caves, which the hero must defeat, or "scary" passageways in folktales where unpleasant "adventures" may occur. In this sense, they also may represent the archetypal "dark night of the soul" experience. In the cave the ego gives up its separateness and merges with the whole,[13] symbolically returning us to our beginnings.

A cave with a glowing star within appears on the distant shore of the Robin Wood Six of Swords, hinting at the higher consciousness to be achieved at the end of the journey. A tiny, dark cave entrance has been hinted at on the opposite shore of the RWS Death card. The Haindl Hermit may well be standing in a cave,[14] and Merlin stands beside his mountain cave in the Legend Arthurian Tarot's Magician card.

centering

Centering refers to meditative techniques to align personal, physical energy with the invisible or ethereal "energy" body. Often it involves visualizing and working with the chakras so that energy flows freely through the body. Some tarotists suggest that centering is an essential component of preparing to do a tarot reading.

See **chakra(s); grounding**.

certification

The Tarot Certification Board (TCB), established June 1, 1996, was disbanded in 2002, and reformed as the Tarot Certification Board of America (TCBA). It offers seven levels of certification: Apprentice Tarot Reader, Tarot Reader, Professional Tarot Reader, Tarot Consultant, Tarot Master, Tarot Instructor, and the honorary Tarot Grandmaster (CTGM). Each level, except the CTGM, requires demonstrating various competencies of tarot reading and associated tarot tasks. At present there are also associated certification boards active in Korea and Brazil, and others are forming in several European countries.[15] They can be reached through the TCBA.

The Canadian Tarot Network is a not-for-profit group focused on teaching ethical tarot reading; helping connect clients to readers in their locales; and offering certification to Canadians and to Americans caught in the pinch over the restructuring of U.S. certification boards. It offers levels similar to the TCBA.[16]

On July 29, 2002, The American Board of Tarot Certification (ABTC), a second U.S. certifying board, was founded, which offers five levels of certification: Tarot Associate, Tarot Professional, Tarot Master, Tarot Educator, and Tarot Sage. Included with certification, the tarot professional may take advantage of the board's referral service. Continuing education units (CEUs) are required for certain levels of certification.[17]

chains

Chains are prominent in The Devil card of many decks, often binding two people together (Ancestral Path, RWS, Light and Shadow, Mythic). In the New Palladini card, the goat-headed devil holds the chains of material slavery, representing, as do all chains, the ways we bind or imprison ourselves with false ideals and concepts, and the ways in which we limit ourselves. A broken chain aptly sends its message on the Osho Death card.

chakra(s)

Several Eastern religions teach an energy concept called the chakra system. A chakra (Sanskrit for "wheel" or "disk") is an invisible, spinning center of activity or energy that receives, assimilates, and expresses life force. Based on their location in the body, chakras are associated with various states of consciousness, open or blocked energy levels, archetypal elements, and philosophical constructs. They are like floppy disks containing vital programs that lie deep in our core,[18] inner power centers. Each one represents a spiritual life-lesson or challenge that directs us toward greater consciousness.[19]

Traditionally, each major chakra is assigned one of the colors of the rainbow and, as the Hindu serpent goddess Kundalini rises through each, she creates a personal, internal Rainbow Bridge, the legendary mythical metaphor for the evolution of consciousness.[20]

Although there are more than three hundred chakras in some systems, the most well-known are seven: the root (coccygeal plexus), the base of the spine (sacral plexus), solar plexus, heart (cardiac plexus), throat (pharyngeal plexus), ajna or third eye (carotid plexus), and crown (cerebral cortex) chakras. Several theories have an eighth chakra that resides above the head outside the physical body (although some would say this corresponds to the crown chakra). Its color is magenta. Different authors attribute different tarot cards to the chakras, plus many tarot books present a seven-card chakra spread.

Careful examination of tarot cards shows that often items of clothing or jewelry, and objects of nature (butterflies, birds) appear at the level of, or on, certain chakra areas. Their own symbolism, plus an understanding of the power of that particular chakra, can provide additional information about the meaning of the card for personal development.

In the RWS Four of Swords, the three swords on the wall pointing to the head, throat, and chest chakras may refer to a Masonic resurrection-initiation ceremony, since these were the three chakras struck to slay Hiram Abiff, the Master Mason of King Solomon's temple.[21] In the Robin Wood card the three swords all seem to point to the solar plexus or survival chakra. We must temporarily retire to survive or revive physically and emotionally.

See **snake(s)**.

Chariot, The (VII)

In the fifteenth century at least one version of this card showed a female in profile carried in a triumphal chariot drawn by two winged horses, likely symbolizing the winged figure of Victory.[22] A seventeenth-century card showed Venus in a steedless chariot, holding reins that extend downward through a cloud.[23]

In the RWS and neo-RWS cards, the charioteer is often represented by a young man or adolescent who has left home (the village in the RWS background). He prepares to "head out" for his adventures, the destiny he will make for himself. Psychologically, The Chariot carries us on our outward journey to find our place in the world and on our accompanying inward journey of change. This is aptly demonstrated on the Ancestral Path's Chariot card, where black (unconscious knowledge) and orange (conscious knowledge) lions pull the chariot. In ancient Egypt, the double lion motif represented a turning point, the move from death to resurrection,[24] suggesting this card illustrates the initiatory life lesson of learning to hold one's polarities together in paradox.

A few card designers focus on the chariot as a cube (representing earth or material manifestation) and connect it with the cube (*see* **cube**) on which The High Priestess sits, and The Emperor in some versions of the deck.[25] In both the RWS and Spiral cards, the charioteer is encased in a stone cube, by which the designer of the Spiral deck means to indicate that the charioteer has control over his instinctual and sexual nature.[26] Others define the situation as representing being "blocked" in these capacities. With the latter interpretation, the charioteer is perceived as immobilized rather than actually moving forward, partly because he is not yet free of the ties of home (the town remaining in the background). In both decks, the charioteer has no reins. He relies on his intellect and consciousness to guide him in making this journey.

Even though there are a number of traditionally spiritual symbols (a starry crown and canopy, zodiacal images representing starry forces, magical geomantic signs, sphinxes, winged solar disk, and the Hindu lingam/yoni shield) in the RWS card, the charioteer's planes of victory are to be considered material or external.[27] The tests of initiation—rites of passage—through which he must pass are to be understood rationally. So caught up is he in the bondage of logical understanding, that if he were to encounter The High Priestess, he could neither answer her questions nor open her scroll.[28] He has been, or will be, busy making his successful mark in the world; hence, The Chariot card also speaks to the fact that not all of life can be an inner journey. Certainly at the appropriate time we must make an outer journey to find our place in the larger society.

Still, the many spiritual symbols in the card suggest that the world of spirit is very much alive within. We can turn everyday life into spiritual exercise if we so desire. The card also suggests the yearning that will eventually "drive" the charioteer to seek his spiritual center. Accordingly, several contemporary artists are turning away from a thoroughly material/worldly viewpoint for the card.

Sevens have a "breakthrough consciousness," the ability to view old things in new ways and to revitalize their usefulness.[29] Esoterically, seven is a symbol of the transformation that can occur with initiation. In the Light and Shadow card, a figure holding a crab (Cancer, the card's astrological attribute) sits cross-legged in a chariot, meditating. He is a warrior who seeks truth, not battle—a seeker and a seer. The Thoth charioteer, possessed of great spiritual power, also meditates, encased in massive golden armor.

The Wheel of Change's Chariot card links a silhouetted figure with a wheel superimposed on her body to a series of additional wheels: one formed by ancient standing stone monuments, one formed by the spokes of a wheel, one formed by the planets of the solar system. This card stresses our inevitable relationship with the greater universe, with universal cycles, and with our true inner power. The Spiral card links the charioteer to cycles, as well as to Hercules, a solar king/hero, who died and rose again—rebirth motif (*see* **Heracles/Hercules**).

In the RWS card, the water of The High Priestess (the mother of emotions) "backs up" the charioteer, although he faces away from it, and it is largely obscured by his chariot. The water represents the emotional break we all must experience when we leave home, and the necessity of learning to control our emotions. The chariot's canopy is supported by the four pillars/corners of the earth (material order) and the four elements, while the eight-pointed star on his crown links him to The Star card.

The lingam-yoni shield on the RWS Chariot refers to the combining of opposites (*see* **lingam-yoni**). Since only one person is in the chariot, the implication is that he is on the way to becoming androgynous.[30] The resolution of opposites (also represented by the black and white sphinxes) is always before him (an unseen part of each of his tasks, yet evident to others?). It leads the way in his journey. In some cards (Robin Wood, Morgan-Greer, Spiral, Light and Shadow) the charioteer's horses/sphinxes appear to be pulling in opposite directions or have their heads turned to opposite sides (*see* **twin motif**).

The square on the breastplate of the RWS charioteer at the heart chakra represents order and the material. One of the spiritual challenges of the charioteer is to learn compassion. He has been so busy in the physical world—having built his foundation in the walled city behind him—that he has forgotten, or has not had time to learn, compassion or how to give love either to himself or to others (typical of a striving workaholic). It is one of the challenges of this card and of life: how to be successful in the workaday world and also in your love life, how to observe and acknowledge the spiritual, loving energy around us, as we look straight ahead, pursuing our goals.

One of our adult tasks is that of generating an internal sense of emotional steadiness or harmony, from which we can allow all other emotions to be expressed and to which we can return as an inner haven. The Chariot card serves to remind us of this task. It is a card of finding new directions or, perhaps, simply of finally being able to determine or define a direction for oneself.

The Robin Wood charioteer sings and strums his harp, while unicorns, which will only obey the pure of heart, pull his chariot so fast they stir up a cloud of dust. Yet the absence of reins tells us he "reigns" by "being in tune with destiny."[31] It is "spiritual horsemanship."[32]

The tarot charioteer and chariot symbolically represents the dynamic or active situation of exerting control over human conditions or conflicts such as those between the baser and higher self, conscious and unconscious thought, the material and the spiritual plane, humanity's need for preservation and destruction. The chariot may also symbolize the world with its earthly cube, starry sky, and the world axis or *axis mundi*, which connects the two domains.

The Hebrew word for this card, *Cheth*, means a field and the fence enclosing it. This can refer to restriction or a boundary into which flow inner, or spiritual, forces, or it can refer to the emotional or intellectual "fence" we build around ourselves to establish boundaries so that all that is within, conscious and unconscious, is united and maintained, rather than being scattered. Remember, however, that when appropriate, fences can be moved to restrict the field differently, or removed to expand it.

In the Haindl card, a red boat with wheels rushes through a rough sea, carrying a white-robed figure. In the sky behind him looms a mythical figure, part boar, part wolf, signifying wild, unmanageable fears and archaic terrors. It is a confrontation between willpower and those fears. On the Osho card (Awareness) the veil of illusion starts to burn from a shadowy figure. What emerges is a bright blue Buddha-like figure. It is a card of no-mind, of revolution in action as we become aware of, and release, crippling, inhibiting thoughts of the past and expectations of the future.

Keywords/phrases: gaining control of one's instincts and impulses; self-determination; endurance; willpower; ambition; conquest; finding one's path or place in the world; controlling one's direction in life; roads to travel; using mental abilities to govern emotions.

See **arch/archway; Cancer** (sun sign); **lingam-yoni; winged disk.**

checkerboard pattern

The pattern is related to the number two and to the Gemini myth, the contradictory and contrasting forces of life, the light and shadow of the personality. As a floor pattern, it may represent the bipolar nature of earthly existence and/or the dual paths (positive/negative; good/evil; light/darkness; spirit/matter) of destiny or wisdom. Together the blacks and whites represent the germinal, or primal, stage of a process and its ending (illumination or purification).

They also represent a sorting process that leads to transformation and, as such, suggest life cycles. In early Christian art, black stood for penitence or the penitent, and white for purity and forgiveness. In heraldry, the pattern is called "embattled" (the forces of dark and light battle).[33] Found in the flooring of mystery temples and Masonic lodges, the pattern also appears on the floor of the RWS Hierophant, the Spiral Emperor, and the Mythic Justice cards. On the wall of the RWS Ten of Pentacles, it is seen as the black-and-gray border of a tapestry, and as a black-and-yellow sash in the RWS Three of Wands.

Chiron (centaur)

See **Hierophant, The (V)**.

Christian, Paul (1811–1877)

The pen name of French journalist and historian Jean-Baptiste Pitois, a librarian with the French Ministry of Public Education in the nineteenth century. A follower of Eliphas Lévi, Christian produced a manuscript in 1863 titled *L'homme rouge des Tuileries*, which described a circle of seventy-eight gold leaves purporting to contain images used in ancient Egyptian mystery religions and to have been recovered from an Egyptian temple. His 1870 *Histoire de la Magie* (published in English as *The History and Practice of Magic*) adapted an Egyptian ceremony taken originally from the Krata Repoa (a pastiche of ancient mystery traditions) into a rite where an initiate was led up a series of seventy-eight steps and then through a hall containing images of the tarot trumps. The images were given appropriate Egyptian names, as in Isis Urania for the third trump, The Chariot of Osiris for the seventh trump, and The Sphinx for the tenth trump.[34]

circle with a dot within

A common symbol for the sun in astrology, the "sun principle" psychologically represents the process of developing our individuality. Thus, Jungians consider the circle with the central dot as the circle of wholeness, which encompasses the "dot" of individuality. The symbol represents, therefore, the ego-Self axis.[35] The angel on the RWS Temperance card wears it on his forehead. We are called upon to transform ourselves into a unified whole.

See **gold** (metal); **Self**.

clarifying cards

These are extra cards sometimes drawn by readers to amplify, enhance, or expand the meaning of a card when they are having trouble fully understanding it. Sometimes clarifying cards are used to suggest the next step for a direction the reader thinks is indicated by the card. Tarot readers with strong feelings against using clarifying cards believe their use means one has not delved fully enough into the meaning of the first card. They caution against becoming sloppy or lax in thinking more extensively about a given card or its relationship to its spread position.

clearing a deck
See **deck clearing**.

client/querent
Traditionally tarot texts and tarotists refer to the person asking the question, and receiving a reading, as the querent. It is becoming more popular, however, to refer to that person as the client, whether or not you're doing a reading for yourself or another, paid or unpaid.

client's card
See **significator**.

cloak and hood
See **hooded cloak**.

clothes/clothing
The figures on almost every tarot card (there are some nude figures) wear one or more garments of clothing. In fairy tales, clothes symbolically represent an attitude the person or figure wants to show to his/her surroundings, an outer presence.[36] Many figures on tarot cards also carry or hold some article of clothing.

Considering the garments and clothing accessories of figures, why they are included, or not (in the case of nude or semi-nude figures), the symbolism of garment colors and any decorations thereon may add depth to an understanding of a card's meaning.

See **naked/nude**; ***persona***.

coffin

Like any closed container, a coffin may symbolize the womb, the feminine principle, and the beginning and end of life; hence, it can be associated with birth-death-rebirth initiation ceremonies and mythologies. In alchemical art, coffins represented the vessel of transmutation.[37] The coffin (sarcophagus) on the RWS Four of Swords suggests the change that needs to come about during a respite. Opened coffins on the RWS Judgement card show "awakened" figures casting off their mental restrictions. The Wheel of Change Tarot's Four of Swords depicts the sarcophagus of an Egyptian pharaoh, along with his four canopic jars. It represents the voluntary actions of a hero (us), whose journey/sacrifice/withdrawal (symbolic death) restores fertility and balance to the people or, personally, to our respective lives.[38]

collective unconscious

A term created by C. G. Jung to represent the storehouse of basic human instincts and the heritage underlying the psyche and common to all humanity. The psyche creates images (stories, dreams, tarot cards) of those impulses or innate predispositions, called archetypes, in symbolic form.

See **archetypes; Self.**

color(s)

Most tarot decks are printed in color and understanding the colors of each item on a card can enhance the card's meaning and significance. The symbolism of red may change if the item is shoes (passionate understanding) or a hat (passionate thought or intention). At different times, certain colors on a card will stand out more than others. When this occurs, pay attention to how this changes your understanding of the card at the moment.

In general, lighter colors symbolize conscious mind, while darker colors symbolize the workings of the unconscious, although this categorization may not have much meaning if all the colors in a deck are either light or dark. Contrasting colors in juxtaposition to one another often indicate "contrast" or dichotomy, e.g., black and white suggest unconscious/conscious; red and white suggest the antithetical ingredients of alchemy. Complementary colors in juxtaposition to one another suggest the combined power and strength of complementary energies. "Flashing" or opposing colors that presumably cause the brain to go into an alpha state are deliberately employed in the Sacred Rose Tarot.[39]

See specific colors and **rainbow.** *Also see* "Color Me Tarot," Chapter 2, Part 1.

column(s)

Columns ensure the stability of a structure.[40] They are associated with the symbolism of trees, the Tree of Life, and the World Axis. Like pillars, they also may symbolize gateways. In the RWS High Priestess card, a black column with the letter B (Boaz) flanks her on the left side of the card, while a gray column with the letter J (Jachin) flanks her on the right side of the card. These refer to the two columns, or pillars, of the Temple of Solomon, although the original pillars were of brass and were not likely to have the Egyptian shape of those in the card. The priestess on the card represents the gateway to their ancient wisdom. An eighteenth-century German drawing of the alchemical process shows the two pillars of the Temple as the two magnetic poles of "The Work" that produces the philosopher's stone.[41] A miniature version of them stands beside the Priestess in the Aquarian Tarot. The Hierophant of the RWS deck also sits between two columns, as does the figure on the Justice card, suggesting the stability of their archetypal principles.

See **pillars.**

combination tarot reading

This refers to using parts of more than one deck, or several divination devices, in a single spread, e.g., using trumps from one deck and Minor Arcana cards from another, or replacing one or more of the card positions with another form of divination device (*I Ching* coins, runes).[42]

comfort deck(s)

It refers to the deck(s) that one reads with easily and comfortably. It's your warm, fuzzy, trusted-friend deck.[43]

Comparative Tarot

An in-depth process named and pioneered by Valerie Sim-Behi, it involves comparing a single card from several decks for additional insight into the meaning of that card, or for comparing cards from several decks for any or all cards in a spread to amplify and enhance the understanding of the layout.

composite creatures

See **Devil, The (XV); Typhon; undines.**

consciousness

The conscious mind includes all perceptions, memories, thoughts, and feelings existing within our awareness. In Jungian theory consciousness is composed of the attitudes of extraversion (oriented to the external world of objective reality) and introversion (oriented to the inner world of subjective reality). It also includes four psychological functions: thinking, feeling, sensing, and intuiting (*see* **Jungian functions**).

Conscious mind operates when we consider the meaning of a tarot card and recognize how it applies to our lives—when we use our intellect to make sense of a card. The Fool represents our conscious desire to develop our personality. The Hanged Man prompts us to realign our personality so that we can more easily incorporate intuitive impulses and images emerging from the unconscious and make them conscious. The Sun card represents joyful consciousness.

See **personality** (Jungian theory).

constellation

Used for analysis or meditation, it is a particular pattern wherein cards are set in columns according to the way in which they numerologically reduce. For instance, a subset of Judgement (Major Arcana 20), would be: 20, 11 (Justice), 2 (High Priestess), Two of Wands, Two of Swords, Two of Cups, Two of Pentacles. Major Arcana are laid out as follows:

19	20	21	22					
10	11	12	13	14	15	16	17	18
1	2	3	4	5	6	7	8	9

The appropriate Minor Arcana cards are then added to these vertical columns.[44]

See **tableau**.

cornucopia

Also known as the horn of plenty, it represents nature's abundance, inexhaustible bounty, and prosperity, as it does in the Alchemical Tarot's Queen of Coins. In Greek myth, it is associated with the horn of Amalthea, the goat-nymph who suckled the infant Zeus. As the horn of a goat, the cornucopia can be associated with Capricorn, the tenth sign of the zodiac. When Persephone returns from the underworld as the goddess of spring, she carries a cornucopia overflowing with flowers.[45] Likewise, when Hades appears in his agricultural aspect, usually as Pluto, he also carries a cornucopia. In the border of the Renaissance Tarot's Queen of Coins, Autumn holds a cornucopia, indicating she is a "cornucopia of delights."[46]

corrected deck

A tongue-in-cheek term applied to tarot cards with keywords and/or borders removed (known as a "borderectomy") by hand-trimming. Mark McElroy[47] coined the term as an in-joke, and as a jibe at occultists who position their personal systems as "corrections" or "rectifications" of earlier decks.

See **snippage.**

correspondences

In a broad sense, correspondences refer to the many ways that the psyche unconsciously conceives to organize the perception of *natural* phenomena (stars, cards, bones) in order to find a way in which it may symbolically display itself.[48]

In tarot work, correspondences are connections between two or more different systems that may expand the understanding of a card, e.g., the symbolism of predominant colors, the cards position on, or relationship to, the Kabbalistic Tree of Life. Hebrew letters, numerological and alchemical principles, animals, plants, musical notes, mythological stories, runes, *I Ching* hexagrams, and astrological symbolisms are other "systems" that contribute correspondences to tarot cards.[49]

Court de Gébelin, Antoine (1719?–1784)

The son of a Protestant clergyman, and himself a Protestant minister, his writings—notably two essays in the eighth volume of the nine-volume *Le Monde Primitif Analysé et Comparé avec le Monde Moderne,* published in Paris in 1782—were the first known published writings on the tarot. One essay by him and a second, attributed to the M. le C. de M***, later established to be le Comte de Mellet, did much to awaken the idea of the hidden symbolic nature of tarot cards. Court de Gébelin asserted that the tarot was of Egyptian origin, the remaining fragments of the *Book of Thoth*, written by the Egyptian god Thoth and provided to Egyptian magicians. He proposed that the trumps be read from highest to lowest (backwards from the way they are numbered and read today). Death prevented him from completing the total volumes he had intended and possibly from writing more about tarot.

See **de Mellet, le Comte.**

court cards

In traditional tarot decks, each of the four Minor Arcana suits contain four court cards: Page (sometimes Princess), Knight (Prince), Queen, and King. In the Thoth deck court cards are the Princess (page), Prince (knight), Queen, and Knight (king).

Court cards are multifaceted and can represent any of the following: strong or influential people in a person's life, the person himself/herself, aspects or qualities of human character at different times in one's life, the personification of an action, stages in the development of maturity, states of mind, and opportunities. Metaphysically they represent levels of initiation, one's progression toward a specific form of mastery and the psychic changes occurring accordingly.

In reading for characteristics, court cards are not gender linked. A masculine figure can refer to a female and vice versa. In divination readings, they often are gender linked, e.g., the King of Pentacles as a rich uncle or lover. Many authors write about court cards separate from the preceding cards of their suit rather than as a continuation or expansion. They are sometimes considered a bridge or link between the Major and Minor Arcana.

See **elements; pages; knights; queens; kings;** and specific Minor Arcana court cards. For their relation to the elements, *see* **elemental/suit dignities.**

court cards (astrological aspects)

In the Golden Dawn zodiacal attribution system, kings, queens, and knights are assigned 21–30 degrees of their zodiacal sign, and 0–20 degrees of the following sign, e.g., the Queen of Wands is assigned 21–30 degrees of Pisces and 0–20 degrees of Aries. The Page (Princess) is regarded as a pure creature of the element of his/her suit.

Wands court cards are the three fire signs; Cups the three water signs; Swords the three air signs; and Pentacles the three earth signs. In addition to being supported or thwarted by the elemental dignities of neighboring cards, court cards also may be helpful or unfriendly by zodiacal rule: the fire and air signs harmonious, the water and earth signs harmonious, and all other combinations either neutral or unfriendly. Thus, the Queen of Swords next to the Knight of Cups struggle to understand each other (air neutral with water). The Queen of Cups is inimical to the King of Wands (water dislikes fire). Court cards are enhanced when same-suit pip cards are near them in a spread, even more if they share the same sign, e.g., if the King of Pentacles appears with the Nine of Pentacles (both Virgo).[50]

court cards (direction and placement in spreads)

Attending to the direction in which court cards face in a Celtic Cross layout is a specialized or advanced technique for additional understanding of a reading. Forward-facing court cards placed anywhere in a layout except the "past" position may indicate an issue or situation or person present in the client's life.

A court card *facing* the client's card (the first position in a Celtic Cross spread, or the card designated the client's card in any other spread) from either side suggests an issue or situation or person coming toward the client. One that is turned away from the client's card on either side indicates something going away from the client.

A court card placed to the *right* of the client's card (facing in any direction) suggests something that will be involved in the client's life in the future. *Facing toward* the client's card, it suggests future help, *facing away*, a possible impediment. For example, this may be a person who "turns his back" on the client, gives the client the cold shoulder, or will refuse to help the client. If the card *faces forward*, it may refer to someone in the client's present life who will also be there in the future.

A court card placed to the *left* of the client's card, facing any direction, suggests an issue or situation or person involved or active in the client's life in the past. *Facing forward* it likely reflects someone in the past still in the client's life. *Facing toward* the client's card suggests someone who was, or is, supportive of the client, someone who "stands behind" him/her. If the court card "*looks away*," it suggests someone who is no longer in the client's life or was a problem in the past.

Court cards placed *above* the client's card suggest someone who is over the client (such as a boss). If placed *below* the client's card, it refers to someone who supports the client in some manner (spouse, good friend, co-worker) and/or may be a part of the problem situation. It may also refer to someone in the client's life who is younger than the client, or a co-worker in a subordinate position. A card can be in a supporting position and still be the reason for the reading or the cause of the problem (the card beneath the client's card typically referring to the foundation or reason for the reading).[51]

See **court cards; direction** (of figures on cards).

cow

The cow has long been a symbol of maternal fertility and nourishment. Its horns link it to the crescent moon. Mythologically it is related to the Egyptian goddesses Nut and Hathor (often shown with the solar disk between her horns). Such a symbol is seen on the head of the RWS High Priestess.

crab

Crabs on the Light and Shadow and Thoth Chariot cards connect the charioteer with the astrological sign of Cancer. The crab crawling out of the conch chalice on the Thoth Queen of Cups represents the archetypal feminine/mother principle. The Thoth Knight (King) of Cups holds a grail chalice from which emerges a crab, representing aggressiveness,[52] although it may also represent inner absorption entering consciousness.[53]

See **Cancer; crayfish**.

crayfish

The crayfish and crab are identified with the astrological sign of Cancer, the only sign ruled by the Moon. Cancer/Moon relate to a sense of belonging, to emotional security, "to the idea of coming from somewhere and something."[54] The Cancer glyph appears on the sword belt of the RWS Charioteer. The crayfish appears on the RWS Moon card, where it represents the dark and hidden process of regeneration, and a need to plunge to the depths of inner emotions. The crayfish/crustacean appears on The Moon cards of the World Spirit, Morgan-Greer, Tarot of the Spirit (representing new life), Light and Shadow, and Mythic Tarot (where it is replaced by a crab). It represents primitive ideas emerging from the unconscious—or, more likely, from the collective unconscious—which still need protection (the shell).

See **Cancer; crab**.

crocodile

The ancient (and unexplainable) belief that crocodiles had no way to procreate or perpetuate their species made the crocodile a symbol of the greatest creative energy possible. In Chinese mythology the crocodile invented singing and drumming, making it an essential player in establishing cosmic harmony.[55] Typically, however, the crocodile has a more sinister or, at least, ambivalent meaning. A deadly predator, it can symbolize a negative attitude "lodged" in the personal or collective unconscious.[56] In ancient Egypt the crocodile was regarded as a devouring divinity of darkness (the underworld) because of its association with the Nile water, yet, that same association rendered it a god of fertility. The Egyptian crocodile-headed god sat below the scales when the hearts of the dead were weighed against the feather of Ma'at, waiting to greedily devour those whose hearts could not meet the balance of truth and justice.

Obviously a crocodile can symbolize danger and primitive instinct, but it can also symbolize something that will psychologically devour us by robbing our energy if we do not overcome a certain sense of inertia (symbolized by the mud in which crocodiles lie).[57] In that sense, it is akin to the devouring aspects of the Great Goddess, the unconscious, and the entire life-death cycle.

Both the Thoth and Light and Shadow Fool cards bear crocodiles, suggesting the instinctual creative energy available to sustain and inspire the Thoth Fool, along with the devouring danger inherent in his journey (the Light and Shadow card). Typhon is presented as a crocodile-headed creature on the Thoth Fortune card, where he represents salt, the alchemical transforming element that both destroyed and renewed (*see* **salt**).

cross

Seen on the gown of the RWS High Priestess, the cross may represent the Hebrew letter *Tav*, which symbolizes the involution of spirit into matter. In general, however, an equal-armed cross represents a uniting (*see* **crossroads**) of masculine and feminine energies—rendering them equal and interdependent—or the wholeness that occurs when the unconscious (horizontal arm) connects with consciousness (vertical arm).[58] The three crosses seen on the vertical strip on the front of the RWS Hierophant's clothing and on those of the bishop in RWS Death card may come from Masonic ritual and represent the three basic initiations the wearer has experienced: apprentice, fellow craft, and master.[59]

cross of St. Andrew

Also called the cross saltire, this cross, which forms an X, appears in a crest on the RWS Two of Wands and Six of Cups. Symbolizing the union of higher and lower worlds,[60] it was earlier the cross of Wotan/Óðinn, god of war and also of truth, ecstasy, and shamanic wisdom. Esoterically the flowered crest in the RWS Six of Cups represents the crossing or meeting of the mystic path (the lilies) and the occult path (the roses). Positioned on the left side of the two RWS cards, it calls for the figure(s) to awaken, and attend, to higher, inner truths. In the Haindl Two of Wands, two crossed wands superimposed over the painting form a St. Andrew's cross, which Haindl associated with the ancient paintings of Osiris, where the arms are crossed over the chest.[61]

See **crossroads; X**.

crossroads

At their center, crossroads represent the union of opposites, but in their crossing, represent ambivalence. Hecate is the goddess of the crossroads, while Hermes is the god of crossroads (statues called Herms were erected there in his honor) and is, therefore, the god of travelers and wanderers. The Mythic Tarot's Magician depicts Hermes standing in the center of where four roads meet.

Crossroads are most often represented in the tarot in the form of a cross with two equal arms. They raise the question of whether there is a "hidden" issue behind, or included in, the more obvious meanings of the cards. An X appears on the breast of the Light and Shadow High Priestess, suggesting she is the mistress of reconciling opposites.

See **cross of St. Andrew; X**.

Crowley, Aleister (1875–1947)

Several biographies have been written about this controversial man who was born Edward Alexander Crowley and who, throughout his life, identified himself with the Beast 666 of the Apocalypse. Pursuing his interest in the occult, Crowley was initiated into the Hermetic Order of the Golden Dawn in 1898. Between 1938 and 1943, working with the talented British artist Lady Frieda Harris, Crowley produced a tarot deck, published only as illustrations for his accompanying commentary in *The Book of Thoth*. Finally published as a working deck in 1969, it is now commonly known as the Thoth deck, the Crowley deck, or the Crowley-Thoth deck, and is one of the two most popular decks sold today. Neither Crowley nor Harris lived to see her paintings published as a separate deck.

Crowley considered the Major Arcana to be pictorial representations of the forces of nature (*see* **archetypes**) and guides to conduct. He also believed that the tarot was based on the Kabbalistic Tree of Life, and his deck is created accordingly.

See **Harris, Lady Frieda**. For a description of the deck, see Chapter 3, Part 1.

crown

In addition to representing authority, it can symbolize the highest expression of the personal Self. The meaning alters depending on its shape, the material from which it is made, and any jewels or other adornments applied to it (what crowns the figure). The circularity of the crown symbolizes perfection and the wearer's relationship to the infinite divine.

A three-leveled crown, such as that worn by some Hierophants, suggests rulership over the three worlds of body, mind, spirit. In many Tower cards, the top of the tower is represented as a toppling crown, suggesting the overthrowing or breakdown of personal ambition, or feelings of inflated pride/greatness.

On the RWS Temperance card, the sun rises in the shape of a radiant crown, which Jung considered the symbol of reaching the highest goal in evolution—"he who conquers himself wins the crown of eternal life."[62] Since Temperance lies on the central path of the Tree of Life in the Golden Dawn system, the goal of the mystical journey suggested by the Temperance card may be reflected as Kether, the crown.[63]

The RWS Empress wears a crown of twelve stars, which links her to the heavens and to the archetypal principles reflected through astrology. The Thoth Death skeleton wears the crown of the Egyptian god of the dead, Osiris, linking the card to a death-rebirth initiation. The RWS Ace of Swords carries a crown, showing its victory over our worldly nature, and the potential development of higher truths.

crustacean

See **crayfish**; **Moon, The (XVIII)**.

crystals

Crystals are a symbol of the spirit; rare or especially precious crystals represent the Self. As something that comes from underground, a crystal can be associated with enlightenment from the unconscious. Coming from or placed in a cave, crystals represent a connection with the womb, and deeper feminine nature. If transparent, they connect with the union of the opposites of spirit and matter—wholeness—demonstrating simultaneously that matter exists and does not exist because it can be seen through.[64]

Crystals, often gleaming, appear on all the staffs in the Robin Wood suit of Wands. They have different meanings depending on the cards, but most often their gleam demonstrates the brilliance, radiance, or active energy of the person or scene. In her Three of Wands, one of them glows to show that the "future looks bright." In the Nine of Wands, it depicts "clear vision."[65]

A bowl of crystals sits on the magician's table in the Ancestral Path Six of Cups, displaying their importance in divinatory magic and in inducing visions.[66] Crystals form along the hemline of the dress of the Thoth Princess of Cups; she is the "faculty of crystallization").[67] The Light and Shadow Tarot's Fool holds a crystal in his left hand, representing a lens or tool through which he can bring things into focus and find clarity.[68] A field of crystals emanates from the Haindl Magician's right eye, suggesting his precarious (because of other symbols on the card) ability to perceive the pure forms of existence.

cube

Its geometric shape was attributed by some alchemists to the philosopher's stone, the ultimate perfection; hence, a cube becomes a symbol for stability, especially if used as a throne. Because it contains twelve edges, six faces, three axes, and a center, totaling twenty-two, the cube is considered one of the quintessential symbols of the Major Arcana.

See **cube of space; philosopher's stone.**

cube of space

Paul Foster Case introduced the idea that, since the esoteric structure of the Hebrew alphabet forms a cube of letters, by assigning these letters to tarot cards and arranging them dimensionally, they, too, can serve as a cosmological model of the universe and of the spiritual evolution of our lives.[69] A recent book illustrates the concept in detail.[70]

Cupid

See **Eros/Cupid; Psyche.**

cups (symbol)

In general, cups represent emotional or physical nurturance, receptivity, the womb. Cups are related to the chalice (used in religious and other rites) and, mythologically, to the cauldron of the Triple Goddess, or witches, which holds the potential for brewing healing (Good Mother) or evil (Bad Witch) potions, i.e., bringing about transformation. Cups are also related to the "alchemical vessel," another symbol for the transforming womb. Any cup's symbolism is expanded according to the number of the tarot card on which it appears, how it is formed or shaped, the metal used, and its decorations and contents (what they are and how they are contained, e.g., balanced, spilling, or overflowing).

See **cauldron; Cups/Chalices** (suit), and all entries for Cups cards.

Cups/Chalices (suit)

The suit of Cups deals with creating emotional fulfillment, which includes not only positive and negative emotions, but also one-sided behavior and conditioned emotional expression. Cups cards lead us to explore our range of feelings, to develop them, and to open up to them as a way of acknowledging and validating ourselves individually and in relationship to others. They also have to do with emotions raised through fantasy and can reflect a sorting out process accomplished through daydreaming, night dreaming, contemplation, and meditation.

Cups represent the element or principle of water, Jung's feeling function, and the yin or female principle. They equate with the alchemical process of *solutio* (solution), a watery dissolution/transformation different from that brought about by fire.

Water, having long been one of the most basic symbols of feelings or emotions, and for the feminine womb is, therefore, bound up with maternal, feminine archetypes and their mythologies. Water-related mythology is associated with Poseidon/Neptune, Greek/Roman god of water and the depths of the sea, symbolic of the unseen depths of emotional reactions.

Mermaid legends are also related to Cups, inasmuch as mermaids or water nymphs are the suit's elemental spirits. Many myths regarding mermaids involve some quality of mystery, some secret the mermaid keeps and requires her human companion not to pursue. Yet, human curiosity being what it is, the human comes to believe he must solve the mystery . . . and we have the notion of the destructive qualities of curiosity, one of the negative aspects of the suit. When the human violates the promise originally extracted by the mermaid, she disappears. So Cups' experiences are important in teaching us about when to recognize the secrets of the unconscious (not too fast and not too soon) and how to transform them into a greater understanding of the feminine within, as well as what is the appropriate way to trust and relate to another person. Both the Renaissance and the Mythic Tarot's Cups suits explore the myth of Psyche (*see* **Psyche**).

Many Cups cards in a reading suggest that emotionality forms the basis of the question. They represent emotional issues needing to be attended to, or ones that are not being dealt with (depending on the positions of the cards).

Cups are replaced by the Suit of Water: Emotions in the Osho deck, by Water in Tarot of the Spirit, and in the Shining Tribe by the Suit of Rivers.

See **Jungian functions; water; Poseidon/Neptune; undines.**

Cups, Ace of

Most decks display the most lavish or ornate cup of the suit. It is often linked with Christian communion or the legend of the Holy Grail, both of which refer to the possibility of connecting to a source greater than oneself. The shadow aspect of the Ace of Cups is getting so caught up in emotional fantasies or the concept of cosmic or unconditional love that we fail to set limits for ourselves or others when necessary, or to do the emotional work needed to recognize/acknowledge all of our feelings.

An "Open Channel" (Tarot of the Spirit), we become the receptor and the receptacle, capable of receiving and containing all that exists. We are open to possibilities, longing to be filled.[71] The "Going with the Flow" Osho card shows us being available to the "currents of life," trusting that they will take us where they want us to go.[72] The Shining Tribe Ace of Rivers portrays water as the nourishment that leads to transformation and creation through expression.[73]

Keywords/phrases: opening to spiritual or unconscious channels; receptivity to love; pleasure; psychological and emotional nourishment and the courage to accept it; opportunity or courage to open up to, connect with, or explore a new attitude related to emotions or feelings or fulfillment.

See **aces; ones.**

Cups, Two of

Usually RWS-type cards depict a male and female holding two cups. If seen as one person, it suggests that under the influence of the inner spirit or Self, the person realizes the need to integrate opposites. It is alchemical work, as symbolized in the

RWS card by a caduceus and a winged lion above the people. As a two, however, it is still early.

More typically the card is seen as two persons coming together in a union. Above them the winged lion (RWS, Ancestral Path), which might at first appear to be blessing their union, symbolizes the whole person that each has the potential to become if they can grow in the relationship (*see* **winged lion**).

In the "Sacred Cord" (Tarot of the Spirit) two chalices overflow with the waters of the cosmic sea. Above them a female "force" and a male "force" intertwine into a lemniscate. Their union represents how both bonding and individuation can occur within a relationship's structure. On the Thoth "Love" card, two cups (equal and balanced love) overflow, filled from an overshadowing lotus blossom of higher spirit. On the Osho "Friendliness" card, branches and leaves of two brightly colored trees intertwine, indicating a readiness to connect without a need to change the other.

The Two of Cups signals the need for the process of individuation, i.e., developing according to our true nature rather than remaining the captive of our *persona*. In fairy tales, marriage represents the unfurling of a new layer of the psyche.[74]

Keywords/phrases: union of two persons; union of inner opposites; a call for the need for individuation and self-development; balance in a relationship; resolution of ill-feeling; reconciliation; a joyful, affirmative view of the world.

See **twos.**

Cups, Three of

As a three, the card represents an early form of completion and calls for a celebration, e.g., dancing one's pleasure in the RWS and Osho cards. The Thoth deck calls it "Abundance."

Mythologically the RWS card is often linked to the Three Muses or the Three Graces (later Christianized into Faith, Hope, and Charity) or, the three fates of Greek/Roman mythology.

Whatever their names, they all are forms of the primordial Triple Goddess, as in the World Spirit Tarot where three women, representing the obvious stages of the goddess, sit in a garden drinking lemonade.

One of the purposes awakened by this card is to connect with the feminine qualities within, whether we are male or female, so that we will be ready to build fully loving relationships with others. A stylized ankh, from which the sacred "Waters of Faith" fall, dominates the "Stream of Love" (Tarot of the Spirit). The Three of Rivers (Shining Tribe) celebrates the female "mystery" of menstruation as a symbol of sharing deep emotions and harmony.

Keywords/phrases: expansion in relationship (possibly a child conceived); opening to life's mysterious, ritualistic, or celebratory opportunities; enjoyment of the moment; an emotional healing; happy conclusion of some phase or stage of life.

See **threes**.

Cups, Four of

Often the card depicts a male person pondering (or ignoring) a fourth cup being offered, while three cups stand elsewhere in the scene. Although reluctance to take a risk can be a mark of this card, it also can suggest that if we take the time for self-reflection, we may learn more about ourselves, our motives, the elements of any situation we are pondering. Thus, the Four of Cups may represent a plateau, or our ability to sit quietly and allow the intuition that comes to shape our direction. The World Spirit Tarot describes the man as lost in thought, although it also says he is emotionally cut off from the world. Two cups in the card have tipped and spilled in the grass before him; one remains standing. A mouse in its own luminous circle gazes at a fourth cup floating above the man in its own luminous mandorla (see **mandorla; mouse**). In the Osho "Turning In" card, a woman with eyes closed watches the "antics of the mind," shown as ethereal faces all around her.[75]

The Thoth card is one of "Luxury." Four chalices radiating white light from their interiors are constantly being refilled by the same light from a pink lotus. The card is one of feeling emotionally fulfilled and internally satisfied, and reminds us to take time to savor this kind of experience.

Keywords/phrases: waiting for intuition or inspiration; ennui; so caught up in inner emotions (turmoil? discontent? conditioned reactions?) that we can't see what is available or offered; boredom; help from an unseen source; weariness of life and a call to again become active.

See **fours**.

Cups, Five of

Many therapists have written of the fact that our own woundedness makes us more compassionate healers for others. True health and healing may result when we acknowledge, rather than hide, our wounds and accept them as an integral part of our being.[76] The Five of Cups can alert us to take our time and grieve for our losses and "Disappointment" (the Thoth card's title).

Out of what seems hurtful may arise something special and valued if we identify and acknowledge it. Can we embrace the remaining two cups still standing in the RWS card (but not necessarily in other decks)? All the cups are toppling in the World Spirit card, although two may still retain some of their contents.

The Five of Cups reflects the message of the Icelandic myth of Kvasir, the wisest of the gods. Formed from the spittle of the Aesir (warrior gods) and the Vanir (fertility gods), he is an ambiguous figure. After two envious dwarfs murdered him, they mixed his spilled blood with honey to form the mead of inspiration and of poetry. The story is typical of the ambivalence expressed by the Five of Cups.

The Greeks placed their temples to Asclepias, god of healing, near healing waterways where a purification ritual and other rites were performed as preparation for spending the night in the temple to receive a healing dream. Could the structure in the background of the RWS card be a healing temple? After receiving a dream, a literary production (a poem, a song, a drawing) was usually required as an offering of thanks for a successful healing—again referring to the notion that something special and valued may arise out of something painful or hurtful.

In the Five of Water (Tarot of the Spirit), three cups spilled inside a dark pyramid (the past) pour out the water, wine, and blood of life. Around the perimeter of the pyramid, the "light of love" flows from two cups, looking very much like the bright lights of fireworks, or like streamers of colored ribbons. From another perspective the pyramid looks like a road (the road of life/of new experience/of the future?) passing alongside the lights and leading into a green distance. In the Five of Rivers (Shining Tribe) rigidity gives way to acceptance as the river bends and turns, and the fish adapt to it.

In the very graphic Osho card, a figure so preoccupied with clutching her box of memories—indeed, it looks like her head is caught in it—is defined as a "Blockhead." She cannot see the "champagne glass of blessing" available to her.[77]

Keywords/phrases: woundedness; need (or time) to grieve; caught up in the past; accepting loss; expanding self-confidence by deepening understanding; disappointment or regret; cherished hopes that have slipped away.[78]

See **fives; Pentacles, Five of**.

Cups, Six of

The RWS card deals with the processes of giving, receiving, and sharing. If, however, we regard the two children in the RWS card as brother and sister, then it may also refer to delving into the sibling relationship. It also refers to developing true inner intimacy by reconciling the inner masculine (sun) and feminine (moon). This reconciliation represents the central organizing principle of many myths as they are acted out in our daily lives and depicted on tarot cards.

Sometimes the male figure in the RWS card is seen as a

"dwarf," even though he is the largest figure. In folklore the appearance of a dwarf or elf often signals the presence of an archetypal child, a healer, a bringer of wholeness. Dwarfs also can symbolize childish or immature personality aspects, or hidden or growing creative impulses, latent potentialities.[79]

The Ancestral Path card shows a bearded "magician" consulting an ancient text, his youthful apprentice behind him. It is a wonderful combination of the past and the present. The chalices before him expand on the theme. One holds an old, dusty bottle. Others contain quartz crystals (potential energy), swimming fish (the flow of the life process), and a flowering herb (growth and healing).

The cartoonlike scene of the Osho "Dream" card reflects the false fantasy of someday finding the perfect mate who will fulfill our every need, in order to avoid acknowledging the fact and fear of our aloneness.

Keywords/phrases: fulfillment; looking for inspiration from past, or childhood, experiences and memories; harmony of the natural forces within or in a relationship; ongoing emotions and issues of childhood.

See **sixes**.

Cups, Seven of

The card deals with personal desires and fantasies, or with being caught up in illusion. It is sometimes referred to as the "castles-in-the-air" or "pie-in-the-sky" card. In a positive sense, it calls upon us to engage in creative imagination and to realize some of our dreams and fantasies. The Seven of Rivers (Shining Tribe) celebrates the power of the vast rivers of the unconscious as expressed in dreams, fantasies, and myths.

The Thoth card portrays a more sinister theme: debauchery and emotional indolence. Tiger lilies fill chalices with poisonous nectar, suggesting an external splendor that hides "internal corruption."[80]

Inasmuch as freedom of imagination often threatens deeply

rooted, familiar attitudes,[81] the card can call upon us to evaluate the "truth" of ideas/ideals we think most dear, to make a choice, perhaps with accompanying ambivalence. We have so much to choose from that we may postpone decisions and delay actions while simply waiting for our dreams to come true. Sometimes the card points to the notion that we are deluding ourselves, or that we are overindulging or overdoing in some way. It also is seen as a card of emotional addiction and indulgences, portraying what we reach for when we are frustrated or depressed.[82]

The visions in the RWS card cover a range of fantasies: wealth (jewels), success (victory wreath), fear (the dragon), adventure (the blue castle), to mythological archetypes (a godlike face, a radiant figure, a snake).[83] The castle also has been connected with power, the dragon to adventure, and the snake to knowledge.[84] The meanings of the items in the cups change with various authors' interpretations, as the content does with different decks.

The top three cups in the RWS card form a triangle symbolizing the mind (human head), body (kundalini energy of the snake), and spirit (yet to be fully recognized in the covered radiating angel). Since sevens represent inner development, the card may depict the tension between the contents of the "higher" (sacred/spiritual) three cups and the lower four ("ego") cups. Sevens offer tests and temptations (as part of our shadow) and show a need to recognize but not get caught up in them. That the person's shadow is activated in the RWS card is shown by the figure's black appearance (ignorance) and that we see only his back.

The Osho "Projections" card deals with illusionary ideas. A couple see their projected image of the other rather than the actual person. In the Tarot of the Spirit "Insight" card, six cups are tossed around in the sea of the unconscious, while the victory cup, which holds the "vision of original purpose" rises out of the swirling pool. It is a card of contemplating your perceptions and discovering your own higher purpose.

Keywords/phrases: looking into emotions and relationships for deeper understanding of Self; illusion/delusion/false hopes; a choice needing to be made; a richness of fantasies or imagination that may be immobilizing or overwhelming; confusion.

See sevens.

Cups, Eight of

"Enough of This!" is the subtitle of the Robin Wood card, while Tarot of the Spirit calls it "Still Waters." The card can refer to leaving a phase of life behind; to withdrawing the value of, or moving away from, old beliefs; or to rejecting the value of material objects for the spiritual search/quest, as shown in the Ancestral Path card, where a caped figure heads toward Stonehenge. It suggests "turning your back" on turmoil, and heading for a renewing, strength-building experience.

The card also can refer to withdrawal (healthy or not), an energy drain, or being filled with a sense of self-pity and turning away from life. Dew rests on lotus leaves and one drop falls into the pond below in the Osho "Letting Go" card, which cautions us to not attempt to hold on too long to things that are finished.

In the World Spirit card, a man walks along a rock-strewn beach, leaving three cups behind. Five more cups are mirrored in the water, hinting that while things may look fine on the surface, we are really "empty vessels, drained of our enthusiasm."[85]

"Indolence" (Thoth) shows a rotting, dying sea. Lotuses wither, and bronze chalices are chipped and broken. It is a cesspool of a card, warning of the rotten swamps we are approaching because we have lost our way.[86] By not honoring our own boundaries and limits and overextending ourselves, by indulging in phony feelings rather than being true to ourselves, we have become like stagnant waters. The card calls for us to recognize this and bring new momentum into our lives.

Keywords/phrases: a relationship is wrapping up, finishing a cycle, or moving to a higher level; searching for deeper meanings; abandoning an unsuccessful or unfulfilling situation; turning away from present emotional state to seek more positive or greater emotional awareness or understanding; "letting go" in the quest for higher insight.

See **eights.**

Cups, Nine of

Names used to characterize this card include: "Fat and Sassy," "Party Hearty" (Robin Wood), "Laziness" (Osho), "Happiness" (Thoth) and "Wishes" (World Spirit).

Typically one person, often a richly clad merchant, is shown with his nine cups. The Ancestral Path card, however, shows a richly dressed *group* seated around a circular table, watching a dancer. It is a card of communal celebration and fellowship/sistership. Negatively it represents meaningless celebrations, or events that have lost their purpose and substance.[87]

The figure in the Osho card sits in an overstuffed chair beside a pool, holding a piña colada. At his right, a mirror cracks. Although he thinks he has "Arrived" (the card's title), his world is about to shatter around him, for he deceives himself that he has reached the pinnacle of achievement.

While nines are a completion and should indicate a success and a celebration of fulfillment, the RWS figure sits with his arms crossed, certainly over his heart chakra and possibly over his solar plexus chakra. The card suggests that it pertains to ego or *persona* satisfaction rather than to true inner, "heart" satisfaction. Is this person able to acquire things (people, possessions) out of love or is he just an arrogant collector? The heart chakra challenges us to generate an inner climate from which we can accept personal emotional challenges as extensions of a Divine plan, which has our conscious evolution as its intent.[88] Jung said that when people live their lives as if there is a higher plan, no matter how they define it, it seems to result in a new level of tranquility. So, perhaps the "nine completion" here is the recognition of that tranquility. It could well be that this man is saying "Look what God—the Goddess, universe, higher power, or whatever words you use—gives me." Or it could be calling upon us to learn to live in that fashion, i.e., as if there is a higher plan.

A strong sense of integrity and inner security is the message from "Rainbow Mirror" (Tarot of the Spirit Nine of Water). White light pours in all directions from the sephiroth of the Kabbalistic Tree of Life. We simultaneously understand them all at once and are truly aligned with cosmic will.

Keywords/phrases: completion of some phase of a relationship or situation; emotional stability; strong sense of self-esteem; financial security; devotion to the enjoyment of the senses.

See **nines**.

Cups, Ten of

Often seen as a simple card of happiness and fulfillment ("Satiety" in the Thoth deck) and of knowing how to truly love, the card actually is much more complicated. In one sense, the RWS card, which shows a family standing beneath a cup-filled rainbow, represents the inner father, mother, sister, brother, child/ parent relationships to which we must all reconcile. It speaks of "being at home with yourself."[89]

Usually considered a card of completion and success, embodying all that the Ace of Cups promised, it can also call upon us to consider a new task: that of identifying the projections that we have dumped onto, or otherwise attributed to, family members, and to claim them as our own.

The Haindl card, showing clouds overhead and a rugged, ancient stone standing in the sea, hints at the ambivalence of "Success" (its title), which can bring both sadness and joy. Not only we as persons, but the world as well, becomes transformed through our individual efforts to become mature and discover our individuality.[90]

On the Osho "Harmony" card, dolphins emerge in a path of glimmering light from the heart of the meditating figure and arc toward the third eye or *ajna* center. The scene represents the playfulness and intelligence that comes when we move in the world according to the heart's message.

The "Fountain of Love" (Tarot of the Spirit) spews forth love like searchlights. Bountiful as love has been, it is now time for it to come into balance with such other great forces as reason, spirit, and physical reality.[91]

Keywords/phrases: fulfillment and contentment; a meaningful relationship; commitment; preparing to move into a higher (emotionally richer?) level of relationship; wholeness.

See **tens.**

Cups, Page of

The RWS page gazes at a cup from which a blue fish emerges, often considered the visualization of imaginative ideas. This page still lives in a world of inner images and fantasies.

The myth of Narcissus, subject of the Mythic Tarot card, represents illusion, the vanity and dangers of self love along with their ability—if considered correctly—to allow the emergence of a true capacity to feel and love (*see* **Narcissus**).[92]

The Seer of Cups card (World Spirit), dedicated to Pamela Colman Smith, addresses the self-nurturing that occurs by attending to our emotions and messages from our unconscious.

The Thoth Princess of Cups dances on the "foaming sea of emotions."[93] She represents the process of diving into the unconscious for exploration and not accepting outer world information too quickly[94] (see **dolphin(s); swan(s); turtle**).

The Polynesian Prince of Cups (Wheel of Change) steers his canoe through the changeable waters of human relationships, learning to recognize their subtle differences with the experience of each "journey." The Osho "Understanding" card shows a bird in a cage, whose bars are disappearing. New understanding dawns.

Keywords/phrases: a dreamer; seeker/seeking; follow your heart; attend to or nurture your intuitive abilities; idealistic, impractical.

See **pages.**

Cups, Knight of

In many decks, the Knight of Cups typifies the romantic spirit. The Mythic Tarot identifies him with Perseus, volatile, sensitive, changeable and, in all his adventures, motivated by the love of women (see **Perseus**).[95] Now he begins to learn to identify and actively express his ideas or feelings. The RWS knight wears a winged helmet, linking him with Hermes/Mercury. He is beginning to be comfortable with contradictions and has higher or spiritual aspirations.

A Native American man sitting astride a horse walks along a stream in the Ancestral Path Seeker of Cups. A dreamer and idealist who worships all that is beautiful, he is more comfortable with love from afar than with everyday relationships.

Representing the airy aspect of water, the Thoth Prince of Cups guides an eagle-drawn chariot through the sky. Heavy rains fall in the pond below. The prince has not yet reconciled with his feminine, and the card is intended to be one of stagnation. He still needs to learn to recognize his deep feelings (water) and express them (air).[96] The Princess of Cups (Wheel of Change) serves ale to the Great River of the galaxy, as she learns how to honor and balance her own emotional needs with those of others and of the cosmos. The "Trust" (Osho) bungee jumper trusts that something immense will open up as she prepares to jump into the unknown without her cord.

Keywords/phrases: developing a new understanding of emotions; psychic development; allowing unknown or unconscious information to emerge; openness; receipt of comforting, loving, or understanding messages.

See **knights.**

Cups, Queen of

As a water card in the water suit, the Queen of Cups is one of the most comfortable queens. Sitting on her throne, decorated with undines (water nymphs), the RWS queen gazes at an elaborate but closed container. What it contains is not to be seen by all.[97] That it is linked with spirit is indicated by the winged angels on the handles.

Both she and the Queen of Pentacles face the left and gaze at their suit objects, suggesting that they are more prone to turn inward, and/or are deeply in touch with their unconscious, or at least unafraid of it. The Queen of Cups represents deep feelings and, possibly, visionary experiences. The ethereal Thoth queen sits atop the water, drenched in blue and white archways of light. She is the "oracle fairy," inspired and guided by images arising from her depths. Simultaneously, she is the *anima mundi*, the soul of the world.[98]

In "Receptivity" (Osho), the queen represents the process of allowing ourselves to be filled to overflowing, and then be emptied and filled once again without expectations or demands, in harmony with the Universe.

In the World Spirit Tarot a blue-skinned mermaid, the Sibyl of Cups, offers sound guidance without judgment. She knows how to blend imagination with action.[99] She is the epitome of all things that rise from our unconscious to nourish our conscious thoughts and actions.

The Wheel of Change Knight of Cups is the third court card, while the Queen of Cups (see below) is the fourth, equivalent to the king in most decks. The Knight plays his horn on the street during a snowy Christmas season, depicting selfless love. The money he collects will be converted to "emotional caring for others" and will bring "community and celebratory spirit" to city streets."[100]

Helen of Troy is the myth embodied in the Mythic Tarot's card. A mysterious, elusive woman who stirs up trouble in others, she also activates their depths and inaugurates action and conflict without seeming to do anything at all. She represents the unconscious pursuing its "secret" purposes and luring us into crisis through its "seductive power."[101]

Keywords/phrases: full emotional understanding and authenticity; sensitivity; self-nurturance; forgiveness; great depth in one's desires; deeply involved in, opening up to, or developing one's inner world; mastery or teacher of emotional integrity.

See **queens.**

Cups, King of

Many consider the King of Cups the least organized and least structured of the kings, at least in the RWS deck. It's as if he doesn't quite know what to do with his kingship and authority, and is not connected with his element of water the way his queen is. As a fire/water combination, his inner forces are weakened. Even as a king, he will still spend a lot of time trying to reconcile his inner conflicts and achieve fulfilling relationships. Although he can talk the emotional talk, he may not really be able to put it into action without inner conflict. The World Spirit Tarot describes him as carrying a "whirlpool" of emotions, which he keeps hidden from others, and perhaps from himself.

Nevertheless, he is a king who shows great perseverance. The Mythic Tarot king is Orpheus, who, having lost his beloved Eurydice, can never heal his own wounds (*see* **Orpheus**). The Osho King of Water, who no longer hides from himself and the wounds of his past, is, therefore, healed, and can help others heal (*see* **lotus blossom(s)**).

The Thoth golden-haired Knight (King) of Cups wears wings resembling a scallop shell from which he seems to arise, riding his white horse. He represents "grappling with emotional spheres"—allowing them more space in our lives.[102]

The Wheel of Change Queen of Cups (the highest, or at least last, of the four court cards of this deck), is a selfless Inuit woman. She gives direct emotional support in order to further emotional development and empathic love in others.

Keywords/phrases: wisdom; compassion; the wounded healer;

expressing feelings in the form of music, poetry, or other artistic creation; taking a new occupation that allows for more enjoyment or expression of feelings; gaining access to deeper inner levels through dreams/myths.

See **kings.**

D

dance/dancing

Dancing relates to sensuousness or sensuality; to celebration of events or seasons; to the "dance of life" concept; and to Shiva, lord of the dance, whose own dancing rhythm creates the cosmic rhythm of everything. Dance can be an active interplay of opposites, particularly when the dancing couple are male and female. In a broader sense, it represents the tension between discipline and self-abandonment.[1] Where one follows the "rules" of the dance, it may represent a microcosmic act of bringing order to the energy of chaos. In many cultures, ritual dances, and often their specific hand and foot movements as well, reenact important mythological stories. Dancing can be an attempt to evoke the benevolence of the gods (rain dance), to contact and release the spirit within, or to reach a higher state of ecstasy or transformation. Dance is a "soul art," and connects with the concept of *musica mundana*, "world music," the prime expression of the world soul.[2]

Dancers appear on the RWS and Robin Wood Three of Cups, the Robin Wood Four of Wands (harmony and festivity), and the World Spirit's Two of Cups (representing the dance of courtship and the dynamic interplay of opposites).[3] The figure in many World cards is identified as dancing in the cosmos, having the capacity to see it clearly and still enjoy its pleasure to the utmost. In the World Spirit deck she dances the world into existence. In the Daughters of the Moon's World card, Shakti, the life dancer, dances her way into our lives. The Light and Shadow Death card portrays the "Endless Dance of Death" between Death and Humanity.

Daphne

Daphne (Greek for laurel) was a water nymph who requested her father, the river god Peneüs, to transform her into a laurel tree as she fled the amorous pursuit of Apollo. Since she would not be his wife, Apollo declared that she would be his tree; that he would wear her leaves for his crown and to decorate his harp, and would weave them into triumphal wreaths for Roman conquerors. For cards on which laurel wreaths appear, *see* **wreath, laurel**.

day (daily) cards

Some people like to draw one card from a deck to determine their influential card for the day. Others select the "day" card from the Major Arcana, similar to the way personality and year cards are chosen. To do this add the day, month, and year together and then further add and reduce the separate digits of the total to a number between two and twenty-two (representing The Fool). If the number is ten or larger, do not reduce it.

See **personality cards; reduction; soul cards; year cards**.

de Mellet, le Comte (1727–1804)

Little is known about the eighteenth-century French noble-man and lieutenant-general in the cavalry, Louis-Raphaël-Lucrèce de Fayolle, le Comte de Mellet. He was born in Périgueux and died in Constance, although the dates of his birth and death are uncertain. During the time he was Governor of the Maine and Perche (1767–1784), he wrote an essay for Volume Eight of Court de Gébelin's *Le Monde Primitif Analysé et Comparé avec le Monde Moderne*. Among other ideas, it presented what is now considered the oldest known tarot spread and linked the cards to the letters of the Hebrew alphabet.[4]

Death (XIII)

Although The Death card serves to remind us of the arche-typal experience of death, traditionally when reading tarot cards, it represents imminent change or a mystical, or initiatory, "death-like" experience. Old traditions and ways of thinking must die or be discarded.

In mystery schools, the initiate had to experience a symbolic death at the end of one phase of esoteric understanding and before entering the next one. This seems especially appropriate for the Death card, since it follows the new revelations experi-enced by the preceding Hanged Man card. Behind The Death card "lies the whole world of ascent in the spirit."[5] The Spiral Tarot's card describes Hecate as the harvest reaper who winnows out what is no longer useful, or prevents new growth, so that new shoots may flourish, and our life may once again become rich and fruitful.[6]

In the Haindl card a bony arm holds a crescent-shaped sickle, suggesting that at the end of life we harvest what we have grown. We are reminded to make a decision and do something with our lives.[7]

The Mythic, Wheel of Change, Morgan-Greer and Renaissance decks all portray Death carrying a scythe, linking him with Father Time and Saturn, Roman god of time. The shape of the scythe links the card to the crescent moon, and to The High Priestess, The Moon card, and the Roman goddess Diana (perpetual maiden and virgin moon goddess—*see* **Artemis/Diana**).

The Death card is related to the archetypal theme of forgetfulness, the "curse" of "ignorance"—the human condition in which we lack awareness of our true identity or true Self—which in various stories is laid upon humans by an evil spell of transformation or sleep (*Sleeping Beauty*), by expulsion from a paradisal garden or, as told in the Indian poem *Gorakṣa-vijaya*, by the great spiritual master Matsyendranāth's amnesia, produced through imprisonment and seduction into physical love.[8] These themes intimately connect the Death card to the Judgement card, where in "awakening" we become aware of the true identity of the soul and recognize our celestial origin.[9]

The Hanged Man and the Death cards, combined with the Judgement card, comprise the archetypal death-rebirth theme. Shining Tribe's Death is represented by a wine-colored goddess, bearing on her gown a fish emblem—symbol of the soul returning to the Great Mother and relating to the fetus in the womb waters—and a butterfly (death-rebirth).[10] The tattered sail in the Spiral Tarot card represents transient life, yet it looks so much like a waterfall flowing from the clouds that it also reminds us of this symbology (*see* **waterfall**).

The RWS card portrays Death as a golden skeleton, connecting it with the golden sunrise and the golden garments of the priest or hierophant. This is the first and only one of two RWS Major Arcana cards (the second being The Sun) where the dominant figure moves from left to right (as we look at the card), from the unconscious toward consciousness, from the imprisonment of the past toward the rising awareness of the future. The great river and waterfall in the background further show that emotional turmoil or change is going on here and link it with the only other card in the RWS deck to have a waterfall, The Empress.

Major archetypal themes are represented by the four smaller figures in the RWS card: the wounded king, the child, the maiden, and the prelate (the wise old man archetype), who wears the three crosses of completed initiation, first seen on The Hierophant card. In the Renaissance card, the bishop's miter and the king's crown lie on the ground at the feet of Death, where they represent the lost vanities of power and prestige.[11]

In terms of actual death, the RWS figures have also been described as representing the nondiscriminatory aspects of death, which comes to everyone.[12] Yet, the horseman's black banner, emblazoned with the "Mystic Rose," and the roses on the bishop's cloak and in the woman's hair signify life, the mystic path,[13] alchemical change. The arrow pointing to the cave entrance in the background of the cliff in the RWS card may be a visual reference to Dante's journey in the dark wood, "the exotic and almost unknown entrance while still in this life, into the state of mystical death."[14]

Many decks portray death as a skeleton (Nigel Jackson, Tarot of the Spirit, Renaissance, Spiral, New Palladini, Light and Shadow, Wheel of Change, Alchemical, Thoth), our basic support system and the elemental structure of our existence.[15] It allows us to stand upright, and makes movement, change, and all else that we do possible.[16] In fairy tales and archetypal symbology, bones represent the indestructible soul-spirit, the Self in Jungian psychology.[17]

Death and anxiety are intimately related, since one aspect of anxiety is the realization that one may cease to exist as a personality. Recognition of our "being" calls into awareness the possibility of "not being," but this does not necessarily mean death. It may consist of the "threat of meaninglessness," that is, of the loss of psychological or spiritual meaning.[18] Further, when we give up old conflicts, destructive ways of being, or rigid thinking after psychological or spiritual work, it almost always feels, at first, like loss, and we often develop a temporary heightened awareness of, and mourning for, the "death" of "old ways."

Surrounded by a forest of birch trees (*see* **tree, birch**), Robin Wood's Death is cloaked in a gorgeous robe the color of heart's blood (where change generally strikes us). The white rose of freedom and rebirth on the black flag of the unknown indicates the seeker will find freedom by following the path he is now shown. We are unable to identify anything about the figure because that is the nature of change; we can't really comprehend it completely until it is all over.[19]

The Death card also has to do with forgiveness (*see* **Hermit, The (IX)**). If you let go of anger toward someone or negative aspects of certain relationships, you have to develop an entirely new perspective. You cannot fully live in the present, when part of you is symbolically dead (holding onto the past). Alchemically this is a card of releasing energy—old demons—and changing consciousness.

The Alchemical deck portrays Death as a skeleton chained to the fiery blackened alchemical vessel, the ongoing process of *nigredo*. In the center of the beautiful Osho "Transformation" card, a black, many-armed figure holds a sword that cuts through illusion, a snake that represents rejuvenation, the broken chain of limitations, and the yin-yang ball, symbolizing transcending duality. Another reaches down to touch the outline of a sleeping face, symbolizing the time for "deep let-go."[20]

Keywords/phrases: new opportunities; the transforming principle that renews all things; liberation from old or worn out concepts, beliefs, and behaviors; examination and exploration of things, principles, and ideas to their true depth; release of outgrown ideas or attitudes; bringing order back into spiritual life.[21]

See **Empress, The (III), Moon, The (XVIII); Sun, The (XIX); twin motif.**

deck clearing

This refers to the many and varied processes to "remove" or neutralize "energy" that a deck "carries," which has accumulated from a reading, or from another's handling of one's cards. Performing a deck clearing ritual is really about what it takes for you to feel you have removed the influence of a previous reading and re-established your own intuitive link with your deck.[22]

The two most simple ways are to rearrange all seventy-eight cards in their original numerical order or to shuffle the cards as many times as necessary until the deck feels "lighter." Cleansing or clearing rituals range from the relatively simple, such as passing the cards through the smoke of incense or sage, or placing a crystal atop the deck overnight and washing it in warm water the next morning, to serious rituals involving ceremonial time, ingredients, and incantations. Many books and websites describe such involved rituals.

Demeter/Ceres (Greek/Roman goddess)

The myth of the goddess of the cornfield, who seasonally ripened the grain, and who governed the orderly cycles of nature, is frequently associated with The Empress card. She was a deity of both wild fertility and tamed harvest.[23] After her daughter Persephone was abducted, Demeter roamed the earth searching for her. When she discovered Persephone's abduction by Hades, Demeter reacted with maddening rage and cursed the land with drought and famine. Eventually a compromise was reached where Persephone would return to Hades for part of the year (some say six months, others say three months). When that happens, Demeter goes into mourning again: leaves fall, the earth grows cold and hard. When Persephone returns above ground, everything begins to turn green and flourish again.

See **Empress, The (III).**

desert

Deserts may be considered places of desolation or isolation, and/or places of spiritual connection and inspiration, depending on the landscape in which they appear. In the RWS deck, deserts figure prominently in the Page and Knight of Wands cards, where the three pyramids suggest Egypt and a pathway of ancient, hidden knowledge or ideas to be learned. The pyramids are only slightly implied in the Queen and King cards of the suit. Wisdom has been internalized.

See **Egypt; pyramids.**

Devil, The (XV)

Not a card of evil, as popular conception would have it, The Devil card speaks to our own inner chaos, our bondage to those mental or emotional things that hold us prisoner, and the demons within, such as addictions of any kind, fears, and prejudices, especially those created by projections.[24] Psychologically, it can represent the "devilish influence of the unconscious."[25] In the Spiral Tarot's card a woman sees herself in a mirror as she really is and doesn't like what she sees.

In the RWS, Renaissance, Mythic and Nigel Jackson cards, The Devil is portrayed as a satyr: part human, part beast. His horns (the goat)—and in the RWS, his raised palm bearing the glyph for the planet Saturn, ruler of Capricorn—tie him to this zodiacal sign; therefore, many Devil cards portray the goat in some way. The satyr figure also connects him with Pan, depicted in the Renaissance and Mythic Devil cards.

Saturn energy represents socially created "reality." It directs us toward others' opinions or truths, and when our personal realities differ, we experience a clash or conflict.[26] The Devil card raises the question, "What is truth?" and its corollary, "Whose truth?" It also represents the false structure of society, one which, admittedly, we need much of the time in order to survive without anxiety. Still, we must remember that this structure is man-made; we create it, and then pretend that it is "truth."

The loose chains holding the male and female figures in the RWS card show that, should they choose, they could remove them. They are imprisoned by their own beliefs and "bullhead-edness," symbolized by the horns on their heads. So, the card relates to the false power of these things to "bind us" and hold us captive.

The arm positions of the satyr figure, similar to those of the RWS magician, suggest that this is the consequence of "worldly magic"—illusion—rather than understanding higher law. A four-armed figure in the Light and Shadow card is identified as the master of illusion, the king of mirages.[27]

The card is related to the alchemical process of *nigredo*, the beginning of purification through the breaking down of the *prima materia*. Jungians understand the process to be represented by composite creatures, which symbolize our attempt to join conscious knowledge (the human part of the figure) with emerging, unconscious material (the beast part). Some consider The Devil card as the ultimate shadow card. It is the act of recognizing and acknowledging our shadow aspects, which can often spur great creativity (*see* **shadow**).

Mirth is one of the qualities attached to *Ayin*, the Hebrew letter for this card. It is mirth provoked by our human foibles, shortcomings, and incongruities—all things that provoke insight, "new truths," and change,[28] and allow us to laugh at illusion. Being numerologically the same as The Lovers (VI) card ($15 = 1 + 5 = 6$), The Devil card is sometimes considered to be a parody of that card. If we ignore, or fail to fulfill, the tasks indicated by The Lovers card, we then become our own internal jailers.

Ayin also means "eye," and the Thoth, Haindl, and Nigel Jackson cards display the eye, which can refer to the all-seeing eye of God, the third eye (as in the Haindl and Thoth cards), the process of discernment, and to Lucifer as the "bringer of light" so that we might "see." Hence, another message from this card is that of becoming aware of one's own inner darkness and, in so doing, of *becoming* the light rather than searching outward for it.

The satyr figure is omitted in the Robin Wood card, where a chest filled with jewels is prominent. It is chained open and when the chains are extended to their limit outside the card's boundaries, they form an inverted pentagram to demonstrate that the attitudes depicted by this card are anti-life.[29] Perhaps they also reflect the concept, contained in many puzzles, that to reach a solution, we sometimes have to look beyond the boundaries and our own assumptions (limitations).

In the Alchemical Tarot's card, we see the sinister, venomous side of Hermes/Mercury chained to a red dragon. The prominent creatures on the Haindl card are a triple-horned, curly haired goat and a snake, all of which symbolize kundalini energy. The "lord of obsession" dominates the World Spirit card, and in the Wheel of Change card, the wild king of the autumn equinox, sitting astride a goat, plays a drum to symbolize heartbeat and the rhythm of nature. The card represents our attachment to extremes, and a warning that we are giving our power away.

Keywords/phrases: gluttony; needing to examine one's greed; self-indulgence; self-deception; facing denied aspects of oneself; false limitations; the pull of self-defeating patterns; needing to recognize, acknowledge, and integrate the shadow; things that bind us (habituation, dependency, or addictions).

See **chains; Hierophant, The (V); opposites, tension of; Pan**.

dignities

Using dignities with tarot cards refers to how two cards affect, or react, with each other—how each card influences surrounding cards. Any two cards side by side, one above the other—and sometimes diagonally placed to one another—either strengthen or weaken each other. Dignities are used by less than half of those who read professionally and are preferred over reversals by those readers with a bent toward astrology or Golden Dawn concepts.[30]

The easiest way to use dignities is when cards are in a straight line either vertically or horizontally. In a circular spread, each card influences both the card before and after it.

If one reads cards *only* according to dignities, the emphasis is not on basic or symbolic card meanings but, rather, on the "energies" (balanced/unbalanced, compatible/incompatible, active/passive, strongest/weakest, excessive/missing) expressed by the dignities. Cards can be well-dignified or ill-dignified.

Obviously, dignities cannot be used with one-card readings (nothing to compare), and their use is often difficult, although not impossible, with two-and three-card readings. They begin to work well with four-card readings.[31]

See **court cards** (astrological aspects); **elemental/suit dignities; ill-dignified cards; numerological dignities; well-dignified cards**.

DIN

This symbol appears at the top of the visible leg in the RWS Magician card. A Hebrew word, *nun-yod-daleth*, it means judgment. Although an alternative name for the sephira Geburah, no one is quite clear on its meaning here. If Waite associated Geburah with the gold that occurs at the end of the alchemical operation, the word's presence may suggest that the magician is an alchemist.[32]

See **hidden letters**.

Dionysus/Bacchus (Greek/Roman god)

The son of Zeus and the mortal Princess Semele, Dionysus/Bacchus was the god of wine. Representing not only the intoxicating power of wine, but also its social influences, he was considered a promoter of civilization.[33] Hera, furious at Zeus's infidelity with Semele, presented many difficulties for Dionysus, eventually driving him mad for a time. In one story, he was torn to pieces by the Titans, whereupon Zeus transformed his heart into a potion of pomegranate seeds. When Hades fed this to Persephone, she became pregnant and Dionysus was thus reborn in the underworld. This gave him the name Dionysus-Iacchos, twice-born.[34] In other stories the name twice-born is considered to apply to him because after Semele was consumed by Zeus's lightning, Hermes saved her six-month-old fetus, sewed him up inside Zeus's thigh to mature, and in three more months delivered the newborn.[35]

Dionysus was often depicted with a wreath of ivy around his head or carrying an ivy-twined staff tipped with a pinecone (called a *thyrsus*). His Dionysian revels taught humanity about temporary liberation from the restraints of civilization. Many cards in which grapes or grape vines are shown connect with the Greek Dionysian revelries or the Roman bacchanalia, which we celebrate today as Mardi Gras or Carnival.

Dionysus is The Fool in the Mythic Tarot deck. The grapes on the Thoth Fool card and on the staff of the Nigel Jackson fool also relate the cards to Bacchus, while the Thoth figure's horns connect him with Dionysus.

See **Fool, The (O); grapes**.

direction (of figures on cards)

The direction toward which the figures in a card face can provide additional symbolic information. When looking at a card, its left side, for instance, can represent the unconscious and the need or desire to delve into it—facing, examining, or caught up in the past. The right side then represents conscious awareness or facing the future. Designs at the top of the card may represent "above" influences regarding the meaning of the card, while what is at the bottom of the card can represent that which supports or undermines the figure.

Some authors consider that the left and right directions pertain to the figure's left and right. If a figure is standing facing forward and looking to the left side of the card, the direction of the eyes are actually to the figure's right. Either theory can be used, but it is important to adopt one and be consistent in defining what are the right and left directions.

See **court cards** (direction and placement in spreads); **profile**.

disks

See **pentacles**.

dog

Associated with watchfulness and fidelity, the dog is often considered a guardian of the home, and the helper and protector of women and children. In antiquity dogs were considered to be guarantors of eternal life. The dog was a favorite animal of Artemis/Diana, goddess of the moon. In ancient Greece the dog also belonged to Asklepias, god of healing; so, symbolically a dog is considered a guardian and guide,[36] a protective force on which we can draw.

The three-headed Cerberus, the guardian Hound of Hell, is tamed by the Thoth Hermit's light, actually the light of Mercury. When the dog is paired with its cousin the wolf, as the two often are on The Moon cards of various decks, they represent the necessity for the recognition of opposites and the need to carefully make our way between our civilized nature and our untamed aspects. A white dog appears on the RWS Fool card, where he may represent The Fool's spirit guide or a "domesticated" warning to avoid the risks of wild adventure.

See **Moon, The (XVIII); wolf**.

dolphin(s)

Dolphins play in the ocean of the Mythic Tarot's Eight of Wands, representing the exciting burst of energy experienced with the release from, or victory of, a previous struggle. They leap toward a goal.[37] A dolphin, symbolizing the perceptive and emotional world[38] and the power of creation,[39] swims behind the Thoth Princess of Cups.[40] Two red dolphins, representing union, twine together about a lotus stem on the Thoth "Love" (Two of

Cups) card. A dolphin appears on the RWS King of Cups, and on the Tarot of the Spirit's One of Water, where it symbolizes the creativity inherent in the suit and its element (water).

See **Apollo**.

door/doorway

Doors represent the opportunity for transition from one place to another. Closed doors may represent a "mystery," or secret knowledge known only to the initiate, or a defense, warning, or blockage. Open doorways represent an invitation or opportunity. An open doorway in the Haindl Empress card symbolizes intellectual creation, therefore culture. It also represents "philosophy," the human urge to abstraction, to turning curved trees into straight boards and to building right angles on a round earth.[41] Layers of colored doorways are present in the Shining Tribe Devil card. The devil stands before the black door of illusion that keeps us from entering the threshold of the occult. The purple doorway suggests the wisdom that can come from overcoming illusion. The green door represents the life we can have if we transform repressed energy and, finally, the red doorway promises the wonders we can experience when we tap into hidden power.[42]

See **arch/archway**.

dove(s)

Doves drew the chariot of Aphrodite/Venus, and were considered her messengers. In Gnostic legend, the dove represents Sophia. Some stories say it was a dove that Noah sent forth during the flood to find land. In Christian legend, the Holy Ghost came to the Virgin Mary in the form of a dove, and ultimately the dove came also to represent her. All of these stories suggest that the dove is a messenger that brings new possibilities. In alchemical art, a white dove often represented the mercurial spirit that carried out the work, or the distillated spirit that reunites with the body after the stage of putrefaction.[43]

146

As the symbol of God's female soul and feminine creative potential, Shekinah, a white dove appears on The Empress card of the Spiral deck and on the Thoth Hierophant card. Representing inner peace, one rests on the right hand of the Tarot of the Spirit Empress. Doves also appear on the Renaissance Lovers card and on the Ten of Rivers of the Shining Tribe deck. A descending dove, no doubt symbolizing holy spirit, carries a communion wafer on the RWS Ace of Cups.

dragon(s)

The understanding of symbolic dragons depends on the culture and historical frame within which they appear. Often thought of as evil (St. George and the dragon legend), they also symbolize esoteric secrets and hidden things. Dragons represent a primal energy, creativity, or vibration that runs throughout the earth and represents the cosmic mind in motion.[44]

A lunar image, when depicted as a huge winged snake, it can represent the ouroboric primal mother or, in Christian iconography, the devil. The fairy tale and mythic tales of the hero who fights a dragon are often related to the archetypal experience of separation from our families. The hero fights the dragon (dependency on family), succeeds (successfully separates from family), and is then able to pursue his own quest for unique self-development.[45] The Fool's Journey through the Major Arcana is a "dragon-fighting" quest.

Green, gold, crimson, and blue dragons coil through the web of the spider-woman in the Shapeshifter card. They represent the elements and the four directions. In the same deck's equivalent of The Fool card, the initiate shapeshifter flows with the dragon energy behind him, giving him spiritual strength, determination, and courage—an inner spiritual fire. A small, horned green dragon (evil subdued by spiritual authority) perches on the right glove of the Renaissance Hierophant. A surprised baby dragon appears on the Wheel of Change Princess of Wands, but a fierce, fire-spitting dragon dominates the Haindl Universe

(World) card. It has been circling the earth and although now uncoiling, it is associated with the Scandinavian World Serpent coiled around the earth. It represents the spirit that has obtained higher wisdom and now returns to more ordinary life.[46]

dualities

See **opposites, tension of**.

E

*

eagle

As the king of the birds, the eagle represents mastery of the element of air. It is often seen flying in Emperor cards, or reproduced on a nearby shield. The Morgan-Greer Empress holds a yellow and red eagle shield (the passion and intellect behind her authority), while an eagle rises above the head of the Empress in the Tarot of the Spirit.

In mythology the eagle was the special messenger of Zeus/ Jupiter. If sent in answer to prayers, it was considered a positive omen. For early alchemists the eagle represented the high, soaring, but also volatile inner spirit.[1] It symbolized the successive "volatizations and sublimations" that took place during their work[2] (the eagle on the Thoth Death card), and also higher spirit/ higher mental faculties "exaltation above solid matter."[3] In the

Thoth "Art" (Temperance) card, the alchemical white eagle has become red in a transformative, mingling process with the former red lion (now white). Thus, the eagle is sometimes understood as the emblem of the soul, especially if colored silver; however, if black, it may be considered the soul "darkened" through incarnation.[4] Half of the shield of the Thoth Empress bears the alchemical white eagle, while the black eagle appears on the "wallet" of the RWS Fool card. It suggests that through his journey, The Fool will now have to purify and transform himself (*see* **wallet**).

ego

That part of the personality that we consciously acknowledge as "I" or "me"—who we think we are or how we define who we are. Spiritually oriented tarot readings aim to get beyond the ego and ascertain a message or guidance from the higher self or the soul.

See *persona*; **Self**.

Egypt

As the land where ancient Biblical people were held in bondage or from which they fled, it represents a journey out of emotional slavery toward higher consciousness. It expresses the tension between barrenness (the Sahara Desert) and fertility (the Nile valley), and symbolizes the tension between an "open crossroads and an isolated oasis."[5] This symbolic tension, and the personal progress of dealing with it, are aptly portrayed in the RWS Page and Knight of Wands—the neophyte adepts or trainees hold budding wands as they stand in a desert before three pyramids. The pyramids loom large in the Page card and grow smaller in the Knight's card, where presumably he has begun to learn the lessons of the Wands. They are well behind the RWS Queen of Wands and nowhere to be seen in the King of Wands.

See **desert**; **pyramid(s)**.

eights

Because of its shape, eight can symbolize the two interlacing serpents of the caduceus (the balancing of opposing forces) or the eternally spiraling movement of the heavens, especially when placed on its side as the lemniscate.[6]

Eight represents the ceaseless in and out breaths of the Cosmos, the "flame of divine breath," by which the soul achieves equilibrium. Lower ideals are withdrawn (exhalation) and higher ones introduced (inhalation).[7] Eight is a number of cosmic balance, as in the symbolism of eight spokes in the RWS Wheel of Fortune card.

In its hourglass shape, eight symbolizes the passage of time and cycles. It represents the four seasons, plus the two solstices and equinoxes.[8] As a double of four, it hints of totality, yet tarot eights also express the rush of uncontrolled energy from the sevens, which may leave us with a sense of imbalance and the need to create a new order out of chaos. Time to ponder and evaluate all that has gone before, sort out and organize priorities, make a plan. Eights are associated with the sephirah of Hod (glory) on the Tree of Life.

See **fours; lemniscate;** eights of each suit.

elemental/suit dignities

In reading EDs (as they are sometimes abbreviated), each suit's elemental association is more important than other meanings assigned to the card. Pentacles are associated with the earth element, Cups with water, Wands with fire, and Swords with air.

Derived from the Golden Dawn, all court cards have two elemental associations: one for the suit and one for the rank or title. Pages are attached to the element of earth, knights to air, queens to water, and kings to fire—although in some systems kings represent air (thought) and knights represent fire (action). They also carry the attributes of their suit; hence the Page of

Wands (fire suit) would be the Earth of Fire, an energetic, down-to-earth messenger. The Queen of Swords (air suit) would be the Water of Air, an intuitive or thoughtful spiritual teacher.

There are two popular ways to read the elemental associations for the Major Arcana. In the easiest, Major Arcana cards are considered neutral and belong to the element of Spirit. In the second, each Major Arcana card is given an elemental association based on its astrological association, usually as determined by the Golden Dawn system.

See **dignities; elements; ill-dignified cards; well-dignified cards**.

elements

The doctrine of the four elements can be traced as far back as the Greek philosopher and poet Empedocles (*ca* 495–435 B.C.E), who referred to them as the roots of all things.[9] It was refined over time by Hippocrates (the "four humors") and Aristotle, who believed that by manipulating the four qualities of dryness, coldness, moisture, and heat, one could change the elemental combination of material things and bring about transmutation—the principle of alchemy. For the ancients, the term "element" meant a set of ideas, a working principle that employed certain qualities and characteristics.

In alchemy the four elements relate to the process of moving from a chaotic mass to a state where they are arranged according to the degrees of their density: earth, water, air, and fire. Oftentimes this final achievement is shown in an arrangement of concentric circles with gold/Sun (the Quintessence or spirit element) in the center.[10] It was the alchemical goal to bring this fifth element down from the fiery heaven to earth through various transmutations.[11] Often Quintessence/spirit is assigned to the Major Arcana cards in their entirety.

The four elements are assigned to each of the four suits of the Minor Arcana, and are often used to assist in interpreting the transmutative actions portrayed by those fifty-six cards. Usually they are fire (Wands), water (Cups), air (Swords), and earth (Pentacles), although in some decks (Nigel Jackson, Shapeshifter) Wands are associated with air and Swords with fire. There are, however, decks where Swords equal earth, Wands equal fire, Coins equal air, and Cups equal water,[12] and even one where Cups equal air and Swords equal water.[13]

The elements are represented symbolically in the four corner figures seen in the RWS Wheel of Fortune and World cards, and the four sphinxes on the Thoth Chariot card. The bull equals earth, the lion equals fire, the eagle equals water, and the human equals air. The Wheel of Change Justice goddess stands at the intersection of the four elements. The card represents a balance between them.

Dating from Golden Dawn time, elements are also assigned to each of the court cards, which allows the introduction of these principles into focused ideas about each court card (*see* **elemental/ suit dignities**).

The popularity and continuation of the idea of four major elements indicates that it is an important archetypal image or principle related to the quartenary, the fourfold structure of consciousness.

See also **Cups; Pentacles; Quintessence; Swords; Wands; Wheel of Fortune (X).**

elephant

The Indian God Ganesh, son of Lord Shiva, bears the head of an elephant and is the patron saint of literature and the overcomer of obstacles. Continuously in communication with each other (although below the human sound range), elephants are the quintessential communicators, always in relationship.

Because of long life and slow movement, they symbolize knowledge and the accumulation of wisdom, particularly ancient wisdom, the reason for the presence of a stone elephant on the

Haindl Eight of Stones, subtitled "Knowledge." The figure also refers to the wisdom of the earth.[14] Elephants, as symbols of power, surround the throne of the Thoth Hierophant.

elevens

In the Major Arcana, eleven is the number of the Justice card, and the halfway point to twenty-two. Since eleven can be broken down into $1 + 1 = 2$, some authors connect Justice with all the twos of the Major Arcana (The High Priestess and Judgement). Some tarotists count pages as elevens.

Numerologically, eleven symbolizes transition, new or expanding energy, excess and peril, conflict and martyrdom, extravagance, exaggeration. Considered by some to be a number of individual initiative, exercised without relation to cosmic harmony, eleven can, therefore, also be considered a symbol of internal conflict, discord, rebellion, and law-breaking.[15] A combination of the holy number seven, and of four, the number of squaring things in our lives, eleven symbolizes preparation for expanded awareness (looking inside and out at the same time).

See **Justice (XI); pages; twin motif; twos.**

Emperor, The (IV)

The Emperor is one aspect of the active male principle or father archetype, the worldly father—The Hierophant representing the spiritual father. Not only is he a "father" representative, but he also serves as a representation of what the hero-adventurer can become: the earthly lawgiver, a reflection of the World Axis or World Mountain, a man whose "word is the wind of life."[16]

He is the Great Father archetype portrayed by all the "father gods" of any mythology. As an archetypal principle, The Emperor represents an outgoing, inseminating force or energy, the Taoist concept of yang. He is rationality, the order and structure that has arisen out of the secrets and creativity of the first three Major Arcana. One would think that such fecundity would result in something more creative, yet structure is precisely what we need to ground us at this time, so that we can once again proceed, adding thinking and planning to our repertoire of mental activity.

For some, The Emperor is the "gloomy sovereign of hell,"[17] Pluto, who rules over concrete and corporeal things, in contrast to The Empress, who rules over souls and pure spirits. As the *animus* or male principle in Jungian psychology, The Emperor is always behind the search for truth.[18] When portrayed with white hair and beard (RWS, New Palladini), he is related to the wise old man archetype, also portrayed in the tarot by The Hermit (IX). The Hermit is The Emperor once the latter has nourished his inner fire. There is the merest hint from the red and white stones in the RWS Emperor's crown that Waite may have identified The Emperor with an alchemical king (red and white being the fundamental antithetical ingredients of alchemy).[19]

In many decks, The Emperor holds an orb in his left hand (yin) and a scepter (sometimes resembling an ankh) in his right hand (yang). He personifies these two contrasting elements, which represent the dynamic balance in all things. They can also represent the Cosmic Father and Cosmic Mother. In the Mythic Tarot, he holds lightning bolts, symbol of Zeus, in his right hand.

In many Emperor cards, rams are someplace nearby, decorating the throne or a tapestry. They connect him to the Egyptian god Amun-Ra, the virile Ram and holy phallus.[20] They symbolize the Emperor's assertive powers and our own power to follow our goals.[21] They also connect him to the zodiacal sign of Aries.

In ancient Egypt the installation of a new pharaoh represented the creation of a new epoch, which would repair the rift between society and nature, a symbolic re-creation of the Universe, with its implied passage from chaos to cosmos.[22] Today this is symbolized in various New Year rituals and celebrations which, by symbolically ensuring renewal of the cosmos, offer hope that the "bliss of the beginnings" can be recovered.[23] So an aspect of The Emperor card deals with our own rejuvenation or strengthening, of reinventing our own connection with nature. This is aptly portrayed in the Shining Tribe Emperor, a shamanistic horned god symbolizing regenerative power.

Ultimately The Emperor points us toward the task of reshaping the inner "father authority" into an "inner masculine with heart." Our inner emperor enables us to set boundaries, establish guidelines, take a stand for principles or ideals and back it up. The card speaks of a time when our reasoning abilities need to be at their uppermost in order to make necessary decisions. At its most extreme, however, The Emperor's organizational ability is about rigidity, about forcing others to "shape up," about "playing by the rules" no matter what and with few or any exceptions. There's no room for spontaneity. He can represent our own "inner tyrant" (*see* **mountain(s)**).

Keywords/phrases: manifesting success and stability; worldly achievement; having or holding to structured and logical beliefs; using logic and linear thinking to resolve issues and make decisions; the lawgiver; facing and resolving one's issues with or about "father" or fathering.

See **fours**.

Empress, The (III)

The Empress is the mother aspect of the triple Great Goddess archetype. Associating her with The High Priestess, we then have the material and the spiritual feminine. So linked are the two cards that it is sometimes difficult to distinguish the myths that apply to them.

The Empress is connected to the mythologies of Hera/Juno, goddess of marriage and childbirth, and all cultural mythologies of the earth mother. She is Demeter/Ceres in the Mythic and Spiral decks and linked with Psyche, the lover of Eros (*see* **Psyche**) in the Haindl card.

Traditionally said to be pregnant, the obviously pregnant Wheel of Change Empress sits on the fertile crescent between the Tigris and Euphrates rivers. The RWS Empress, not so obviously pregnant, wears a gown decorated with what some say are the astrological symbols of Venus, while others believe they are pomegranates, further linking her to The High Priestess. Other Venusian symbols decorate the shield lying against her throne, and one of the cloths at her back. Sumerian astral mythology identified the various aspects of the cosmic female with the phases of the planet Venus,[24] with which this card is associated.

Clearly The Empress is not ethereal, but fruitful and earthy. She is "birthing" in all its aspects: interior, exterior, physically, emotionally, and psychically. Not only does she represent the archetypal concept of mothering, but also the way we mother others and ourselves (our internal mother). She is the "gateway to form."[25]

Shown outdoors, in the light of day (RWS), the Empress reveals, while The High Priestess conceals. The Empress brings us into human life, so that The High Priestess may lead us beyond.[26] The Alchemical nude Empress represents the alchemical vessel that nurtures and eventually produces the philosopher's stone.

The base of the RWS Empress's crown is myrtle, a Venusian plant. The twelve stars in her crown (RWS, Aquarian, Ancestral Path) link her to the signs of the zodiac and, therefore, to The Star and The Moon cards, the early study of the zodiac being linked to the moon and the path of the moon goddess.[27] The twelve-starred crown also hints at the Twelve Labors of Heracles/Hercules, for which she must prepare her children (*see* **Heracles/Hercules**). It may also refer to Revelation 12:1, where a woman appears with twelve stars in her crown.[28]

While others see the Egyptian trilogy of Isis (The Empress), Hathor (The High Priestess), and Nephthys (Justice) hinted at here,[29] Waite wrote that to link her to "the Triad" is completely wrong.[30] Nevertheless, the Robin Wood Empress wears a crown engraved with the three phases of the moon, suggesting that The Empress encompasses all of those.

The armless, semiabstract figure on the Shining Tribe card bridges the gap between reality and the principles represented by The Magician and The High Priestess.[31]

The clearly pregnant Robin Wood Empress spins the thread of life, linking her with Arachne, the maiden whose skill at weaving caused Athena to jealously transform her into a spider. In Icelandic literature, the spinning Empress would be associated with the three Norns who spin the thread of Fate, similar to the Greek *Mœræ*, the Three Fates. Spinning myths and the spinning wheel link this archetype to the Wheel of Fortune card. Psychologically, the web of our fate or destiny has much to do with the pattern of our unconscious fantasies. As we gradually and successively make them conscious, we understand the connection between the events of our lives.[32] This is another type of "birthing" represented by this card.

In the Renaissance card, the figure is Eve. The "mother of runes," Hagall, enclosed in a hexagram, is one of the runes that appears on the Haindl Empress card. As the "framework of the world" rune, it represents cosmic harmony.[33]

The Light and Shadow Empress rises out of a lotus and holds one in her left hand, as she strokes the head of a stork, symbol of charity and material feeling with her right. The queens of the Minor Arcana at the base of the card form her foundation and indicate her contact with the four elements they represent.[34]

Keywords/phrases: thoughts or projects conceived but not yet born or expressed; possessing or exhibiting creative ability or abundance; deep awareness of, or comfort with, one's physical existence; naturalness; fertility and productivity; maternity and motherhood; boundless or unconditional love; possessing feminine sexual vitality; new, growth-producing and life-enriching insights; time for renewal; facing and resolving one's issues with or about "mother" or mothering.

See **Demeter/Ceres; High Priestess, The (I); pearl(s); Proserpina/Persephone; tree, evergreen; waterfall**.

Eros/Cupid (Greek/Roman god)

The son of Aphrodite/Venus, Eros was always getting others in trouble by shooting his arrows at them, often at the instigation of his mother. It was his arrow that caused Hades/Pluto to fall in love with Proserpina/Persephone and abduct her. It was his arrows—one to excite love, the other to repel it—that caused the unfortunate experience with Apollo and Daphne (*see* **Daphne**). The story of his own love for Psyche, as well as the stories of others hit by his arrows, are metaphors for the soul's search for love, and the many choices or problems it can encounter.

Although depicted in ancient art as a gorgeous full-grown person with wings, as Cupid he is frequently depicted as a tiny, winged cherub. Chubby cherubs in tarot cards, as on the thrones of the RWS Queens of Pentacles, Swords, and Cups, may symbolically refer to him. In some decks (Marseilles, Nigel Jackson) he is more deliberately portrayed at the top of The Lovers card, aiming his arrow at the figures below. He appears as a small, symbolic figure in the corner of the Light and Shadow and Renaissance Tarot Lovers cards.

See **Daphne; Proserpina/Persephone; Psyche.**

Etteilla (1738–1791)

Jean-Baptiste Alliette, a French cartomancer, published the first book about using tarot cards for fortune-telling in the late 1700s. He is generally credited with popularizing tarot as a divinatory system. The deck he created (The Grand Etteilla) differed considerably from other decks of the time, since most of them had been created for gaming purposes while his was designed for esoteric use. It has been called the first "mass-market" tarot.[35] Without any supporting evidence, Etteilla determined that Thoth-Hermes was the originator of the tarot, and claimed that his deck restored ancient Egyptian elements. Its Major Arcana cards portrayed signs and planets and represented a Hermetic creation myth.[36] Many of the divinatory meanings he assigned to cards are still used today.[37] His was also the first deck to use a complete system of astrological correspondences.[38]

eye inside a triangle

Seen on the Haindl Hermit card, this is the traditional image of God, the architect of the universe.

F

falcon

Representative of the Egyptian god Horus, whose two eyes were the sun and the moon, a falcon ultimately represents the principle of light and of "seeing all" (enlightenment). Hooded falcons often symbolize hidden esoteric knowledge. A trained and hooded falcon sits on the wrist of the woman in the RWS Nine of Pentacles, representing the disciplined mind, and conscious control of her aggressive or hunting impulses. The Shapeshifter "Sorcerer" (Magician) is part falcon, part human, representing the harmonious joining of personal and divine wills.[1]

See **bird(s)**.

farmer

See **Pentacles, Seven of**.

feather(s)

The quintessential symbol of lightness, the feather as a head-dress or part of a headdress is, nevertheless, related to power, the sun, and high aspirations. Feathers are also related to the symbolism and attributes of the bird from which they came, if identifiable. They represent spiritual flight and the shamanic ability to change shape. Their color adds to the symbolism. Related to flying, air, and the heavens, a feather can symbolize spirit, and is linked to creator/creation deities. In Egyptian mythology, the feather is an attribute of Ma'at, goddess of correct ordering. Her feather was weighed against the heart-souls of the dead to determine if they were in the right balance (as light as a feather) to enter the afterlife.

A red feather appears in the headband of RWS and Morgan-Greer Fool and Sun figures and on the hat of the RWS Page of Wands. Some tarotists suggest that the Fool's feather is from the Phoenix, and symbolizes the rebirth to come (*see* **phoenix**).[2] A white feather, symbolizing peace, sticks in the ground on the Haindl Four of Swords. The feathers in the Alchemical Tarot Fool's cap are red and white, the alchemical colors of opposites which ultimately have to be reconciled. The most gloriously feathered wings of any Tarot figure are born by the World Spirit deck's Temperance angel.

feline animals

See **cat(s)**; **lion(s)**.

fields, plowed

Plowed fields, or fields ready to be cultivated, are shown in the RWS and Robin Wood Page and Knight of Pentacles, and in the Wheel of Change Princess of Disks. They represent the potential for cultivation (new beginning) and the ultimate harvesting of the fruits of the earth. Plowed fields also imply the labor, attention, and care involved to bring about material success. Standing in such a field suggests groundedness or connection with the earth element or energy.

figure eight
See **eights; lemniscate**.

fireworks
Being one of the more explosive characteristics of fire, fireworks represent a burst of intense but short-lived passion. They are a universal expression of festivity. Having originated in China, and spread worldwide, they also symbolize creative invention and experimentation and the transfer of creative knowledge.[3] Fireworks explode in the sky of the Wheel of Change Seven of Wands.

fish
Although fish symbolism has a long and varied cultural history, in general, fish are associated with water. For Christians the fish symbolizes Jesus, as it does in the Thoth Death card.

Many myths tell stories of persons being chased, leaping into the water to save themselves, and being transformed into a fish. They personify the saving transformation—the delving into the deeper, unconscious aspects of ourselves. In Jungian psychology the fish symbolizes the "nourishing" influence to consciousness provided by unconscious material.[4]

Fish symbols abound on the Light and Shadow Magician card. The Magician juggles an interwoven chain of fish to indicate the delicate connection in our chain of existence. He wears "fertilizer fish boots," reminiscent of the Native American tradition of fertilizing corn with buried fish, to bring him earthly mastery, understanding, growth and insight.[5] Likely without realizing it, the authors of the deck have connected the fact that fish were sacred to ancient moon goddesses, with the notion that the moon was considered to be the quintessential fertilizing influence.[6]

The RWS King of Cups wears a golden fish necklace around his neck at his heart chakra suggesting the orderly recognition of feelings and a feminine instinct which has yet to be fully incorporated. Many cards in the Legend Arthurian deck deal directly (The King of Cups) or indirectly with the theme of the "Fisher" King, one theory of which is that he was a man whose internal feminine aspect was wounded.

fives

Because it resembled the four limbs and the head, the five-pointed star symbolized humans for the ancient Egyptians, a symbolism that has been carried forward today. Medieval symbolists equated the five petals of many flowers with the five senses; hence, five expressed in any form came to symbolize the senses. Five is traditionally associated with Hermes/Mercury. In medieval alchemy, five is included in the concept of the philosopher's stone, the ultimate goal, not as a fifth element but rather as the representation of the "realized unity" of the first four numbers,[7] and as the potential for future growth.

In Minor Arcana suits, fives most often represent a crisis or a challenge, possibly the destruction of one aspect of our world in favor of a different one. Although we tend to think of crises as negative and undesirable, they do carry the impetus for change or transition from a solid, fixed, rigid past—or from the stagnation/inactivity of the fours—into new possibilities.

It is in the Minor Arcana fives that we find the quality of mind, but not yet the manifestation, that allows us to transform old ways into new patterns of being. Things are just not as secure or stable as we once thought, so the unrest of the fives may be a "crisis of creativity." Fives can also reflect a situation of ambivalence, or of the anxiety of having to live with the unknown. To end that anxiety, we may be forced to make a choice.

The cards preceding fives depict experiences that allow us to develop our personalities according to the suit's qualities and to feel fairly successful at it—what Jungian psychologists call "inflation of the ego" if carried to extreme. In its most positive sense, inflation permits us to imagine that what we are doing is actually "right on target." Fortunately for our personal development—although it may not seem so at the time—the psyche subsequently deflates any "puffed-upedness" about that in order to allow us to move along to the next needed experience. And that is what the fives represent, an end to ego-envisioned "glamour" and an eye-opening experience. They are associated with the sephira of Geburah (judgment) on the Tree of Life.

See the fives of each suit.

flower(s)

Flowers appear on many tarot cards, and specific flowers carry their own symbolism. In general, however, flowers symbolize the seasons of spring or summer, youth, manifestation arising out of the elements of earth and water, and the fleeting nature of beauty and life.[8] Yellow flowers grow in the grass at the feet of the Robin Wood Empress to show her joy at the abundance of growth (represented by the green grass).[9]

See **fives; wreath, flowered.** Where flowers are identifiable in a card, see the listing for the specific flower.

fluer-de-lis

See **lily/lilies.**

flute

The flute, said to be invented by Athena/Minerva, is one of the attributes of Hermes; hence, The Fool in the Robin Wood card plays a flute.

See **Fool, The (O); music.**

Fool, The (O)

Usually numbered zero, sometimes twenty-two, the present-day fool is typically depicted as an innocent youth beginning the journey toward self-knowledge. He is the archetypal wanderer, the person with a quest. He (sometimes a female in contemporary or feminist decks) is naïve and doesn't know what he doesn't know, especially if the card appears in the early part of the reading. If it appears in the later part of a longer reading, it may suggest that by that time in his journey, he now knows that he knows nothing and has no illusions but rather possesses a "wonderful freedom."[10]

In some decks (RWS, Osho, Shining Tribe, Renaissance, Tarot of the Spirit, World Spirit, Light and Shadow, Haindl, Morgan-Greer, Spiral, Robin Wood, Aquarian, Songs for the Journey Home), The Fool faces left, the feminine or yin side, and the direction of the unconscious (*see* **direction** (of figures on cards)). In others (Marseilles, Alchemical, Nigel Jackson, Mythic), he faces toward the right, the masculine or yang side, conscious knowledge and future direction. The Fool looks straight ahead in the Ancestral Path, Wheel of Change, and Thoth decks, the latter sometimes referred to as the April Fool, because of his green clothing. He is the Green Man, the personification of spring, yet also linked with the Parsifal legend, as on the Legend Arthurian card, where he looks toward the castle of Camelot. On the Spiral card, he is young Parsifal before he becomes one of King Arthur's knights and begins his search for the Grail castle.

In the Mythic card, he is Dionysus (*see* **Dionysus/Bacchus**), already having stepped half off the cliff, as he has done in the Osho card. The Shining Tribe androgynous fool, dressed in a rope of braided colors, sails off the cliff, arms outspread and, following the blue bird of instinct, flies.

Dressed in ridiculous clothing with mismatched patterns (surely his mother didn't see him before he left the house), the flexible fool in Songs for the Journey Home uses a sapling to reach the other side of the abyss.

In the Shapeshifter equivalent card, "Initiation," an androgynous person rises from his ocean birthplace, takes the first step into shapeshifting, and flows with a dragon. As the sun rises in the Daughters of the Moon "Dreamer" card, an Indian maiden in reverie stirs the waters of a stream while her nearby horse (*see* **horse**) nibbles grass. She may be on a vision quest to meet her spirit guides, to release logic, or to search for her ideal self.

Most fools are accompanied by an animal, often a dog. Sometimes the dog—a tiger in the Thoth card—nips at the fool's heels (RWS), or tears a hole in his pants (Marseilles). The Light and Shadow fool is about to put his foot into the open mouth of a crocodile (*see* **crocodile**), while his accompanying monkey (*see* **monkey**) pulls on his leg. The Nigel Jackson fool is accompanied by a cat (representing the panthers of Dionysus) and the blindfolded (*see* **blindfold**) Alchemical fool by a hare (*see* **rabbit/hare**). The animals are variously identified as spirit guides, instinctual energies, or the intellect giving warning or suggesting urgency.

In a move away from the animal tradition, the Ancestral Path fool is a blonde, female tarot reader holding upright the card of herself. Behind her the frame of a mirror is engraved with court jesters (*see* **mirror(s)**).

The Fool gives us the spirit, the impetus to find our own way, and is related to both the compassionate healer and the wily trickster, who outrageously flaunts social and personal incongruities. Many trickster stories tell how certain natural or geological processes occurred and how possessions (fire, for instance) came to be acquired through the trickster's antisocial or obscene behavior.

The Fool (O) and The Magician (I) are intimately connected as provocateurs of our inner journeys. Both carry some of the same symbolism, not so much in their artistic depictions as in the overall understanding of their functions. They are the two cards in the deck that show totality, while all other cards merely show *aspects* of our inner opposites (masculine/feminine; yin/yang).[11]

The Fool represents a wonderful combination of our need to explore new places and ideas, our unfettered inquisitiveness, our desire to have adventure in our lives, our capacity to laugh at human foibles—our own and those of others—and our recognition that sometimes even twisted plans or schemes have a benefit.

The Fool is related to the archetypal wanderer, those people who discard the *status quo* of society in an attempt to find out who they truly are or what they truly desire. Each time we begin a new experience in our lives, The Fool archetype is activated within, as we experience feelings of curiosity, excitement, ambiguity, and fear of risk or embarrassment.

Often thought to have survived as the Joker card in modern playing cards, the TarotL group says this attribution is incorrect, since the Joker originated in the United States around 1857 to be used as a wild card in poker.[12]

Keywords/phrases: adventurous spirit; the sense of spontaneity; trusting your feelings; following your hunches; the soul at play; spirit of the tarot; learning to be a child of the universe; the beginning of a quest or search, especially into the unknown; willingness to risk; being at a place of innocence; naïveté; impulse to change.

See abyss; feather(s); Fool's Journey; Magician, The (I); mandala; Quintessence; Tetragrammaton; wallet; zero.

Fool's Journey

This is a popular way of understanding and learning the Major Arcana by regarding the naïve and spontaneous fool as "traveling" through and encountering, in turn, the "lessons" of each card. Looking at the cards in a sequence, rather than each card for itself, interconnects them all. Part of a card's meaning relies on its place in the sequence and the cards that precede and follow it (*see* tableau). Although in "real" life, we do not have these experiences in the order in which the Major Arcana are arranged, it is, nevertheless, an effective metaphor for understanding our individual life journeys.

The Fool's journey has been likened to the hero's journey, which we make as we learn to be true to ourselves and to honor what matters to us individually. It is the oldest story in the world.[13] It represents the alchemical individuation process, the pull between moving forward (cooking, action) and remaining inert (cooling, waiting), between developing individuality (consciousness) and remaining in a secure state of safety and belonging.

The twenty-two Major Arcana, "archetypal milestones"[14] symbolize just such a life process. The hero Fool who makes the tarot journey has not yet been immobilized by the tension of opposites, thus enabling him to follow every path available to him.[15] The search for the Grail in Arthurian legend is one example of such a journey, and Parsifal is the equivalent of the tarot Fool. Dorothy's journey to Oz is another example, and is aptly portrayed in David Sexton's 2002 Tarot of Oz (Llewellyn).

See **individuation; tableau**.

forest

As a dark, hidden place, often filled with strange or dangerous beings or creatures, the forest represents a realm of the unknown; hence, the unconscious, and the potential within. For some it is a feminine symbol which, depending on the person, can be seen as dangerous or as the germination or potential of the feminine principle. A forest serves as part of the background of the RWS Empress card, where it emphasizes her association with nature and feminine development.

See **tree(s)** and names of specific trees.

fours

Since the time of the ancients, four has been a sacred number with magic properties. If you add the first four digits (1 + 2 + 3 + 4), you get ten; reduce it, and you're back to one. Four marks the end of one cycle and furnishes the impetus for the next. It represents a time of stabilization, in which some sort of foundation has been laid. Order and structure are now present. C. G. Jung observed that our urge toward awareness of our unconscious processes functioned in rhythms of four (a quartenary), and more so if the quartenary was integrated within a circle (*see* **squaring the circle**). He regarded four as the ordering pattern of the psyche, and the number representing the individuation process (*see* **individuation**).

Four is associated with wholeness (the four elements, the four cardinal points, the four rivers of paradise, the four Gospels, the four Evangelists, the four cardinal virtues, etc.) and with paired opposites, which also total four (above, below; left, right). Because we have four limbs, fours are often considered the number of mankind, although many prefer that this symbolism be applied to the fives (*see* **fives**).

The tarot fours encourage us to turn into our depths for understanding, to begin our quest for a deeper meaning to life. This inward turning holds the potential to release our identification with our own *persona* and to develop a greater sense of the process represented by the suit. Tarot fours may show us what precipitates the crisis reflected in the fives, especially as it relates to our biological family, and childhood emotions. They suggest emotions and behavior we have been living with habitually or without thinking that cause trouble for us and about which we may now be required to make our own decision.

Fours represent an organized structure and the presence of limits or limitation, which can be either positive or negative depending on the surrounding cards. Although fours can reflect stability as a result of resolving issues raised by the first three cards of a suit, it is of a limited nature. Psychologically, the tarot fours can represent that stage in personal development when there is a stalemate, a period that often seems necessary for unacknowledged emotions or dilemmas to come into consciousness so we can experience them, and get on with growth or healing. The downside of this is that we can get stuck in an unchanging attitude, a determination to maintain the *status quo* no matter what. If we look at it positively, this "stuckedness" or "delay" can give us time to gain insight.

Fours are associated with the sephira Chesed (love) on the Tree of Life.

See **square** and fours of each suit.

G

*

Gemini (astrological sign)
Third sign of the zodiac (May 22–June 21).

Element: Air
Modality: Mutable
Polarity: Yang
Ruled by the planet Mercury

A card attributed to Gemini partakes of its dual nature, its need for communication and the exchange of ideas, and the friendships and associations developed during childhood, including siblings. Gemini takes the products of Taurus to the marketplace, and relates to circles of friends, business associates; the core community of a daily life. The Twins, Castor and Pollux, are a symbol of relating, discussing, contrasting, and multiplicity. The pair of figures in the constellation may refer to twins, brothers, lovers, friends, or a hero and his sidekick. A well-dignified Gemini card may be interpreted as: cleverness, facilities and skills, mastery of language and speech, sense of humor, adaptability, broad field of interests, an extensive social circle with diverse friends and acquaintances, acting skills, multitalented. Meanings for an ill-dignified or reversed Gemini card include: contradiction, confusion of ideas, shallowness of thought, indiscriminate choices, flippant remarks, infidelity, vacillating moods, opinions, and sentiments, knavish manipulation.[1]

See **Mercury** (planet).

geometric design(s)

Geometric designs are an integral part of many tarot cards. Indeed, all the cards of the Thoth deck rely heavily on geometric designs. In ancient times, geometry and geometric designs were considered representations of the sacred because they organize chaos into form.[2] In the Thoth Tower card, falling figures have become geometric designs to show that they no longer cling to their human shape and have become emancipated.[3]

See **circle; circle with a dot within; cube; mandorla; square; tattvas; triangle.**

girdle

See **belt/sash.**

globe

Depending on where and how it appears in a card, it can represent dominion over nature or the world (New Palladini Emperor), or the process of unlimited worldly creations or manifestations. In several Two of Wands cards (Morgan-Greer, RWS, Robin Wood, Spiral), it suggests a person with far-ranging interests.

See **royal orb.**

gnome(s)

As small creatures who lived underground, they were believed to possess treasures made from underground metals and riches; hence, they represent hidden knowledge, and the elemental spirit forces alive in nature (suit of Pentacles). They bring flashes of knowledge and enlightenment. A male and female pair occurring together symbolize the tension and/or conjunction of opposites, partly because the women are considered beautiful and the men ugly and misshapen.[4] Gnomes appear on the Haindl Hermit card.

goat

The goat head on the RWS Queen of Pentacles's throne refers to the Capricorn astrological association with this card.

gold (color)

Associated with the sun, gold shares similar symbolisms with yellow, including illumination, reason and intellect, understanding and insight. As a solar symbol, it is related to all the sun gods, and corn gods/goddesses of every culture, and was the color attribute of Apollo. As a hair color, it may symbolize radiant energy (the RWS Hanged Man). In earlier, esoteric decks, it sometimes represented the final result of the alchemical process.

gold (metal)

The metal of the sun and of Aries. Its alchemical symbol is a circle with a dot or point in the center, representing the end of the quest, perfection.[5] This symbol appears in the RWS deck on The Hierophant's throne, the handle of the sword in Justice, and on the forehead of the Temperance angel.

See **circle with a dot within; colors; yellow.**

Golden Dawn

See **Hermetic Order of the Golden Dawn.**

grain

Grain represents life, its cycles, harvest, and new seed. Growing at the feet of the RWS Empress, and in Empress cards of other decks, it represents fertility. It associates The Empress with nature's cycles, nourishment, and creative abundance. Wherever it appears, it connects with the Greek/Roman grain goddesses Demeter/Ceres. When it appears near a waterfall (RWS Empress), or beside the endless river of life,[6] it represents the Gnostic symbol of fertility, later adopted by the Freemasons to symbolize earth-sea fertility,[7] and the slow, continuing process of spiritual maturity. Various grains from around the world are featured on the Wheel of Change Seven of Disks, symbolizing the soul needs of cultures throughout the world.[8]

grapes

Grapes in the Renaissance and Thoth Fool cards represent inspiration, intoxication, and symbolize all the ancient rituals where fermented beverages were used.[9] Grapes may symbolize truth or truth-telling (when inhibitions are released), but also debauchery, frenzy, and the drunken ecstasies of Dionysus, who gave the gift of wine to mankind. He is depicted as The Fool on the Mythic Tarot card. While grapes do not appear on that card, their effect is implied by his presence, as well as a relationship to the Dionysian mysteries, which celebrated both death and rebirth or renewal. Grapes on the Thoth Fool card represent intoxication with the sweetness of life.[10] Decorating the robe of the King of Pentacles (RWS, Morgan-Greer), and growing in the garden on the Nine of Pentacles (RWS), they more likely represent abundance, fruitfulness, and the achievement that occurs from having successfully attended to one's "vines." In the same sense, grapes are also seen on the wealthy merchant's robe in the Robin Wood Six of Pentacles. Grapes on the RWS and Morgan-Greer Three of Cups and Four of Wands cards celebrate the fullness of life's pleasures. A hand reaches for a branch from a vineyard on the Haindl Six of Swords ("Science"). Together they represent the values and danger of technology on some of humanity's oldest cultivations.[11]

See **Dionysus/Bacchus.**

grapevine

The grapevine was portrayed as a motif in much ancient religious art. In Greece it was sacred to Dionysus, in Egypt to Osiris. Jesus is sometimes referred to as "the Vine" (John XV). Because of its five-pointed leaves, it also was considered sacred to the ancient Great Goddess (*see* **apple**).

See **grapes.**

grasshopper

In ancient Greece, the grasshopper was sacred to Apollo. In its relationship to the locust, however, it can symbolize voracity and destruction. In China locusts were seen as expressing a disturbance in the cosmos.[12] It is in that sense that the grasshopper appears on the Wheel of Change Seven of Disks, representing chance and the unpredictable nature of the world.

gray

As a color midway between black and white, it often symbolizes neutrality, achieved wisdom, integration, unification, and the balance of opposites.

green

The predominant color of vegetation, it typically symbolizes growth, potential, adaptability, balance, cycles of life, renewal, fertility, creativity, ripeness, prosperity, and worldly purposes and functions. It is the color attribute of Venus and Mercury. As a combination of blue, the color of heaven, and yellow, one of the earth colors, it has mystical value, representing dual natures coming together. If dark green, it expresses the most powerful aspects of the color, while light green suggests more calm or subtle aspects at work. Blue green (aqua) indicates the healing aspects of blue interacting with or affecting the action possibilities of green.

See **colors.**

ground

The ground in a scene can represent conscious awareness, that which we know already, or being grounded. Look for whether or not a figure's feet are shown to get a sense of stability or lack of it.

grounding

A technique some tarotists find helpful before beginning a reading or a meditation on a card, it refers to tapping into the earth or universal energy, usually with a meditation or visualization, in order not to deplete one's own personal energy. Many books have exercises to assist readers in tapping into this energy.

See **centering.**

H

Hades/Pluto (Greek/Roman god)

The underworld (psychologically, the realm of compulsions and phobias, and the eruption of suppressed memories from the unconscious) was ruled by Hades/Pluto, along with his sometime queen Proserpina/Persephone. Inasmuch as he was one of the least known and least personified of the gods, his mythic qualities are few but distinct. As the god of the dead, he was apart and isolated from the other gods.

His most prominent departure from his subterranean region is recorded in his abduction of Persephone. That story—the principal myth associated with Hades—is followed in the Renaissance Suit of Coins.

Hades was the god of buried treasures, hidden wealth, and the riches found beneath earth's surface (petroleum, coal, gems). He is not at all synonymous with the Judeo-Christian devil. Not an enemy of mankind, Hades is simply a ruler, whose kingdom includes Tartarus, a place of torment, and Elysium or the Elysian Fields, a paradise of perpetual spring, sunlight, happiness, and song.[1]

In general, behavioral models for Hades lean toward qualities of ruthlessness and destruction, and that of the recluse who has lost his vitality.[2] More positive models of Hades include great healers and counselors for those deeply troubled by life crises. The archetype implies a pervasive understanding of human nature, and the capacity to battle the forces of death and destruction. It is our Hades aspect that allows us to have an understanding of dreams, unconscious messages, and to understand the riches of our inner experiences. In this the Hades/Pluto archetype is related to the crone aspect of the Moon, particularly Hecate, Kali, or other dark goddesses.

The Hades/Pluto archetype allows us to eventually, usually with hindsight, understand the impact of death, destruction, and upheaval in our lives, and the part they play in helping us transform and grow into new life phases.[3]

See **High Priestess, The (II); Moon, The (XVIII); Proserpina/ Persephone; Scorpio.**

Hall, Manly Palmer (1901–1990)

The founder of the Philosophical Research Society in 1934 in Los Angeles, and a prolific author, Hall is perhaps best known for *The Secret Teachings of All Ages: An Encyclopedic Outline of Masonic, Hermetic, Qabbalistic, and Rosicrucian Symbolic Philosophy*, which describes the theories and practices of Western wisdom traditions. Under his auspices in 1929, J. A. Knapp drew a black-and-white deck generally patterned after Oswald Wirth's deck. Long out of print, the most unusual facet of the deck is that every card has a shield or crest containing a symbol or object, about which, unfortunately, Hall offered no explanation. The deck has been re-released in a colored version by U. S. Games.

halo

See **nimbus**.

hand(s)

As with all left-right symbology, the left hand is typically considered the feminine hand (intuition) and the right hand the masculine one (assertiveness, conscious awareness). For most tarot cards, the symbolism of hands is not particularly significant unless the position (hidden or upraised, open or closed) or the object(s) held suggests something more, e.g., the masculine hand holds a feminine object. Then one needs to consider the opposite hand to determine if together they express balance, or if one suggests dominance over, or emphasis upon, a particular masculine or feminine principle. In some Magician cards, the Magician extends his right (action) hand skyward (RWS, Morgan-Greer, New Palladini, Shining Tribe) as his left points to the ground. In others it's just the reverse. In both cases, he is a conduit for the manifestation or materialization of heavenly forces, but the manner through which he receives it may change the meaning of the card slightly. In the Marseilles, Shapeshifter, and Mythic cards, he extends his left hand suggesting passive reception of divine energy and the grounding of it in earthly manifestation through masculine or assertive energy. The hidden left hand of the Robin Wood magician shows that he operates in both seen and unseen worlds.[4]

With their right hands, the RWS and Spiral Hierophants give the esoteric ecclesiastical sign that distinguishes "between the manifest and concealed part of doctrine,"[5] the known and the unknown. The Hierophant uses his downward left hand in the Tarot of the Spirit card. He grounds cosmic secrets into the physical world.[6]

For an explanation of the finger position of the figure's right hand in the RWS Ten of Swords, *see* **Swords, Ten of**. For an explanation of the arm positions of the figures in the Judgement card, *see* **hidden letters**.

Hanged Man, The (XII)

Many authors have speculated about the origins, original intent, and meaning of The Hanged Man. Court de Gébelin, believing the upside-down man was a printer's error, reversed the figure and renamed the card Prudence, as the one cardinal virtue missing from the tarot deck,[7] the other three being Temperance, Strength (or fortitude), and Justice.

The myth most often connected with the card is that of the Norse god Óðinn (Odin). Wounded in the genitals, he hung upside down from the world tree Yggdrasill for nine days and nights in order to retrieve the magical runes of power and poetry from Niflheim, the realm of eternal mist and darkness. The RWS card depicts the tree as an ash (Yggdrasill) and portrays the person as blonde, as was Óðinn. The blue man in the World Spirit card also hangs suspended from Yggdrasill by a cord of flowers. He holds a staff decorated with bits of shell, bone, and feathers; he is a shaman with psychic powers. The very ethereal body of the bearded Haindl Hanged Man begins to merge with the rainbow behind him, while his hair merges with the ground below (*see* **rainbow**).

The Wheel of Change solar king hangs from an oak tree at winter solstice, ready to begin his cyclic journey into the darkness. His is the sacrifice of the sun's light. The card also is linked with the Grail quest and the legend of the wounded Fisher King. The card refers to making a personal sacrifice for the greater benefit of others. Likewise the Mythic Tarot card relates to voluntary sacrifice, portraying the story of Prometheus (*see* **Prometheus**).

On the Spiral card, Dionysus hangs above an abyss between the past and the future, "sacrificing" old hurtful, painful experiences that keep us feeling victimized. We are willing to give up beliefs or attitudes in which we are stuck, or which we have carried in our psyches for a long time. The Thoth figure, crucified upside down, represents the crucifixion of the ego so that we might be "resurrected" into the higher or divine self, symbolized by the ankh to which he is bound.

The hair of the Light and Shadow Hanged Man, also bound to his tree from an ankh, roots with the roots of the tree; he is assimilating with the World Tree.[8] The earthbound figure in the Osho "New Vision" card grows wings to fly into the unbounded because we have opened up to the insight of the "ultimate" and are no longer separate.

The card can be connected to the experiences an initiate might have during a shamanistic journey or mystic initiation, where isolation or length of endurance propel the person into a timeless world from which he emerges with a new sense of inner strength and resourcefulness.[9] Certainly the inversion of values is the first step of the mystical journey.[10] In the Alchemical card the man, suspended by a snake, hangs from a gallows. He loses his gold, representing the loss of worldly possessions, self-esteem, and a "sense of our role in the world."[11] The Hanged Man has also been linked to one of five "dark night of the soul" experiences (the others being The Devil, The Tower, Death, and The Moon), as a result of which new insights may emerge.[12]

During the Renaissance, the card was often referred to as *Il Traditore*, The Traitor, representing cowardly or disloyal behavior, but most present-day cards emphasize an inversion of commonly held values.[13] Still, the Nigel Jackson card connects the Hanged Man with Judas Iscariot suspended from an elder tree, having renounced allegiance to the "normal" world.

The RWS figure wears the red of The Emperor, The Hierophant, and Justice on his leggings, and the blue of The High Priestess in his tunic. A golden halo surrounds his head. On his feet, the foundation of under*standing*, he wears golden slippers. He has head-to-toe comprehension of divine law. His body forms the secret sign of alchemical sulphur (*see* **sulphur**), indicating inner activity or transformational work.[14] We cannot see his hands, suggesting his work is inward. Further, the RWS card's symbolism may be related to the Adeptus Minor Ritual of the Golden Dawn where the initiate was bound to a cross. A red cross (formed by the man's tights) above a triangle (formed by the position of his arms) is one of the emblems of the Golden Dawn, although technically the cross should be white.[15] Likely it is no coincidence that the upside-down RWS figure shares the same leg position with the female in the upright RWS World card.

Two birds, identified as Óðinn's twin ravens Hugin (thought) and Munin (memory) fly toward the Haindl Hanged Man (*see* **raven(s)**), who represents the worst and the best of humanity. He gives himself back to the earth in order to find harmony with the natural world.[16] The Shining Tribe Hanged Woman expresses the message that we achieve "genuine" independence by attaching ourselves to the rhythms of the universe and dissolving artificial barriers between ourselves and all that exists.[17] Children's toys decorate the tree from which the woman hangs, suggesting that surrender need not be solemn nor grim.

In the Ancestral Path "Hanged One" card, a fetus grows upside down in the womb, depicting transition and a period of rest. The Tarot of the Spirit's Hanged Man is immersed in a geometrically shaped "cosmic womb," where he can tap into universal mind.

The card calls upon us to let go of false perceptions,[18] yet this is much more complicated than it sounds. In 1922 sociologist Walter Lippmann, investigating stereotyping and prejudice, presented the idea that we do not make a direct response to our external environment. Rather we respond to a "representation" of the environment that we have created ourselves.[19] We decide how something is or what it means, and then operate on that decision as if it were the truth. This is true for all our perceptions, not just those involving stereotypes and prejudice. One might say, "There is no there there," except as we create it. Certainly the ideas of quantum physics suggest that if we don't create our own world, our interactions with it, and observations of it, change and shape it considerably.

In the Jungian understanding of alchemy, the number twelve (three times four) refers to the relationship between three and four, central to the problem or process of individuation. Clearly The Hanged Man is a card of *reprocessing* what we have learned so that we may correctly incorporate that expanded understanding into our own sense of Self or Spirit. The Hanged Man represents a task that will recur throughout our lifetimes. If we continue to grow in self-analysis and Spirit, we will never be through with this card.

Keywords/phrases: reversing false images; crisis or confrontation that results in greater understanding or perspective; a major turning point in attitude; letting go of control; examining a different point of view; identifying where you are "hung up"; "hanging in there."

harbor/cove

A harbor represents a place of leave-taking and of arriving; hence, it offers challenge or adventure, as well as the culmination of a journey and respite. Related to the symbolism of sea, ocean or water, a harbor implies that the journey we make will be one of learning to identify interior mysteries, while the cove being smaller than a harbor suggests that we will be more protected in those journeys and experiences, or that they will not be so dramatic.

The figure in the RWS Two of Wands looks out above a small cove or harbor, and perhaps the figure in the RWS Three of Wands also looks out on a busier harbor. The harbor in the Songs for the Journey Home "Luminary" (Hierophant) card specifically represents a place of future departure and exploration where we will be called upon to leave behind what is safe and known.[20]

hare

See rabbit/hare.

Harris, Lady Frieda (1877–1962)

Born Marguerit Frieda Bloxam, Lady Frieda Harris was the wife of the liberal member of British Parliament, Sir Percy Alfred Harris. The illustrator for Aleister Crowley's Thoth deck, she worked with him for five years in its creation. Lady Harris incorporated ideas from art nouveau, cubism, and futurism, and introduced the element of movement into the cards by changing the straight lines of previous decks into curves. She wanted all the cards to convey the continual play of opposites. After her husband's death in 1952, she lived the last ten years of her life in India and died in poverty.

Hecate

See crossroads; Moon, The (XVIII).

Heracles/Hercules (Greek/Roman god)

The son of Zeus, Heracles's many successful, but excessive, battles caused Hera, Zeus's wife, to drive him mad. In that madness, he killed eight children, six of his own. The oracle at Delphi commanded him to serve King Eurystheus for twelve years of arduous labor as expiation. Metaphorically, Heracles's Twelve Labors can be likened to the "heroic" tasks we all take on when we leave home and learn to live and survive in the world. They are also linked to the sun's journey through the zodiac and, as such, represent cycles of life. His labors are represented throughout the Renaissance Suit of Staves, and on the Renaissance and Mythic Strength cards.

Hermes/Mercury (Greek/Roman god)

Hermes/Mercury was only semi-divine, but bamboozled his way into being recognized as a fully divine being. Clearly precocious, he left his birth cave when he was one day old and stole Apollo's cattle. Commanded by Zeus to return them, Hermes created the lyre from the shell of a tortoise, and swapped it to Apollo for his cattle.

Like all trickster figures, he had a double-sided nature. Because he amused Zeus/Jupiter, he became a messenger of the gods and, as Hermes Psychopompos, was responsible for guiding the dead to Hades. At Zeus's request, he traveled to the underworld to bring Persephone back to her mother (*see* **Proserpina/Persephone**). He is, thus, considered a liminal god, the archetype present during times of transition.[21] In alchemy he was Mercurius, the spirit that united all opposites.

Hermes was often called upon to aid mortals in their adventures when guile and stealth were needed. He was the god of commerce (transactions, exchanges, trades), and sacred to merchants and trade guilds. He was appointed the patron of gamblers and travelers. After the Thriae (Three Muses) showed him how to tell the future from pebbles dancing on water, Hermes invented divination using knuckle-bones. He assisted the Three Fates in composing the alphabet, inventing astronomy, the musical scale, and the arts of boxing and gymnastics.[22]

As an archetypal figure, Mercury represents the inventive, clever aspects of us, as well as the ability to communicate articulately, and respond quickly.[23] The Gemini-type Mercury is oriented toward verbal skills, debate, and virtuosity; the Virgoan Mercury focuses on research, analysis, technical skills, and the drive for creative perfection.

Hermes was depicted with wings on his hat and ankles and carried a wand of wood or gold, twined with snakes and surmounted by wings (a caduceus). In Egypt he became Thoth, god of wisdom and magic and scribe of the gods. Several early authors attributed the creation of the tarot to him, through his Book of Thoth, presumably handed down through the followers of the Greek teacher/magician Hermes Trismegistus.

In the tarot, he is associated with The Fool and The Magician, both of whom set our feet on the tarot journey.

See **Court de Gébelin, Antoine; Etteilla; Judgement (XX); Gemini** (astrological sign); **Magician, The (I); trickster; Virgo** (astrological sign).

Hermetic Order of the Golden Dawn

Founded on March 1, 1888, in England, and lasting only a brief fifteen years, the group elevated the ideas of the tarot into esoteric principles and linked them with features from the Kabbalah, alchemy, astrology, in the context of studies and rituals for learning elemental magic. The group, founded by Dr. William R. Woodman, Dr. W. Wynn Wescott, and MacGregor Mathers—all members of a secret occult group called the *Societas Rosicrucians*—created its own tarot deck, the exact origin of which remains obscure. It had to be individually copied by each disciple. Apparently it employed Egyptian, classical, Oriental, and primitive symbology and mythology to help members arrive at a deeper understanding of life-structuring forces and of themselves.

In the 1970s Robert Wang painted a Golden Dawn tarot deck based on those early designs, under the guidance of former member Israel Regardie. Two members of the group—Arthur Waite and Aleister Crowley—and Paul Foster Case (member of an offshoot organization) produced tarot decks still used today. There is much debate about how accurate or distorted their decks are; i.e., how much incorrect or garbled symbolism they used from the original Golden Dawn deck in order to reveal or preserve its occult secrets.

See **Case, Paul Foster; Crowley, Aleister; mystery schools; Regardie, Francis Israel; Waite, Arthur Edward.**

Hermit, The (IX)

With his white hair and beard, the RWS Hermit (also Haindl and Tarot of the Spirit) is related to the wise old man archetype, considered to represent the inner spirit and the notion that spiritual wisdom takes experience and effort and does not come about easily. The Hermit is The Emperor once the latter has nourished his inner fire, and the card speaks of the loneliness of that spiritual quest.

The Spiral Tarot's Hermit is represented by the wise old woman (crone) archetype, and the Roman goddess of the hearth, Vesta, whose flame was tended by the vestal virgins. She calls upon us to tend our own inner flame through meditation and centering.[24]

In earlier cards, the figure was often portrayed as Father Time, carrying an hourglass. Indeed, the Mythic Tarot's Hermit is the time god Cronus, carrying his scythe, which symbolizes the harvest ending and beginning.

A recluse, The Hermit represents the contemplative silence that occurs before creation. The card's number is nine, that of the Greek muses of inspiration. We become The Hermit recluse whenever we move into a meditative state and connect with our higher self to seek guidance and inspiration.

The RWS hermit stands atop a snow-covered mountain. Clothed entirely in the gray of wisdom, his head is bowed to receive higher spiritual impressions, and his eyes are closed, allowing him to turn inward. He is the union of personal consciousness with Cosmic Will.[25] The Hermit typically holds his light (representing both the light in the darkness and his own inner light) at the level of his heart chakra, the powerhouse of the human energy system. The heart chakra mediates between the body and the spirit, and its energy allows us to accept our place as part of a divine plan.[26] It is the chakra of compassion and forgiveness, making The Hermit card, then, one of inner- or self-healing.

Coming ninth in the Major Arcana, The Hermit likely does not signal the end of a journey, but rather indicates that there are times when he/we reach some pinnacle of enlightenment or insight that is complete within itself or, perhaps, inspires further introversive exploration. We will travel to the top of this mountain many times.

The Robin Wood Hermit stands atop a snowy mountain in

rather ragged clothes. He carries the red feather of the deck's Fool on his staff—he *has* come a long way. His new slippers are also bright red to indicate that he walks in courage and that "old knowledge is constantly expressing itself in new ways."[27] His staff holds two small medicine pouches to show that he has fewer, but more powerful, possessions than those carried in The Fool's backpack. These "possessions" are the insights that we gather and distill throughout our life journey.

The Hermit card is one of acknowledging profound personal mysteries, which must always include the mysteries of Spirit. The card anchors us in worldly and spiritual time, and reminds us of the lessons to be learned in both. It calls upon us to contemplate or reflect on the meaning of our lives and how any action we take will best express our inner Spirit. It represents the psychic state of being in search of our own "myth of consciousness."[28]

The "wet, sludgy stuff" at the bottom of the alchemist's vessel (typically shown on a mountaintop in this card) needs to be "heated and distilled before it can be explored with imagination."[29] The card reminds us that before making a decision we need to "distill" all the information as it relates both to the situation and to us individually. In addition to a sense of ripening, we must also make a place for incompleteness, ambiguity, and wonder.

Keywords/phrases: time for introspection; soul-searching; pursuit or achievement of wisdom; discernment that comes from solitude and detachment; seeking inner or higher knowledge; solitary spirituality; knowing or learning the ways of the unconscious; illuminating the shadow aspects of oneself.

See **lantern, wheat**.

heron

Said to stand at the gateway between life and death, the bird is active in the battle between opposites, e.g., light/darkness, good/evil. In Celtic mythology, the heron acts as the mediator on the soul's journey to the otherworld.[30] Associated with the Sun principle, yet at home in the world of water, it sometimes symbolizes reincarnation. A heron stands to the right of the Thoth Queen of Cups, representing vigilance and circumspection.[31]

hero's journey
See **Fool's Journey.**

hidden letters
In some versions of the RWS Sun card, tiny marks below Pamela Colman Smith's signature appear to spell the word "love."[32] Although not exactly hidden, people often overlook the letters PAX (Peace) in the halo of the stained glass figure in the RWS Four of Swords, hinting that one of the reasons for the withdrawal suggested by this card is to achieve peace.

Several authors suggest that the center child's upraised arms, and those of the background figures, in the RWS Judgement card represent the Hebrew letter *shin*. When shown graphically, it resembles a three-pronged flame, representing the fiery spirit.[33] It also forms the center of the back mandala on the hem of the RWS Fool. The postures of the foreground figures in the RWS Judgement card form the Latin letters L (the woman), V (the child), and X (the man), which means "light."[34] There likely are many other pictorial clues associating Hebrew letters to the RWS cards.[35]

See **DIN; Tetragrammaton;** *yod.*

Hierophant, The (V)
Although older decks sometimes call this card The Pope, or The High Priest, in the RWS deck those ideas are rejected as leading people to assume or identify a very specific person. It is one of the built-in dangers to understanding this card, and provokes a great deal of discussion among tarot readers, particularly those who have left what they perceive as a strict or restricting childhood religion. Some readers regard it as representing rigid, demanding religious authority. Others perceive it as providing

the stimulation or impetus to begin to create a personal awareness of the sacred, in whatever ways we define it.[36]

Hierophant was the name of the high priest of the Greek Elusian mysteries. Waite's choice of this term may be a hint that he meant for this card to depict the notion of "the hidden way."[37] Hierophant also was the name of a Golden Dawn official in initiation ceremonies, while the rose/lily theme (on the garments of the RWS acolytes) appears in the Golden Dawn Zelator-grade initiation ceremony (*see* **roses and lilies motif**). Sashes with three vertical crosses (RWS, Tarot of the Spirit) were worn in Golden Dawn ceremonies (and in Masonic ritual) to indicate completion of the three basic initiations.[38] Together they suggest that initiation ceremonies may have been one of the themes of the RWS card.[39]

In ancient alchemy, paired white/red colors and white/red roses represented the conjunction or sublimation of opposites (*coniunctio solis et lunae*). It may represent the "invisible quintessence."[40]

The two clerics at the feet of the RWS figure are defined in various ways, for instance, as representing theology and mysticism (*see* **twin motif**). In esoteric work, the occult initiate wears the garment with red roses and the mystic initiate wears the lily-decorated robe.[41]

The Hierophant is one aspect of the active male principle or father archetype. The Emperor represents the worldly father. The Hierophant represents the spiritual father and the religious process whereby we create a certain type of order so that we may cope with the unfathomable.

There's no speculation about the Robin Wood Hierophant, clearly described as a bishop in the Catholic Church, and representing repressive conformity, captivity, servitude, and empty ritual. He is not life-affirming (sallow complexion). No breath of fresh air can get through the solid wall of tradition and dogma (gray, block wall) behind him.[42]

On the other hand, the "Luminary" (Songs for the Journey Home) stands on a hill, his arm around a young man wearing a baseball cap. They are the Guide and the Fool. The Guide points out a distant mountain, the complicated inner aspects of which (potential for growth and knowledge) are only revealed through his act of pointing.

With their right hands, the RWS and Spiral Hierophants give the esoteric ecclesiastical sign that distinguishes "between the manifest and concealed part of doctrine,"[43] the known and the unknown. Is The Hierophant a conduit to esoteric tradition or merely the outer, ruling power of religion in its "utmost rigidity of expression"?[44] In the Wheel of Change card, followers honor a golden idol, symbolizing the commonality and conformity of our religious perspectives. By our beliefs we create our reality. The card calls upon us to examine and determine our religious perspectives for ourselves.[45]

The Light and Shadow Hierophant rides a great, snorting bull representing both determination and power, and inflexibility and trickiness. The World Spirit Aztec priest wears leopard skins and a feathered headdress as he fosters knowledge of the "sacred forces that lie behind everyday reality."[46]

The RWS Emperor's white shoes, marked with the St. Andrew's cross, suggest crossroads, as well as the union of higher and lower worlds. The Thoth card speaks to the essence of all "magical" work, i.e., that of uniting the microcosm with the macrocosm.[47] The crossed keys to that union rest below the shoes of the RWS figure, and much has been made of them. They have been variously defined as the keys of the kingdom, the keys of St. Peter, the keys to the temple of wisdom. They link The Hierophant to Hades, holder of the keys to heaven (higher consciousness) and hell (unconscious or instinctual life). The keys in the Morgan-Greer card are gold and silver, symbolizing the sun and the moon, outer and inner ways.

The decoration at the top of the gray pillars flanking the RWS

Hierophant has been identified as an acorn or a pinecone;[48] however, it also resembles a woman's uterus, suggesting that The Hierophant protects the "feminine" secrets of The High Priestess.

The Mythic and Spiral cards focus on Chiron, king of the Centaurs, and a priest and teacher of young heroes. As a Centaur, he represents our human instincts, our spiritual existence, and the need to balance them. Wounded by an arrow from the bow of Heracles, he becomes the mythological "wounded healer." This archetype symbolizes the inability to generate and sustain relationships and reflects those limitations that each of us has that deepen us and make us compassionate.[49] The wounded healer archetype links The Hierophant to the wounded Fisher King of Arthurian legend. Lord of the Castle of the Grail, he holds the secret key to the question the knight Parsifal must ask.

As with most Major Arcana cards, to ultimately comprehend its full meaning, The Hierophant card cannot be considered alone. In addition to The Magician and The High Priestess, as indicated above, it also has to be considered in conjunction with The Lovers and The Devil. In the RWS deck, all three cards show a similar scene, a larger-than-life figure towering above two smaller figures. In The Hierophant, it is the two acolytes. In The Lovers, an angel hovers above two lovers, while in The Devil card, they are chained at the feet of the devil himself.

Psychologically, a one-sided, (deficient?) intractable position forces the psyche to compensate, not only as an attempt at balance, but also as a way of expressing or recognizing the full and paradoxical qualities of the archetype. If we stick with Waite's conception of The Hierophant as expressing a religious, but rigid, channel of grace, we have in The Hierophant and The Devil cards the archetypal content of spirit (but not free flowing) and shadow. Between them is the love principle (The Lovers card). Where we have religious or other similar beliefs expressed pontifically, we must have the shadow. And only love, or the greater feminine principle, can fill the gap. When one or the other of these three cards appears in a reading, we have to consider whether the other two are in the reading and, if not, why not.

In most decks, whatever the various symbolisms, the card has come to mean a link between, or synthesis of, two paths, in whatever worldly or hidden way they are defined. One of the challenges of the card is to clarify one's own direction and one's worldly/spiritual balance. A strong identification with religion and a religious pursuit is often considered an unconscious, archetypal longing for the comfort of a paradise lost,[50] and the wish or need to let go of responsibility and to be carefree.

Keywords/phrases: adherence to, or problems with, religious hierarchy or religious issues; abiding by or examining tradition (religious or otherwise); spiritual and religious values teachings; needing to find a higher dimension to one's life; enlightened conscience; problems or benefits related to organized religion; being true to your spiritual self.

High Priestess, The (II)

The High Priestess represents the virgin, spiritual, or maiden aspect of the feminine archetype. In many decks, she sits between two columns, one black, one white. These two pillars introduce us to the concept of twos and the recognition of opposites in life. The Robin Wood priestess stands between silhouetted black and white trees ready to bud (potential growth). The green and red columns in the Shining Tribe card represent the plant and animal worlds, and the "growth and blood mysteries" of life and death.[51] The Renaissance High Priestess walks between a lotus plant (incongruously growing on land and representing sweetness) and a thistle plant (difficulties and hardships). Two lotuses opening at the feet of the Light and Shadow Priestess symbolize the "immanence of flowering."[52]

Often the Priestess sits in front of a curtain or veil, suggesting hidden knowledge or secrets and linking her with Justice, when that figure also sits in front of a similar veil (as in the RWS deck). Behind the veil, a body of water can sometimes be glimpsed. Traditionally the water in the RWS High Priestess card is the source of all the flowing rivers shown in subsequent cards. It also is possible that their appearance in the Empress, Emperor, Chariot, and Death cards represents the four rivers that flowed from the Garden of Eden (Genesis 2:10).[53] Esoterically water symbolizes hidden or secret doctrines, which the High Priestess shields from the view of the uninitiated. Clearly this is a "mysterious card," hinting at the revelation and understanding of life's hidden secrets through the feminine guardian. This is aptly portrayed in the World Spirit card, where a nude, blue woman stands in a circle of stones at the entrance to a forest (*see* **forest**), the mysterious realm of which she guards.

Usually there is a moon on the card, linking her with the "sister" Moon card. This, and her link to Justice, suggest that The High Priestess is the quintessential holder of secret, intuitive knowledge related to natural or universal truths or laws, and is the mistress of unconscious knowledge. For this reason, she can be mythologically linked with the prophetesses of classical and Renaissance Europe, such as Apollo's oracle at Delphi.[54]

The High Priestess's crown (RWS) is her insignia,[55] and connects her with the Egyptian goddess Isis, sometimes represented by a "moon boat." She is one aspect of moon goddess personification. In the Thoth deck, she is the most spiritual form of Isis. Clothed in a brilliant, luminous veil of light she is Eternal Spirit, the body and soul of light, and the truth behind the veil of light.[56]

As the mother goddess of Egypt, Isis, and The High Priestess, are again linked with The Empress. One of Isis's symbols was the *mu'at* ("foundation of the throne"), which also represented Ma'at, "the motherhood principle called Right, Justice, Truth, or the all-seeing Eye."[57]

Sometimes a cross overlays the front of the Priestess's mantle (RWS, Morgan-Greer), while she holds a scroll (sometimes a book) in her hands. In the RWS, she holds the "Tora" in her left hand. Her right hand of power is hidden. Typically, a crescent moon at her feet, an attribute of Isis, once again connects her with The Moon. The lunar crescent also represents the beginning of esoteric cycles.

Inasmuch as two produces three, The High Priestess represents the beginning and the subsequent birthing (seen in the following Empress card) of a lifelong study of human, earthly, and esoteric laws, and our personal attempts to come to terms with them. She represents the fundamental polarities or dualisms inherent in worldly and psychological structures and the choices we make in response to them. The Light and Shadow High Priestess wears an X at the center of her body to demonstrate that she is the mistress of the crossroads where opposites meet and are reconciled.[58]

The Wheel of Change High Priestess is uniquely depicted as an older woman who teaches "women's mysteries" to younger women.

In ancient decks, the card was often labeled as the "Papessa" or the "Popess." This may relate to one or both of two stories, the most well-known being the legend of "Pope Joan," who presumably hid her gender and ultimately became pope sometime in the Middle Ages. The second story centers around the zealous fourteenth-century followers of Abbess Manfreda of the Umiliata order. They elected her Pope, believing her to be a kind of female John the Baptist who would inaugurate a new age, and pave the way for a female savior.[59] Incensed, the Catholic Church burned her at the stake. Identified as Maria Visconti, a member of the ruling family of Milan, she appeared, shown in her habit, as the popess or papess when her descendants commissioned a deck of tarocchi cards.[60]

Keywords/phrases: realization of one's hidden self or hidden aspects; trusting unconscious wisdom; listening to one's inner voice; being emotionally sensitive; unafraid to work with information from both the conscious (known) and the unconscious (unknown); beginning to recognize and work with one's opposites; developing feminine spirituality; being in touch with or trusting one's lunar cycles; trusting one's feminine aspects (for a male).

See also blue; camel; veil/curtain; Justice (XI); Moon, The (XVIII); pomegranate; Tree of Life; tree, palm; water.

hills

As opposed to the sharp mountains they once were, rounded hills suggests their age, hence, ancient wisdom, like those in the background of the Robin Wood Empress card.[61] Rounded hills can also represent the nourishing (breast) function of Mother Earth and/or earth goddesses. Hills, with unique explanations, figure prominently in many cards of the Shining Tribe Tarot.

See Swords, Ace of.

hooded cloak

Hooded figures in stories and mythology represent both spiritual and evil persons. They serve to keep the wearer unseen, almost invisible; hence, they symbolize that which is hidden or unknown. Although Jung considered hoods to represent the celestial or divine world, more commonly the idea of the hooded cloak is as a disguise to prevent identification, rendering the wearer free from "socially prescribed functions and responsibilities"[62] and carrying the connotation of persons who are "up to no good."

The RWS Hermit wears a hooded gray cloak of wisdom. He has given up social dress and social ideals; he is of a higher world. To understand the Morgan-Greer Magician's hooded cloak, *see* **red**. The Morgan-Greer Death wears a deep purple hooded robe, suggesting his connection with ancient deities. The indigo hooded figure in the same deck's Five of Swords suggests the darkening of hope, yet at the same time it is the color of the third-eye chakra also suggesting that something has yet to be clarified with this card.

Although not hooded, the black cloak the RWS Five of Cups figure wears suggests that by grief and/or inattention, he/she is alienated or separated in some way. Much of grieving must be done alone, or at least inwardly, although help lies in the distant building across the river (unconscious).

horn(s)

Horns represent force, strength, male virility, and inner aggressive and instinctual forces. Rams' horns are solar and are related to Amon, who became the ruling god of Egypt (*see* **Emperor, The (IV)**). In Celtic worship, antlers were related to the horned god Cernunnos, symbolized by the cap worn by the Robin Wood Magician. He is the central figure in The Horned One card in the Arthurian Legend deck, representing one's primordial nature and animal instincts.[63] With the advent of Christianity and the devaluation of paganism, horns came to be associated with Satan (*see* **Devil, The (XV)**). Cow horns represent female protective and reproductive elements,[64] and are related to lunar goddesses and their characteristics. When seen as a container, horns are definitely feminine but still associated with procreative power.

See **cornucopia.**

horse

Dedicated to the god Mars, the horse psychologically represents the instinctual aspects of a person and refers to power. A horse and rider together may symbolize the union or the workings of the conscious (rider) and the unconscious or instinctual (horse). In some folk tales, the horse is the bringer of messages; hence, the knights of the tarot deck are often considered messengers. In the World Spirit Five of Cups a steed stands on a hill, suggesting the promise of recovery from regret and sorrow and "the ability to ride on in search of wholeness."[65] In the Daughters of the Moon "Dreamer" (Fool) card, the horse nibbles grass, fortifying itself for when the dreamer arises from her reverie and will need to draw on its energy.

horse (winged)

Wings on any creature that does not ordinarily have them suggest an association with air and spirit; hence, a winged horse represents the elevation of the soul—the capacity for spiritualization—and the sublimation of instinctual desires. The most well-known mythological winged horse was Pegasus, which sprang from the blood of Medusa when her head was cut off. A winged horse pulls Hades's chariot as he carries Persephone off to his realm on the Renaissance Four of Coins. The Robin Wood Knight of Swords rides a winged horse, representing the element of air.

See **Pegasus; wings**.

Hyacinthus

A beautiful Spartan prince, Hyacinthus, was desired by many mortal and divine creatures alike, including Apollo and Zephyrus, the west wind. One day, as Apollo was teaching young Hyacinthus the skill of hurling quoits, jealous Zephyrus blew the airborne discus back into Hyacinthus's head, killing him. As Apollo lamented and vowed to create a song to celebrate the young man, a hyacinth flower sprang up from his blood, shown growing beside the two young men in the Renaissance Sun card.[66]

I

✳

I Ching

Dating from between 1,122 and 770 B.C.E, the Chinese *I Ching* (Book of Changes) is one of the oldest known divination systems. It consists of sixty-four hexagrams each comprised of six continuous (yes/yang) and broken (no/yin) "advice-giving" lines associated with prophetic meanings believed to describe all of the basic human situations. The hexagrams are interpreted by means of commentaries. Tarotists associate various of the hexagrams with specific tarot cards. With the exception of the aces and the court cards, the Haindl Minor Arcana cards have hexagrams superimposed over the picture. Selected after the paintings were completed, they are meant to extend a card's message, give it a wider meaning, or balance an idea that could become too extreme.[1] *I Ching* trigrams decorate the cups in the Wheel of

Change's Eight of Cups where they focus our attention on the change of creation.

ibis

Legend says that Thoth, Egyptian god of wisdom, took this bird's form to hover over, and teach occult arts to, the Egyptian people; hence, it is a symbol not only of Thoth, but of the transmission of Hermetic wisdom and of communication in general. Hermes, himself, hid as an ibis when the giant Typhon chased the gods from Olympus, and thus it also became associated with grammarians and communicators.[2] The curved shape of the bird's beak connects it to the crescent moon, while its length symbolizes the ability, and the capacity, to delve into the depths of wisdom,[3] or unconscious material. Because of its supposed ability to stand on one leg for extended periods of time, the ibis has become a symbol of the meditative spirit.[4] As the bird in the RWS Star card, it oversees the transformation of unconscious material into consciousness.

See **heron**.

Icarus

About the only story we have concerning Icarus involves his imprisonment with his father Daedalus by King Minos of Crete, and their subsequent escape. A renowned Athenian craftsman, Daedalus created eagle-feather wings fastened on with wax for their escape. Icarus ignored his father's warning to not soar too near the sun, lest the wax melt. Rebel child that he was, Icarus, rejoicing at his skill with his great sweeping wings, pridefully soared upward. The waxen fastenings melted, the wings came off, and the youth dropped into the sea and drowned.[5] Icarus falls on the Renaissance Tower card.

ill-dignified cards

Ill-dignified cards are antagonistic, adverse, or unfavorable to each other. They weaken the meanings of the cards next to or above them. For suits, Cups (water) and Pentacles (earth) are ill-dignified to Swords (air) and Wands (fire). Fire and water elements are ill-dignified and weaken each other, as do air and earth. The meaning of a Wands (fire) card lying between a Cup (water) and a Pentacle (earth) card would be weakened or unfavorable.

For numerological dignities, even- and odd-numbered cards lying in relationship to each other are ill-dignified. Even-numbered cards are ill-dignified to Wands and Swords; odd-numbered cards are ill-dignified to Cups and Pentacles.

See **dignities; numerological dignities; well-dignified cards**.

individuation

A Jungian concept, it refers to the process of bringing unconscious, divided elements—notably the *anima, animus* and shadow—into consciousness so that a person moves toward inner integration. We seek to become all that we can be, "to render fruitful our [perceived] negative dimensions,"[6] and to become whole within ourselves.

As an ongoing process, individuation may never be fully realized or finished. It often is highlighted as a "midlife crisis," where one realizes that old goals are no longer appropriate or achievable and must be changed or reconciled with the remaining years available.

Individuation is a kind of alchemical rebirthing, continually adding a new dimension to our lives. Ideally we become one with Spirit or the Self—a construct that represents an overseeing composite of all the elements of the psyche—and make our decisions with that awareness. When their messages are taken as "nudging" teachers of wisdom, tarot cards and spreads can serve as one path toward increasing Self-realization.

See **Fool's Journey; opposites, tension of; personality** (Jungian theory); **self**.

Iris (goddess and flower)

Winged, swift, and carrying a caduceus, Iris was the Greek messenger of the gods, the female equivalent of Hermes. She carried a pitcher which contained water for putting perjurers to sleep. The rainbow is considered both the essence of Iris, and the pathway by which she traveled, so when the rainbow or the flower appears in a card (as it does in the Renaissance Tarot's The Stars), it relates to her qualities as a divine messenger, as do the irises on the Morgan-Greer, Spiral, and RWS Temperance cards.

See also **bridges; rainbow.**

Isis (Egyptian goddess)

As the "mother goddess" of Egypt, every living being is said to have a drop of Isis's blood. Believed to hold the secrets of life and death, "ageless wisdom," she is commonly identified with the tarot High Priestess. Mythologically, she is also identified with Athena/Minerva, goddess of wisdom, and Demeter/Ceres, goddess of earthly fruitfulness, who is herself associated with The Empress card.

See **Athena/Minerva; Demeter/Ceres.**

island(s)

The purple islands on the Songs for the Journey Home Luminary card (Hierophant) symbolize aspects of our higher selves we have yet to recognize. Often we only come upon them through an emotional shipwreck, which forces us to look more closely at previously ignored talents and possibilities.[7]

J

✳

Judgement (XX)

Numerologically twenty reduces to two (2 + 0 = 2), which links Judgement to The High Priestess (personal or inner truth), and Justice (social or community truths). The proper combination of those truths, which will be different for each individual, is an important component of self-realization.

Often erroneously thought to depict "the Last Judgement," the true intent of the RWS card asks, "What is that within us which does sound a trumpet and all that is lower in our nature rises in response—almost in a moment, almost in the twinkling of an eye?"[1]

The RWS angel—identified variously as either Gabriel, the angel of completion and of water, or Michael, the leader of the forces of light and the archangel of fire (*see* **wings, red**)—makes the sound that causes the final transformation[2] that awakens the higher self. The card acts as an alarm clock.[3] The angel emits seven sound waves (vibrations) from his horn, stimulating the seven chakras and awakening gray figures, who arise from floating coffins (*see* **coffin**).

In esoteric terms "awakening," and the archetypal concept of birth-rebirth, correspond to initiation, a new way of being in the world, a new way of perceiving oneself and others. We awaken from the sleep of ignorance and rise into a higher state. In all the previous RWS Major Arcana cards showing the waters of the High Priestess (The Chariot, Death, Temperance, The Star), an important transforming event occurs. Now the water flows before the snow-tipped mountains first seen in The Fool.

A huge Anubis looms over a crowd of waiting souls in the World Spirit card, which refers to personal reckoning. It's time to re-evaluate the past or make crucial decisions that allow one to move forward differently.

Hermes dominates the Mythic Tarot card. He represents the "summing up" process that occurs when we come to understand past experiences ("the dead") as parts of a pattern. Our efforts produce a synthesis and the potential for new development.[4]

Certainly the impulse to ascend is magnificently portrayed in the Robin Wood card, where a nude woman, golden in every way, emerges from the fire of the Cauldron of Ceridwen (*see* **cauldron**), the womb of the Great Triple Goddess from which all things are cyclically reborn.[5]

Mythological stories that tell of a folk hero entering a cave (the unconscious) and eventually returning safely—and usually with an important treasure (the now recognized Self or Spirit)—are also expressions of the death-rebirth-transformation process expressed by this card.

Jung wrote that one of our greatest temptations was to be what we seem to be—the *persona*—because we are usually rewarded with paychecks for doing so.[6] Yet "richness in mind consists in mental receptivity, not in the accumulation of possessions."[7]

A male, female, and child (our inner aspects) are the predominate human figures in the foreground of the RWS card. An equal-armed Greek cross—not only a Christian emblem, but also an ancient emblem of Hecate, goddess of the crossroads—is attached to the angel's horn. The way of spiritual ascent, the time of transition, is through the "reconciliation of opposites in a higher unity"[8] and with community (the other figures in the card). Judgement represents the task of recognizing the call to discard deadened aspects of ourselves. The reality of life has changed; the only choice is to follow.

A nude child (Wheel of Change Tarot) emerges from the soil of a flower garden (the womb of Mother Earth), showing the birth of "genuine consciousness" when we awaken to experience free from "outmoded assumptions and judgments."[9] Likewise, "Beyond Judgment" (Songs for the Journey Home) deals with the need to move beyond the limitation, labels, and categorization we attach to experiences. A white bird represents our flight away from all that has held us back, and our new ability to soar. An anchor inside an egg represents our ability to hold on tight in rough times. No more expectations, no more conditioning. Just true being.[10] In "Beyond Illusion," (Osho) an illusionary butterfly flutters before the face of consciousness. We are cautioned to drop our illusory, opinionated mind and look within to our own deepest truths.

Keywords/phrases: re-evaluation; new/altered perceptions, possibly radical in nature; shedding ego illusions; moving beyond past experiences; rising to a higher calling; hearing or attending to a new message or call; the ongoing birthing or renewal process. *See* **Death (XIII)**.

Jungian functions

Swiss analyst C. G. Jung developed a typology of the four ways in which consciousness functions. We perceive reality with our senses (*sensing* function) or with our intuition (*intuitive* function). We evaluate our perceptions via the *thinking* and the *feeling* functions. Theoretically, each of us uses predominantly one of the four functions, assisted by one or two "helping" functions. A fourth "inferior" function is usually poorly developed, frequently because parents or cultures accentuate other functions as more important, and look down on that particular way of behaving.[11] The inferior function(s) is/are fertile grounds for projection.[12]

The most popular or well-known correspondence between Jung's four functions and the Minor Arcana suit is: Swords equal thinking, Wands equal intuitive, Cups equal feeling, and Pentacles equal sensing. Sometimes the functions of Wands and Cups are reversed, making Wands equal feeling and Cups equal intuitive.[13]

See **opposites, tension of; projection.**

Jupiter (planet)

Fifth planet from the Sun, and the largest planet in the solar system, Jupiter rules Pisces and Sagittarius.

Cards attributed to Jupiter partake of the noble and jubilant qualities of the planet. Jupiter is the king of the gods, and the largest planet. Thus it rules the highest levels of understanding, wisdom, sovereignty, faith, and immortality. Jupiter compounds and expands anything it touches—qualities of intellect, passions, drives, even the physical body through weight gain. It is called the "greater benefic," the luckiest planet in the sky. A well-dignified Jupiter card's meanings include: great faith and optimism, *joi de vivre*, potency and fecundity in all things, blessings from the gods, talents, a capacity for rulership, divine protection or guidance, events that show the hand of God. Meanings for an ill-dignified Jupiter card include: excess; egocentricity; overbearing will; exaggeration; bad luck; the inability to manifest a desired vision; infidelity to or betrayal of family, friends, or spouse; obesity; complaisance in unhappy situations; hubris; or denial of divine powers.[14]

See **Pisces; Sagittarius**.

Justice (XI)

When it follows the Wheel of Fortune, Justice deals with the consequences of our actions. She is the more down-to-earth representation of The High Priestess (both cards are a number two; $11 = 1 + 1 = 2$). Like the Priestess, in the RWS deck she sits in front of a veil or curtain between two pillars, all symbols of higher mysteries to be known, even though the veil of Justice opens onto different mysteries than those of The High Priestess.[15] In the early Golden Dawn deck, Justice wore an Egyptian headdress and was identified as Nephthys, the twin sister of Isis.

The RWS Justice wears a crown (she is the ruler or administrator of the law) with a jewel over her third eye and a cape with a squared, jeweled clasp over her heart chakra (*see* **squaring the circle**). Her judgments are backed by higher wisdom or insight, coupled with love and compassion. The strips of cloth extending beneath her cape to below her knees represent etheric currents (kundalini energy), which the interplay of heart and third-eye chakras will "bring under law and order."[16] To emphasize the dual aspects of justice, the Marseilles figure wears a double crown.

Justice represents the active principle of cosmic law.[17] To the ancient Egyptians, that principle was personified in Ma'at, frequently described as the goddess of truth or justice, but more accurately representing "right order."[18] So powerful was she that although her symbol was the feather, seen resting in the scales of the Spiral card, she could stand in for all other Egyptian goddesses,[19] which, in effect, links her to every female in the tarot deck.

The Alchemical Justice (VIII) represents Ma'at and the death aspect of the triple goddess. She balances fire (masculine) and water (feminine) and expresses the alchemical process of disposition. Standing between two pillars, she represents, as she does in many Justice cards, the three pillars of the Tree of Life. She holds her scales (*see* **scales**) in her right hand (the pillar of severity), her upraised sword in her left hand (the pillar of mercy), and her body becomes the central pillar of equilibrium.

Spiral's Justice represents both Ma'at and the Greek/Roman goddess of justice, Themis/Iustitia, who is definitely the Nigel Jackson Justice. Seated above the clouds on a leveled promontory, she is unreachable and unassailable by mere mortals.

Robin Wood's Justice wears a laurel wreath in her fair hair (visual pun) to show that clear thinking will be victorious. Her cape is clasped with a silver (intuition, looking inward) square (perception, looking outward) set with a red jewel at her throat chakra (she speaks the truth). Behind her a lush natural background demonstrates that her justice is alive, vibrant, and "ancient as the hills."[20] She personifies the balance and harmony of the cosmos.

Athena, goddess of justice, represents the faculty of reflective judgement in the Mythic card (*see* **Athena/Minerva**), whereas "Breakthrough" (Osho) reflects the shattering of old patterns.

The World Spirit card is one of the few that portrays Lady Justice blindfolded. She can listen, and give a fair hearing, to the voices within, allowing her to make decisions with integrity.[21] The Haindl card contains no figure. It presents a solid set of scales. Huge, yet fragile, peacock feathers—which could be disrupted with the slightest breeze—dominate. The card is one of balancing duality with clear sight and detachment.

An ominous Lady of the Lake, garbed in a "scale-like" gown (visual pun), rises in the Legend Arthurian Justice card, reminding Arthur that there is a mightier court than his.

When drawn, Justice indicates that it is time to weigh our internal lives and refine them if necessary: the actions we have taken and the consequences, the values we actively live by, and how we "justify" our positions. Do we need to take action to balance past or present behaviors, or to balance the depletion of current energy levels? How are we not honoring ourselves and our needs? In what ways are we giving away too much power?

Keywords/phrases: impartial decision making; a call to balance objective and subjective thinking, feeling, and responding; taking care of legal matters.

For a brief discussion of the alternative positions of Justice as the eighth Major Arcana and Strength as the eleventh, *see* **Strength (VIII)**.

K

Kabbalah (also Qabalah, Cabala)
One part of a greater Hebrew system of knowledge, the Kabbalah is a complex collection of mystical or esoteric ideas first expressed in Judaism around the twelfth century. Its most popular expression is the Tree of Life, which has been illustrated in many ways over time, and widely used in Tarot work.
See **Tree of Life**.

keys (crossed)
See **Hierophant, The (V)**.

kings
Kings and queens represent the male and female principles of maturity. Together they symbolize oneness, wholeness. Kings

represent the outer, conscious expression of the values of their suit; queens represent its inner expression or understanding.[1] Kings may also represent, or reflect, the father within, or our attitudes toward male parental and authority figures. Some decks rename king cards as father, warrior, prince, chief, or sage. In the Thoth deck the king cards are called knights, but carry the characteristics of the kings, as the most "sublime, original, active" part of their element.[2] This is sometimes confusing because like the knights of other decks, they also are depicted on horseback.

Given the knowledge acquired through the experiences of the suit, the king takes action, expressing the responsibility and leadership qualities of his suit. He is the assertive aspect of the element of fire, acting from his nature, his wisdom, or laws, as he chooses. He makes and breaks, or remakes, the rules. Esoterically the king is the adept of outgoing spiritual energy. He is a decision maker, unafraid to take action based on what he has learned and can plow ahead, regardless of others' experiences or feelings, based on what he knows or believes to be historically correct. Past experience is an important guide.

If numerology is used for kings, it usually corresponds to the number fourteen, which represents organization and justice administered according to the law. If reduced (*see* **reduction**), it is related to numerical information regarding fives (1 + 4 = 5). Kings are associated with the sephira of Chokmah on the Tree of Life.

Keywords/phrases: authority; the archetypal masculine; inflexible; outward show of power.

See **court cards; queens;** and the Minor Arcana kings.

knights

If numerology is used for the knights, it usually corresponds to the number twelve, the symbol of cosmic order and salvation. As the number of the months of the year and the signs of the zodiac, it is related to notions of time and life cycles. If broken down, twelve is associated with the numerical information regarding threes (1 + 2 = 3) at a higher or more skilled expression. Knights are associated with the sephira of Tiphareth on the Tree of Life.

Some decks rename the knight as the son, prince (where princess is the page), seeker, and warrior. Most knights ride horses, representing our animal or instinctual nature. Their movement refers to our inner vitality, forcefulness, and ability to change our thinking and propel ourselves forward. Symbolically the "horse-body carries the soul."[3] Knights represent the energy of the quest of their particular suit and the power to perfect and integrate the use of that energy. In the RWS deck, all knights wear armor to protect the physical body while the psyche and soul develop.

The knight leaves. He is separation. He is associated with all those myths of leaving home, with leaving childhood behind, with adventures or battles toward achieving autonomy. He represents a developmental stage similar to early adulthood. Knights have the motivation to explore and test their skills; they are totally focused and committed to completing their goal. The daring knights represent courage, often naïve, and action. However, knights seldom know as much as they think they do. Like Parsifal in his search for the Holy Grail, they, therefore, often fail to ask the right question and must wander for awhile, encountering numerous worldly adventures and opportunities for insight.

Knights test the rules and regulations, not just as a defiance of authority (as the Page might), but as a way to sort out and determine exactly what they believe in and what rules they will keep and maintain for themselves. They are an example of the active process of the element of air. Esoterically, Knights are equated with working disciples and have a greater investment and energy expenditure than pages.

Knights may indicate different rates of timing for a situation, the Knight of Swords being the swiftest. Then Wands, Cups, and that slowpoke, the Knight of Pentacles.[4]

Keywords/phrases: spirit commanding matter; action (sometimes hasty); skill testing; role exploration; courage; impatience; being self-absorbed in reaching a goal.

See **court cards**; and the Minor Arcana knights.

L

＊

lakes/ponds/pools

Lakes symbolize inner reflection or the possibility of such reflection. A pond figures prominently in the RWS Temperance card, suggesting the connection between, or need to balance, upper and lower worlds, the conscious and unconscious. Similar symbolism applies in the RWS Star card, and also suggests the "work" must be deeper or more profound (ripples stir the pond). The pond in the RWS Moon card represents our personal and racial watery origin.

See **rivers/streams.**

lantern

A lantern symbolizes insight, wisdom, and a light in the darkness. Often appearing on The Hermit card, the lantern identifies it as the archetype of the light-bearer, the way-shower for developing spirituality and for opening to unconscious knowledge. The Hermit is one aspect of the Wise Old Man archetype, the power responsible for bringing unconscious knowledge to awareness through dreams and other experiences. The Hermit's lantern symbolizes the light or spirit within; he carries the opening to the light of our soul. The Thoth Hermit's lantern is a gleaming diamond with a sun in the center. It sends rays of enlightened perception in all directions, pervading upper and lower worlds, both of which we must learn to understand for wisdom. The Ancestral Path Hermit's wisdom is cosmic, since his "lantern" is a handful of trailing stars.

lemniscate

A "horizontal halo,"[1] a figure eight on its side, it is the mathematical symbol for infinity or eternity. In the tarot, it stimulates us to consider how divine force expresses, or wants to express, itself through our action. It encourages us to bring ancient, or higher, wisdom, into consciousness. Time to look beyond the mundane and the personal ego for more information and insight, or to connect our task to a higher spiritual level.

Typically seen somewhere on The Magician's card (forming the hat brim on the Marseilles card), it represents The Magician's connection with universal principles, and his infinite spiritual potential. We must partake of universal and eternal truths to transform ourselves.

The lemniscate on the Two of Pentacles of the RWS and Robin Wood decks represents the infinite problems and possibilities of establishing balance and harmony. It often floats above the head of the female figure in the Strength card (Ancestral Path, RWS, Spiral, World Spirit), and connects the two male and female forces on the Tarot of the Spirit's Two of Water. At the base of the World Spirit Two of Cups, a serpent lies coiled in the sign of infinity. The lemniscate merges with the third eye of the mother on the Light and Shadow Tarot's World card, indicating that she represents the infinite galaxy. On the Tarot of the Spirit's Two of Earth ("Cause and Effect") the lemniscate "denotes continuous change, action and reaction."[2]

See **eights**.

Leo (astrological sign)

The fifth sign of the zodiac (July 23–August 22).

Element: Fire
Modality: Cardinal
Polarity: Yang
Ruled by the Sun

Cards attributed to Leo enjoy the vitality and strong will of this fiery sign. Leo is connected with children, love affairs, creativity, and the development of the individual personality. It is a playful, risk-taking sign, prone to gambling, excess pride and a loud roar with no bite. A well-dignified Leo card may be interpreted as: optimism in original ventures, leadership skills, tremendous self-confidence, persistent dedication to triumph in challenges, love of children and small pets, originality and creativity, generosity, a deeply loving and protective nature, a desire for the best life has to offer, and clever risk-taking. Meanings for an ill-dignified or reversed Leo card include: entanglement in personality battles, sexual predator, excessive dominance, tyranny, depression, uncompromising obstinacy, excessive gambling or spending, and obsessions about love affairs to the detriment of other areas of life. Problems with the heart or circulation may also be indicated by neighboring cards.[3]

See **Sun** (planet).

Lévi, Eliphas (1810–1875)

The pen name of Frenchman Alphonse Louis Constant, derived by translating his name into Hebrew (Eliphas Lévi Zahed). A religious student who left the seminary before becoming a priest—but did later become a deacon—Lévi became an advocate and practitioner of magic, which is when he changed his name. Two of his most well-known books on magic are *Transcendental Magic: Its Doctrine & Ritual* and *The History of Magic*, both translated by A. E. Waite.

Like others of his time, Lévi believed that the tarot came from the Egyptians and was the ancient Book of Hermes. He revived and popularized an eighteenth-century idea that the twenty-two trumps of the tarot corresponded to the twenty-two letters of the Hebrew alphabet, and were linked to the twenty-two paths of the Kabbalistic Tree of Life. He was the first to connect the ten sephiroth of the Tree to the ten numbered Minor Arcana cards, and the first to associate the four suits with the four elements, associating wands with air and swords with fire.

See **de Mellet, le Comte; Court de Gébelin, Antoine.**

Libra (astrological sign)
Seventh sign of the zodiac (September 24–October 23).

Element: Air
Modality: Cardinal
Polarity: Yang
Ruled by the planet Venus.

Cards attributed to Libra partake of its focus on relationships, marriage, and balance. Libra is the sign of harmony, reflecting the aesthetic, cultured and artistic side of Venus. While Taurus rules the more earthy and passionate aspects of love, Libra reflects the intellectual and chemical aspects of love and compatibility. This sign also rules law, negotiations, arbitrations, and dialog. Libra aspires to perfection and beauty in all things, the fruits of the labor of Virgo. A well-dignified Libra card's meanings include: social dexterity, artistic or architectural design, compatibility in all forms of relationships, peace-making and diplomacy, musical harmony. An ill-dignified or reversed Libra card may mean: indecisiveness, a compulsion for revenge when thwarted, fanatical idealism, shrewish treatment of a spouse, and a managing temperament. Libra is called "the iron fist in the velvet glove," implying that although natives of the sign approach their goals with gentility and grace, they are capable of bossing people around until they get their way.[3]

See **Venus** (planet).

lightning

It symbolizes an "electrifying" or insightful idea and, sometimes, a wake-up call. Lightning also may symbolize a clash of opposites, the storm in which it appears dissolving (resolving, solving) tension. In many cultures lightning symbolizes the terrifying power of the sky god, the highest god (Zeus/Jupiter) or, as in the Bible, the wrath of God. More benevolently, however, it simply served as a signal of God's presence. Zeus's bolts on the Thoth Fortune card are those sent to blast Typhon when he attempted to obtain supreme authority over the Greek gods. In like fashion, when we become ego-inflated, lightning strikes personally at our ego tower, as it does in many Tower cards.

See **Tower, The (XVI); Zeus/Jupiter.**

lily/lilies/water lilies

The white lily has long been a sign of purity and sometimes light/higher spirit. A royal symbol, it sometimes appears as the heraldic three-sided fleur-de-lis (the triple lily), likewise a symbol of illumination. The figure in the World Spirit Four of Cups is flanked by lilies, reflecting the purity of his original intentions. The RWS Page of Cups' clothing is adorned with three-petaled flowers, variously identified as either tulips or lotuses/water lilies, the Golden Dawn's elemental symbol for water.[4] As such, they float on the water of the RWS Ace of Cups.

See also **roses and lilies motif; tiger lilies.**

lingam-yoni

The lingam-yoni shield (phallic spear attached to a female disc) appears frequently in Tantric iconography. The yoni expresses the idea that the world's existence is a continuous birth; the lingam expresses the notion of continuous fertilization.[5] The symbol appears on the RWS and Spiral Tarot's Chariot cards.

linking themes

This technique involves identifying all the cards from the same deck where the same symbol appears, and examining them as a bridge to deeper understanding of their meaning, relationship to one another, and their relationship in a reading. To add depth to a reading, discuss and compare other cards in the deck not appearing in the spread but containing linking symbols to those that do appear.

lion(s)

The lion is a well-established solar symbol and of alchemical and Christian resurrections. The red lion of alchemy has been changed to white (opposites transformed) in the Thoth "Art" (Temperance) card (*see* **eagle**). "King of the Beasts," the lion symbolizes power, male energy, animal energy, sovereignty, spiritual power, and divine justice. The lion as divine energy has been expressed in mythology (many gods rode on lions), and in many religious beliefs. In Christianity, the Lion of Judah culminates in the person of Christ. In Hinduism the avatar Nara-simha takes a lion's shape, while Buddhism likens the teaching of Buddha to the lion's roar.[6]

Earlier, however, lions were the emblem of Artemis, the Anatolian goddess of the moon. As her cult developed, and before she was adopted by the Greeks, she became known as Cybele (Kybele), Mother of All. She was often portrayed standing in a chariot drawn by lions,[7] as does the charioteer in the Ancestral Path Chariot. He is a spiritual warrior.[8]

Lions appear on the Strength/Fortitude card of many decks (Ancestral Path, New Palladini, Mythic, RWS, Spiral, Robin Wood, Renaissance, Nigel Jackson, Alchemical, Morgan-Greer) and indicate that we have "tamed" the beast—instinctual energy (passion, power) within—or that we acknowledge and are friends with it. The card is associated with the myth of Cyrene, who overpowered a fierce lion on the slopes of Mt. Pelion. In the Thoth "Lust" card, a seven-headed lion simultaneously represents an angel, a saint, a poet, an adulterous woman, a man of valor, a mythological satyr, and the lion serpent (for an explanation of the latter, *see* **Strength (VIII)**).

Lions (usually winged) appear on several Wheel of Fortune (RWS, Spiral, Aquarian) and World cards (RWS, Spiral, Nigel Jackson, Morgan-Greer, Renaissance, World Spirit, Marseilles), where they represent the element of fire, the astrological sign of Leo, the evangelist Mark, and the archangel Michael. On the Shapeshifter card of "Valor" (Seven of Wands), a woman is becoming a winged lion.

A lioness rests at the feet of the Mythic Queen of Wands, demonstrating her strength, mental agility, ingenuity and reservoir of available energy. A charging heraldry, representing the astrological sign of Leo, decorates the New Palladini King of Rods's robe. A lion, for Leo, decorates the border of the Renaissance Knight of Swords, while on the deck's Two of Staves, Heracles defeats the Lion of Nemea, the first of his twelve tasks (*see* **Heracles/Hercules**). In the Alchemical Two of Coins, the alchemical lion (representing fixed nature) swallows the volatile eagle and represents "fixation" on the material plane. The glorious Alchemical King of Coins lion represents the essence of satisfaction and the balance of harmony with nature.[9]

See **Artemis/Diana; sphinx; winged lion**. For the double lion motif, *see* **Chariot, The (VII)**.

lotus blossom(s)

The lotus plant, growing as it does at the bottom of its water source, and sending its flower high above the water, represents the soul or psyche rising from the darkness (unconscious), or from matter, into the clarity of consciousness and enlightenment. The thousand-petaled lotus of Eastern religions symbolizes The One; therefore, it also serves as one of the symbols of the Self.

The stylized lotus topping each of the pillars in the RWS High Priestess card is an Egyptian symbol for the watery origins of the world and human life. The Light and Shadow cosmic Empress rises from lotus-like robes. Lotuses serve as the suit's elemental emblem on all of the Thoth Cups cards except the Seven and the Knight (King). The Morgan-Greer Empress holds a lotus blossom along with grains of wheat in her left hand, suggesting inner and outer cycles. The Thoth Empress holds the lotus of Isis meant to represent feminine creativity and the life force that "blossoms from the female womb."[10] The lotus garland worn by the Thoth Devil identifies him as the son of good.[11] A lotus replaces the head of the Osho Queen of Water, and lines extending from it form a matrix pattern. Together they represent the perfect harmony of the universe when we are receptive to it rather than solely to ego messages. On the Osho King of Water, lotuses of light, carrying healing crystals or patterns, inspire us to recognize and heal our wounds. Lotuses in the pond of the Spiral's Star card represent hope for renewal. The several blooms suggest that we are always given more than one chance when we have failed. Here the lotus also represents the four elements: the earth from which the plant grows, the water that supports its stalks, air into which its perfume escapes, and the fire of the sun which provides its growth energy.[12] The enormous mother on the Light and Shadow's World card sits centered on a huge cosmic lotus blossom.

For the meaning of lotus blossoms on several High Priestess cards, *see* **High Priestess, The (II)**.

See **lily/lilies/water lilies**.

Lovers, The (VI)

The Lovers card represents the feminine/masculine (yin/yang; *anima/animus*) within each of us and speaks of attempts to keep these separate, or to acknowledge and reconcile them in order to become whole (*see* **Self**).

One of the card's early designs showed a young man standing between two women—often Virtue and Vice—who represented different choices and destinies. This is akin to the Tarot de Marseilles scene.

Such a choice may be related to the story of Heracles/Hercules who met Duty and Pleasure at the crossroads, and chose the gifts offered by Duty. In the Mythic Tarot, the Trojan prince Paris is commanded by Zeus to judge a beauty contest between the goddesses Hera (offering worldly authority and rulership), Aphrodite (offering love), and Athena (offering to make him the mightiest warrior of all). Paris chooses love, and his decision sets off the downfall of Troy, which Athena and Hera begin to plot.[13] These myths suggest the card is one of being at the crossroads of choice or of transcendence (integration of opposites).

In other early cards, a marriage occurred beneath the sights of a bow-aiming cherub or angel. This version linked the card to the myth involving Aphrodite/Venus, her son Eros/Cupid, and Psyche, an allegorical story of the search of the soul for love.

The young man's need to make a choice and the "challenge to mature and commit"[14] has been removed from many cards (RWS, World Spirit). The nude RWS male looks to the nude female. She, in turn, looks upward at the archangel Raphael (Regardic calls him Michael), dramatically robed in regal purple (higher truth and healing) with fiery red wings (spiritual passion). In the Spiral card, this is understood to mean that while the male's primary motivation is love, the female realizes their relationship must also encompass the spiritual. We are challenged to connect our spiritual life with our emotional one to achieve new harmony and inner healing.[15]

The Tree of Life behind the RWS male contains twelve triple flames, representative of the signs of the zodiac and the three decanates into which each is divided. The Tree of the Knowledge of Good and Evil with the serpent twining around it, behind the female, links the card with the story of Adam and Eve and to the archetypal myth of a golden age or paradisal time. Psychologists believe the universality and popularity of this archetype refers to the comfort we once experienced in the womb and our "fall" (birth) into mortality and consciousness.

In alchemical symbolism, and sometimes in mythology, winged figures represent the unconscious. So, another way to interpret the RWS card is that the naïve (nude) couple come into their relationship bound by tradition and their respective natures (the trees in the background) and overseen by their unconscious which expresses passion and fervor and swirls in clouds of the unseen or unacknowledged. Before they truly can come together, this couple will have to deal with the "wildness" (the unrecognized fantasies and expectations) within.

The nude Robin Wood lovers walk with their arms around each other, demonstrating commitment and the concept of becoming more whole and open within a relationship.[16] In the Spiral card, the angel holds a pot of gold, representing wholeness and integration.

That there are two women in older cards and only one in the more contemporary versions may reflect the attempt to portray the difficult Jungian concept of the Self, which, while appearing as opposites, is in fact a totality and unity in which the opposites are united. Or it may suggest that either woman of two can be chosen, for to choose one "constellates" (unites it with) the other.[17]

In numerology, six is the only number considered both masculine and feminine, further suggesting this card as one representing the joining of the opposites for healing and the lush garden of inner balance that would follow (New Palladini card). For men, it may represent the sacred marriage where a man and his own feminine nature join together, preferably before he chooses a wife.[18] The same in terms of the masculine nature is true for women.

Writing about The Lovers card from the Golden Dawn, Wang says its true meaning is the "liberating effect of illumination on the individual" and union with the Divine.[19]

All of these stories and ideas deal not only with attempts to balance the internal masculine and feminine, but also how we will be as a male or female dealing with the opposite sex and how we will define, or redefine, our sexual relationships, given the parental grounding of the first set of four cards. The card also speaks to how we determine our relationship with The Divine, i.e., whether spirit has both feminine and masculine aspects, and is perceived as benevolent or wrathful, or some combination thereof.

Keywords/phrases: life cycles of attraction and repulsion; a decision required (often regarding love); opportunities available and a choice to make; union of the opposites under the auspices of the higher self; a call to consider the values, instincts, or implications reflected in our choice.

See *anima*; *animus*; **Hierophant, The (V)**; **Psyche**; **wings, red.**

M

Magician, The (I)

Related to the tradition of "magic healers," and shamans, The Magician is the archetype that teaches about creation, bringing new ideas into being, and self-realization (note that the number one symbolically refers to the self and also to potential, e.g., the alchemical phrase "out of the One comes Two"). He is focused will and intention.

As one of the archetypes of spirit, The Magician is related to the Wise Old Man archetype (*see* **Wise Old Man/Woman**). He also is related to, and appears in additional guises/aspects, as The Emperor (IV), The Hierophant (V), and The Hermit (IX). Another archetypal image of the Wise Old Man is Merlin, The Magician in the Legend Arthurian deck. Garbed in a purple robe, Merlin guards his sacred spring with his wolf (*see* **wolf**). Over his shoulders he wears a cape of feathers, symbolizing his shamanic ability for spiritual metamorphosis. When we begin to seriously work to understand the link between something apparent and something obscure in our lives, our inner Magician is alive.

In many cards, The Magician stands in front of, or near, a table (the altar of life-potential or of life-about-to-become-manifest) containing symbols of the four Minor Arcana suits, suggesting the various paths available for personal fulfillment. They also represent the four symbols or hallows of The Grail search and the four elements. The Magician can take spiritual energy and transform it into physical matter. The Voyager "Law of Talent" card refers to this transformative ability. Items on the Renaissance Tarot Magician's table express the same concept except they are portrayed as the basic forms of matter: square/cube, circle/sphere, triangle/pyramid, and a dodecahedron (twelve-faceted sphere) representing all complex forms.

Sometimes The Magician juggles (Nigel Jackson) and/or is dressed as a jester, linking him to the qualities of The Fool. The implication is that The Magician is about to juggle (rearrange) the elements, or the life qualities of the Minor Arcana cards, because he has such influence over the powers of nature.[1] The Magician does not seek power for his personal gain, but, rather, acts as a vehicle or instrument of transformation. That the magician is in the process of creation is very evident in the Tarot of the Spirit "Magus" card. His moving right hand brings down swirls of colored energy, the force of "universal essence."[2] The Songs for the Journey Home Magician kneels beside the planet and appears to be brushing it. He has global vision and the ability to change the "stuff" of everyday life.[3]

In the Marseilles deck, "Le Bateleur" (the baton wielder) is a working cobbler, wearing a large-brimmed hat shaped like the lemniscate. In some form, this symbol of eternity (see **lemniscate**) is often present in The Magician card, as well as an ouroboros belt (see **ouroboros**). Frequently he stands in a garden, or at least a flowering arbor—one of nature's sacred spaces. The four-armed, youthful figure on the Wheel of Change card stands between the portico pillars of a temple, representing the creation of sacred space by and for humankind. The Ancestral Path's Magician stands inside a Paleolithic cave, the walls covered with prehistoric drawings (horse, stag, spiral) that show the earliest use of magic.[4] He is a priest of the Horned God in the Robin Wood card.

Many decks (Spiral, Renaissance, Mythic, Alchemical) link The Magician with Hermes/Mercury, which connects him with the mythology associated with The Fool. The Alchemical Tarot's Magician is *prima materia*, the base ingredient of all alchemical processes.

In the giddy Light and Shadow card, The Magician's legs and arms extend outward from within a modified six-pointed star, as he juggles a chain of fish (*see* **fish**), representing the interweaving of the food chain and the chain of existence.[5] The naked female on the Osho "Existence" card sits on the lotus leaf of perfection, floating in a sky filled with stars, directing us to develop the inner quality of "home." The Daughters of the Moon "Witch," stirring her bubbling cauldron, represents the natural ability to create our circumstances.

Drawing The Magician awakens us to consider our choices, and the role our own illusions or fantasies play in our situation. A card of spiritual strength and focus, it may, like The Hermit card, suggest a spiritual or inspirational teacher.

Keywords/phrases: using initiative; employing discernment and comprehension; creative energy available; ability to shape or direct one's future; bringing spirit into matter; grounding ideas into reality; willed or willful action; the ability to link the spiritual and the material; eloquent communication, especially of Hermetic or secret wisdom.

See the symbolism of specific colors, flowers, and clothes shown on fool cards. *See also* **DIN; Emperor, The (IV); Fool,**

The (O); Hermes/Mercury; Hermit, The (IX); Hierophant, The (V); lemniscate; ones; trickster; Wise Old Man/Woman.

Major Arcana

Comprising twenty-one "trumps" (an earlier term coming back into popular usage), plus an unnumbered Fool card, this group of tarot cards represents archetypal energies, therefore "higher," more complex energy than the fifty-six Minor Arcana cards. They indicate major forces active at the time they are drawn, and/or a message from one's higher self—something definitely not to ignore. Depending on where they are placed in a spread, they also can be considered a "central theme" striving to be recognized.

See archetypes; Minor Arcana; trumps; twenty-one; and individual Major Arcana cards.

Major Arcana (elemental and astrological associations)

According to the Golden Dawn system, the following are the elemental and astrological attributions of the Major Arcana, based on their associations with the Hebrew alphabet, as compiled by MacGregor Mathers:[6]

    0 The Fool (Air/Uranus)
    1 The Magician (Air/Mercury)
    2 The High Priestess (Water/Moon)
    3 The Empress (Earth/Venus)
    4 The Emperor (Fire/Aries)
    5 The Hierophant (Earth/Taurus)
    6 The Lovers (Air/Gemini)
    7 The Chariot (Water/Cancer)
    8 Strength (Fire/Leo)
    9 The Hermit (Earth/Virgo)
   10 Wheel of Fortune (Fire/Jupiter)
   11 Justice (Air/Libra)

12 The Hanged Man (Water/Neptune)
13 Death (Water/Scorpio)
14 Temperance (Fire/Sagittarius)
15 The Devil (Earth/Capricorn)
16 The Tower (Fire/Mars)
17 The Star (Air/Aquarius)
18 The Moon (Water/Pisces)
19 The Sun (Fire/Sun)
20 Judgement (Fire/Pluto)
21 The World (Earth/Saturn)

See **court cards** (astrological aspects); **zodiacal attributions**. Other systems of astrological attribution are mentioned in Part One, Chapter 2.

male/female
See **masculine/feminine; opposites, tension of**.

mandala
A Sanskrit word, it represents the cosmos in miniature, the whirling motion of the creative universe. Several are prominent on the outer garment of the RWS Fool.

The construction of a mandala is equivalent to a magical re-creation of the world; hence, it represents an *imago mundi*, a world image.[7] To qualify as a mandala, an image must be constructed in such a way that it (1) symbolizes the central axis of the cosmos, (2) depicts the union of opposites, (3) equates cosmic space and time with temporal space and time, (4) illustrates the powers that exist at both cosmic and mundane levels, (5) and has structural components based on multiples of either three or four, or, typically, both.[8] Buddhist mandalas, for instance, often show a circle within a square representing cosmic or eternal harmony (*see* **squaring the circle**). A diamond-shaped mandala, with all its complex symbolism, is held by a goddess on the Light and

Shadow Wheel of Fortune. To get out of a recurring cycle, we can move toward the mandala's still center.

Mandalas suggest a passage between different dimensions whereby humans may be projected into the universe and the universe into them.[9] They represent a unifying and healing passageway that helps us attain a more cosmic realization of life rather than remaining stuck in our own ego aspirations.

In Jungian psychology, the mandala represents the ordering principle of the unconscious, i.e., the Self, one's inner spiritual core. The mandala symbolizes through its center the ultimate oneness of all archetypes. It is the inner psychic equivalent of the *unus mundus*, the one world.[10]

The Wheel of Change Tarot makes ample use of mandalas on many of its cards, particularly the fives of the Minor Arcana, where they have their own complex symbolism, and also symbolize a way out of the crisis of the fives (although the fives in this deck do not necessarily indicate crises). In the problem lies the solution. Mandalas are inherent in the design of many Shining Tribe cards, especially in the images that fall from the sky (gifts from the Great Above) in the "Knower of Birds" card, and in the "Tradition" (Hierophant) card, which reflects many pathways of sacred teaching.

mandorla

The *vesica piscis* (vessel of the fish), the third shape formed at the center of two intersecting or overlapping circles. Almond-shaped (mandorla is Italian for almond), it can be associated with all the symbolism of the almond (virginity, sweetness, watchfulness). It represents perfection (opposites are joined) and often surrounds artistic presentations of virgin queens of heaven.[11] In esoteric tradition it represents a secret, something hidden in a dark place, therefore the treasure hard to find—the Self. In Jungian psychology, the mandorla is an image that reflects the healing of the split between shadow and conscious ego, the perfect symbol of conflict resolution and union.[12] A mandorla is shown in the upper left-hand corner of the Haindl "Alchemy" (Temperance) card. The figure in various World cards often dances in a mandorla, representing the overlap between heaven and earth. The Irish Ardagh Chalice floats in a mandorla on the Wheel of Change's Ace of Cups, representing the *yoni* and the gateway of life.[13] Employing the same symbolism, the single wand and sword in the World Spirit Tarot aces float in a mandorla/yoni, gateway to the powers of their suits.

See **yoni**.

Mars (planet)

The fourth planet from the Sun, Mars is the ruler of Aries and Scorpio.

A card attributed to Mars emphasizes the flow of healthy root aggression energy that is needed to achieve goals, and assert needs and drives. Mars is libido and passion without a brain, so neighboring cards will indicate whether the Mars energy is going to be channeled intelligently, or released as an unrestrained destructive force. A well-dignified Mars card will include interpretations such as: pronounced libido and physical drive, single-minded focus on ambitious goals, athletic prowess, skilled marksmanship, forceful determination, independence, courage, and honor. An ill-dignified or reversed Mars card's meanings include: discord, ruthlessness, violence, destruction, quarrels, abrasive or abusive dialog, action without thought of consequence, bloody injuries, serious wounds and fevers.[14]

See **Aries; Scorpio**. For mythic qualities associated with this planet, *see* **Ares/Mars**.

masculine/feminine

Some card descriptions define aspects of the card as referring to either the "masculine," the "feminine," or some combination of both. Sometimes other words will be used, such as assertive or creative, or receptive or regenerative. These are not meant as value judgments but rather as a common understanding of the polarities of energy, of the oppositional and complementary qualities of nature within and without all of us.

The symbolism of many tarot cards deals with the task of realizing and acknowledging the dual nature of our personalities, and it is often shown as a pair of black and white pillars, trees, animals, or in checkerboard floors and sashes. They call for us to find or acknowledge within ourselves what we have not yet recognized as our own and have allowed members of the opposite sex to "carry," or live out, for us.[15]

See **opposites, tension of**.

mask

The mask has a double meaning. It is used to express an aspect of the illusory personality and conceal the true self (*see* **persona**), sometimes even to oneself. In some instances, however, putting on the mask of a deity or spirit represents a way to come closer to the divine. If we consider each of the Major Arcana cards as the mask of an archetype, then drawing a card and "wearing" the mask of that archetype may give us insight into how it is expressed in our life. The faces of Major Arcana cards in the Sacred Rose Tarot are masks, inasmuch as the figures are deliberately meant to be reflections of archetypal energies.[16]

Mathers, S. L. MacGregor (1854–1918)

Leader and co-founder of the Order of the Golden Dawn, Samuel Liddell Mathers added MacGregor to his name as a gesture of Celtic pride and identification. He wrote much of the Golden Dawn's rituals, and is thought by some to have created the Golden Dawn deck (possibly painted by his wife, Moina MacGregor Mathers[17]) which was used in those rituals, although others believe he simply refined existing decks.

meditation

See **card meditation; moving meditation**.

mercury (alchemical)

Mercury was one of two primal alchemical essences, the other being sulphur (salt was later added as a third reactive element). The female mercurial essence symbolized the fluid principle or force, the changeability of metals, and the personality and power of transmission. The alchemical sigil for mercury appears at the top of the inner wheel of the RWS Wheel of Fortune, beneath the letter "T" on the outer circle.

See **alchemy; salt; sulphur.**

Mercury (planet)

The first planet from the Sun, Mercury rules Gemini and Virgo.

Cards attributed to Mercury emphasize transactions, exchanges, and the transmission of information. This planet represents the intellect, the multilayered conscious mind, logic and rational thought, skills of speech, knowledge, and foresight. Mercury, in its aspect of Thoth or Hermes Trismegistus, gives sacred knowledge to humanity in the Book of Thoth—another name for the tarot. Neighboring cards will determine which aspect of Mercury is being emphasized—the literary, medical, magical, or integrative. Meanings for a well-dignified Mercury card include: pronounced mental and verbal skills, keen logic or intuition, dexterity, skills in commercial negotiations and transactions, extemporaneous wit, inventiveness, and mastery of tools. Meanings for an ill-dignified or reversed Mercury card include: manipulation, lying, deception and illusion, thievery, fickleness, jokester or prankster, amoral or corrupted ethics, gossip, forgery, superficiality or illiteracy.[18]

See **Gemini; Virgo.** For mythic qualities associated with Mercury, *see* **Hermes/Mercury.**

mermaid

See **undines.**

Minor Arcana

The fifty-six cards of the four suits of the tarot deck are considered to be the more mundane cards, representing life experiences in which we will engage in order to understand the archetypal energy of Major Arcana cards. Each suit represents its own life functions, and their broad range of experiences are thought to be more within our control than Major Arcana concepts. In older decks, the Minor Arcana as a group were referred to as "suit cards." Although there is a new debate about this, it was thought that until the production of the RWS deck in 1910, Minor Arcana cards bore no illustrations.[19] They displayed "pips," symbols corresponding to the numerical value of the card. The Golden Dawn deck specified titles, preceded by the word Lord, for each Minor Arcana card, i.e., Lord of Dominion for Two of Wands. The key meaning of the card lay in its title. It is possible that these descriptive titles were used in developing the RWS images.[20]

See **Major Arcana**; individual Minor Arcana suits (**Cups; Pentacles; Swords; Wands**); and cards in each suit.

mirror(s)

As a reflector, the mirror is a symbol of consciousness—ego— and can be linked with the myth of Narcissus. Mirrors also show us a reversed image, perhaps a negative reflection; hence, the mirrors on the Spiral, and Light and Shadow, Devil cards. The mirror on the Ancestral Path Fool card, and presumably on each smaller card, extends The Fool into eternity. The broken mirror on the Renaissance Death card represents the lost vanity of youth and beauty.

See **Narcissus**.

missing suits

In readings involving five or more cards, some readers find it useful to determine if any suits or Major Arcana cards are absent from the reading. No Major Arcana cards may suggest that no major internal or spiritual issues are aroused, or need to be dealt with, in taking care of the situation.

A missing suit may be a signal to take another look at things. It may represent what is missing and what needs to be done to resolve the issue, e.g., no pentacles might suggest to stop dreaming and get to work. The missing suit might hint at the need to respond in a different way to achieve more balance (no cups means to use your heart instead of your head). Then again, it may be that the missing suit is taking care of itself and is not involved in the answer to the question; we don't need to look at whatever area the suit represents.

Usually, other cards will provide clues to understanding the meaning of the missing suit. Any tarotist will advise that there are always exceptions to the rule, times when they do the opposite of what they advocate precisely because of other cards in the reading or the nature of the question. If, in a question involving a love or relationship issue, no Cups are drawn, the "missing Cups mystery" will have to be addressed (other issues may be more important right now?), whereas no Cups in response to a financial question might be quite positive.[21]

Moakley, Gertrude C. (1905–1998)

A library cataloger for the New York Public Library system, Moakley became interested in the Visconti-Sforza cards as a way to test the usefulness of the library as a research tool. Her 1996 book *The Tarot Cards Painted by Bonifacio Bembo for the Visconti-Sforza Family* was the result. In it she created an imaginary parade of tarot figures on floats, based on the paradigm of the triumphal parade in Petrarch's epic poem *I Trionfi*, and on Renaissance triumphal marches and festivals. She offered an alternative explanation for why there was "a Popess" card: that she was a nun, Sister Manfreda from the extended Visconti family (for more on this story *see* **High Priestess, The (II)**).

monkey

Monkeys symbolize agility, frantic activity (hopping from one thing to the next), the chattering of the mind and, in some cultures, a trickster figure. Like most animals, the monkey also represents primitive or unconscious instincts and may represent a way of renewing one's contact with the instinctual. Such a monkey appears as the animal companion of the Light and Shadow Fool, although he is described as the "intellect" trying to warn The Fool of danger, specifically the crocodile's jaws into which he is about to step.

Moon (goddesses)

The moon has long been one of the primary symbols of the Great Goddess or the Great Mother, the triple goddess of antiquity. This trio representing a single goddess enacting the lunar phases was venerated in many cultures. Sometimes she was Aradia, as maiden; Artemis, as mother; and Hecate, as crone. Sometimes Persephone represented the maiden, and Demeter the mother. In Celtic mythology Hecate was replaced by Cerridwen, Celtic moon goddess of inspiration.

As a behavioral model, the Moon represents core ties to family, emotional conditioning in early life, and the infant's bond with the mother. The Moon symbolizes emotional needs and emotional style, inner security and a feeling of unity or the lack of it (despairing emptiness, insecurity, abandonment). Moon patterns emphasize the power of core (unconscious) emotions, the capacity for intimacy and emotional sharing, the influence of phases and life cycles. The Moon signifies the quality of emotional flow between individuals, whether familial, platonic, or romantic.[22]

See **Cancer; Moon** (planet); **Moon, The (XVIII)**.

Moon (planet)

Earth's sole satellite, it is illuminated by the Sun and rules Cancer.

A card attributed to the Moon emphasizes flow, cycles, liquids, the unconscious mind, dreams, and emotions. Moon rules the hidden, inner self and secrets; the night; and the lunar influence on the tides and plant growth. Neighboring cards show if the Moon's vibrations are harmonious and flowing (waxing); or are deteriorating and losing influence (waning). The Moon is connected with the Triple Goddess of antiquity—the maiden (new crescent), mother (full), and crone (waning and dark phase) aspects of the feminine. The meanings of a well-dignified Moon card include: cherished memories of the past, mothering, the eternal feminine, flowing emotions, precognitive or clairvoyant visions, dreams, emotional stability, and public recognition. The meanings for an ill-dignified or reversed Moon card include: depression, moodiness, female problems and diseases, resistance to change and evolution, dark and devouring emotions, evil magic, jealousy, traumatic memories of the past or negative conditioning that operates on a unconscious level.[23]

See **Cancer**. For goddesses associated with the moon, *see* **Moon, The (XVIII)**; **Moon** (goddesses).

Moon, The (XVIII)

Since the Moon's number (18) can be reduced to nine, and then again to three, much is made of this as a representation of the Triple Goddess. Associated with the three distinct phases of the moon, the card links to the three aspects of the Mother Goddess. On the Spiral card, Hebe represents the new moon and virgin; Hera, the mother (full moon); and Hecate, the crone (dark moon). Hera holds an embryo contained in an egg symbolizing creative potential and a gift from the unconscious.[24] In the Mythic Tarot, Hecate is shown as a three-headed goddess with the three-headed hound Cerberus, guardian of hell's gates, and her animal form. Likely this refers to the moon goddess sometimes being called Hecate-the-Three-Headed, a combined form of Artemis, Selene, and Hecate.

Great Goddess symbolism links The Moon card to The Empress and The High Priestess, who, in the RWS card, wears a moon crown and has a crescent moon at her feet. Being related to a nine links the card with The Hermit and with all nines of the Minor Arcana. "Nine" tasks often represent journeys of the mind and the discovery of meaning. Although The Moon card represents the "life of the imagination apart from life of the spirit,"[25] we are cautioned that the imaginative visionary may see things in a false light, thereby failing to perceive their real essence.[26] Whether the card reflects or hinders inner illumination (and fosters illusion) can depend on where it lies in a spread.

The Moon card is one of emergence, presenting (in the RWS and neo-RWS cards) a treacherous, twisting, yet rising path between our animalistic (wolf) and our more civilized (dog) natures, between the realm of magic and the rational world,[27] between inspiration and understanding—another example of the tension of opposites. The wolf was also one of the creatures of Artemis, the maiden aspect of the Great Mother. A shadow aspect of this is the werewolf, which appears when the moon is full (instincts out of control, or the dark side of our instincts), and can only be destroyed by a weapon made of silver, the moon's traditional metal.[28]

We dodge this way and that, pulled in one direction, then the other, acknowledging conscious and unconscious material, until we find a balance and an appreciation for both in our lives. It is a journey geared toward learning to survive and to comfort ourselves in the process. Jungians link The Moon card to the archetypal "night-sea-journey," or "dark night of the soul," wherein the hero, like Jonah, must overcome the monster or whale. The battle symbolizes our victory over the regressive pull of the unconscious. The card is also an expression of unavoidable cycles, in which what's emerging is sometimes seen and sometimes not— yet we are called upon to honor and accept those sometimes strange ideas and to have the cyclic patience to wait for understanding, if necessary.

On the RWS card a crustacean (our most primitive aspect)

rises from a pool that may be the same as that shown in the Temperance and Star cards, the "great deep of cosmic mind-stuff."[29] We are not totally helpless in the journey since our shell and pincers (ego defenses) will protect us somewhat. Yet, there is always the possibility that the regressive pull of the water will "win," and we will retreat into our past.

In the Robin Wood card, unseen things move in the pool, which is bordered by large rocks, symbolizing society's attempt to keep unconscious material walled in. The struggle between wildness and domestication, between the hand of man and that of nature, is portrayed in the wild, uncut—but once tamed—grass, the dog, the wolf, and the monoliths put there by a long-gone civilization.[30]

The large unicorn (see **unicorn(s)**) on the Haindl card links dream and myth with kundalini energy (see **chakra(s)**). The white-haired Grandmother Spider weaving beside a moonlit stream or waterway (Ancestral Path) suggests that life cycles "possess" their own knowledge, and that their work in our lives brings us higher or universal wisdom as we are ready to receive it. The repetitive design in the rug or blanket hints that the "patterns" of the past may repeat themselves and cause us trouble until we learn from them.[31] (see **weaver/weaving**).

The huge, emerging crustacean on the Nigel Jackson card needs to travel along a relatively small stream to enter a larger ocean. It may address the idea of the movement of the ego (which thinks itself quite large and important) toward the greater collective unconscious. Identical dogs bordering the stream cast shadows; the crustacean does not, hinting at the shadow aspects we need to recognize as we discover the hidden truths of our nature (the narrow, possibly constricting stream).

The Tarot of the Spirit card focuses on the idea that by experiencing our shadow "monsters," we learn to realize that each ordeal through which we move is a ritual of passage and that wherever we plant our feet, that becomes holy ground.[32]

On the Shining Tribe card, the sickle moon is represented as a bow, associated with the Greek archer Artemis/Diana, another famous deity frequently associated with the moon. She appears in the upper right-hand corner of the Renaissance card. Two young maidens create music to remind us that when Artemis/Diana wearied of the chase, her respite was music and dancing. On the Alchemical card one of Diana's black hunting hounds (the passive principle) reclines. The white one (active principle) stands. The card represents the white stone that marks the end of the albedo, or whitening, phase.[33] For the stone to become the philosopher's stone, the moon must join with the sun; hence, the entire card in itself is one aspect of the archetypal tension of opposites.

Two dark towers in the Thoth card form a gateway (the threshold, the Way), guarded by two jackal-headed figures (Anubis, Egyptian god of the dead). Even though a scarab (Khepri, the Egyptian god of transformations) rolls the rising sun toward the two gates, Crowley describes his scene as sinister. Other interpreters of the card do not.

The two towers in the RWS card were first seen across the river in the RWS Death card (*see* **twin motif**). To cross the river and emerge at the towers, the mystic initiate "has been transformed into an aquatic creature" and submerged into the unconscious.[34]

On the Osho "Past Lives" card, the hands of existence form the opening womb of the cosmic mother, which contains many faces from other times. Yet, we are advised to not work so hard to identify karmic issues, rather to identify the roots of the patterns of our present lives so that we may emerge from an endless cycle or trap of unconscious behavior.[35]

Keywords/phrases: cycles of inner development; facing and dealing with ambivalent forces to achieve clarity; balancing the wild (unconscious) and the tame (conscious) aspects of personality; creative intuition; identifying and learning to portray one's authentic self; examining emerging ideas and information, especially as they appear in imagination and dreams, to achieve inner integration.

See **Artemis/Diana; dog; Moon** (goddesses); **Moon** (planet); **opposites, tension of; roadway/path** (twisting); **Wheel of Fortune (X); wolf.**

mountain(s)

Mountains appear on many tarot cards and depending on other items or figures in the card, they may represent the height of awareness, isolation, peak experiences, spiritual retreat or ascension, wisdom or higher truths and/or the willingness to search for them. Mountain symbolism changes depending on color, location in a scene, or how a figure moves toward, away from, or stands on them (as does the RWS Hermit where they represent the far-seeing wisdom the Hermit alone possesses). The snow-capped (spirit-capped) mountains in the background of the RWS Fool card represent both The Fool's pilgrimage and the goal of personal pilgrimages and mystical journeys, i.e. psychological ascension—finding the Self. They suggest that The Fool's need for this journey has always been in his psychic background. The stark, harshly colored mountains in the background of the RWS Emperor card suggest he may have lost some of the lushness of mental clarity, now expressed as rigid thinking. Simultaneously, they can represent how long and hard was the struggle to reach his present position.

Their upward-intruding shape often give mountains a phallic meaning, as in the purple mountain between the two figures in the RWS Lovers card. It may symbolize their union and sexual strength and passion, while also representing the road they have to travel together to attain wisdom.

The mountains on the Robin Wood Temperance card are almost obscured by clouds, representing the uncertainty encountered through this archetypal experience or process.[36]

"Mountains of enlightenment" and majesty appear in the

background of the Robin Wood Empress card, symbolizing her personal majesty and the depth of her knowledge.[37] Mountain symbolism can be very complex, for as one artist-author observed, the essence of a mountain is in the colors in its shadows.[38]

See **hills.**

mouse

In some folklore traditions the mouse has been thought of as the soul. Because they prefer dark places and can spread pestilence, mice also are associated with the demonic, whereas their haste and perseverance make them good symbols for work and endeavor. A mouse in a luminous circle gazes at the figure in the World Spirit's Four of Cups, as if to wonder when he is going to "get it together" and get busy again. Perhaps he represents the person's patient soul, standing by until attended to. The mouse appearing on the Wheel of Change's Seven of Disks represents Apollo, who had oracular shrines of mouse priestesses.[39] Mice, representing stealth, caution, and cunning, scamper behind the initiate on the Shapeshifter "Journey" (22) card.[40]

moving meditation

This is an active meditation process created by Mary K. Greer to add depth to one's personal understanding of a card. After grounding and centering yourself, settle into a position suggested by the main figure in the card. Then "move through" the figure's position, considering the kinds of gestures, postures, walking movements, and energy it would express. Add songs, or other noises if desired.[41]

mushroom(s)

In older traditions mushrooms are associated with good fortune, longevity, and immortality. In modern western symbology, they often represent rapid growth and also destruction (the mushroom cloud).[42] Actually the fruiting body of the mycelium of a fungus that grows underground, mushrooms may symbolize hidden nourishment coming forth, e.g., messages from the unconscious rising to consciousness. Tiny mushrooms grow around the rocks in the Robin Wood Moon card. They represent restlessness, wildness, and change—"going fey."[43] Two people dance within a mushroom fairy ring (mushrooms growing in a circle)[44] on the World Spirit's Two of Cups, implying the joy of nature's magic.

music

Music is implied in many tarot cards where dancing occurs (Robin Wood Four of Wands) or bells appear (Haindl Fool). In some Judgement cards, an angel plays music or, at least, his trumpet emits sounds. The poet/bard Taliesin—The Hierophant in the Legend Arthurian deck—introduces three children to his harp, because music is a passage to the Otherworld.[45]

Paul Foster Case associated a musical tone for each of the Major Arcana, with the exception of The Sun and The Hermit cards.[46] In some cases it was derived from the musical note associated with the astrological planet or sign assigned to the card, and in others from the predominant colors of the card and the planet with which they are associated. His designations are:

The Fool, The Magician, and Strength: E
The High Priestess, The Hanged Man, and Temperance: G♯/A♭
The Empress: F♯/G♭
The Emperor, The Tower, and Judgement: C
The Hierophant: C♯/D♭
The Lovers: D
The Chariot: D♯/E♭
Wheel of Fortune and The Star: A♯/B♭
Justice: F♯/G♭
The Hanged Man: G♯/A♭
Death: G
The Devil and The World: A
The Moon: B

Mary K. Greer assigns D to The Sun and F to The Hermit cards.[47]

See **Quintessence**.

music (inner)

There is music (sounds made by instruments and voices) and then there is *music*, audible only to the inner ear and tuned to the fundamental and psychological "overtones of the soul."[48] It refers to understanding the elements of the soul, its consonance and dissonance, and its tempering and tuning, as creating an archetypal harmony. In this concept, the gods of mythology become the scale or scale-tones out of which experience is composed. The archetypal concepts and mythologies associated with the tarot cards express these soul tones.

mystery schools

Mystery schools have been around for centuries and refer to organizations where students/initiates receive mystic, metaphysical, or esoteric "teachings" available only to them and believed to be not appropriately understood until one has undergone lengthy and progressive training. The teachings usually consist of specialized knowledge regarding universal and natural laws and principles— sometimes referred to as "Ageless Wisdom"—that guide members into developing "higher" knowledge of their own individual personalities and their relationship to the greater universal community and the cosmos. The most famous school related to the tarot was the Hermetic Order of the Golden Dawn. Several of its students (Waite, Crowley, Regardie) created, or helped create, decks considered to include selected aspects of the Order's hidden knowledge or secret teachings. Although thought of as a mystery school by others, its members actually considered themselves members of a magical order. The first mystery school to come out of the Golden Dawn was Paul Foster Case's Builders of the Adytum (*see* **Case, Paul Foster**).

While the original Golden Dawn disbanded a number of years ago, a more quiet version of it does still exist, and dozens of offshoots, as well as schools of "magic and mystery" that include tarot in some way, exist in the United States, Europe, Australia, South Africa, and New Zealand. Many tarotists consider the tarot deck itself as a mystery school in the sense that it may be a "coded" system for preserving and presenting Ageless Wisdom.

See **alchemy; Case, Paul Foster; Hermetic Order of the Golden Dawn; Regardie, Francis Israel; Waite, Arthur Edward.**

N

❋

naked/nude

Portraying a person without clothing may symbolize or express the inner divine or Self; a state of being free and unfettered from socializing influences; open to opportunity; connection with higher nature; an initiatory state. In part, the symbolism relates to the age of the figure(s) shown in card illustrations, and to their relationship (if more than one figure).

In the RWS nude figures appear on The Lovers, The Devil (where nakedness appears to relate to the Christian story of the fall of Adam and Eve from primeval innocence into shame), The Star, The Sun, Judgement, and The World cards. The Robin Wood nude "Sun boy" represents the innocent and pure spirit, unconfined joy and freedom untroubled by modesty or societal conventions.

See **Sun, The (XIX)**.

Narcissus

Narcissus, the beautiful son of the blue Nymph Leiriope and the river-god Cephisus, eventually became the embodiment of self-love and conceit. Originally he was quite unaware of his beauty (identity) because Leiriope never permitted him to see his reflection. When finally he did see his reflection in a river, he became enraptured with it. Unable to leave his unattainable "love," and pining away for it, Narcissus plunged his dagger into his breast. The narcissus flower, with its red corolla, sprung from where the earth soaked up his blood,[1] and became the flower sacred to Hades/Pluto. They grow in the grass beside the young Narcissus, whose story is the subject of the Mythic Tarot's Page of Cups.

Neptune (planet)

The eighth planet from the Sun, Neptune co-rules Pisces along with Jupiter.

Neptune, named for the god of the oceans, is the planet of mystery, of unknown ocean depths, of spiritual heights and unconscious depths. In all, Neptune is a planet of contradictions and slippery intangible qualities. Unlike Saturn, Neptune knows no boundaries or limits as it seeks contact with the divine. This planet is also connected with the international flow of wealth and long-term economic cycles. A well-dignified Neptune card's meanings include: artistic skills, romantic or unconditional love, theatrical abilities, divine inspiration and visions, prophetic dreams, love of the sea, enchantment, and spiritual blessings. Occasionally, it may also indicate vast riches, or wealth derived from public adulation. An ill-dignified or reversed Neptune card may mean: confusion, swamped by excessive empathy or compassion, deceit, foolishness, forgetfulness, unconsciousness, being conned or quacked, excessive use of drugs or alcohol to escape reality, hard-to-diagnose illnesses, lost purpose, feeling invisible to others,

ineffectual efforts in the arts, possible suicidal tendencies if indicated by neighboring cards.[2]

See **Jupiter** (planet); **Pisces**.

nimbus

A circular area of rays, radiance, or golden light around a
person's head. Also called an aureole or halo, it is a symbol of
divinity, of unusual holiness, of possessing higher powers and,
especially in the RWS Hanged Man, of illumination.

nines

Once again we have the end of a cycle (7-8-9), and the end
of the third cycle of threes (1-2-3, 4-5-6). Tarot nines reflect the
collecting of energy for the final steps we need to take to bring
the 1-10 cycle to a close. Alternatively, they can represent a cyclic
end in itself, with the tens beginning the transitional work toward the experiences of the court cards.

Either way, nines symbolize a time of reflection, of gathering
and organizing information, of ruminating, of compiling inner
and outer resources in order to finish what was begun and/or to
prepare for the next experience. There is calmness—and maybe
some regret—and sometimes excitement in the process, or possible anxiety in the anticipation of what comes next.

Depending on the cards around them, nines can reflect either a
time of restoration and appreciation of the gifts one has received or
developed from previous efforts, or one of desperation. They coun-
sel patience to prepare for integration (of suit components) and imply that isolation or solitariness may be necessary. Nines sometimes
symbolize stability through transformation and are associated with
the foundation sephira, Yesod, on the Tree of Life.

See nines of each suit.

numbers

Jung believed that numbers were the most primitive expression of spirit, the dynamic (moving and creating) aspect of the unconscious. For the Pythagoreans, natural numbers were expressions of cosmic divine principles that constituted the basic structure and principle of the universe, of all existence.[3] As an ordering archetype, numbers are not only abstract concepts but also have "character" or "personality" (a fact even conceded by some mathematicians),[4] signifying "different rhythmic configurations" of one continuum.[5]

Long-standing controversy exists as to the numerical sequence of the tarot cards and of the numbers assigned to specific cards, notably those of Strength and Justice. Reproductions of cards from some of the earliest decks show no numbers at all on the cards.

See specific numbers for their archetypal meanings and associations.

numerological dignities

In using numerological dignities, numbers rather than suit elements control the influence of each card to its neighbor. The most common form of numerical dignity[6] is to consider that all even numbers are well-dignified to themselves (2-4-6-8) and to the feminine suits (Cups and Pentacles). Ten can either be not reduced and considered an even number or reduced ($1 + 0 = 1$) and considered an odd number. All odd-numbered cards are well-dignified to all other odd numbers (1-3-5-7-9) and the masculine suits (Wands and Swords). Court cards are reduced to their numerological value. Pages $= 11 = 1 + 1 = 2$, and Queens $= 13 = 1 + 3 = 4$, both even numbers. Knights $= 12 = 1 + 2 = 3$ and Kings $= 14 = 1 + 4 = 5$, odd numbers. Even- and odd-numbered cards lying in relationship to each other are ill-dignified.

See **dignities; ill-dignified cards; elemental/suit dignities; well-dignified cards.**

O

✳

ocean/sea

The ocean, as a body of water, symbolizes the unconscious, but
being larger than lakes and streams (which feed into them),
oceans and seas also simultaneously symbolize a collection place,
e.g., the collective unconscious, and the "primordial, undifferen-
tiated state"[1] from which we all arose. They represent a source
of unending creation and vitality. More specifically, they can symbolize the personal as well as the archetypal mother.

Oceans complete the landscape in many Renaissance Tarot
cards. They are present in all the Aces of the New Palladini
deck, except the Ace of Swords, and represent the boundlessness
and vastness of the new energy now available. In the RWS and
New Palladini Two of Wands, a man is separated from his "sea
of life" adventures by the wall of his home. In both decks' Three

of Wands, he is, likewise, still contemplating his journey, although he can see by the ships that others are already making theirs. The King of Cups in several decks (RWS, New Palladini) sits on his throne in the midst of an ocean. It may represent mastery of his emotions or remind us how easily we can be overcome by them.

See **rivers/streams**; and specific cards in which the ocean or the sea appear.

ones

As the only natural integer that does not follow another, one represents the mystic center, the origin, the active principle of creation, the beginning of form. Often considered a synonym for wholeness—"oneness"—it symbolizes totality and unification. More mundanely, its phallic shape also renders one a symbol of the masculine principle, i.e., power and directed consciousness.[2] Ones, or aces, in the tarot typically represent the availability of a new creative impulse or energy. Major Arcana cards that carry the number "one," or that can be reduced to one, are said to "oversee," or in other ways influence, the aces and the tens ($10 = 1 + 0 = 1$) of the Minor Arcana suits. These include The Magician (I), The Wheel of Fortune ($X = 10 = 1 + 0 = 1$), and The Sun ($XIX = 19 = 9 + 1 = 10 = 1 + 0 = 1$)

See **aces, tens.**

opposites, tension of

Holding the tension of the opposites refers to recognizing the oppositional and complementary energies or qualities within and learning to hold them in balance. Jungian psychology postulates four functions of consciousness (four ways we interact with and understand the world): sensing, intuiting, thinking, and feeling, each of which is associated with one of the Minor Arcana. Theoretically, one of these four is more conscious than the others, and a second, known as the "inferior" function, is repressed.

Most of us expend a great deal of energy resisting the recognition and use of our hidden function. Such recognition and acceptance becomes part of the great attempt to reconcile opposites. Many cards in the tarot deck refer to reconciling opposites, to becoming aware of what's operating within and choosing how we will express it rather than being dominated by it.

Although the ordering of the universe into a dual structure may be archetypal, by deifying the principle of evil into Ahriman, king of the underworld, Persia became the first culture to codify dualism.[3]

An equal-armed cross is one symbol of the tension of opposites or their reconciliation (balance) and, as such, is reflected in the cross on the breast of the RWS High Priestess, and the flag on the RWS Judgement card. Some believe that The Hierophant, in occupying the central position between two columns and listening to acolytes of two different natures (as indicated by their clothing), is called upon to become the middle way between linked opposites (right and left, above and below).[4] On the Wheel of Change Eight of Cups every symbol on the card refers to the interaction of the two complementary forces, or polarities, which together create the richest of all possible worlds.

See **Jungian functions; masculine/feminine; polarities; yin/ yang**.

orange

This color carries much of the same passionate and ardent meaning of red, yet is considered to hold less aggression. Related to the symbolism of flames and fire, it is linked with solar energy and the sun. It is a color of determination, confidence, creativity, spirituality, ambition and authority, yet also of impulsive action. It can represent changing process, as in turning away from the physical toward the emotional.

See **colors**.

orb

See **globe; royal orb**.

Orpheus

The most famous poet and musician ever, Orpheus was the son of the Thracian King Oeagrus and the Muse Calliope. With his lyre he enchanted wild beasts, and caused trees and rocks to move as they followed his music. His wife Eurydice, fleeing the advances of Aristaeus, was bitten by a serpent and died. Orpheus descended to the underworld, soothed the heart of Hades with his music, and won the right to leave with Eurydice as long as he didn't look behind him until she was safely back. When he reached the sunlight, he turned to see if Eurydice was still with him, and lost her forever. Subsequently Orpheus spent his time teaching sacred mysteries to the men of Thrace until he was murdered by maenads of Dionysus. Orpheus, as an archetype of the wounded healer, is embodied in the Mythic Tarot King of Cups.[5] Orpheus and Eurydice are portrayed in the Spiral Tarot's Lovers card.

Ouranos/Uranus (Greek/Roman god)

Mythic qualities of the Roman Uranus draw on the ancient stories of the Greek progenitor god Ouranos, the personification of the Great Sky God, who, with his wife Gaia (personification of Earth), sired the Titans, the Cyclops, and many of the elemental spirits. Eventually Ouranos was overthrown and killed by his son Cronos/Saturn.

As a behavioral model, associated with tarot cards having the zodiacal attribute of Aquarius, Uranian traits encompass the eccentric, the misfit, the revolutionary personality. A completely amoral god, Uranus was willing to destroy old forms in order to seed new forms. The Uranian personality could be considered a "geek," or coldly intellectual inventor. The sheer intellectual brilliance of this god-type can become detached from material reality, leading to fanatical visions, or ideas far ahead of society's ability to absorb and enact them.[6]

See **Aquarius**.

ouroboros

An ancient symbol of a serpent or a lizard bent in a circle to bite its own tail (the "tail eater"), it is another image of the resolution of opposites. It represents alchemical work as a circular, self-contained process of distillation and condensation. Sometimes the alchemical figure was presented as a winged snake or dragon (universal spirit) above a lower snake (matter), each swallowing the other's tail. The meeting of opposites produces a "flow," which the alchemists called the "meaningful flux of life,"[7] the continuity and constancy of the changing cosmos. The mercurial serpent devouring itself in fire refers to the destructive emotions or instincts burning themselves out until their essential unconscious fantasy content becomes conscious.[8] It embodies the concept of regeneration and, therefore, of cycles and of immortal time, the entirety of time and space.

The clothing of the figures on the RWS Wands court cards (except for the queen), all bear the ouroboros, showing their dedication to higher service and self development. The Page and Knight are, perhaps, alchemists in training. One wraps around the bodies of the figures on the Light and Shadow Two of Pentacles, showing how they are becoming open to each other's souls and becoming one (the alchemical marriage). The Spiral's Queen of Wands holds one in a ball of light in her hands, symbolizing the continuity of life.[9] In the Alchemical, Tarot of the Spirit, and Mythic Tarot World cards, the figure dances within a wreath or frame formed by the ouroboros. The Great Work is finished; wholeness is achieved for all time.

See **salamander**.

owl(s)

The symbol, or familiar, of the goddess Athena/Minerva, owls represent wisdom; the clear perspective that empowers (especially that of the night or underworld); death/renewal; and initiation.

They appear on the Mythic Tarot Justice card and in the border of the Renaissance Justice. In the Shapeshifter deck, an owl-person dominates the center of the Shapeshifter "Circle" card (Wheel of Fortune), representing the seeker with all-seeing eyes. A white owl, representing goddess wisdom, flies on the "Nature" (11) card, and represents animal powers on which the initiate can call in the "Journey" (22) card. The Welsh Goddess of Air: Arianrhod (King of Wands) walks as an owl-woman. A night predator, she can see into the darkness of the soul. Here the owl symbolizes death and renewal, moon magic, and initiations.[10] Similarly, an owl sits in a tree watching the Daughters of the Moon Tarot's "Witch" (Magician). An owl representing the soul appears on the Shining Tribe Ace of Birds, while owl eyes decorate the deck's Six of Trees, a forest of souls.

P

✳

pages

The first court card of each suit, the page may also be called a princess, maiden, daughter, or seer (World Spirit). Generally, the page is like an adolescent, characterized by energy and ambivalence. Pages are "the least developed [of the court cards] but the most open and willing to take risks."[1] They tell us we are getting ready for independence but still have a lot to learn.

Pages represent higher aims. Esoterically, the page is the beginning adept and enthusiastic apprentice in the task of moving toward higher learning and understanding and, as such, can be considered more a "follower" than other court cards. Yet pages, like knights, are also reflections of the archetypal experience of "crossing the threshold," leaving behind the known and entering the realm of the unknown. In the Shining Tribe deck, they are

"Place" cards, and depict entering a state where we are learning to know what the suit truly can give us.[2]

The RWS pages wear no armor. Their protection is their innocence and naïveté. This is the first time they dare to take a stand. They are entering a new stage of life or study, with a certain amount of risk involved, and although pages believe they have calculated those risks, they are yet unaware of the difficulties and confrontations that lie ahead. In that sense they are also quite courageous, although if you suggest that, they will tell you simply that this is the pathway they have to take, because the "old ways" are no longer appropriate.

Most people don't employ numerology for the court cards, but those who do usually consider the page an eleven. Pages also can incorporate the symbolism of the number's reduction into two (1 + 1 = 2) and be related to all the twos in the tarot deck. Or one can simply consider the symbolism of the number eleven itself. Either way, note that numerically the page doesn't start at the beginning. As an eleven, he is already at the twos. All the Minor Arcana experiences have prepared him to make that leap and to not have to start at the beginning again.

In divination, pages often represent children, or a beginning event or action of the basic elemental energy of their respective suits. Pages are linked with the element of earth and are associated with the sephira of Malkuth on the Tree of Life.

Keywords/phrases: message bearer; a new stage of initiation; new cycle; communication; limited responsibility; fresh attitude; a hotheaded or impulsive response.

See **court cards; elevens;** and the Minor Arcana pages.

palm tree(s)
See **tree, palm.**

Pan
The best known of the Greek satyrs (a composite creature, half man, half beast), Pan, with his cloven hooves and goatlike

horns (linking him with Capricorn), was a personification of nature. His music, played on a reed pipe, expressed his passion for the chaste nymph Syrinx, a follower of Diana. Rather than accede to his desires, Syrinx had herself transformed into a reed. Not sure which one she was, Pan gathered several together and produced the syrinx or "panpipe." The nymph Pitys similarly escaped his lusty advances by becoming a fir tree.

Pan is, above all else, a god of joy, revelry, fertility, and the license to engage in these and similar behaviors. Perhaps that is why Christian legend made Pan the only god who has died, his death having occurred at the moment Jesus was born.[3] All the oracles became silent thereafter. Such a satyr figure, often associated with Pan, is prominent on many Devil cards.

panther

The panther was an attribute of Dionysus. A cat, representing the panther, walks with the Nigel Jackson Fool. A panther itself crouches in the border of the Renaissance Fool card, symbolizing both brutality and beauty, ferocity and playfulness.[4]

Papus (1865–1916)

The pen name (which means physician) of the Spanish-born French physician Dr. Gérard Anaclet Vincent Encausse. A prolific writer on esoteric topics, he became one of the leading French occultists of the nineteenth century. His most famous book, commonly known by its translated title, *The Tarot of the Bohemians*, was in the original titled *The Tarot of the Gypsies: The Most Ancient Book in the World*. One of the most influential tarot books to come out of France, it was illustrated by cards designed by Oswald Wirth. The editor of the second edition was A. E. Waite, who also wrote its preface. Like many others of the time, Papus believed tarot cards originated in Egypt, where they represented initiation tests. It's likely that some of his ideas were influential in both Waite's and Crowley's deck designs.[5]

peacock

An ambivalent symbol, it can represent vanity (probably because of the bird's pompous courting behavior), yet it is also associated with perception, vision, and insight. Its feathers are said to ward off evil. Sacred to Hera, the tail feathers represented the goddess's all-seeing eye and her vigilance to watch for Zeus's infidelities. Her peacock appears on the Renaissance Empress card. Legend says the bird acquired these eyes when hundred-eyed Argus, a monstrous but beloved son of Hera, was defeated by Hermes. Juno then spread his eyes throughout her peacock's tail so that their "light" might not be closed.

In Christian and other traditions, the peacock is often considered a solar symbol because of the way its tail feathers spread to form a wheel.[6] For this same reason, and because of its many colors, esoteric tradition considers the peacock a symbol of wholeness. In some cultures, it represents the soul and immortality (reincarnation and karma in India). In medieval alchemy, the peacock represented the "phase of bright colors," the synthesis of the elements. The peacock on the Thoth Knight (King) of Cups symbolizes the "fluorescence" or brilliance of water in its most active form.[7]

In Jungian psychology, the peacock represents the collective unconscious. Because they renew their plumage each year, peacocks sometimes symbolize resurrection, renewal, and cyclic processes, as well as pride, ostentation, and splendor. Peacock feathers figure prominently in the Haindl Justice card. Their symmetrical precariousness represents the fragile "orderliness" of reality, and the eyes in the feathers represent "seeing" our emotions.[8] A peacock head dominates the Haindl Death card, where it symbolizes looking at the truth regarding death. The peacock feathers behind the head of the Spiral Tarot's Justice card symbolize the starry night sky and the watchfulness of the Egyptian goddess Ma'at, against whose "plumes of justice,"[9] the hearts of men were weighed at death (see **Justice**).

pearl(s)

In many decks (RWS, Morgan-Greer), the Empress wears a pearl necklace, a lunar/yin symbol. It shows that she is the ultimate creative feminine principle,[10] the "guardian of the inexhaustible well."[11] Associated with water, pearls represent special insights from our unconscious, i.e., "pearls of wisdom," to which the Morgan-Greer Queen of Swords has access (the pearl in the center of the rose before her). Because pearls are rare—or at least once were—and precious, they are considered a symbol of the Self by Jungians.

Pegasus

The quintessential winged horse, Pegasus sprang full-grown from the blood of Medusa after Perseus beheaded her. Tamed by Minerva and given to the Muses, his kick opened the Hippocrene (Hip-poe-CREE-knee) fountain on their mountain. Wherever his hooves strike the earth, springs (creative inspiration of the unconscious) bubble forth. The winged steed is said to have been ridden by the poets from time immemorial.[12] The Robin Wood Knight of Swords rides a winged steed that is mythologically associated with Pegasus. This Knight represents the soaring of the instincts into higher realms; hence, spiritual creativity.[13] Bellerophon rides Pegasus on the Mythic Tarot's Knight of Wands.

Pentacles (suit) ✗

The Minor Arcana suit of Pentacles is linked with the element of earth, and Jung's sensation function. It represents the body and our relationship with the material world. The five-pointed star reminds us that this suit deals with what we can perceive and experience with our senses and what we can create with them.

Called coins or disks in some decks, it is a suit of physical work and of bringing inner thoughts, ideas, and fantasies into manifestation. Pentacles' cards are concerned with our financial

✗ *how we relate to the aspects of the physical world*

security, material resources, and other worldly needs. Many pentacles in a spread may indicate that the need to deal with practical matters is paramount, or that things are moving sluggishly.

Psychologically, Pentacles' experiences contribute to ego development and to sensory experiences that help us function in the world. Esoterically, the suit refers to the development of work as service and spiritual exercise, and with learning to understand the deeper meaning of our work if we can get past money concerns. Earth energy equates with the alchemical process of *coagulatio*/coagulation, the stage in which vapor (spirit) was reunited with ash (the body). Negatively, Pentacles cards may refer to the impoverishment of the soul.

In the Haindl and Shining Tribe decks, Pentacles are the Suit of Stones. In the Tarot of the Spirit, they are the Suit of Earth. In the Osho deck, Pentacles become the Suit of Rainbows: The Physical. They are the Suit of Sacred Circles in the Ancestral Path deck.

Pentacles, Ace of

Typically, the Ace appears alone held in a large (Nigel Jackson) or gleaming (RWS) hand, floating against some background, (Alchemical), mounted on a column (Robin Wood), or otherwise dominating the card. In the Spiral Ace, a nude earth-mother goddess stands on a pentacle. Her arms and hair extend into and become the World Tree. On the Wheel of Change Ace of Disks, planet Earth, surrounded by a border of colored beads and seasonal trees, forms a mandala. A card of primary inception and sustenance, it represents being centered in one's body.

Like all aces, these variations represent a new opportunity or a new direction—in this case, one of material experience, fortune, activity. Some aces focus largely on the promise of materiality, sensuality, economic power. Others suggest that the card deals with the opportunity for inner and outer wealth. It calls for grounding or centering oneself in order to begin a new cycle of creation.

On the RWS card, the lilies of the mystical path and the roses of the occult path offer a "higher" choice. For those who care to pursue it, we are being called to embark on an esoteric, spiritual journey, one of understanding how our attitudes or behavior toward outer work reflect our inner life—or how we want to make it do so.

Keywords/phrases: new financial security; energy to begin new financial ventures; new sources of income; new ways of spending money; new affirmation of self-worth; the start of a new project or hobby.

Pentacles, Two of

In many depictions of this card, a figure juggles, attempts to balance, or holds two pentacles within a ribbon-like lemniscate. It represents the paradox of maintaining the fluid flow of stability, as when, in the Osho Tarot's "Moment to Moment" card, a Japanese figure steps lightly across stones placed in the ever-swirling, ever-changing waters of life. The Tarot of the Spirit's Two of Earth card deals with the awareness that for every action, there is a reaction, and that life is in a continual process of creation.[14]

In the background of the RWS card, two ships sail on a rolling sea (the fluctuations of emotional life). The Robin Wood juggler walks a tightrope (she is out of her element, yet in complete control) and creates a glowing lemniscate (seen on so many versions of this card) as she balances two pentacles. She is a more advanced representation of The Fool, but in her case her choice is courageous, joyful, and deliberate, not the result of naïveté.[15]

The Two of Disks (Wheel of Change) reflects the interplay and relationship between the earth and the sun as the opposing and complementary qualities of life and their interconnected rhythm. On the Two of Stones (Shining Tribe) a toad (yang energy, action, quickness, creative power) is engraved on one stone and a tortoise (yin energy, intuition, inaction or slow, thoughtful, careful action) on the other. The card is read according to which stone appears on the top in the reading.

On the Renaissance Two of Coins, Eros shoots an arrow toward Hades, symbolizing an unusual or unexpected turn of events. The Haindl Two of Stones ("Harmony") represents constantly shifting energy and an exchange of energy between people, even though no people are shown in the card.

The Two of Pentacles is a card of playful decision-making. With a certain amount of playfulness in juggling life's situations, we can adapt to the ups and downs of life in our search for equilibrium. This is portrayed well in the World Spirit card where a barefoot female balances herself on a rock amidst swirling waters, while also balancing a pentacle in each hand.

Keywords/phrases: balance or skillful manipulation of financial affairs; a need to keep things moving without taking them too seriously; ambivalence regarding life's fluctuations; juggling two possibilities; balancing two opposing issues (money/time, friend/family) in order to maintain financial balance.

Pentacles, Three of

As a three, the card represents an initial completion, or a success, but an early one; therefore, it simultaneously represents a decisive step, and the developing skill and dedication that leads to more accomplished levels of creation. Like all cyclic cards, it represents the ending of one phase, the hint of another. The Osho "Guidance" card cautions us to attend to our inner truth and use it for direction, so that we go exactly where we need to be.

Many cards show someone working or preparing to work, usually in a holy or sacred place. They represent the "birth of invention" wherein we apply the creative mind to the physical world.[16] In the Alchemical Tarot's card, three coins sculpted with the signs of the alchemical trinity (mercury, salt, sulphur) symbolize bringing unconscious creativity into physical awareness.[17] On the Nigel Jackson card, a monk works on a manuscript. Through an open window we see workers harvesting wheat—a hint that physical and spiritual work can be meaningfully combined.

The Mythic Tarot associates the card—and the entire suit of Pentacles—with a reward for Daedulus, an Athenian craftsman. Persephone gathers fruits (well-being and satisfaction) in the Renaissance card. The Spiral Tarot's ballerina stands in the spotlight. Roses thrown at her feet show a successful performance. The Shapeshifter's otter-woman (Three of Earth Element: "Success") symbolizes our abilities to come through crises and renew our spirits by acquiring wisdom.[18]

Keywords/phrases: growing in or sharpening professional ability; new threshold of physical mastery; successful effort using creative and practical skills; new undertakings that bring material rewards; planning and initial work toward a financial goal.

Pentacles, Four of

Traditionally the card of the miser, the Four of Pentacles addresses our need for material structure, stability, and security, our anxieties about it, and our attempt to control those anxieties. At a deeper level, our attitudes toward money can reflect our sense of self-worth, so the card also suggests that an obsessive or unreasonable outer need for security and achievement reflects a need to order our inner life as carefully as our outer life.

Frequently the card shows someone holding tightly to coins or pentacles, hinting that, in addition to a miserly attitude toward wealth, our fixed ideas and stubbornness prevent us from being open to new circumstances and insights. It reflects the fear of "letting go," not just of wealth but also of one's very way of being in the world, of giving up decaying attitudes and approaches to life, or whatever else we're holding onto so tenaciously. In the Shapeshifter's card (Four of Earth Element: "Legacy"), a male and female "elk-person" lead a small herd through a canyon (the birth canal). We need to evaluate how we become the "steward" of our own energy.[19] The Tarot of the Spirit "Power" card represents a closing off of the outside world to allow inner power to unfold and to think about the kind of reality we want to construct. The radiating keyhole on the card represents the opening we can select to move into the next level of development.

Keywords/phrases: gaining control of financial situation; financial stalemate; monetary or work obsession; need for security; possessiveness or hoarding; fear of change; acquisition without enjoyment.

Pentacles, Five of

A frequent Five of Pentacles illustration shows two people in ragged clothes (sometimes crippled) outside on a dark, snowy night. Often the bright light of a church is nearby, but the figures do not see it. They fail to see the positive that remains in a desolate situation. Nevertheless, the figures in the card usually *are* moving forward—except in the World Spirit card, where a single figure huddles at the church door.

The "Material Difficulty" Haindl card represents a test of strength, and possibly financial and/or inner impoverishment. The crippled beggar in the Alchemical card holds out his hand for alms, oblivious of the coins lying on the ground at his feet. He has not realized his own inner light or spirit.

Self-esteem is at a new low. The cold or barren ground may represent insecurity or a shaky, possibly crippled, *persona*. The Renaissance card likens this to the period when Demeter, disguised as an old woman, roamed the world, mourning her daughter's disappearance, cursing the earth's fertility (*see* **Demeter/Ceres**). The Alchemical Five of Shields ("Wasteland") refers to the barren country that surrounded the Grail Castle due to the Fisher King's wound.

A small child looks through a chained but unlocked gate in "The Outsider" (Osho's Five of Rainbows). The scene reflects feelings of helplessness when we are excluded, yet because of past experience fail to see a way out, or to realize we are still connected to the greater universe. Depicting rock art figures from the wall of Horseshoe Canyon, the Shining Tribe Five of Stones represents an inner journey or healing experience out of which something substantial will emerge.

Keywords/phrases: spending too much money; financial or work difficulties; a change in social status; an inner feeling or sense of poverty; spiritual impoverishment; so involved in our own plight or drama that we can't see available help and opportunity.

Pentacles, Six of

In the RWS card, a merchant drops coins into the outstretched hands of one of two beggars draped in tattered blankets. For one of the myths that can be connected with this card, *see* **beggar(s)**.

The New Palladini and Haindl (Six of Stones) cards express success, which in the Haindl card is derived from the low point of the material difficulties of the Five of Stones. A king, a female, and a bearded old beggar entwine their hands about a balancing scale on the Spiral card, denoting equality between all people and the karmic message that you reap what you sow.[20] A child gives a coin to another on the Alchemical Tarot's card, expressing the message of giving freely and lovingly.

Keywords/phrases: a time of, or need for, give and take; time to recognize the divine in everyone; overcoming financial difficulties; financial help required; being open to help; willingness to share wealth and resources with others; ability to give from a place of wholeness; understanding the process of giving and receiving; generosity.

Pentacles, Seven of

In RWS and related decks, a young man—clearly a farmer in the Robin Wood card—leans on his hoe and gazes at seven pentacles growing from a vine.

In fairy tales, farmers represent the "keepers of tradition," exhibiting the value of common sense.[21] They are linked with the saving hero who has yet to be recognized,[22] and with cyclic time and renewal. Like the alchemist, they must obey the seasonal laws rather precisely. Indeed, alchemy has sometimes been called "celestial agriculture."[23]

So, the Seven of Pentacles represents a pause in our labors to review, evaluate, and decide our priorities or next steps. The success we have achieved may not yet be obvious.

The Haindl Seven of Stones ("Failure"), however, represents standstill. Activity that is without a sacred connection has lost its purpose. It is the reversal of this card that represents recovery and a fresh start. The Shining Tribe Seven of Stones is one of birthing and nurturing and contains an Indian medallion colored like the rainbow to refer to the seven chakras. On the Alchemical card, seven coins aligned on an obelisk represent the seven metals of alchemy. On the Wheel of Change Seven of Disks, grains from around the world reflect a synthesis of cosmological differences and polarities.

All of these cards call upon us to consider practical and sacred knowledge in order to nourish ourselves in a new way by our next step. The Thoth "Failure" card refers to not taking the time to use introspection and imagination to create what we want to manifest. The Shapeshifter Tarot's "Growth" card is dominated by a woman beginning to shapeshift into a horse. It reflects the joy of using our psychic powers on the inward path to spiritual growth, the horse symbolizing swiftness in overcoming obstacles (*see* **horse**).

Keywords/phrases: time to recognize tradition; cyclic time or renewal; looking inside to discover direction; reaping the fruits of one's labor; pausing for appreciation, assessment, or planning; preparation; following natural cycles.

See **rainbow**.

Pentacles, Eight of

A card of talents and skills, this card nevertheless suggests more work needs to be done. It is a card of slow, steady achievement. It sometimes takes tedious repetition to learn life lessons.[24]

In the RWS, Morgan-Greer, Spiral, New Palladini, Mythic, and Alchemical cards, artisans are at work. A young lad learns to carve on the Robin Wood card. In the Wheel of Change card, spiders weave their webs, representing the web of life and strong network connections with others. The village in the background of the RWS card and the yellow road leading to and from the work area suggest that work unrelated to community lacks meaning.[25]

One of the eight "stones" in the Haindl Tarot's "Knowledge" card is a bubble indicating that practical activities require opening ourselves to the world of spirit for true knowledge.[26] The Shapeshifter Tarot's "Skill" card reflects the notion of a centered consciousness.

Keywords/phrases: perfecting one's craft for increased prosperity; perseverance; a hobby or skill may now become a moneymaking possibility; new financial or material application; apprentice stage of some new skill or ability; paying one's dues; focused, disciplined, and meticulous effort; careful attention to details.

Pentacles, Nine of

Many RWS-like cards show a lavishly or exotically attired woman in a garden with fruiting grapevines. If she is not shown in the garden, grapes often are included somewhere (New Palladini, Morgan-Greer). The card deals with realizing and enjoying the "fruits of our labors," and of the time being right, or ripe, to create our happiness. We have found or identified the real values of our work and can contemplate our material endeavors. We are at our "Zenith" (Tarot of the Spirit). The Shining Tribe card addresses the issue of self-creation, the idea not of attempting to overcoming our nature but of transforming what nature gives us.[27]

Depending on the deck, "Lady Nine" frequently has a bird with her. In the New Palladini and Alchemical cards, it is an exotic white bird with a lavish tail, representing her higher self.

In the RWS, Morgan-Greer, and Shining Tribe cards, a hooded falcon reflects the discipline needed to create a good life. A snail appears at her feet on the RWS and Spiral cards, reflecting both the end of a cycle and the promise of a new one.

Keywords/phrases: completion of a financial project; taking solitary pleasure in material success; self-contained; a (possibly new) sense of inner richness; abundance; completion of a creative cycle; fulfillment; utilizing your own abilities and self-control to follow your dreams.

See **falcon; grapes; snail**.

Pentacles, Ten of

The card's traditional meaning is one of financial stability and a firm foundation for home and family life with the capability to create it. The RWS card speaks not only of material culmination and harmony, but also of emotional or spiritual prosperity, since the pentacles are grouped in the pattern of the Kabbalistic Tree of Life.

On the RWS card, a family of three stands within an arched gate. A bearded, white-haired man sits outside the gate, petting one of two gray dogs. His coat is decorated with grapes (growth or harvest) and magic symbols that represent power over nature. Some tarotists regard the old man as an outsider and link him to the god who, disguised as a beggar, tests a family's hospitality, as only the dogs recognize the stranger's divinity.

The card marks the stirrings of interest in higher service after financial success. It directs us to choose a path of enlightenment and further growth. The old man outside the arch suggests that eventually we have to step outside of the family compound to further our perspective. Other decks expand on this concept in several ways, marking family success (Spiral) and community relationships (Ancestral Path).

Despite the harsh landscape of the desert, the Shining Tribe Ten of Stones, painted with sacred images, gives a sense of abundance. The images represent the accumulation of what we have made of our lives and the card is one of great success.[28] The World Spirit's Legacy card asks us to consider what we will leave to future generations and reminds us to honor the magic and mystery of everyday life.[29]

Keywords/phrases: finishing or starting a new financial project; attending to family tradition; family nurturance; being materially settled, satisfied, or fulfilled; becoming conscious of one's true wealth; gateway to spiritual knowledge.

Pentacles, Page of

An earth card of the earth suit, the Page of Pentacles is a most comfortable young man or woman (Alchemical, Spiral, Robin Wood, Wheel of Change). Typically the Page simply holds his/her pentacle; the RWS Page looks as if he is about to set it afloat. He is ready to begin bringing his ideas into fruition or manifestation, yet he takes the opportunity lightly and is not wholly caught up in it. The Wheel of Change Princess of Disks, a brightly dressed young Rajasthani girl, holds a tray full of chapatis, round flat breads. She symbolizes past preparation and readiness to put her learning into action.

Keywords/phrases: immersed in a new aspect or understanding of work, material things, or values; messenger of a new venture or project; new investments; learning business and financial acumen; good business hunches; news of a new job offer or opportunity; readiness to start new endeavors; awareness of new ideas that could propel a new career; dreaming about future financial ventures.

Pentacles, Knight of

As an air card of the earth suit, the Knight of Pentacles contains antagonistic elements, perhaps learned as the page. He is sometimes perceived as a character with many ambivalences. In facing his challenge, he develops will and strength of character. He is a hard worker, sometimes doggedly so, and exceptionally dependable. He shows plenty of determination, and is usually shown on or near his unmoving horse and often near a plowed field to show the potential cultivation of his work (RWS, Robin Wood). The Spiral Tarot describes him as being so thorough that he sometimes can be seen as boring and slow.[30]

The Alchemical knight stands beside a huge pentacles shield. He is the "protector of wellbeing."[31] Although deeply rooted in the outer world, the RWS knight seems to stare "over" his pentacle, not at it. By dedicating himself to practical matters, has he lost sight of the source and meaning of his strength in life?[32] He is careful, cautious, and conservative.

Keywords/phrases: steadily plowing through the quest for understanding material values; perseverance; resolution of long-term situations, breaking out of limitation; steadfastness; rootedness; pride in accomplishment.

Pentacles, Queen of

A water card of the earth suit—these two complementary elements describe a person who tends toward compromise, balance, and moderation. She would be inclined to look after another's physical needs, and give practical advice to students or followers rather than allowing them to find their own way. For some this would be a welcome security, for others it would be restricting.

She is often shown in lush surroundings, although the simply dressed Renaissance Queen of Coins sits outdoors with the basilica of Maxentius and the Colosseum rising behind her.

The Queen of Disks (Wheel of Change) weaves a circular food tray. Surrounded by trays filled with food, she is definitely a skilled, confident, and bountiful queen. The Earth Mother (Tarot of the Spirit) is quintessential manifestation. Because she understands herself so well, she compassionately controls the elements and trains material force.[33]

Keywords/phrases: practical business help or advice; awareness and appreciation of good things in life; great attention to physical surroundings; reliability and steadfastness; passion for the world around and making life plentiful; having abundance and willing to share and nurture others; fecund queen in harmony with nature's cycles.

See **cornucopia; cow; goat; rabbit/hare.**

Pentacles, King of

As a fire card in the earth suit, this king can give mature and thoughtful guidance on how to successfully survive in the world, particularly in a prudent way. He has a keen eye for opportunities and is a shrewd bargainer.[34] Fully aware of the pleasures of the earth—the bull's head on his RWS throne denotes his love of material possessions—he is pragmatic, sensible, and methodical. In some decks, he is considered the epitome of fertility and fertilization (Tarot of the Spirit, Light and Shadow).

On the RWS card there is the question of whether the castle in the background is the fruit of his labors or whether his hard work has estranged him from home and family, as evidenced by the wall behind him, separating him from the castle.

On the Alchemical card he is shown as a crowned lion, expressing the embodiment of courage and strength due to his own harmony with nature.[35]

Keywords/phrases: enterprising achievement; financially responsible and successful; acute sense of what is feasible and practical; a card of cunning action that leads to tangible results; workaholic; strength of character; uses material possessions to create relationships; ability to turn insights and ideas into material comfort.

Perseus

Perseus was conceived when Zeus appeared in a shower of gold to the mortal woman Danaë, daughter of King Acrisius. Having been warned by an oracle that his grandson would kill him, Acrisius had previously shut his virgin daughter into a tower. After Perseus's birth, Acrisius had Danaë and her infant sealed in a chest and cast into the sea. Rescued by a fisherman on the island of Seriphos, Perseus was reared by King Polydectes, whom he later killed for falling in love with Danaë. Eventually, he also accidentally killed his grandfather in a discus-throwing contest.[36] Perseus setting off on his adventures is the subject of the Mythic Tarot's Knight of Cups, and represents us setting off on our journeys of mental or spiritual prowess. The destruction of the tower in which Danaë was imprisoned is the focus of the Spiral Tarot's Tower card.

persona

In Jungian theory, the *persona* is an archetype representing a "mask" or, more accurately, an adaptation. It is that aspect of ourselves we employ when playing a role (abiding by the rules). Sometimes this is necessary to be successful in dealing with various situations and people. Such a mask appears in the Morgan-Greer Seven of Cups. The *persona* is necessary for keeping a job and living in civilized society, but can be dysfunctional if we fail to develop our personalities further, or if we believe that the *persona* is truly who we are. In tarot cards, clothes may represent the *persona* we show to the world. Many Tower cards show the toppling of an inflated *persona* (shaped like a crown).

See **clothes/clothing**.

personal unconscious

One aspect of the personality, according to Jungian psychology, the personal unconscious refers to personal memories, thoughts, or experiences no longer available in conscious awareness, but relatively easy to remember. Also active in the personal unconscious are "complexes," clusters of memories, emotions, or thoughts of which we are unaware but which may control or influence much of our conscious behavior. Sometimes material from the personal unconscious can be retrieved and identified by viewing certain tarot cards individually, or by a number of cards laid out in a tarot spread.

personality cards

A process first developed by Angeles Arrien and made popular by Mary K. Greer, it consists of adding the month and date of your birth to the year of your birth, and reducing the separate digits of the total to the higher of two numbers between one and twenty-two, so it can be associated with a Major Arcana card (The Fool equals 22). For instance, $2002 + 10 + 1 = 2013 = 2 + 0 + 1 + 3 = 6$ (The Lovers). The personality card indicates essential characteristics that one develops easily because they resonate with or reflect one's essential nature.[37] Pay particular attention to this card when it appears in a reading, as it may denote an important development.

See **reduction; soul cards; year cards.**

personality (Jungian theory)

In Jungian psychology, the personality is composed of three separate but interacting systems: the ego, or the conscious mind; the personal unconscious; and the collective unconscious. An influx of energy and information from the unconscious fuels consciousness, since the latter is incapable of producing psychic energy by itself.[38] The experiences of the collective unconscious exist as tendencies called archetypes, of which we are not aware but can become so through images. Although there are many archetypes, the five major ones consist of the *persona*, the *anima*, the *animus*, the shadow, and the Self. These archetypes and others are expressed in the many images of tarot decks.

See ***anima*; *animus*; archetypes; collective unconscious; *persona*; personal unconscious; Self; shadow.**

Phaëthon

Helius, who daily drove the sun chariot across the sky, finally yielded to his son Phaëthon's persistent demands to be allowed to drive the chariot (some stories say Phaëthon's father was Phoebus Apollo). The horses, sensing that the weight in the chariot was lighter than usual, dashed about as if it were empty, and Phaëthon, in a panic, forgot their names and, further, did not have the physical strength to control them. Consequently, they flew so high that the clouds, the constellations, and the earth were scorched, and waters dried up. In a fit of rage, Zeus killed Phaëthon with a thunderbolt.[39] He is seen falling on the Renaissance Tarot's Tower card. In most decks the Tower reflects the "toppling" experience of an ego/*persona* that believes it is more ready or capable than it truly is.

philosopher's stone

Often associated with The World card, it reflects the ultimate goal of the alchemical process. In psychological terms, this means that the personality in transformation was projected into the stone, i.e., the alchemist projected an inner event onto an outer object, so he could more easily comprehend and deal with it. From that point on, the stone becomes the symbol of the totality of the inner experience. For Jung, the "Philosopher" was Hermes and the "Stone" was Mercurius, the Latin Hermes.[40] In the tarot they are represented by The Fool and The Magician.

See **alchemy; Self.**

Phrixus

Phrixus was the son of King Athamas of Boeotia and Nephele, a phantom woman, whom he married at Hera's command. Athamas then secretly wed Ino, a mortal woman. Nephele complained to Hera, who issued a vow of eternal vengeance. In retaliation Ino persuaded the women of their village, who were devoted to her, to parch the seed-corn so that it wouldn't sprout. She bribed the messenger that Athamas sent to the Delphi Oracle to say that Zeus had declared that the land would only regain its fertility if Phrixus was sacrificed. As the sacrifice was about to occur, a winged ram flew down to rescue Phrixus. When he was safe, Phrixus sacrificed the ram to Zeus, and it was the ram's golden fleece that the Argonauts sought a generation later.[41] Details of Jason's search for the golden fleece are told in the Minor Arcana suit of the Spiral deck. On the deck's Page of Wands, Phrixus rides the ram out of danger.

phoenix

In Greek mythology, the phoenix is an attribute of Venus. In alchemical illustrations, which characteristically portrayed "chemical mysteries" using animals, a phoenix often represented the rubedo, or reddening, phase—the alchemical flames. The rubedo created the "solar tincture," the "red elixir," which could result in solidification into the lapis. A phoenix rises from the fire of the Alchemical Tarot's Ten of Staffs, representing the transformation and renewal that occur through the "tests" of life experiences. A phoenix hovers over Isis in the Spiral's Star card, representing the human soul and rebirth. The golden shadow of a phoenix with red-tipped wings backs the nude female in the Robin Wood Judgement card to show that she is reborn from the ashes of her old self.[42]

pillars

As man-made objects, pillars are related to structure and to the "upholding," "supporting," or "encompassing" of some concept. They also are related to the "outside" as opposed to the "inside" (*see* **cave/cavern**) and to duality. Of interest in the tarot cards is what is placed between the pillars, making them a sort of gateway. Many tarotists believe that the two pillars of The High Priestess, Justice, and Hierophant cards represent the left and right columns of the Kabbalistic Tree of Life. The figures then represent the central pillar of equilibrium.

In the RWS Death card, a rising (or setting) sun is seen between two pillars on the horizon. A similar set of pillars are seen on the RWS Moon card, where the path between them appears long and winding. Possibly the two together constitute a death-rebirth theme and/or initiation.

See **columns**.

pinecone

For the Greeks the pinecone was a masculine generative symbol, likely because of its flame shape. It was sacred to Zeus/Jupiter. Dionysus was often shown holding a pinecone in his hand like a scepter, or carrying a pinecone-topped scepter, the *thyrus*, representing his intoxicating force over nature.[43] For the Romans, however, the pinecone, and its tree, were sacred emblems of Venus, and celebrated in the later cult ceremonies of the mother goddess Cybele. It was therefore considered a feminine symbol of fertility. The Haindl Empress, associated with Venus, holds a staff topped with a pinecone.

See **Aphrodite/Venus; Dionysus/Bacchus; tree, pine**.

pips

See **Minor Arcana**.

Pisces (astrological sign)

The twelfth sign of the zodiac (February 20–March 20).

Element: Water
Modality: Mutable
Polarity: Yin
Ruled by Jupiter, co-ruled by Neptune

Cards attributed to Pisces partake of the mystic and compassionate qualities of this sign. The constellation depicts two fishes, forever bound at the tail. This sign rules the passing aeon that is giving way to the aeon of Aquarius. Pisces is another dual sign of the zodiac, symbolizing the union between the human and divine. Pisces is the sign of unconditional love, forgiveness, mercy, compassion, and healing, and is connected with the oceans, saints, and martyrs. A well-dignified Pisces card's meanings include: gentleness; loving compassion; the desire for unity and peace; absolution, and a connection with the divine; all varieties of mystical inspiration; acting, theater, and cinematography; and all forms of fantasy and illusion. The meanings for an ill-dignified or reversed Pisces card include: deception, despair, whining and weak-willed acceptance of every obstacle, chronic complaints about health, befuddlement, intoxication through drugs and alcohol, addictions, moodiness, disconnection from reality.[44]

See **Jupiter** (planet); **Neptune** (planet).

Pleiades/Pleiads

The seven daughters of Atlas, they fled from Orion's lusty pursuit. Hearing their pleas, Jupiter transformed them into stars. And, still, in the heavens today, Orion, killed by Diana's arrow, and followed by his dog Sirius, gives chase to the Pleiades flying before him.[45] They, and the "dog star," are sometimes included in the mythology attached to The Star card and its seven stars.

Pluto (planet)

The ninth planet from the Sun and the furthest known planet in the solar system. It co-rules Scorpio.

As the outermost planet, Pluto takes the individual beyond known boundaries to the realms of the underworld or unconscious mind, a place of fears, compulsions, buried memories, tragic losses, abuse, and addictions. This planet represents the processes of death and loss that lead to rebirth. As such, cards attributed to Pluto evoke the invisible, terrifying gods of the underworld; things deeply hidden beneath surface appearances; collective upheaval and mass destruction, yet with the possibility of apotheosis and transfiguration at the completion of the journey; healing or shamanic skills, the use of power for the good of all; and historic events that irrevocably change the collective paradigm. An ill-dignified Pluto card can mean: senseless destruction and annihilation, genocide, abuse of power, cold-hearted manipulation and abuse, psychopathic or violently sociopathic behaviors, deadly force and tyranny, dangerous obsessions.[46]

See **Hades/Pluto; Scorpio.**

polarities

Although many symbols on tarot cards point to the need for recognition and reconciliation of opposites, better words for "opposites" are "polarities," "dualistic principles," or even "paradoxical ideas," since they do not contain the judgements of positive/negative, and good/bad. According to the ancient Zohar, the two dualistic principles correspond to the two H's (Heh) in the Tetragrammaton (*see* **Tetragrammaton**).[47] Some of the common polarities depicted in tarot cards include: creation/destruction, young/old, masculine/feminine, conscious/unconscious, attachment/separateness, instinct/intellect.

See **masculine/feminine; opposites, tension of**.

pomegranate

Seen on the veil behind some High Priestess cards (RWS, Aquarian), pomegranates represent reconciling the diverse "within apparent unity."[48] The fruit also represents one creative source becoming many,[49] inasmuch as its seed, its blood-red juice, and its shape symbolize fertility and new possibilities.[50]

Several myths connect the pomegranate with Dionysus/Bacchus. One says the fruit sprang from his blood. Another says that when he was torn apart by the Maenads, his heart and soul were preserved within a pomegranate held in the land of Hades. Thus, when the abducted Persephone (*see* **Proserpina/Persephone**) was fooled into eating one or more of the seeds, not only was she doomed to return to Hades annually, but she was also impregnated with Dionysus's soul and gave birth to their son Iacchus.[51] So, pomegranates are also a "new birth" symbol. Persephone eats the seeds of the pomegranate on the Renaissance Eight of Coins.

Once considered an exotic and exquisite fruit reserved for visiting royalty, the pomegranate cups on the Thoth Three of Cups represent the ability to communicate the riches we have received from others.[52]

Some say the design on the gown of the RWS Empress is that of pomegranates, and a pomegranate does rest at the foot of the Morgan-Greer Empress. They also grow in the garden of the Spiral Tarot's Lovers card. In all cases, they represent creative, receptive, and feminine energy. The pomegranate in the Shining Tribe Three of Rivers (Cups) symbolizes the lifeblood of menstruation and birth.[53]

See **Proserpina/Persephone; tree, palm.**

Poseidon/Neptune (Greek/Roman god)

Poseidon rules the great realm of the ocean. Married to Amphritite, Poseidon was a philanderer, often disguising himself in animal form to seduce maidens.

Poseidon was also greedy, acquisitive, and desired the patronage of great cities often belonging to other gods and goddesses. When thwarted, he caused tidal waves and floods, destroying all that humans had built. When we experience waves of intense feelings arising from our depths, we are having a "Poseidon experience."[54]

Poseidon is credited with having invented chariots and horse races. One of his most notable offspring (with Medusa) is the winged horse, Pegasus, and Poseidon's symbolic animals were bulls and horses. As befits a water god, his symbol was the trident, the triple phallus, suggesting that one of his earlier functions was as mate of the triple goddess.[55]

Behavioral models connected with Neptune range in the extreme. On one end is the saint, the martyr, the holy prophet of god, who offers unlimited compassion and forgiveness, and the redemption of humanity. Then there are the con man, the deceiver, the one who comes disguised to steal virtue, wealth, or goods. In between, there's an underlying emotional depth to which the Poseidon person has access, and which can be expressed in artistic or theatrical spheres or in tormented visionary qualities so often endemic of great artists.[56]

See **Cups/Chalices** (suit); **dolphin(s)**; **Neptune** (planet); **Pegasus**; **Pisces**; **water.**

pouring water

A figure pouring water symbolizes the changing or transformation of consciousness, the stirring up of unconscious material and bringing it to awareness. The RWS Star figure pours water from a pitcher held in each hand. From one pitcher five streams of water pour onto the earth, representing the physical, the sensual, consciousness (the five senses). From the other, water pours into a pond, rippling its water, i.e., stirring the unconscious or possibly the collective unconscious, from which we are called upon to retrieve ancient and universal knowledge.

The RWS Temperance angel, as do many Temperance angels, "pours" water back and forth between two chalices, one lower than the other and representing the unconscious. He blends the two levels of the psyche so they flow more smoothly.

The movement and effect of pouring water, as in these two cards, relates to the concept of vibration. One Aramaic word for vibration is *shemaya* ("heaven"), so when we want to shift the shape of reality, we work with *shemaya*'s tools.[57]

profile

A figure seen in profile says that only one aspect of the forces he/she represents is visible. The upper body of the Thoth Empress sits with her face to the right, which permits her to face the Emperor, who also sits in profile. Her posture suggests a conflict (but possibly a balance) between her upper body (assertion and intellect) and her lower body (turned to the left, and reflecting sensuality and instinctual drives). Although the Thoth Emperor faces left (toward his Empress), his body faces forward, suggesting his need to receive feminine information, which he will then develop and express as material law or rules.

See **direction**.

projection

The recognizing and/or attributing of certain qualities (positive and negative) to another person because you refuse to recognize, or are unable to admire or express, the same qualities within yourself. Many tarot cards deal with projection or, more precisely, the need to own one's own inner characteristics in order to become a more self-realized person. Projection of one's own needs onto card meanings is a possibility that needs to be guarded against when reading for others.

See **shadow**.

Prometheus

Said to have created humans from the earth and his tears, Prometheus, whose name means "forethought," then stole fire for them because Zeus was withholding it. As punishment, Zeus had Prometheus chained to a rock. Each day he endured the torturous punishment of having an eagle or vulture devour part of his liver, which then grew back nightly. Prometheus gained immortality when Chiron bequeathed him his own immortality.[58]

The myth of Prometheus is the subject of the Mythic Tarot's Hanged Man.

Proserpina/Persephone (Greek/Roman goddess)

Persephone (per-SEF-oh-knee) was the beautiful maiden daughter of Demeter/Ceres, the earth mother. Impaled by one of Eros's (Cupid's) arrows, Hades/Pluto fell in love with her as she picked flowers in a meadow, and carried her off to his underworld kingdom. Persephone's mother, Demeter, searched the world for her, wreaking havoc, cursing the land, and forbidding trees to fruit and plants to grow. Finally Zeus/Jupiter intervened on the condition that Persephone should not have taken any food during her stay. Hades offered her pomegranate seeds, and she unwittingly accepted, condemning her to spend only half the year with her mother and the rest with Hades (hence the seasons).

One Jungian explanation of this myth is that it symbolizes in older women the loss of the inner daughter—one's young and carefree aspect—which prepares a woman for the discoveries of meaning that are the task of the second half of life. Women who have no contact with the Demeter mystery experience difficulty in giving up their unconscious clinging to youth and their yearning for the status quo.[59] Persephone is linked with The High Priestess, and the maiden aspect of the Triple Goddess, shown in many Moon cards.

See **pomegranate**.

Psyche

Aphrodite, goddess of love, wore a magic girdle which made her the most beautiful being of all, among both mortals and deities, but Psyche was so beautiful that when she passed people abandoned Aphrodite's temples to admire her. This so angered Aphrodite that she instructed her son Eros/Cupid, who carried arrows of desire, to infuse Psyche with a passion for some low, unworthy being. Unfortunately, Eros accidentally wounded himself, and subsequently took Psyche for his bride. Yet she did not see him or actually know who he was, because he came in the darkness and left before the dawn. At the urging of her jealous sisters, Psyche viewed him with a lamp as he slept, whereupon he left her with the words "Love cannot dwell with suspicion." One look, however, and Psyche had fallen in love with Eros. In order to win him back, Aphrodite imposed four labors on Psyche, which symbolically prepared her for soulful love. In addition to the mythology of Eros and Psyche often being associated with The Lovers card, it is also the story behind the Cups suit in the Renaissance and Mythic decks.

See **Cups/Chalices** (suit).

purple

The color associated with Zeus/Jupiter, purple is the color of royalty, authority (worldly and ecclesiastical), and esoteric and spiritual knowledge/insight. The color of perfect attainment, it combines the active energy of red with the passive energy of blue.[60] As violet, it is the color of the crown chakra, which represents the point where heaven and earthly consciousness meet. Its ruling planet is the moon.

See **colors.**

pyramid(s)

Pyramids are associated with the symbolism of the world axis, their apex symbolizing the highest point of, or connection with, spiritual attainment.[61] Some believe that in ancient times initiation rites were performed in the pyramids; hence, they can also symbolize initiation into the "higher mysteries. Pyramids on a card call attention to life's deeper, more cosmic mysteries; a desire for spiritual aspirations; hidden secrets; or introduction to an esoteric system of learning. Pyramids appear in the backgrounds of the RWS Page and Knight of Wands, suggesting that the secrets or skills they are about to learn are backed by higher knowledge or ancient wisdom teachings.

Q

※

queens

Tarot queens represent a stage where, through dedication and work, skills are fully developed. Passion is lessened but the confidence that comes from experience is heightened. We add new behaviors to our repertoire.

Queens and kings are the most mature figures in the suit sequence. They have lived through the sequences of their respective suits, resulting in expanded perspective. With the kings of their suit, they represent the male and female principles. Together they symbolize oneness, wholeness.

In myths and fairy tales, queens and kings represent the ruling powers of consciousness.[1] The mother-queen transmits eros and life-habits; the father-king transmits spiritual values.[2] It is the queen who first explains the "higher" rules and regulations—she sets the tempo, defines the path—and then makes us aware of our basic nature and encourages us to move into our higher natures. She is an adviser, partner, and support system, nourishing and directing each student individually as is appropriate to consolidate and further their learning.

Queens may represent or reflect the mother within, or our attitudes toward female parental and authority figures. Some decks have renamed the queen as the mother, matriarch, guide, or priestess.

Queens represent the receptive aspect of the element of water. As such, they represent the inner expression of the values of their respective suits, while the king represents outer expression.[3] Esoterically, the queen is the adept of incoming spiritual energy. She understands what must be nurtured for both inner and outer worlds to remain fertile. A mother figure, she must, of necessity, represent the more mundane or worldly aspects of the mother archetype, which are expressed through her suit.

If numerology is used for the queens, it corresponds to the number thirteen. Frequently considered a number of "bad luck," in classical antiquity it was a symbol of strength and one of the most powerful and exalted numbers (Zeus was the thirteenth and highest member of the Olympians).[4] If reduced, thirteen is related to all the numerical information regarding fours (1 + 3 = 4). The queens are associated with the sephira of Binah on the Tree of Life.

Keywords/phrases: feminine authority; the archetypal feminine; inspiration; highest feminine potential for integration; receptive qualities; concepts and conception; direction giver; nurturer; behind-the-scenes mover; role model for inner control.

See court cards; kings; and the Minor Arcana queens.

querent
See client/querent.

quest

As children, mother usually was protecting, comforting, and nourishing us. Mythologist Joseph Campbell calls her the "bliss that once was known" and believes that the recovery of that feeling is at the base of our every quest[5] and is, therefore, the basis of the Fool's journey, and our own tarot journeys.

See **Fool's Journey.**

question phrasing

The most effective way to do a tarot reading is to have a question, although many readers will not require a question, allowing "the wisdom of the cards" to reveal itself. In myths and fairy tales, asking the proper question is the key to transformation; it opens the secret doors of the psyche.[6] In general, the better the question is worded, the better the information obtained from a tarot reading. Asking the right question sets up a resonance in the unconscious which facilitates arriving at an appropriate conclusion regarding the reading.[7]

"What" questions (What do I need to know about . . . ?) often lead to fruitful readings. "Should" questions (What should I do . . . , or Should I . . .") are "trap" questions, asking for the reader, or the cards, to make a decision for the client. Ethically, the job of a reader is to provide information which empowers clients and offers them some choices in making their decisions.

Quintessence

Both Indian and Western Hermetic traditions recognize five elements, associating them with the five senses. The fifth element, called Quintessence, or Ether (sometimes Spirit), is the element associated with the Major Arcana. The symbol for Quintessence is a dot, signifying zero. Hence The Fool is considered the quintessential card of the tarot deck.[8] The element of Quintessence is associated with sound and the Robin Wood Fool plays a flute.

See **music.**

quintessential card

For their final card, many tarotists add the total of the numerical value of the cards in a reading (pages equal eleven, knights equal twelve, queens equal thirteen, kings equal fourteen), and reduce the total to a number below twenty-two (if higher than ten, but twenty-two or lower, retain the higher number). An alternate numbering system suggests all court cards have a value of zero.[9]

The resulting Major Arcana card serves as the quintessence of a reading, or the quintessential message. Others regard this process as nothing more than drawing an "extra" card at the end of a reading, and have their own rules about whether or not, and how, to do this.

R

✳

rabbit/hare

The rabbit/hare was the original symbol for the zodiacal sign of
Virgo, the Virgin Goddess.[1] It is one of the animals of Freya,
Norse goddess of beauty and love. In the Celtic tradition, the
hare is the symbol of the initiate, and sometimes can be said to
represent regeneration through sacrifice. It is mythologically associated with the moon in numerous cultures. In Sanskrit, the
moon was *cacin*, "that which is marked with the Hare."[2] In alchemy the hare is the guide to the interior of the earth, and in
archetypal psychology, serves as a guide to the underworld (unconscious), its purpose in the Alchemical Fool card. The rabbit
also appears on the Alchemical Ace of Coins (in its relationship
to the earth element), the RWS Queen of Pentacles (the earth
queen), and in the Shapeshifter Tarot's "Nature" (11) card.

rainbow

Made up of the spectrum of all of the colors, there are traditionally seven colors attributed to the rainbow, although in some cultures, there are less. The seven colors correspond to, or are linked with, the seven chakras, the seven notes of the musical scale, the seven days of the week, and in Christian terminology, the seven virtues, the seven deadly sins, and the seven faculties of the soul. After the biblical flood, the rainbow was a sign of God's covenant, and a symbol of hope; hence, rainbows have come to represent promise and renewal.

Rainbows, and specifically the goddess Iris, represent joining and conciliatory actions that restore natural peace.[3] Her rainbow, as well as other mythological rainbow bridges, connected the upper and lower realms of mythological worlds, the known and the unknown, the sacred and the mundane. In some folk legends a rainbow represented the androgynous blending of opposites. The rainbow that rises from the alchemical cauldron and forms the cape of the androgynous figure in the Thoth "Art" (Temperance) card represents the spiritualization of the inner alchemical work.

A rainbow (fragile but indomitable love) connects the Robin Wood Lovers. A rainbow is common in Ten of Cups cards (Alchemical, Robin Wood, RWS, Ancestral Path, Morgan-Greer, New Palladini) where it represents fulfillment. In the Spiral deck, the rainbow on The Hierophant represents the centaur Chiron, the Rainbow Bridge between upper and lower worlds). The rainbow on the Spiral Tarot's Hanged Man card bridges the gap between two rocky cliffs representing the left and right pillars of the Tree of Life. That on the Temperance card symbolizes the connection with Iris.

The rainbow flowing into one of the New Palladini's Seven of Cups refers to "hope with rewards."[4] The Thoth Fool's relationship to both spiritual and divine realms and conscious ecstasy is reflected in the rainbow surrounding his head.[5] In the Tarot of the Spirit's Nine of Water, a rainbow pillar or bridge links the sephiroth of Kether and Tiphareth. It is the secret bridge of the knowledge of true love.[6] The nude, ethereal Haindl Hanged Man almost seems to merge with the rainbow behind and crossing him. The rainbow colors match and cross the appropriate chakra locations in the man's body. Inner awakening occurs.

The rainbow on the Tarot of the Spirit's Two of Earth ("Cause and Effect") represents continuity and the "rainbow covenant" (to know and serve truth), while that at the core of the deck's Six of Earth ("Beauty") also refers to the rainbow covenant.[7] The suit of Pentacles is replaced in the Osho deck by the Suit of Rainbows.

See **Iris** (goddess).

ram(s)

As the first sign of the zodiac, represented by the ram, a ram on a tarot card not associated with Aries may suggest an impulsive "beginning" of whatever is the greater meaning of the card. In the New Palladini Emperor card, it is the enforcer of organized structure.[8]

See **Emperor, The (IV)**.

raven

Depending on the culture, a raven has a positive image (in Africa, it is a guardian spirit) or a negative one (in India, where it brings messages of death). In ancient Greece, the raven, a solar bird sacred to Apollo, was associated with his oracle at Delphi. Likewise, in Celtic legends, ravens are birds of prophet.

Clearly, in whatever time or culture, the raven was regarded as a message bringer. Like all birds, it can represent messages from the upper or divine realms, yet as a bird with black feathers, it may represent messages from the underworld (the unconscious, the shadow). A raven also may represent the conjunction or union of the two psychological realms. In alchemical illustrations, the raven often indicated the ongoing state of putrefaction from which the royal couple (the sun/Sol, the moon/Luna) would emerge, cleansed of their blackness (shadow). As a representation of the nigredo state, a raven appears on the shoulders of the Alchemical Hermit and Death cards.

A raven brings a vision for the Wheel of Change Tarot's young Prince of Wands. The Robin Wood Emperor sits on a stone throne decorated with the ravens of the Norse Great Father Óðinn on the back and ram's heads on the arms. Folk tradition says that Britain's immortal King Arthur—shown as the Arthurian Emperor—lives on in the form of a raven.

reader

A person who "reads" or interprets tarot cards and spreads to answer questions for himself/herself, or for another.

reading frequency

Some Tarotists believe one should only do self-readings occasionally. Others advocate daily readings with one, two, or three cards to set the day's intent and focus (*see* **day cards**). Most consider that daily readings pertain only to that day.

Readings laid out to resolve a major question or issue usually require more time and consideration. The conventional understanding is that for readings involving a major issue, one should not ask about it again until the client (self or another) has followed through on at least part of the work (course of action) suggested by the initial reading.

One school of thought says that all major issues or crises, and associated readings, relate to the greater question of whether or not you are in alignment with, or on, the proper "path" for you, so that the reading may need to be dealt with on two levels: the actual crisis or issue, and the deeper question of how it fits in with the unfolding of your personal inner life (*see* **Self**). Most tarotists agree that whether or not you like the "answer" the reading gives you, or do not understand it, the same question should not be asked repeatedly. Stick with the original reading until you can understand it further.

red

The color of fire and blood, it is associated with the life force and, therefore, often symbolizes action, willpower, purpose, passion, courage, sensuality, outer worldly activity as opposed to inner, spiritual activity, might and forcefulness, and power. It is associated with the planet Mars. All these ideas are incorporated into the shades of red comprising the Thoth Emperor card.

Red also pertains to alchemical sulphur, and may symbolize an alchemist or an alchemical process depending on whether it appears as a color for clothes or for other articles. Red and white together are alchemical colors, and it is appropriate that the RWS and Morgan-Greer Magicians wear an outer robe of red over a white garment of purity.

See **colors.**

reduction

A process for selecting a Major Arcana card for special insight, meditation, connection with other cards, or to add a quintessential card to a reading. It consists of adding together a series of dates, then reducing the separate digits of the total to twenty-two (The Fool) or less, e.g., $2002 + 8 + 15 = 2025 = 2 + 0 + 2 + 5 = 9$. Depending on the card desired, the higher number is kept (for personality, year and day cards), or once again reduced to a single-digit number, as in $12 = 1 + 2 = 3$, for determining soul cards and associating higher numbered Major Arcana cards to lower numbered ones.

See **day cards; personality cards; soul cards; storytelling; year cards.**

Regardie, Francis Israel (1907–1985)

A member of the Golden Dawn after its heyday, and a one-time disciple of Aleister Crowley, Regardie angered many Golden Dawn members by publishing books exposing four volumes of the group's papers. A deck "based" on the symbolism of the Golden Dawn cards was illustrated by Robert Wang under Regardie's direction, and published in 1977. It is reputed to be the first published deck generally to conform to the specifications of the Golden Dawn's *Book 'T'—The Tarot*.

repeat readings

See **reading frequency.**

reversals

Interpreting reversed (upside down) cards is one way to modify or expand on a card's meaning. One of the conventions of working with reversals is that you decide beforehand whether or not you are going to use them. If you decide not to use them, then any reversed cards are turned upright.

Reversed cards can be understood in many ways and Mary K. Greer has written an entire book on working with and understanding reversals.[9]

The most common understanding of reversals is that they simply change the meaning (energy or intensity) of the card in some way, possibly emphasizing other aspects of the card or giving it a new twist. For many, the easiest way to interpret reversals is as the exact opposite of the upright meaning, or the negative. Another simple way to understand them is as a "red flag" that indicates a choice point or problem area to which you need to pay particular attention, perhaps something that needs to be released in order to allow you to move forward. Reversed cards may also send the message, "This is what it is not," so if you are looking for "what it is," you skip the reversed card and turn over another.[10]

A few of the many additional ideas for understanding reversals include: the card now has a weaker, reduced (less intense), or more vague meaning; the message of the card may be delayed, i.e., extended into the future; it represents an energy force or message attempting to make itself known by moving from inner to outer expression; it represents an inner attitude you don't want others to know about you; it expresses an aspect of yourself that you are ignoring, putting off dealing with, or that you may not consciously recognize (shadow aspect). It can also suggest the client not take the action suggested by the upright meaning of the card. The cards surrounding the reversed card may point toward a more specific meaning.

Some readers think it important to pay attention to the total number of reversed cards in a reading, suggesting that a preponderance of them may indicate being in a blocked or "stuck" place or that the situation or purpose is not clearly defined. When only the cards of a particular suit are reversed, it may suggest the client is confused about, or having difficulty with, that aspect of his/her life. If cards of the same number appear reversed, consult the symbolism of the number for clues about what may be troubling in the client's life.

rivers/streams

While all bodies of water share some similar symbolisms, rivers and streams as moving bodies of water suggest action, and the progression or "flow" of life. Rivers often divide the tarot landscape, separating one aspect of life from another. The river in many Six of Swords cards (RWS, New Palladini) suggests either or both of these meanings.

Some famous rivers, such as the Styx, are linked specifically with death, and this may be the river shown in many of the Death cards. Often the river includes a boat, sometimes shown guided by Charon, the Greek boatman of death who ferried souls to Hades.

By tradition all rivers in the RWS deck flow from the waters on The High Priestess card. Depending on the card, they are also sometimes identified as one of the Four Rivers of Eden, which flow to the four cardinal points of the earth. In the RWS deck, rivers appear in The Empress, The Emperor, The Chariot, Death, Judgement, the Ace and Eight of Wands, and in the Ace, Five, Ten, and Knight of Cups.

See **ocean/sea**; and specific cards in which rivers/streams appear. *also, access to the unconscious*

roadway/path (twisting)

The dipping roadway symbolizes the cyclic nature—the ups and downs—of our spiritual journey. We must make our way toward wholeness and wisdom (usually hills in the distance) without getting emotionally killed or devoured along the way; that is, while learning what we need to know in our life travels, we must not let our essential spirit get trampled or destroyed. Such a path typically appears in The Moon cards of many decks (also the Temperance card of the RWS), sometimes replaced by a winding waterway (Ancestral Path, New Palladini, Nigel Jackson, World Spirit).

rose(s)

The *quinta essentia*, the essential symbol of alchemical perfection, the rose is often associated with the pentagram because of its basic five-petal structure. The stylistic red-and-white rose was an alchemical symbol for the sacred womb and virginity; however, the slang of several languages equates the rose with female genitals and losing that virginity. Horticulturally, the rose is linked with apples, also a member of the rose family. Both were sacred to Aphrodite/Venus and to the Egyptian Isis.

Roses appear on many of the RWS cards—sometimes white, sometimes red—and for most, their original intent is long obscured. Red roses are sometimes considered a symbol of desire, and of passionate feelings (not necessarily sexual), while white roses can represent abstract thought, as well as our connection with spirit or soul. In several decks (RWS, Robin Wood, New Palladini) Death's banner bears the white Mystic Rose of life, while a large white rose simply appears in the forefront of the Morgan-Greer Death card. In some early alchemical drawings, the white rose represented the lunar "philosophical tincture," and the red rose, the solar "metallic tincture."[11]

When roses are clearly depicted as having five petals, they relate to the five senses, to sensory awareness and expression, to passion. They also connect to the inner five-pointed star of the cut apple.

In the Morgan-Greer deck, roses appear on the Four of Wands, and the Ace and Queen of Swords, where one has a pearl in its center. Red roses appear on the Empress's gown in the Spiral deck because the red rose is sacred to Venus, while they comprise her shawl in the Tarot of the Spirit's Empress. A red rosebud dominates the Haindl Sun card, and represents the "merging" of the feminine with the masculine.

See **pearl(s)**.

roses and lilies motif

Roses and lilies appear in the RWS Magician card and refer to the Rose of Sharon (*flos campi*), and the lily of the valley (*lilium convallium*), from the biblical Song of Songs 2:1, now changed into garden flowers.[12] Roses and lilies decorate the garments of the acolytes in the RWS Hierophant where they represent the occult way (red roses) and the mystic way (lilies). They may express the same pathways in the Morgan-Greer Ace of Pentacles. A rose and lily decorate the shield of the Morgan-Greer Two of Wands, suggesting choices (as in the heraldry of the RWS Two of Wands). The rose and lily motif also appears on the World Spirit Lovers card.

See **Hierophant, The (V)**.

royal orb

A round ball held by a royal figure, it is a feminine symbol of temporal power and sovereignty (note in which hand it is held). If topped with a cross, the symbolism of spiritual authority is added. When combined with the masculine scepter, it symbolizes combining the creative forces of the world,[13] the union of opposites. The RWS Empress and King of Pentacles hold such orbs. Bearing various decorations, the orb is often held, with or without the scepter, by the emperors in various tarot decks, where it represents not only human domination of the physical world, but also the soul of the world, which the emperor holds in his hand. As a circle, it is a symbol of completeness and fertility and suggests that we create our own lives.

See **circle; globe**.

ruby

The birthstone of Leo, rubies are regarded as emblems of good fortune, power (the gem of royalty), and passion, and are said to protect warriors, banish sorrow, ward off poisoning and evil, and suppress disease. Its color associates it with the planet Mars. Rubies or red gems appear on a number of tarot cards, and their placement (in a crown, at the throat, on a belt) can enhance a card's symbolism.

See **gems; red; Mars**.

runes

Runes are a secret and sacred alphabet first used by the early Northern European and Scandinavian peoples to ask for divine protection and to ward off evil. There are several runic alphabets. Ostensibly the runes were received by Óðinn when he hung upside down on the world tree Yggsdrasil. When carved or written on wood or stone, they became an early divination device. It has become fashionable to associate runes with certain tarot cards and, as yet, there are no specific rules for this association other than the intuition or inspiration of the person making the choice. Selected after the paintings were completed, runes are superimposed over the pictures of all the Haindl Major Arcana cards. Along with Hebrew letters also placed on the cards, they show, among other ideas, how the traditions of various cultures could work together. In the Robin Wood Magician card, the sword on the magician's table shows a man holding the Tyr rune, which refers to the god Tiw, known for his honor and for having the courage of his convictions.[14]

S

※

Sagittarius (astrological sign)
The ninth sign of the zodiac (November 23–December 21).

Element: Fire
Modality: Mutable
Polarity: Yang
Ruled by Jupiter.

Cards attributed to Sagittarius partake of the universal and humanitarian qualities of this fire sign. Knowledge and wisdom are the aim of the Archer's arrow. The Archer is half man, half horse (a "twin" sign like Gemini and Pisces) thus contrasting physical and intellectual qualities. The search for enlightenment leads to higher education, world travels, and a relationship with nature. Lengthy works, like books and symphonies, publishing and the judiciary are other areas ruled by Sagittarius. A well-dignified Sagittarius card may be interpreted as: optimism; belief in higher powers; luck in unusual situations; marksmanship or the ability to achieve aims; an inquisitive or expansive intellect; the search for knowledge or wanderlust for adventures; higher education; foreign countries and languages; judges, diplomats, hunters, athletes; publishing, and large-scale written works; the abstract ideas and concepts typically found in physics, philosophy, and religion. An ill-dignified or reversed Sagittarius card may mean: loss of temper or physical equilibrium, crude or coarse language, random violence, the degradation of accepted forms, excessive behaviors that are offensive to others, atheism, prejudice, or hatred.[1]

See **Jupiter** (planet).

salamander

The ancients thought the salamander, the elemental spirit of the suit of Wands, survived fire by quenching it with its frigid body. As one of the alchemical symbols for the *prima materia*, its purpose was to help the substance under transformation give up its secret fire.[2] The salamander appears in the Alchemical Tarot's Ace of Wands, and as the ouroboros (tail-eater) in the RWS Wands court cards, except the queen.

See **ouroboros.**

salt (alchemical)

Salt, as a preservative of food, has many cultural meanings and was often used in religious and purification rituals. Corresponding to the body, "alchemical salt" was the catalyst that typically worked in tandem with alchemical sulphur, the soul. It was at the center of Hermetic mysticism, as the "secret central fire," the "salt of wisdom."[3] The alchemical sigil for salt appears on the left hand side of the inner wheel of the RWS Wheel of

Fortune, to the right of the "O" on the outer circle. The posture of the Thoth Empress forms the alchemical symbol of salt.[4]

See **alchemy; crocodile; mercury; sulphur**

sarcophagus
See **coffin**.

Saturn (planet)
The sixth planet from the Sun, Saturn rules Capricorn and Aquarius.

Cards attributed to Saturn reflect this planet's structuring principle as it is applied to time, reality and manifestation. Before telescopes, Saturn was the outermost planet visible to the human eye, thus considered the lord of boundaries and limits. Saturn reflects the enforcement of worldly power, control and authority. A well-dignified Saturn card's meanings include: careful maintenance and preservation of all things material, authority in earthly matters, good management of time and resources, earthly authority, inherited qualities and family structure, discipline of talents, patience, fulfilling family obligations, conscious acceptance of appropriate limits, strong teeth and bones. An ill-dignified or reversed Saturn card may mean: rigid control; oppression; depression; sorrows; losses; bitterness; anxiety; difficult tests; illness or death; a harsh parent; ruthless domination of others; a deleterious lack of appropriate boundaries with others; chronic physical ailments, particularly arthritis, dental problems, loss of hair.[5]

See **Aquarius; Capricorn; Saturn/Cronos**.

Saturn/Cronos (Roman/Greek god)
The images of Saturn show him as Father Time, or as the Grim Reaper, equipped with a sickle. This was the weapon he used to destroy his father, Uranus (a titan). Saturn was the father of many children by Rhea, so has a patriarchal quality. But Sat-

urn needed to stay in control, and oppressed and repressed the development of his offspring, the great Olympian gods. Zeus/Jupiter eventually overthrew Saturn's control, yet Saturn remained as the grandfather of the gods and the lord of time. As a behavioral model, Saturn represents the wise old man, the person who has gained wisdom through hard experience. In parenting roles, Saturn shows how one balances the need to control children with the ability to encourage them to grow and develop over time.

See **Aquarius; Capricorn; Saturn** (planet).

scales

Scales are a symbol of authority, and serve to remind us to balance inner self-nurturance with nurturance of the outer world. Scales are engraved on the archway of the RWS Ten of Pentacles and also appear on the World Spirit's Empress card. They are typically a part of most Justice cards, and associate the card with the astrological sign of Libra.

Scorpio (astrological sign)

The eighth sign of the zodiac (October 24–November 22)

Element: Water
Modality: Fixed
Polarity: Yin
Ruled by Mars, co-ruled by Pluto

Cards attributed to Scorpio partake of the dark intensity of this sign. Scorpio has long been regarded as the sign of death and decay, but modern astrologers focus on its regenerative qualities. Scorpio rules the organs of regeneration; sexual intensity; the birth-growth-death cycle; goods of the dead; and shared resources of the spouse or partner acquired in Libra. Scorpio is possessive and cautious, and seeks knowledge of things concealed beneath surface appearances, including occult studies and medical research. A well-dignified Scorpio card may be interpreted as: tenacity, will power, understanding the deep and dark sides of life, sexual fertility, healing skills, and an unshakable determination to survive. An ill-dignified or reversed Scorpio card may mean: wrathfulness, treachery, illness and death, compelling forces of change that cannot be stopped, morbid curiosity, sexual or social deviance.

See **Mars** (planet); **Pluto** (planet).

scroll

See **book(s)**.

Self

A complicated Jungian concept closely connected with the Jungian concept of individuation, the Self is the archetype of wholeness and the regulating center of the psyche, sometimes referred to as the soul. It contains both light and shadow aspects, which do not derive from each other and which are irreducible. They co-exist and comprise a unity.[6] Values do not exist in the Self. It is paradoxical, i.e., it unites opposites or polarities without considering whether one is more valuable than the other.

The Self is unknowable except through artistic works and dream symbols. It is often experienced as a "transcendent" occurrence, after which the person feels decidedly different. Jung believed that the purpose of our lives was to shift the psychic center of gravity from the ego to the Self, i.e., to move from the mundane into the sacred domain.

The Self is often depicted in tarot cards as a wise old man with a white beard (sometimes The Emperor, frequently The Hermit), and is reflected in The Fool's journey toward greater awareness and self-realization. Other artistic renderings of the Self such as mandalas, wheels, squared circles (see **squaring the circle**), gems, certain flowers, and the mandorla wreath in the

RWS World card also serve as representations or expressions of the Self. One Jungian suggests that the light-radiating figure covered by a sheet in the RWS Seven of Cups represents the Self.[7]

See **circle with a dot within; individuation; personality** (Jungian theory).

sephiroth

Embedded, as part of the Kabbalistic Tree of Life, as disks, the sephiroth (singular, sephira) are the ten primal numbers believed to embody the various aspects of the Godhead and to form the measure of all things. They are the structure of the universe. The concepts associated with these numbers have been presented in many diverse diagrams and shapes by different occult and alchemical writers. In the traditional Tree of Life formation they are, in descending order:

1 Kether, the crown, is at the top and begins the middle pillar of the tree.
2 Chokmah, wisdom, on the right pillar of the tree, is paired with:
3 Binah understanding, on the left pillar.
4 Hesed, Mercy, on the right is paired with:
5 Geburah, severity, or judgement on the left.
6 Tiphereth, beauty, is on the center pillar.
7 Netzach, victory, on the right pillar, is paired with:
8 Hod, Glory, on the left pillar.
9 Yesod, foundation, is on the center pillar and directly below it is:
10 Malkuth, kingdom.

In the tarot, the ten Minor Arcana of each suit are associated with the ten sephiroth, from Kether for the aces through Malkuth for the tens. Their full pattern appears on the RWS Ten of Pentacles.

sevens

Seven represents a slow process of evolution and development, self-expression through progress. It is connected with the planets (the five known planets of the ancients, plus the sun and moon) and, as such, represents cosmic rhythm or cycles. Seven days in the week remind us that sevens can refer to a shorter temporal cycle. Comprised of the union of three (the number of spirit) and four (the number of matter), seven is often given sacred meaning.

Tarot sevens begin a new cycle of threes (7-8-9), a turning point. A new restlessness—possibly a breakthrough in awareness—causes us to reevaluate and willingly try new things, which may result in a changed understanding or perspective. Sevens begin a new phase of inner work and self-reflection, but their numerological order indicates that it may be a short-lived victory and one that involves challenge and a struggle. We have to prove ourselves anew. The insight that occurs with the sevens propels us right into the situation of the eights. On the Tree of Life sevens are associated with the sephira of Netzach (victory).

See sevens of each suit.

shadow

A Jungian concept that refers to dark aspects of ourselves that we don't recognize and haven't accepted or integrated as being some part of ourselves. As we grow and our personalities develop, the shadow develops side-by-side with the ego; it is part of the maturation process. Aspects of ourselves that adults teach us are inappropriate or not to be expressed are disavowed and move from ego to shadow. Shadow is understood as being both personal (pertaining to an individual) and collective (pertaining to a nation or culture). One of its values is that those aspects of ourselves which we have learned to neglect or suppress also make it possible for us to cultivate their opposite strengths and virtues.[8]

Every person's psyche is motivated toward wholeness or integration. This can only happen when shadow aspects of our personality are once again recognized and accepted as equally important parts of all our developmental experiences. In fairy tales this is most often expressed when "ugly" or misshapen characters (guess who?) turn out, in the end, to have been transformed princes or princesses, who can only become their true selves after someone loves them.

Often our first recognition of the shadow, if we are an observant adult, occurs in seeing the qualities that we dislike most about ourselves being expressed in someone else. We don't recognize them as an aspect of ourselves, rather our experience is usually one of not being able to tolerate some aspect of that "different" or "difficult" person (*see* **projection**).

Each archetype—and, therefore, each Major Arcana card—also has its shadow aspect. Some Major Arcana seem to be related simply to the expression of shadow (The Devil and The Moon are commonly accepted ones). Others seem more related to calling upon us to integrate our shadow aspects, e.g., Strength and Judgement.[9] A dark figure emerges from the Haindl Magician's crown, suggesting the Magician has not integrated his own shadow emotions.[10]

There are several ways to identify one's shadow aspects using the tarot. One tarotist defines shadow as a person's unresolved inner conflicts and unexpressed emotions, gives guidelines for working with these, and identifies the shadow and "shadow gifts" of each of the Major Arcana.[11] Another tarot expert connects or "constellates" the cards to create combinations that include a Major Arcana (personality card) and a hidden factor (personal shadow) card.[12]

When shadow aspects are released (expressed alchemically as transforming lead to gold), energy that was used to keep them hidden from the ego often provides or supports a great burst of creative energy.

See **archetypes**.

shell

Scallop shells relate to the scallop shells carried for "good luck" by medieval pilgrims. The one predominant on the Morgan-Greer Queen of Cups and that held by the Thoth Princess of Cups (the "Queen of the Thrones of Water") likely relate to their suits' water element.

shield

See **eagle**.

ship(s)

Traditionally ships are considered feminine (we refer to ships as "she"). They are vessels that sail above the waters of the emotions (the unconscious), but are also partly in the unconscious.

Ships can represent commerce and the diffusion or introduction of cultural information. A ship can suggest that awareness may come through attending to other cultural values or practices, such as the man watching ships in the RWS Three of Wands.

See **boat(s)**.

shirt

In fairy tales, a shirt, because it is worn between outer clothes and the bare skin, represents an intimate attitude that is not quite yet the naked truth. Therefore, we also have to look at the color and design of the shirt for further understanding.

significator

Sometimes called the client's card, it is a card chosen to represent the client in a reading. One of the most common ways to select a significator is to allow the client to choose one that seems to favor the client in personal characteristics (blonde/dark, blue eyes/brown eyes, older/younger, male/female).

Another method is to assign categories to the court cards. Kings represent married men/older men (married or unmarried)/

widowers. Queens represent the same category for women. Pages are unmarried men/women learning their skills (new in a job, still in school); knights represent unmarried men/women who have completed their skills/job/educational training.

A third method involves drawing the first card in a reading and designating it as the client or significator card, representing the client at the time of the reading. Interpret it as you would any other card in the spread.

Many tarotists think that choosing a significator means one less card available to appear in the reading.

sixes

Six is an important number in ceremonial magic. It is presented geometrically by the six-pointed star—the Hindu Sign of Vishnu and the Hebrew Star of David—which shines from the Hermit's lantern in several decks. Psychologically six can be considered a symbol of the Self in that it is related to the geometry of the circle: the circumference of a circle contains 6×60 degrees, each containing sixty minutes of sixty seconds each.[13] Six also refers to spirit's connection to life in all directions (north, south, west, east, above, and below).[14]

Tarot sixes represent the end or completion of a second cycle of threes (4-5-6) and offer clues as to how we have integrated a new understanding that results from the crises or revolutions of the fives. They reflect the coping skills, abilities, and success achieved, challenges overcome, and the resulting stability, comfort, or respite. A temporary, but very satisfying, state of balance has been achieved, which serves as a base and a pivot for new experiences.

There are frequently at least two figures in the Minor Arcana "six" cards raising the question of reciprocity. How or what is the exchange of energy between the figures?[15] Sixes are associated with the sephira of Tiphereth (beauty) on the Tree of Life.

See **wreath, flowered**; sixes of each suit.

skeleton

See **Death (XIII).**

Smith, Pamela Colman (1878–1951)

Called Pixie by her friends, Corinne Pamela Colman Smith, an artist and theatrical set designer, created the artwork for Arthur Waite's Rider-Waite deck (Rider and Son was the first publisher). Like Waite, she was a member of the Hermetic Order of the Golden Dawn, and followed him when he left to create his own splinter group. Receiving only a token payment for her tarot artwork, she died penniless, her other artistic contributions being only occasionally accepted by the public. As her contribution to Waite's deck becomes more recognized and appreciated, the deck is beginning to be popularly referred to as the Rider-Waite-Smith (RWS) deck.[16]

smoke

A combination of the elemental principles of air and fire, it blends the principles of spirit and matter, the relationship between heaven and earth. In the RWS deck, smoke appears on only one card, the Seven of Swords, and is a tiny puff in the background of this stage card (*see* **stage cards**), suggesting that there is more that is going on in this card than is obvious. "Look behind the scenes" when you draw this card.

snail

Appearing mostly at night, snails are a lunar symbol, therefore a symbol of feminine energy and the cycle of death/rebirth, ending/beginning, continuity, and fertility. Because of its shell, it is linked to the symbolism of the spiral and to self-sufficiency. A snail appears on the RWS and Spiral Tarot's Nine of Pentacles, reminding us of the cyclic nature of this success. On the Light and Shadow Hermit card, the snail represents slow and steady progress made in the journey "home" (toward enlightenment).[17]

See **Pentacles, Nine of.**

snake(s)

Because of the ability to periodically sheds its skin, the snake became a symbol of enlightenment, transformation, and rebirth or rejuvenation. Regenerating snakes appear in the cups of the Thoth Six of Cups. The tail of the lion on the Thoth "Lust" (Strength) card is a snake, related to the lion serpent Abraxas. It represents the masculine and feminine impulses, and inner polarities of the will to live (Eros) and the will to die (Thanatos).[18] Abraxas appears again on the Thoth Tower card.

Intertwining snakes represent the Hindu serpent goddess Kundalini, the evolutionary life force within each of us. As she "dances" her way along the spine, ascending through each chakra, she awakens the Ida (feminine) and Pingula (masculine) energies. The kundalini "snake of redemption" is nailed around the head of the Thoth Hierophant[19] (*see* **chakra(s)**).

A snake twines up the Tree of the Knowledge of Good and Evil in the RWS Lovers card (linking it with the Adam and Eve story), while twining snakes appear on the RWS Two of Pentacles. A snake coils around the scepter held by the Haindl Empress. Together the scepter and the sinuous, curved snake symbolize the masculine and feminine principles.[20] A snake representing Typhon, one of the Greek gods of destruction, descends the RWS Wheel of Fortune, while two snakes (symbolizing action and reaction) appear on either side of the Alchemical Tarot's Wheel of Fortune. The snake on the Haindl Wheel card represents deeper truth within. Snakes representing the flow of psychic energy reside in one of the fantasy cups in the RWS and Morgan-Greer Seven of Cups. A snake, symbolizing the goddess, spirals up the leg of the Wheel of Change Tarot's Strength card.

The snake "serpent" on the Thoth Death card symbolizes immortality. The entire illustration of the Haindl Strength card is based on the attribution of the Hebrew letter Teth, which means snake. A nude woman (Shakti, female creative energy), kneeling in ceremony under a waxing moon, holds a snake. Spiraling around her, it connects upper and lower regions, the conscious and the unconscious. The woman's control of the long snake shows that part of her strength lies in the ability to activate and control kundalini energy.[21]

See **caduceus.**

snippage

The bits and pieces of card stock left on the table after a commercial deck has been "corrected."

See **corrected deck.**

soul cards

A process created by Angeles Arrien and made popular by Mary K. Greer, it consists of first determining your Major Arcana personality card (by adding the month and date of your birth to the year of your birth), and reducing the separate digits to the higher of two numbers between two and twenty-two (The Fool). Then reduce the higher double-digit number to a single-digit number, e.g. August 19, 2002 = $2002 + 8 + 19 = 13 = 1 + 3 = 4$, The Empress. Soul cards portray inner qualities we must express and use to feel fulfilled in our daily activities and life purpose.[22] Pay particular attention to a soul card when it appears in a reading as it may denote an important development.

See **personality cards; year cards.**

sphinx

The most well-known sphinx, that on the Giza plateau in Egypt, symbolizes the invincibility of man, although its human face is believed to be that of the ruler Kephren. In Greek mythology, the female sphinx of Thebes devoured those who could not answer her riddle, until Oedipus was successful. The sphinx is the guardian and holder of secrets. Not only does she symbolize the riddle of human existence on the RWS Wheel of Fortune card, but being blue, the color of the goddess, she is linked to The High Priestess. Light or dark sphinxes appear individually on other Wheel of Fortune cards (Light and Shadow, Spiral, Thoth, Aquarian), and as light and dark pairs on the Chariot cards of many decks (horses on the Morgan-Greer), where they represent the pull or tension of opposites. If the pair is not black and white, they often face different directions to express the same concept of duality and its contradictions.

spider

The spider, spinning its web, is associated with the Three Fates who spun the web of life. It can also represent the devouring aspect of the Great Mother Goddess, yet in Hindu mythology the spider represented Maya, a virgin aspect of the Great Goddess and, likewise, a spinner of magic and fate. Spider-woman, Life Weaver of Pueblo legend, is the Daughters of the Moon equivalent to the Wheel of Fortune, and is portrayed in all three goddess aspects. A spider in its web looms large in the tenth Wind Song (Songs for the Journey Home). It addresses the issue of relationships in which we may have become entangled, and the type of fixation that draws us into seduction.

See **Pentacles, Eight of**.

spider's web

Can symbolize the pattern of life and its fragile qualities (fate), but it also can symbolize a "web of illusion" and the possibility of entrapment therein.

A spider-woman lies, with quiet awareness, in a web woven like an eight-pointed star in the Shapeshifter Star card. She represents the gateway between the manifested and unmanifested and knows that silence points to this cosmic mystery (*see* **dragons(s)**).

The spider web above Wheel of Change Tarot's High Priestess suggests the overshadowing influence of Athena, goddess of wisdom and ancient knowledge.[23] The eight webs in the deck's complex Eight of Disks represent the manifest world, strong connections or networks, traps we fall into. It asks you to follow the threads, webs, and patterns of your life.[24]

spinning

See **weaver/weaving**.

spiral

The very shape of the spiral conveys the motion of the ever-widening and expansively complex life process. Every form of energy in the Thoth Star card is represented as a spiral, except one, which sends the message that the illusion of straightness blinds us to the wonder of the universe.[25]

The flat spiral corresponds to the maze and may represent the one-way process of evolution from the center, or the involution of returning to the point of beginning (center). The double or helical spiral symbolizes the same movement simultaneously, the polarity and balance of the two cosmic polarities.[26] It can be found in the caduceus of the RWS Two of Cups, the DNA spiral on the Robin Wood Ace of Wands, and the unicorn's horn on the Haindl Moon card. The spiral is an integral part of the Wheel of Change Tarot's Star card and of the Robin Wood Tower card. The World figure in the Light and Shadow deck sits on a spiral, symbolizing the universe and endlessness. Red and green spirals representing the as-yet-undivided basic patterns of light and dark, yin and yang, intellect and emotion swirl on either side of the magician's table in the Tarot of the Spirit Magus card and also represent his powers to divide the world into component parts.[27]

square

Like all geometric figures, the square is an attempt to bring order into chaos. One of the four basic symbols (along with the center, circle, and cross), it expresses the symbolism of the earth (the four cardinal points) and materialism. It represents temporality, whereas the circle represents eternity.[28] Squares on the jacket of the Haindl Fool's costume symbolize the jester's function of providing social direction and the truths of reality to society's rulers. In the Thoth Nine of Cups, the overflowing, lavender chalices are arranged in a square, to represent the "complete and most beneficent aspect of the force of water."[29]

See **fours.**

squaring the circle

Squaring of the circle, or a circle shown within a square (*see* **mandala**), is a Freemasonry concept,[30] as well as an important Jungian idea. It represents unity within the quartenary of elements, a balanced fourness. It unites sacred and profane, heaven and earth, the eternal with the now,[31] and is one representation of the Self. All these principles are expressed in the broach worn by Justice (RWS, Morgan-Greer).

staff

Staffs typically symbolize support for a journey, but appearing as it frequently does in The Hermit card, it is also related to all the magic wands of mythology (as in Merlin's wand), to the healing staff of Asclepias (in this card referring to spiritual healing), and to the powerful wand of Moses. It implies that the Hermit has acquired special knowledge and training (as in The Pope's scepter). It is an emblem of his high ability and spiritual clarity, and an indirect, albeit modest, statement of his power.

See **Hermit, The (IX); royal orb; wand(s).**

stage cards

Inspired by the fact that RWS artist Pamela Colman Smith was experienced in theater and costume design, Wald Amberstone and Ruth Ann Brauser Amberstone, directors of The Tarot School (New York), noticed that the RWS deck contains a number of scenes where the figures stand on a smooth, flat surface in the foreground, separated from the background with a dividing line. Suggesting that the figures can be perceived as standing on a "stage," with the scenery presented on a painted backdrop, they developed several possible ways of interpreting these cards. One is to consider that what appears to be going on may be an illusion or a fiction, in which case you need to consider what might be going on "behind the scenes."

A second possibility is that by their intention, the people in the card are projecting the image on the backdrop "skrim." They envision the scene, and manifest it through their will and focused attention. Yet a third possibility is that what is seen in the card is something the querent is projecting onto his/her situation.[32] The RWS stage cards include: the Two, Five, Eight, Ten, and Page of Cups; the Two, Five, and Seven of Swords; the Two, Four, Six, and Eight of Pentacles and, finally, the Four, Nine, and Ten of Wands.

Referring to the same artistic depiction, Isabel Kliegman calls the cards "separation cards." She suggests they refer to a sense of existential isolation, a separation of feeling, or a distancing, from the existing world that is part of the deep truth or need(s) for the figure(s) on the card.[33]

Star, The (XVII)

The figure in most Star cards is a nude female pouring water from two (sometimes one) containers into a pond, although in the Alchemical Tarot's card, she is the fountain of life. Blood and milk pour from her breasts. Typically, however, the "star lady" kneels, with one foot on land and one foot on, or in, the water. She thus establishes her rule and authority over the material and the spiritual plane—or in psychological terms, over the conscious and the unconscious. She is the worldly realization or manifestation of the principles of the Temperance angel. She freely pours the "waters of life" and the "gifts of the spirit."[34]

The eight-pointed star above the RWS female links the card to the eight spokes in the Wheel of Fortune card, and to the star in the crown of the charioteer in The Chariot card. Stirred into vibration by meditation, the pool is that of the collective unconscious filled with archetypal knowledge. Supporting herself on the earth with her left knee, the figure's right foot rests on the surface of the water. She helps support herself by receiving impressions (ripples) from the unconscious.

The RWS figure kneels beneath one large eight-pointed star (a double star in the Marseilles and Haindl cards) and seven smaller ones, possibly representing the seven stars/planets referred to in Revelation 1:16–20, 2:1, and 3:1 and, therefore, the star or birth planet unique to each of us.[35] Some connect the seven stars to the seven Greek sister/nymphs, the Pleiades (*see* **Pleiades/ Pleiads**).

In the Haindl card, Gaia, the first Greek divinity and mother of life and of Uranus, the sky, washes her hair in a stream in an "act of unity with the Earth."[36] On the Alchemical card she is Sophia/Aphrodite. Rising from the sea as a messenger from the unconscious, she spreads her two mermaid tails on either side of her.

Only one star shines in the Shining Tribe card, where Persephone pours water into two cracks in the earth, referring directly to the final celebratory act of the Greater Mysteries of Eleusis, which honored Persephone. Her brightly colored Greek clothing bears a Tree of Life design. She is the High Priestess unmasked, her clothing indicating her responsibility to share her wisdom.[37]

The central star has been identified by some tarotists as the North Star—long considered symbolically to be the center of the universe—but also identified by others as the Morning Star,[38] the light of the planet Venus. A symbol of the life principle, it is the last star seen in the morning, and the first and brightest evening star, where it represents descent into the underworld.[39] Both ideas link the card to the mythology of the Sumerian mother goddess Innana, later identified with the Babylonian goddess Ishtar (*see* **star, eight-pointed**), associated with the planet

Venus. Ishtar was a double-sided goddess, possessing both compassionate mother attributes, and those of lust and war. Others connect the card to the goddess Astraea (meaning "starlike"), who later became the constellation of Virgo (see **Astraea**).[40]

The female on the Golden Dawn card represents a synthesis of Isis, Nephthys, and Hathor. A large star in the sky, surrounded by seven smaller stars, representing the stars of the then-known planets, has seven principal and fourteen secondary rays, and represents Sirius, the dog star, and an attribute of Isis-Sothis. In addition, there is an eight-pointed star above her.

On the Spiral card, the vessels of Isis, great mother of Egypt, contain the jeweled "waters" of renewal, gifts to revive shattered dreams. Above her hovers a phoenix, symbolic of available hope. In the sky are the stars of the Pleiades. Lotuses bud and bloom in the pond at her feet (see **lotus blossom(s)**).

The scarlet ibis on the bush behind the RWS female is sacred to Thoth, Egyptian god of wisdom, and to Hermes/Mercury— thereby linking the card to The Magician and to Isis. At the Egyptian temple of Philae, now preserved on an island in the Nile, Isis, goddess of the Nile, is shown pouring out the saving Nile waters onto the parched earth.[41]

The Wheel of Change Tarot's blue goddess represents the virgin aspects of the Triple Goddesses Artemis, Athena, and Blodeuwedd. She nurtures herself by standing in the center of a spiral galaxy created as she pours stars from a crescent-shaped cup in her left hand. Her right hand pours fiery energy from the sun's spiral into her heart (see **spiral**).

As an eight (17 = 1 + 7 = 8), The Star is linked with Strength in the RWS deck, reflecting the strength that occurs with spiritual regeneration. As the sign of infinity, eight also links The Star to The Magician. We have worked our inner magic and come through our inner trials with a new sense of confidence based on a trust in inner guidance or awareness of higher spiritual centers. The Osho "Silence" card shows a face deep in meditation in a star-filled sky. It is time to come home to yourself.[42]

The water in the silver bowl in the right hand of the Robin Wood figure reflects the hidden spiritual world. The clear crystal bowl in her left hand indicates that she sees the physical world with clear sight. Fitted together, the hemispherical bowls form the "sphere of all that is."[43]

As in the RWS card, the water she pours on the earth forms five rivulets, for our five senses, which are nourished by meditation. One of the streams runs back into the pool, symbolizing the connection between the information we take in with our senses and the processing of it in the unconscious.

On the Mythic Tarot's card, Pandora opens the chest of worldly afflictions. The Spites, portrayed as insects, fly into the world. Fortunately Hope, who had somehow also gotten locked into the chest, does not fly away, but hovers over the scene and over us all.

The Star card represents the beginning of an initiation—the unmasked truth—that will continue in the next four cards (The Moon, The Sun, Judgement, and The World). We have the beginning of a vision that has yet to be fully realized. We are being urged to "follow our own star," to trust in our own inner light.

Keywords/phrases: attending to or balancing inner and outer awarenesses; regeneration and renewal through meditation; allowing Universal wisdom, guidance, or cosmic energies to flow through one; truth unmasked; realization of spiritual hopes or dreams; renewal of life forces or energy; new threshold of consciousness.

star(s)

Typically a symbol of light and of awareness and luminosity, stars also may be associated with personal "shining." Rarely having one meaning or appearing alone, their meaning is modified by the number of points, where they appear, how many there are, and other characteristics, such as shining or sending out rays.

star, eight-pointed

The sacred emblem of Ishtar, Great Mother Goddess of Babylonia and Assyria, and Innana, the Sumerian cosmic mother. Ishtar's myth is a predecessor to that of Demeter and Persephone. While she rescued her lover Dumuzi/Tammuz from the underworld, nothing grew above.[44] The myth, in whatever form, alludes to that time of inner "seasoning" from which we emerge fresh and creative. Also linked to Venus, Ishtar became so identified, and confused, with other female goddesses that eventually her name became simply a generic term for "goddess."[45] Eight-pointed stars appear in many Star cards and on the crown of the RWS charioteer.

star, five-pointed

One meaning of the five-pointed star, dating from Egyptian hieroglyphs, was that it indicated "rising upward toward the point of origin."[46] The blazing five-pointed star of Freemasonry represents the mystic center. Five-pointed stars within a circle or disk are called pentacles in the tarot.

See fives.

star, seven-pointed

The seven-pointed star brings in all the symbolism of seven. Geometrically comprised of a square and a triangle, it represents cosmic and personal wholeness.[47] In the Thoth Star card, it is used once to represent Venus (love), and again to represent the Star of Babylon, both symbols of renewal and highest inspiration.[48]

star, six-pointed

Called the Star of David or the Seal of Solomon, it is comprised of interlaced equilateral triangles, one with its point facing upward, one inverted. It represents the harmonic rhythm of ac-

tive and passive, masculine and feminine, spirit and earthly principles. In Tantric doctrine, the two triangles represent the
interpenetration of Shiva and Shakti. The upward pointing triangle represents Shiva, the static aspects of the supreme reality.
The downward-pointing triangle represents Shakti, the kinetic
energy of the objective universe.[49] As a hexagram, the six-pointed
star can represent dominion over the laws of the greater world,
the macrocosm.[50] A six-pointed star shines from the lantern of
many Hermit cards, and twelve small ones adorn the crown of
the RWS Empress.

stone wall

Depending on where a figure is placed in proximity to the
stone wall, it can be that it protects the "back" of the figure, that
it "walls off" the figure from something, or that it makes only
forward movement possible (as in the RWS Sun card).

Stone walls can represent the "human adaptation of natural
conditions,"[51] e.g., changing stone into something needed in the
human world.

In the Golden Dawn Sun card, three children stand before a
circular stone wall of five levels, representing the five senses. In
its entirety the wall represents the circle of the zodiac, and the
stones, its various degrees and divisions.[52] One "unofficial"
Golden Dawn document suggests the wall exists to protect the
"pilgrim" so he can present himself humbly and without fear to
the "searching Light."[53] The stone wall in the Thoth Sun card
tells us that aspiration also involves self-control.[54]

storytelling

As a vehicle for symbols, storytelling may work in ways similar to rituals, bringing order into chaos, and allowing the teller
or the listener to connect at a visceral level with archetypal messages. A common tarot game is to have persons draw cards and,
in turn, tell a continuing story suggested by the cards.

Stories or myths connected with tarot cards can enhance a

given person's connection with the greater universe, within and without. Telling the "story" of a card can also clarify or deepen its personal meaning (*see* **amplifying**).

We can also tell some aspect of our life pattern by deliberately selecting cards to symbolize or represent certain life experiences. Tarotist Nina Lee Braden has created a number of exercises that help accomplish this.[55] Tarotist Diane Wilkes suggests integrating storytelling techniques (eye contact, empathic approach, finding a common ground, setting the stage, appealing to all the senses) into her readings. She perceives tarot cards as metaphors for life that help the client see his/her own life story in a new context. Each reading literally illustrates a subplot of the querent's journey, providing ways for the individual to plot his or her life in a desired direction.[56]

Strength (VIII)

Although in older decks (and some contemporary and European decks), tradition specified the eighth Major Arcana in the Trumps' sequence as Justice, with Strength as the eleventh card, in RWS-style decks, Strength is the eighth card. The switch apparently occurred with the Golden Dawn deck, and was followed by Waite. It is not clear why. Some suggest a major reason was to make certain Hebrew letters and their zodiacal equivalents match the symbolic images on the cards e.g., the obvious astrological association of Strength with Leo (Hebrew letter Teth) and Libra with Justice (Hebrew letter Lamed).

The RWS card depicts the fiery life-force (the lion) or energy that is at the basis of all our actions. A maiden closes the lion's mouth. The card illustrates the power of the female principle.

Above the RWS maiden's head floats the lemniscate linking her with The Magician's qualities and magic skills. She is his feminine aspect, although in the Haindl card, she is considered the *source* of his power, the life energy of the universe.

As the maiden, the woman is also connected with The High Priestess and The Empress. She is the young Empress practicing her skills. She is a cousin to The High Priestess (in some decks she wears the colors of The High Priestess) come out of her temple into the discipleship of nature, represented by the crown or wreath of flowers around her head. She is power passing into action,[57] the strength to take control of one's life.

The woman is sometimes described as opening—and more often as closing—the lion's mouth; however, the card does not refer to strength in subjugation. The higher self, represented by the maiden, pets him with her left hand and places her right hand in a vulnerable spot near the lion's mouth, the instinctual aspect of human nature.

The strength depicted here is one of trust and love. In return, the maiden's instinctual self opens up to her with a lick rather than an attack.

The card also is another representation of balancing opposites, in this case the masculine-feminine resolution (logic vs. *eros* or love. Inner strength lies in the acknowledgment of both our mental, spiritual, and physical aspects, not in competition between them, or repression of one. They are not rivals; they are partners. Our objective (conscious) and subjective (unconscious) aspects are in balance, or we are working to achieve that balance.

This strong love/acceptance relationship is apparent in the Robin Wood card where the smiling maiden appears to be almost leaning against the giant lion and has placed in his mane some of the flowers she has gathered. It is a card of moral strength, and of spiritual power, energy, and conviction—the kind of strength that is infinite.[58]

Strength, power, and control are all intertwined. The Strength card suggests that spirituality (as symbolized by the lemniscate) must always be a part of those situations. They cannot be properly utilized without it, and are more likely to be misused if it is missing.

The young African woman in the Wheel of Change Strength card rides a lioness. The two figures are so in harmony that the woman sits astride the lion, not needing reins. It is a card of women's journeys of attempting the new and difficult with passion, and with the strength within to achieve those goals.

The Mythic Tarot depicts Heracles in the first of his Twelve Labors for King Eurystheus, that of slaying the lion of Nemea and acquiring his magical pelt, which rendered the wearer invincible. When we wear the skin of our conquered impulses, especially anger, we are armored with vital power and an indestructible sense of identity.[59]

The Thoth "Lust" card (the eleventh trump) refers to "joy of strength exercised."[60] A nude woman with flowing hair (sexual ecstasy; love of life) sits astride a seven-headed lion (instinct). The card refers to the passionate and lascivious side of our lives, the "divine drunkenness . . . completely independent of the criticism of reason."[61]

On The Alchemical Tarot (also the eleventh trump) the virgin aspect of Fortuna rides a tamed lion. She carries a flaming heart-shaped vessel into which the sun and the moon pour masculine and feminine alchemical fluids to ferment and bring matter to a higher form.[62]

Keywords/phrases: balance and integration between instinct and passion, and intellect; mastery, especially self-mastery; time to use gentle force; spiritual power over material; inner fortitude, strength, and courage.

suit cards
See **Minor Arcana**.

sulphur (alchemical)
One of the "philosophical" elements of alchemy, it represented the "fiery" or volatile, masculine principle (sometimes called Sol-Sulphur), the opposite of its feminine counterpart, mercury (Luna-Mercurius). In alchemical art, the two were sometimes personified as a couple being led by a cherub into the labyrinth of transformation.[63] Their sexual liaison produced cinnabar or red sulphide, considered the medicine of immortality in ancient

times.[64] The symbol for sulphur appears on the RWS Wheel of Fortune card (*see* **Wheel of Fortune (X)** for location). The Thoth Emperor sits with his arms and legs in a position that forms the symbol for sulphur. In the RWS Strength card, the lion may represent the "red king" or alchemical sulphur.

See **alchemy; mercury; salt**.

sun (mythologies)

The sun has always been a predominant symbol of strength and energy. It brings light and, therefore, symbolizes consciousness and enlightenment. In many cultures, the sun was either the singlemost supreme deity or, if not, then certainly one of utmost importance, and was often the ancient symbol of kingship.

Some deities associated with the sun include: the Titan Hyperion, Helius (early Greek), and the more sophisticated Phoebus Apollo (later Greek). These were life-giving deities, intricately involved in the journey of the sun through its daily course across the sky. Others include Sol (Roman), Marduk (Babylonian), Mithra (early Persian), the archangel Michael (Christian). The Egyptians had three sun gods over a 2,000 year period: Osiris, Horus, and Amen-Ra. They equated the sun's journey through day and night as equivalent to man's journey through life and the afterlife. The rising sun was Horus; Ra, the noon sun; and Osiris, the setting sun.[65]

In several cultures distant from one another, the sun is considered the eye of the sky god.[66] For Greeks, it was the eye of Zeus; for Scandinavians, the eye of Óðinn/Woden. In the Islamic faith, it is the eye of Allah. The oriental mystics regarded the Sun as the source of *prana*, or *chi*.

On the other hand, the southeastern Yuchi Indians, the Eskimo, the Cherokee, and some Nordic peoples regard the sun as female. In such cases, however, the goddess's attributes are "masculine" in the sense of being dynamic rather than passive. For instance, the Egyptian solar goddess Sekhmet, daughter of the sun god Ra, was portrayed with a lion's head crowned by the disc of the sun, and was a deity of battle and bloodshed.[67] In Iceland, Freya, the goddess of sunlight, must do battle with the strong forces of winter, ultimately being temporarily overwhelmed by them. As a behavioral model, the sun archetype is best shown in the proud, sometimes disdainful Apollo (*see* **Apollo**).

The sun's masculine energy, or yang, is the counterpart of the moon's feminine, yin energy. In the tarot The Sun and The Moon cards are often seen as pertaining to the light (conscious) and shadow (unconscious) in our lives.

The meaning of various suns depicted in tarot cards may be changed by their color or by the shape and number of "energy" rays that radiate from them.

See **Leo; Sun** (planet).

Sun (planet)

The central star of our planetary system, it rules Leo. A card attributed to the sun partakes of its powerful life force, radiance, and heat. The sun is a symbol of the personality traits of the current incarnation (the sun takes 364 days to travel through the entire zodiac, spending about thirty days in each zodiac sign). The sun represents the divine potential within the individual, the highest possibilities for achievement, fame and glory. A well-dignified sun card may be interpreted as: energy, vitality, optimism and self confidence, distinct and authentic individual qualities, the drive to achieve a purpose joyfully, illumination, honor, recognition, fame and glory. An ill-dignified or reversed sun card's meanings include: despotic control, excess heat, fevers, a weak physical constitution, uncontrolled temper, brutality, weak will or perverse obstinacy clearly against one's best interests, dishonor, exile, prodigality, hubris, possible heart or circulatory problems, public notoriety for cruelty or anti-social achievements.[68]

See **circle with a dot within; Leo.**

Sun, The (XIX)

Mythologically, The Sun card is linked to the sun gods of any culture, all of whom symbolized the rising spirit, the generative principle, "in-*light*-enment," higher truths or the "true light," the mystery of divine energy, and at the same time one-half of a cycle—night and day, death and rebirth (*see* **Sun** (mythologies)). Mithras (Persia/India/Rome), the Greek gods Helios (representing the sun in its daily and yearly course), and the Olympian sun god Apollo/Phoebus (shown as the central figure on the Mythic Tarot's card), are all well-known sun gods.

Apollo, the enemy of darkness, appears in one corner of the Renaissance Tarot's Sun card, while his dolphin shape appears in another (*see* **Apollo**). The Spiral Tarot depicts beautiful Eos/Aurora, goddess of a bright and beautiful peach and magenta dawn, preceding the horse-drawn chariot of Helios.

Historic solar symbols include the disc, which sometimes has wings, the swirling swastika, and the spoked or revolving wheel, which links The Sun card to the Wheel of Fortune (X). When the halo or nimbus, also a symbol of solar radiance, is extended around the entire body, it becomes a mandorla, the union of opposites.[69] We see this fully developed in The World card (*see* **mandorla**).

In the tarot, The Sun principle, concept, or mythology embodies both the Divine Child and the mythic hero. Together they represent all that we have yet to become, potentialities that will be shaped and "crystallized" by our experiences and the understandings we acquire in response to them.[70]

In the RWS card, the child (our psyche's urge to realize itself) rides bareback (*see* **horse**) with outstretched arms, using no reins. The scene symbolizes the perfect balance between conscious and unconscious. Consciousness has no need to control unconscious forces and instincts (the horse) because they trust one another and can work together to bring information, knowledge, and insight "into the light." The child's red banner, which he holds lightly and easily (no burden), suggests unfurling energy—action and "vibration."[71]

Clearly this is a divine child, a son/sun child. Simultaneously it represents the inherent divinity and unity in us all, the distillation and combination of all our preceding consciousness, out of which we can make a new form.[72] The child archetype as the "personification of vital forces outside the limited range of our conscious mind" embodies "possibilities of which our one-sided conscious mind knows nothing."[73] In Jungian terms, the child in the card may also represent the eternal child archetype, a composite of opposites that constitutes wholeness—wonderful combination of the simple and the complex, of "consciousness in spirit," of "innocence in the sense of wisdom."[74]

The RWS sun child wears a wreath and the red feather we first saw in The Fool card in this deck. The wreath, now of flowers instead of the leaves The Fool wore, intimates the near approach to the harvest of final realization and liberation.[75] The six flowers may be related to the sixth sephira on the Kabbalistic Tree of Life, which corresponds to the sun.[76] In alchemical analogy, the nude child represents the alchemist who has been reborn as a spiritual child. The remainder of the alchemist's work is "mere child's play." The *prima materia* has been turned into the gold of the sun. The only step remaining is to turn the gold into the ultimate result, the philosopher's stone.[77] Indeed, the Tarot of the Spirit calls The Sun card one of spiritual realization, of having come through deep darkness. "All things are illuminated and show themselves truly."[78]

RWS child and horse sit in front of a gray stone wall—only forward movement is possible. The child, having come out of the walled garden of the sensitive life, is on his way "home."[79]

Although traditionally thought of as a male child, the sex of the RWS child cannot accurately be determined from the illustration; therefore, it bears a characteristic often attributed to The World card, that of androgyny. A huge anthropomorphic sun (solar intelligence) with alternating straight and wavy rays dominates the card. They may indicate direct and indirect, radiating and vibrating, positive and negative influences. Traditionally, the four sunflowers represent the four Kabbalistic worlds and the four kingdoms of nature, that is mineral, vegetable, animal, and human.[80] Together the stone wall and the sunflowers symbolize the human and the natural world.

The young boy on the Robin Wood card, representing untroubled innocence and pure spirit, rides bareback to show mastery of the bright, daytime forces. Sunflowers pointing toward the child show that he shines brighter than the sun.[81] In the World Spirit's Sun card, a nude child sits in the center of a lotus, arms upraised to the sun. He *is* the "sunflower." In the New Palladini card, a personified sun sends its beams throughout the universe, as drops (some resembling yods) fall on the blooming lotus below (*see* **lotus; yod(s)**).

Earlier cards often showed two children; hence, The Sun of the Marseilles deck looks down on two children within a walled garden, the wall of which shows five levels, similar to that found in the early Golden Dawn Sun card (*see* **stone wall**). Being the same color as the sun in the picture, it may be that it reflects the sun's strength and protective powers.[82]

Twin fairy children (*see* **twin motif**) with wings dance beneath a sun whose spiraling rays create and separate the twelve signs of the zodiac on the Thoth card. Their dance represents awakening energy and bliss as we strive for fusion with the divine.[83] In the Nigel Jackson card, a nude male and female, poised in the Garden of the Sun, raise their arms to the sun, as they kneel before a flaming altar, carved with rams' heads. Two nude boys, the twins of the Great Goddess, hold hands in the Wheel of Change's Sun card. Above them the sphere of the sun creates the twelve colors of the zodiac, which is duplicated beneath their feet (what is created above, is created below). This is a cosmic card of macrocosm and microcosm.

While most of the cards show a smiling sun either alone in

the scene or above one or more persons, on the complex and beautiful Haindl card a labyrinthine sun shines a huge red rosebud. The rose, placed before a tree-lined field, dominates the lower half of the card and speaks directly to the union of opposite principles (*see* **rose; opposites, union of**).

Keywords/phrases: comprehensive understanding [of the components of a situation]; "casting light" [on the complexities of a situation]; having an enlightened or illuminating perspective; new confidence; turning one's focus toward knowledge; transforming one's life; attaining clarity; unconscious workings becoming conscious awareness; practical inspiration.

See **androgyny; naked/nude**.

sunflower

In Greek legend the sunflower is the symbol of the water-nymph Clytië (CLY-tee-ee), who pined for Apollo and was ignored by him. After sitting for nine days without eating, her eyes fixed only on the sun god as he rose and traveled across the sky, her limbs took root in the ground and her face became a flower, perpetually turning to follow her love. She is considered a symbol of constancy.[84] Sunflowers appear on the Ace of Wands (Robin Wood) and in the RWS in The Sun, and the Queen of Wands.

swan(s)

Apollo was fond of riding in a chariot drawn by swans; hence the swan is sacred to Apollo, as a sun god, and also sacred to the sun. Brahma and Saraswati, Hindu creation gods, also rode upon swans. As an emblem of pure soul, it was also associated with Astraea, daughter of Zeus and Themis, and goddess of innocence and purity (*see* **Astraea**). Both Astraea and a swan recline in the border of the Renaissance Tarot's The Stars card.

In many fairy tales, people are turned into swans, the birds conveying the idea of transformation. In alchemy a swan often depicted the albedo or whitening phase. A swan, representing renewal and rebirth, flies above the Thoth Princess of Cups. For the Robin Wood Six of Swords, a young prince glides across the water in a swan-shaped boat propelled by an ethereal figure.

In the Grail myth Parsifal wounds a swan and his recognition of woundedness begins his quest. Such a wounded swan on the Haindl Fool card represents "the Fall," the loss of paradise. It also reminds us that, like Parsifal, we must heal the broken connection between ourselves and our animal existence.[85]

Swords (suit)

In most decks, and for many people, Swords cards are seen as negative, especially since most of the swords depicted are double-edged. They raise the issue of whether we will focus on problems or opportunities.

Swords cards connect with one of the most inspiring and crucial events related in every mythology, the awakening of the human capacity to reason. When associated with the "element" or principle of air (spirit)—as they most often are—they reflect making sense out of the spirit within, and of understanding social and personal abstractions such as truth.[86] Connected with breath or breathing, they also reflect a connection with the breath of the soul. On the negative, more physical side, those "possessed" by the element of air can become too involved in abstract thinking and lose touch with physical reality.

Air cards have a strong social quality, but that does not necessarily refer to close intimacy, since the actions of persons with a great deal of air element would more likely occur in activities such as organizing social situations and concern for the working of community, or the greater world. The air principle is that which gives us the capacity to see social problems and the energy to work for social change. Swords is the suit that deals with the kind of discernment that banishes error.[87] Swords represent Jung's thinking function—that of ordering and making sense out of what we perceive.

The suit deals with the development of logical sorting-out

skills, ethical considerations, and the consequences of our decisions. Swords experiences help us develop our sense of morality and presence of self. Perhaps that is the reason so many of the cards are seen as negative or painful, since nothing spares us from the torment of ethical decision-making.[88]

Swords equate with the alchemical process of *sublimato*, the process whereby instinctual content is spontaneously transformed into an image, often as a bird or other winged figure.[89] Hence, after much of the mundane work has been engaged in, we observe birds flying in the RWS court cards of this suit, while the Robin Wood Knight of Swords wears a winged helmet and soars on a winged horse, like Pegasus (*see* **Pegasus**), symbol of poetic inspiration.[90]

Sublimato also occurs when we transform our desire for an external object or person into an internalized image that gives meaning, purpose, and regenerative capacity to our life.[91] If we properly honor those feelings rather than deny them, we begin to realize that the beautiful and desired beloved "is really a dimension of our own soul."[92] Such realization often results in a burst of creative activity. The sword can be likened to the blade of the alchemical "conjuror," its cross-shape representing the fusion and cooperation—the fruitful union—of opposites, of male and female principles.[93]

An overabundance of Swords in a spread may indicate too much thinking, not enough attention to action or emotion, or may suggest that the person needs to slow down and think things through.

In the Shining Tribe deck, Swords are now Birds. The suit becomes Wind in the Tarot of the Spirit deck; in the Osho deck, it is Clouds: The Mind.

Swords, Ace of

The element of air, or the principle of integrity, is activated. New energy begins to move within to inspire or motivate us to create from a rational or analytical base rather than intuitively.

Depending on the position in which the card falls it can refer to the personality or psychological patterns we have, or will need to develop, to relate to the external environment.

The build-up of energy to use in the pursuit of knowledge is foremost when we draw this card, and our task is to become aware of the need to express ourselves thoughtfully, to allow time for our organizing and ordering abilities to set in rather than to rush into action. It calls upon us to think clearly and to re-evaluate values, possibly those derived from childhood conditioning rather than personal thoughtfulness.

In the RWS card, the glowing right (active) hand of higher spirit holds the sword above purple mountains, symbolizing the wisdom that can occur when we use our minds. A crown rests over the tip of the sword and from its right side hangs a palm branch (triumphal victory). The left branch is from an olive tree, said to be the world tree, the *anima mundi*, in Islamic traditions. Its branches were also triumphal emblems. Six *yods* float above the handle of the sword, representing the potency of activity, power, and direction. Higher guidance is inherent in the card.

In the Robin Wood card, a gleaming, upright, double-edged (knowledge cuts both ways) sword hangs in front of a background of clouds (the confusion and ignorance the sword is about to dispel). A laurel wreath (victory) circles the tip of the sword, from which hangs a garland of olive leaves (peace and fruitfulness) and one of white roses (freedom of spirit and thought), twining to form a double helix of DNA (a beginning, new life).

The eye of truth appears amidst swirling air behind the upright sword on the Spiral Tarot's card. The Haindl Tarot refers to the Egyptian myth of Nun. From her chaotic waters (female principle), emerges a single hill (male principle) supporting a sword—the divine mind activating nature.[94]

Although most cards in the Osho Suit of Clouds are either troubled or cartoon-like, the Ace is called "Consciousness." The large Buddha figure, who appears in the vast universe beyond the stars, represents the "crystal clarity" available to us all in the deep stillness at our core.[95]

Keywords/phrases: strength in adversity; enlightenment; inevitable change; intellectual energy; learning to express ourselves thoughtfully; achieving clarity; developing of organizing and ordering abilities; triumph and conquest through intellect.

See **tree, olive; tree, palm; rose; ruby; wreath, laurel;** *yod.*

Swords, Two of

Most RWS-type cards typically show a blindfolded woman holding two crossed swords (representing dilemma, possibly because of two equal choices). Her clothing, placement (sitting, standing, walking a tightrope), and her relationship to a body of water differ in various decks, and change slightly each card's meaning.

The Robin Wood figure sits on a stone wall in an inlet of a rolling, foaming ocean (it's too late to avoid the situation), beneath dark ragged clouds (she may not be thinking as clearly as she might). The various shades of indigo in the card (*see* **chakra(s)**) suggest she inwardly knows how to get out of the situation. Her bare feet show she is still in touch with essential knowledge.[96] The Spiral Tarot's female walks a tightrope over a rough sea, reflecting the precarious situation and emotional turmoil that can occur when we attempt to balance inner forces.

The Thoth card shows two crossed swords penetrating the center of a blue flower and forming four sections (a quartenary and the double of two) in which four-sided pinwheels of light, the essences, stream from the flower. On the tip of a small sword above, a crescent moon rests, while on an identical sword below, rests the astrological sign for Libra. Together they suggest emotional or feminine balance, hence the card's title, "Peace," the same title for the Haindl card. Contrary to its title, however, the double motif of twos suggests the psychological concept of "tension of the opposites," as well as unconscious content striving to cross the threshold and make itself known. The Osho "Schizo-phrenia" card refers to those aspects of our personality where we are stuck in our conditioning and in the dualistic aspect of the mind.

On the Nigel Jackson card, two armored knights stand in a grass-strewn landscape holding upright between them a shield imprinted with a crowned, fiery dragon. It represents compro-mise, truce, and restored equilibrium, whereas its reversal rep-resents the indecision shown by cards from other decks.

Swords and knives as symbols of the masculine principle also suggests that part of our problem may be that we are caught up in masculine energies and are failing to "see" or allow the fem-inine viewpoint or feminine energies (empathy, intuition) to work in our situation. On the Wheel of Change Two of Swords, a pair of scissors, representing the mind at work, cut a paper snowflake, demonstrating how something can be manifested from a specific, formed goal in which the trivia has been cut away.

Although the card is often considered one of stalemate, it more appropriately refers to the task of learning to hold on and to let go, of action or assertion, of inaction or passivity. As a two, our indecision will be short-lived, but the card does suggest a time of contemplation and waiting, of turning inward. It may be important to live with the ambivalent balance for a time as we think through our situation and prepare to make our decisions. While we may feel like we are powerless, the swords in RWS-style cards are usually balanced across the heart chakra, suggest-ing that we have more power than we are able to realize or to feel at the moment. We blind ourselves as we are caught asking, "Do I hold onto this for awhile longer? Do I let go and trust that I, or a higher power, know what to do? Do I throw away these heavy swords right now, rip off this blindfold and get out of here?"

Keywords/phrases: dilemma between two equal choices; stale-mate; being intellectually immobilized; action or assertion vs. inaction or passivity; learning to hold on and to let go; contemplation and waiting; balance of ideas.

See **clouds; fire; dragons; stones.**

Swords, Three of

Although logically it would seem that by resolving the conflict that appeared in the Two of Swords, or by ending its state of "blinded" ambivalence, we should arrive at a suitable solution, it is not yet to be. The Three of Swords that pierce the RWS stylized heart show that giving up the conflict may result, for a time, in a sense of loss and heartbreak. Here the three with its rain combines the principles of air and water, which are somewhat incompatible and together indicate disorganization, friction, and the subtle undermining of experiences.

Many see the RWS card as "false heartbreak" because the swords are not dripping blood and so have not pierced the true heart. Although the Robin Wood swords, and even the heart, drip what appears to be blood, it is actually water, when you see it at the tips of the blades. A major question to ask yourself concerns your personal symbolism of rain. Is this rain a light, healing, renewing, fertilizing shower—the release of tension? Is it about to become a deluge, suggesting a sense of being overwhelmed?

On the Spiral Tarot, a woman stands in rain, next to three swords. She holds a red rose over her heart (*see* **rose**), while a diminishing male figure in the background (her masculine aspect?) recedes from the lamplight (inspiration).

The Haindl "Mourning" card depicts a wound with a single, clear tear oozing from it. It refers not only to personal pain but also to that brought about by patriarchal cultural values, e.g, wars and subjugation. Colored tears ooze from the eyes of the iceman in the Osho "Ice-olation" card, representing the process of having drawn ego boundaries and separated ourselves from the flow of our lives and of the greater Universe.

Two purple-cloaked figures (a man and a woman?) stand on

mountains separated by a cloudy abyss in the Nigel Jackson card, reflecting one of the major meanings of the card: the painful, but necessary experiences we all must endure, out of which arise new understanding, insight, healing, and wisdom if we do not get caught up in bitter recriminations. Have we identified all the conflicting emotions present in and relating to our situation or issue, including those hidden in past situations and "crying" to be recognized?

Keywords/phrases: loss; heartbreak, possibly false heartbreak; painful experience we must endure for new understanding, insight, or wisdom; flash of insight that provides new perspective for some sorrow or loss; decision made in opposition to or ignoring feelings; time to release some aspect of the painful past.

See **clouds; rain.**

Swords, Four of

The active conflict, tension, and pain of the Two and Three of Swords in the RWS cards now give way to the experience of contemplation and withdrawal, or to "Truce" (a moment of calm) as in the Haindl card.

The Four of Swords suggests both ending and beginning. We need a time of introspection to end the previous experiences of tension and indecision and to arrange our understanding in order to prepare us for the next cycle in which more active intellectual activity and difficulties occur. We are called upon to gather strength to prepare for those activities and tests that lie ahead (*see* **hidden letters**).

The downside of the Four of Swords is that too much internal ruminating can result in paralyzing fears that keep us immobilized as in the Osho "Postponement" card. A woman looks through a frame at a gray landscape. She is unable to give up the "what-if?" activity of her mind and step through the frame into the real world.[97]

Keywords/phrases: contemplation, withdrawal, and introspection; "sleep on your problem"; time out for reconciliation of issues; recognition of "dormant" energy or life force we have failed to recognize; lack of awareness; gaining control of one's ideas; becoming more focused; need to, or time for, recuperation and renewal; enforced rest.

See chakra(s).

Swords, Five of

The Five of Swords depicts a crisis with respect to our intellectual processes or moral integrity. In the RWS card, a storm threatens. Change is on the horizon, and strong emotions are about to be acknowledged, and likely expressed, especially regarding who "wins" and who "loses" in an encounter. Much as most of us would like to avoid certain *persona* or ego experiences, they do occur in our lives and we must learn to respond to them.

Perhaps all three of the figures in the RWS card are aspects of ourselves, subpersonalities. There is our "bully within," which expresses itself outwardly in this card, while the two retreating figures turn away from the outer *persona* and turn inward, toward the water (the unconscious).

Balding and bare chested, the Spiral Tarot's bully stands victorious on a floating raft. A figure in the water clings to the side of the raft and another floats face down in the turbulent ocean. The bully is not open to negotiation and it is a no-win situation for everyone.[98] On the Haindl "Defeat" card, five broken swords collapse before the background of a dying unicorn.

Moving away from the defeat theme of many Five of Swords cards, the Wheel of Change's card depicts five sickle knives like those used by the Druids to cut sacred mistletoe. That act symbolizes the recognition and understanding of seasonal cycles on our lives, and of honoring the cycle of thought that moves from unconscious energy to initial conscious recognition (manifestation). From a more spiritual viewpoint, the card emphasizes attempts to live or relate on a more soulful level, and our inner struggles to penetrate higher planes of existence.[99]

Keywords/phrases: moral crisis; defeat, degradation, loss, or dishonor and how one deals with them; taking advantage of others; someone who will or does not play by the rules; overwhelmed by too many ideas; acknowledging limitations (self- or other-imposed); arrogant self-importance or superiority; time to move in a new direction; time to check or clarify priorities; taking resources that others have left behind; crafty victory; tending to ego needs at the cost of others; disregard for the concern of others; the ability to deal with rejection, losing, and winning.

Swords, Six of

Journey is the keynote of most RWS-style cards.[100] Perhaps it is the journey of insight or of the mind, as shown in the Ancestral Path card—a lightening of our burden, a new level of self-awareness or harmony—that has come about as a result of our participation in the Five of Swords engagement. Disaster overcome by a focused and attentive mind allows for further progress. On the Thoth "Science" card, it refers to the work of testing, retesting, and careful observation. The journey of "Science" is also reflected by the Haindl card, which expresses the need to take an objective view to discover inner and outer truths (*see* **grapes**).

In some cards the journey is toward a new "land," as shown by the trees on the distant shore of the RWS card. Unlike the seemingly burdened figures in the RWS card, a young man in the Robin Wood card sits in a swan-shaped boat propelled by an ethereal figure (letting go and trusting the higher self). Across the way a star twinkles in a cave (higher spiritual awareness, deeper inner development). The guardian angel in the Spiral Tarot guides the figure in the boat toward a "light in the night" on the opposite shore. The flounce on the Alchemical boatman's cap duplicates the boat's figurehead, that of a quail, longtime symbol of the soul. Fate directs the boat toward distant lands on the Morgan-Greer card.

Keywords/phrases: rite of passage; transition; overcoming fears and moving ahead; soul's journey toward enlightenment; influence of biological family in present situation; moving from rough waters into smooth waters; leaving rough times; ideas coming together.

Swords, Seven of

Once again we find ourselves challenged to achieve mental clarity, but perhaps not as we expected. In the background of the RWS card, a campfire burns with the black (shadow) silhouettes of men sitting around it. A cloud of gray smoke, the symbol of air, the major element of this suit, rises from the fire. So we have the burning phase of alchemy (attending to the shadow secrets of the unconscious) giving rise to a more spiritual element. Instinctual nature is being transformed.

More mundanely, some see the figure in the card as "sneaky Pete," a person who would betray us or the betrayal aspects of ourselves. Others see him as having made a plan, taking care of himself, and taking only what he needs, leaving behind the tension and possibilities represented by two remaining swords. The concept of the Haindl's "Uselessness" card is that of defeating patriarchal power, "useless old men." The scattered swords represent a time when society moves in the wrong direction, making individual energy more difficult.[101]

Keywords/phrases: instability; carelessness; planning to get what you want; neglected ideals; lack of power; cunning; direct tactics will not be appropriate; taking the best from a situation to make it part of oneself; examination of one's ideas (those that worked and those that didn't) for future progression; abandoning a former allegiance or ideal.

Swords, Eight of

The young woman first shown in the RWS Two of Swords may have made some progress, but she is still blinded and life now is infinitely more complicated. At its simplest, the task suggested by this card is that of freeing ourselves of those parts imprisoned by early hurts and the distorted perceptions that have grown from them.[102] Esoterically, the card sometimes represents the *persona* that has become distanced from the soul or Self, the awareness or realization of that separation, and the anguish or misfortune that it brings about. The woman is tied by wraps around the four lower chakra centers (root, spleen, sacral, and solar plexus), leaving open only those centers capable of expressing the soul: the heart, throat and *ajna* chakras.[103] She is the initiate and to be successful must rely on her soul qualities, her inner, highest self, and free herself of the bonds of limited insight.

The Haindl card speaks of "Interference," which can be helpful or hurtful, and of our moral responsibility in the face of worldly wrongs and sick spirituality.

Keywords/phrases: the *persona* distanced from the soul or Self; the imminence of a major identity shift; move only when mindful of both physical and emotional components of situation; ignoring family values; time to rely on inner, highest qualities for success; restriction through inaction due to fears and inhibitions; paralysis due to indecision; being so overwhelmed by a task that one is unwilling to face it; viewing oneself as helpless.

Swords, Nine of

The Nine of Swords is typically a card of worry and oppressive concerns. In the RWS card a woman, her face covered with her hands, sits upright in a bed placed before a wall of swords. The Spiral Tarot's card describes her as a woman gripped by fear. The Haindl card refers to the self-destruction brought about by the cruelty of human culture. Unlike the immobility suggested by many cards, the Wheel of Change Nine of Swords card is one of action. Blowing wind and whirling windmill blades reflect the idea of clear and considered thought.

Keywords/phrases: sorrow; unwillingness to face one's fears, instincts, or unconscious; worries that interfere with the search for self-awareness or insight; repetition of same problem, choice, or situation over and over, therefore, related to compulsion and addiction; rumination over issues rather than taking action to resolve them; sorting out of beliefs and determining which to retain and which to discard.

Swords, Ten of

One of the most powerful and complex cards in the RWS deck, the swords along the spine of the figure symbolize the giving up of old mental constructs and developing a new alignment with higher energies (*see* **chakra(s)**). The man's right hand forms the Japanese "kichijo-in" mudra (symbolic finger position) symbolizing good fortune or joy.[104] In Japanese mudra theory, the fingers represent chakras. In this mudra, the ring finger (the second chakra of decision) touches the thumb (the fifth chakra of communication) of the right (active) hand, signaling a conscious decision to evolve toward emotional integration, integrity, and harmony. In Chinese, the position is called the "sword" mudra and represents the act of cutting through perceptual difficulties.[105]

Although many decks produce a picture that defines the card as totally ominous and hopeless, in fact the card represents both a completion and a new beginning. It is in this sense that the Haindl card is titled "Ruin," i.e., out of ruin comes renewal.

In many cards the swords are not aligned (the death of old ideas or training), pierce different areas of the body (random activation of old memories), or have different hilts (diversity of thinking available). Sometimes the figure does not bleed from the wounds, suggesting a false or symbolic death, an initiation. In whatever way it is portrayed, the card simultaneously shows the pain that may be experienced at the end of a cycle and the dawning of new spiritual insights. It has been called the card of "greatest activity, wakefulness, and livingness" in the deck.[106]

If you consider it an "acupuncture" card, then the figure is receiving a generous jolt of endorphins (peptide hormones that activate the body's opiate receptors), as well as sending old emotional messages (thought by pharmacologist Candace B. Pert to be stored in the ganglion of the spinal cord) up the spine to the brain's limbic system where they can be consciously recognized, expressed, and integrated. So the card can represent a physical process of heightened self-awareness and satisfaction that assists healing.

Indeed, the lines of rocks on the Haindl card resemble photographs of brain neurons, although the card suggests pain disrupting pathways of thought and energy. In cards where swords puncture other areas of the body, all muscles have peptide receptors and connect via nerves to the spinal cord.

To remind us that we all have a vulnerable point, the Renaissance Tarot's card depicts Paris striking Achilles's heel, which results in his death. The contents of the Wheel of Change garden shed reflect the tools and knowledge we need in life, while at the same time suggesting old age and wisdom. It also reflects the death of each moment "as it passes into what has been and will never be again."[107]

Keywords/phrases: feeling overwhelmed; a build-up of problems; stabbed in the back; the lifting of a false perception and new insight; release; surrender.

Swords, Page of

As an earth card in the air suit, this page is too often at cross-purposes with himself, and frequently in a crisis. He may encounter more obstacles, stress, and conflict than other pages, but if he can stay with these and not become discouraged—and he surely is determined and dedicated—he may develop great skill in his ability to carefully think through his own ideas and those of others and fit them into his developing ethical scheme.

He is beginning to realize that people may have hidden motives in their interactions with others, and he begins to look for them, but does not yet have the training to fully fathom them. Still nothing prevents him from rushing headlong into situations with a righteous attitude and the need to make others "see it his way." He is quite disdainful of anything he encounters that he judges as "stupid" or "unthinking."

The Page of Swords is the only page in the RWS deck not looking at his suit symbol, suggesting that he/we may be remote and defensive at the time when the card appears. Sometime he is seen as not holding the sword firmly enough; therefore, the card may caution against false defensiveness, i.e., being defensive when there is no true reason to be. He is, after all, a new student or adept and presumably receptive to the new stimulation of ideas he will be receiving. Perhaps he is not quite ready to face and integrate the mental clarity his teachings will provide.

The Wheel of Change Prince of Swords represents just the opposite. In an ornately decorated room, he learns a sword dance, which requires concentration, balance, flexibility, and control. He is learning to focus and to transform these intellectual concepts into an active part of his personality and life.

Mythologically the Page of Swords is related to the union of Mother Earth and Father Sky and to Arthur because of the image of the sword in the stone.

In the Shining Tribe deck, the Place of Birds card presents an imaginary landscape created by an observant person and celebrates "the mind with its ability to see forms and construct ideas."[108]

Keywords/phrases: dedication to shaping analytic abilities and ethical values; temporarily being at cross-purposes during time of sorting; having more energy than sense, more action than judgment; detachment; caution; cunning; calculating.

Swords, Knight of

An air card in an air suit, the RWS knight is obviously action-oriented, bent on fighting for or learning the truth. He is easily bored and wants to move on. In the process of developing a daring and quick mind, he needs constant mental stimulation. And he gets it, or creates it, in the Spiral Tarot's card where he rushes headlong into the wind.

In the RWS deck this, and all the suit's remaining court cards, show clouds and birds, symbols of the element of air. They suggest that now we are entering a phase of mastery of the air principle, the ability of the logical mind to cut through the air of spoken words.[109] The birds also symbolize the drive toward developing a thoughtful sense of ethics, and the "flightiness" of this knight's personality.

Facing the left side of the card suggests that part of his learning will only occur when he clarifies the "truths" of past or unconscious experiences.

The Robin Wood knight charges across a stormy sky on the back of a winged horse. His helmet, decorated with lightning bolts, and his sword, crackling with lightning, display the wit and power of his personality. His task is to learn to direct it appropriately.[110]

The Shining Tribe Knower of Birds, a finely robed diviner and master of images, represents our ability to set up a system of thought, intuition, and symbolic understanding.

Keywords/phrases: the dichotomy of expanding energy and the need for discipline in the continuing quest for reshaping ethical values and personal ideals; blindly seeking the truth; caught up in an adrenaline rush of excitement; time to cut through illusions and find the truth within; intellectual creative activity at an all-time high; time to protect self or defend ideas; discrimination; intense focus.

Swords, Queen of

As a water card in the air suit, the Queen of Swords is, above all, an articulate truth-speaker, although she does it in a compassionate, sympathetic, and tactful way. Many see her as a woman who has experienced sorrow and bears her pain with courage. Experienced enough to not rush headlong into an emotional relationship, once committed, she can be fiercely and unswervingly loyal. She will join you on the picket line, but doesn't trust easily and will be hard to get to know.[111]

Not so approachable is the World Spirit's Sibyl of Swords sitting on a throne high in the Himalayas. As mentally sharp as the surrounding clear, crisp air, she remains ever-ready to cut away untruths.[112]

The Queen of Swords speaks and guides from her own inner integrity. She can be very discriminating in her analysis of situations, and is excellent at dissecting them and getting at their core. With her quick perception, she is the quintessential problem solver. She is a good teacher, directing and guiding, carefully observing her students' progress. Sometimes, however, she tends to be a bit excessive in her teaching, not always knowing when to back off because of her own inner certainty about the task at hand and her abundance of knowledge and ideas. She is quite skilled, however, at teaching how to use logic and courage to transmute fear and emotional distress into focused energy. Forthright in her approach, she also can bring mental subtleties to a situation.

Although the bird-headed shaman in the Shining Tribe Gift of Birds card can defend himself against mental aggression, his greater skill is that he can nondefensively open himself and create—or inspire others to create—art, music, and poetry.

Keywords/phrases: strong willed; determined; sharp and penetrating mind; ability to be totally honest; self-righteous.

Swords, King of

Being an "air of air" king, he is one of the most integrated of the kings, and is very charismatic. His actions are effortless, but he shows little attempt to compromise or to adjust his position. He is united in his thoughts and action, no dissension there, but will never be able to inspire the way his queen does, or the way some other kings do. His shrewdness and commanding bearing have some perceiving him as too dominating. He is a role model of focused confidence in his ability to think things through and arrive at a committed position. A harsh judge, he is not easily swayed from his beliefs. A brilliant strategist, he is intolerant of any kind of "thinking" that reeks of the emotional or the mystical.[113]

The King of Swords realizes better than anyone that reality is only the result of intellectual concepts. He is a person of great emotional reserve, the "strong, silent type," yet he can help others develop the great analytical abilities and insights that he possesses.

The Shining Tribe Speaker of Birds, depicted in an African dance posture, employs the invisible body of the mind to share ideas and information and to communicate from deepest truths.[114]

The Ancestral Path card refers to the Japanese ancestral deity Izanagi, who stands on the Bridge of Heaven. As a result of his churning of the waters of chaos, it thickens like butter and creates the heavenly island of Onokoro. The card represents the essence of creative skill.[115]

Keywords/phrases: judgement or judgemental; close-minded; clear thinking; deep, ethical commitment; strength of character; quick, intelligent mind dedicated to objective, logical thinking; intellectually domineering.

symbolism

One of the most ancient and fundamental methods of artistic expression, symbols can, and usually do, embody more than one level of meaning (see Part One, Chapter 2). Expressed as larger art productions, symbols are extremely powerful ways to represent archetypes and other complex ideas, although, as Jung has indicated, they always rank below the "mystery" of psychic truth they seek to describe. While general meanings for symbols do exist, a particular item in any tarot card may also have personal meanings that can significantly change the understanding of the card.

See **archetypes**, specific items shown on cards.

synchronicity (synchronistic phenomenon)

As used by Carl Jung, the term referred to a combination of acausal inner and outer events that come together in such a way to have extremely important meaning for an individual, often having a seemingly magical, mythological or unique symbolic quality about their appearance or occurrence. Synchronicity is not the same as coincidence. For synchronicity to occur, an archetype is activated within the psyche and in some inexplicable manner also appears or emerges in the outer world, often in several ways (an overheard conversation, a dream, the appearance of an animal or other creature, a symbolic artwork).

Synchronicity is one of the important principles behind the drawing of tarot cards. Those cards needed for one to receive an important message related to a question, idea, or situation are drawn, and the theme or image appears provoked by the querent's inner wrestling with that issue and, therefore, the activation of unconscious energy.

T

✳

tableau

A way of grouping Major Arcana cards to form a pattern in order to analyze horizontal and vertical relationships between cards. The most common is three groups of seven, beginning with The Magician. The Fool card is outside the pattern because it represents the journey through archetypal experiences. With each row of seven, The Fool moves deeper and deeper into self-understanding. Sometimes the three levels of development are named "conscious" (cards 1–7), "unconscious" (8–14), and "superconscious" or "higher consciousness" (15–21).[1]

Several unequal ways of organizing the cards exist, including dividing the cards into the four gateways of "childhood" (cards 0–7), "adolescence" (cards 7–13), "adulthood" (cards 13–18), and "wisdom" (cards 18–21);[2] or dividing them into "basic drives" (cards 0–5), "ego construction" (cards 6–12), and "integration of conscious and unconscious" (cards 13–21).[3]

See **constellation**.

tarocchi

A card game developed in the fourteenth century and typically played with seventy-eight cards, twenty-two of which were used for trumps. Originally such cards were called *carte da trionfi* (cards of the triumphs). Apparently the word *tarocchi* began to be used to distinguish them from a new game of triumphs or trumps played with ordinary playing cards.[4] In the fifteenth century (c1460), a deck known as the Tarocchi dei Mantegna was created containing fifty cards ranked by number so the deck could be played as a game. A modern copy of the Mantegna Tarot has been created by Lo Scarabeo of Italy (now distributed by Llewellyn). The deck contains five classes of figures corresponding to social, intellectual, and spiritual aspects of the Middle Ages. Within each of those are ten iconographic figures representing human conditions, artistic expressions, arts and sciences, universal principles and virtues, and planets and celestial spheres.

tattvas (also Tatwas)

Indian geometrical symbols, often painted on separate cards, and sometimes worked into tarot illustrations, they act as gateways into the astral world for purposes of divination, meditation, and scrying. Tattvas were introduced to a general audience by Madame Helen Blavatsky and her Theosophical Society. Apparently MacGregor Mathers, inspired by one of Bulwer Lytton's novels, where the hero escapes poisoning by using the tattvas, introduced them into the Golden Dawn system.

The elements are represented as a red triangle for fire (called *Tejas*), a silver crescent for water (*Apas*), a blue circle for air (*Vayu*); a golden square for earth (*Prithvi*); and a black or blue-violet oval for ether (*Akasha*).[5]

When combining the elements, a smaller elemental symbol is

placed into the center of the main element, which dominates. For instance, the watery part of fire would show a red triangle (usually against its complementary color green as a background) with a smaller silver crescent in its center.[6]

The five basic shapes appear on the Thoth Five of Disks. It is believed that Waite and Paul Foster Case encoded tattvas in many of their cards (not necessarily with the original colors).[7] The Akasha black oval clearly appears in the center of the alchemical vessel on The Devil card of the Alchemical Tarot,[8] while the wreath in the RWS World card is sometimes thought to represent this tattva.[9]

Taurus (astrological sign)

The second sign of the zodiac (April 21—May 21).

Element: Earth
Modality: Fixed
Polarity: Yin
Ruled by the planet Venus

A card attributed to Taurus partakes of its developmental, fertile earth energy, and is abundant with growth. Taurus stabilizes the momentum of Aries, rooting ideas in the soil. The Taurean bull is a symbol of rampant potency, but in earlier legends the horns were a symbol of the Mother-Moon Goddess. A well-dignified Taurus-attributed card may be interpreted as: acquisition of money and possessions; sensual passions and desires; endurance and determination to succeed; exceptional talents in math, music, the arts, or business management; a high valuation of the self. An ill-dignified or reversed Taurus card may be interpreted as: inflexibility, inertia, intemperance and uncontrollable passions, greed or possessiveness that borders on obsession, a pessimistic or self destructive viewpoint, problems with stability in love or money.[10]

See **Venus** (planet).

Temperance (XIV)

At its simplest, Temperance cautions us to proceed with moderation; however, Temperance is linked to The Star (XVII), at least in the RWS deck where both figures have one foot in water and one on land. Both cards deal with working with, or acknowledging, unconscious material, and with reconciling spiritual and worldly matters—of becoming a unified whole.

After the initiation suggested by The Hanged Man and Death cards, we move to a new phase of transformation, that of learning to recognize and own our projections. To do that we have to begin to discriminate between what is "in here" and what is "out there,"[11] and to recognize what is conscious and what is unconscious.

It is not insignificant that the temperance angel often wears a white garment (RWS, Mythic cards, the female Renaissance angel), representing the *albedo*, or whitening, phase of alchemy (dissolving and integrating prime matter). It is the beginning and the basis of all practical work in spiritual alchemy.[12] In alchemy, moderation (*temperantia*) was particularly important, lest any of the elements of "The Work" assume predominance, resulting in disharmony and chaos.[13]

On the Alchemical card, the mother aspect of the Great Goddess pours the waters of time. She has learned to harness the world's natural rhythms. Representing a continually renewing process, she is the alchemist who distills and blends our fragmented aspects into something of value.[14]

The RWS angel has been identified variously as the archangel Michael, and as the archangel Raphael, the healer angel of Tipareth.[15] The image of the orange triangle in a white square over the angel's chest may represent the solar emblem of Tipareth,[16] as well as forming the septenary (triangle equals three, square equals four). Above it, we see the Hebrew letters for the Tetragrammaton at the neck of the gown (*see* **Tetragrammaton**). The symbol for gold on the angel's forehead has been replaced with the alchemical rose on the Marseilles card.

Alchemically, the winged figure also links the card to the wizened Winged Mercurius, spirit of the unconscious. Irises often bloom on a Temperance card (RWS, Robin Wood, Spiral), connecting the card with the Greek goddess Iris, who frequently served as a messenger of the gods. She is, indeed, the angel alchemist portrayed in the Spiral Tarot's card, and the winged woman in the Mythic Tarot's card.

As the goddess of the rainbow, Iris is linked to various rainbow bridges, which connect the known and the unknown, the upper and lower realms (*see* **rainbow**). In Icelandic mythology, the quintessential "bridge of bridges," *Bifröst*, was a "quivering," fiery rainbow guarded by Heimdall to protect Asgard, the realm of the gods, from invasion by the frost giants.[17] The Hebrew letter attached to Temperance, *samekh*, means "quivering" or "vibration," the fundamental power that provides creativity, and that transforms energy into matter or manifestation.[18]

Behind the RWS angel, a rising sun in the shape of a crown (*see* **crown**) glows between two mountains. Since the symbology of mountains and columns are often interchangeable, we understand that this sun is the same one we see in the RWS Death and Moon cards and symbolic of the columns from the RWS High Priestess, Hierophant, and Justice cards. The pathway of the mystical journey they create is now clear. Dawn denotes a state where we are on the threshold of a new consciousness, of developing an awareness of inner luminosity,[19] and of understanding "some part of the Secret of Eternal Life, as it is possible to man in his incarnation."[20]

The Robin Wood angel juggles three balls: one silver (spiritual wealth, the unconscious mind, the present), one gold (material wealth, the conscious mind, the past), and one made of crystal (mental aptitude, mystery, the future). The angel has his sleeves rolled up because he is not adverse to hard work.[21] Yet, on the Tarot of the Spirit card, an armless Michael stands between the sun and the moon. They represent the multidimensional layers of the personality, which must be peeled back at a spiritual level; hence, Michael's "balancing act" does not require material arms.[22]

The female angel in the Nigel Jackson card represents the "angelic influence" that "pours the clarifying waters of spirit into our troubled earthly existence."[23]

While Temperance appears a seemingly calm card, tarot fives $(14 = 4 + 1 = 5)$ are often crisis cards and this card is one of tempering the soul.[24] Perhaps the crises implied by the following two cards (The Devil, The Tower) lurk in the rippling (tempestuous?) water flowing between the cups. The symbols on the third eye or ajna (wisdom) and heart chakras (RWS card) suggest a connection between "forgiveness or love" work and mental evaluation. Ajna activities are those of retrieving our power as we give up "false" truths, of learning to act on internal direction rather than the direction of others, and of learning to discriminate between thoughts motivated by strength and those motivated by fear and illusion.[25]

A diagonal line dissects the Haindl "Alchemy" card, dividing it between blue and red, water and fire. It deals with the "alchemical marriage" of our polarities. Such a "marriage" is shown in the Thoth "Art" card where an androgynous figure created by the alchemical union of two lovers (mercury and sulphur), pours and blends the elements.

The Temperance card encourages us to develop a new sense of internal balance between discrimination and love, in part by raising our consciousness, or our level of vibrational understanding. Adaptation is an important concept associated with this card.

Keywords/phrases: the higher self in action; blending or integrating polarities; taking one's "measure" and then taking control; "finding the 'right mixture' of inner certainty and outer expression."[26]

temporal readings

An easy way to handle time ("when" questions) in a tarot spread is in terms of events that need to happen before something can occur. For a one-, two-, or three-card reading, interpret each card as an issue the client has to resolve, before the "when" question will occur. Example: When will my marriage get better? Draw three cards and interpret them as at least three things the client has to resolve for the marriage to get better.

As an alternative ask how many major events need to occur before the hoped-for event happens. Draw a card. Its number tells you the number of events. Court cards say ten, plus draw another card. If the second card is another court card, that means an additional ten more events plus draw another card. The Fool (zero) means "there's nothing you can do to attain this goal."[27]

More complicated ways of answering temporal questions involve assigning months, days, and years to specific cards or suits, or to consider the astrological signs (dates) of the cards. These vary considerably depending on the reader.

tens

Tens mark the completion of a cycle of work, concern, or achievement. They honor the rhythms of nature; they are the beginning $(1 + 0 = 1)$ and the end. As such they represent realization and satisfaction, *and* the stirring of the restless energy preparing for a new cycle. Sometimes this feels like a definite burden (Not again!); hence, the "heavy" RWS Ten of Swords and Wands.

Tens typify perseverance in its best and worst senses (compulsion, or doggedly struggling along without insight). Sometimes tens represent a transitional or liminal state. We have ended the more mundane cycle of nine and await the higher level work promised by the court cards. We experience a brief respite before making a decision to repeat the cycle of nines or to move into court card lessons. Tens can also be viewed as showing an "indeterminate" energy that will change or be made apparent, depending on the cards around them. Tens are associated with the sephira of Malkuth (kingdom) on the Tree of Life.

See tens of each suit.

Tetragrammaton

The fourfold division of the Divine name, and the universal creative process, expressed in the four Hebrew letters: *Yod, Heh, Vau* (or *Vav*), *Heh*. In Jewish tradition the name can be spelled YHVH, but not pronounced, substituting the word *Adonai* ("Lord"). As a condensation of the three forms of the verb "to be," it signifies the timeless, unknowable source and context of all being.[28] Tradition says that God used the four letters to create the universe.[29]

In the RWS deck, the letters are embroidered at the necks of The Fool's shirt and the Temperance angel's gown, and appear on the Wheel of Fortune, interspersed with the letters TARO. They are also associated with each of the four Minor Arcana suits (*Yod* equals Wands, *Heh* equals Cups, *Vau* equals Swords, *Heh* equals Pentacles). According to Golden Dawn tradition, God's descent into matter occurs in this order, while our spiritual ascent progresses in the opposite direction (Pentacles, Swords, Cups, Wands).

See **Yod**.

Theseus

In an act similar to that of Arthur of British legend, when Theseus reached an appropriate age, he removed a rock beneath which his father Aegeus had hidden his sword and sandals, learned whose son he really was, and headed to Athens, where his father ruled. On the way he bested or killed many tyrants and marauders. Once in Athens, he survived an attempt by Aegeus's wife Medea to poison him. Identifying with Hercules and bearing the self-image of a hero, Theseus was equally as reckless and brazen in love and carried off many a woman to his bed in addition to his several wives.[30] Theseus is the archetype of the fiery, impulsive youth who eventually channels his energy into becoming a vibrant leader and strategist. He is the subject of the Mythical Tarot's King of Wands.

Thoth

See **Hermes/Mercury**.

threes

In religious and mythological symbolism, threes often represent the triplicity of the deity and, simultaneously, the creator, the act of creation, and the thing created. The Thoth's triad is Isis, Osiris, and Horus. The deck's Hierophant holds a scepter of three interlocking rings representing their "interlocking magic."[31]

Many cultures and traditions consider three a most mystical number. The division caused by twos is resolved but not completed; the process continues. It is a number of expansion and growth, of creativity and vision. Distance and perspective now come into play. Tarot threes refer to increased understanding and confidence as a result of having resolved, perhaps only temporarily, the conflict reflected by the twos. Threes may call for re-adjusting some of our plans. As a result of our acquired knowledge, we become more than we were previously, and grow in insight and understanding. Threes are associated with the sephira Bina (Understanding) on the Tree of Life.

See threes of each suit.

threshold

A threshold can symbolize many things related to transition: movement from one state or level of being to another, the process of entering and exiting, and rites of passage or initiation that mark a new level of attainment. Like crossroads, thresholds call upon us to stop, think, and make a decision or commitment. Many cultural myths also include a guardian of the threshold, to assure that only appropriate persons or spirits enter or cross the portal.

There are a number of threshold symbols in the tarot. In the RWS Tarot, The Fool stands on a cliff threshold. The Chariot is on the threshold of forward movement, or has already begun movement, depending on how one interprets the card. The Hanged

Man, Death, and The Moon cards also refer to threshold experiences. All the pages and knights in the court cards are at a threshold experience where a decision has to be made or new actions taken.

See **bridges; crossroads.**

throne

Thrones appear in many of the queen and king cards of the Minor Arcana suits (depending on the deck), as well as in various Major Arcana cards. In general, a throne stands for power, stability, authority, and rulership. The meaning of a throne, and the card on which it appears, may be further enhanced by considering the jewels or carved decorations on it.

The hieroglyph of the goddess Isis's name, and the symbol often seen covering her head, resembles a throne. Isis was originally thought to be the personification of the throne from which were born the kings of Egypt;[32] therefore, at some level the throne is always associated with the Great Mother.[33]

tiger lilies

In the Thoth Seven of Cups, the lotus blossoms that bloom on all other Cups cards have become tiger lilies, dropping their poisonous nectar into the sea.

toad

The toad, an ancient symbol of the birth-giving goddess, appears on the Shining Tribe Seven of Stones. For its meaning on the Two of Stones, *see* **Pentacles, Two of.**

Tower, The (XVI)

Upheaval, crisis of the soul, extensive destruction and rebuilding of everything we hold near and dear—that's the first and most obvious message of The Tower. Too late to be careful and cautious—things are being stirred up, the established rearranged. It is "a whack on the side of the head."[34]

The Tower card represents the *persona* and the lifetime of defenses we build up to help us protect it and to counter anxiety. Now, they are toppling—or need to be—and although it feels like a crisis, repair will serve us better in the long run.

The Tower represents a "lightning flash of revelation," the sudden insight that releases us from illusion.[35] It causes us to question what our life structure has been about, and what we now want it to be about in the future.

The Alchemical Tarot's Tower represents the oven of alchemy wherein a higher or second dissolution (breakthrough) occurs. Lightning threatens to destroy the oven, making it is a moment of "shattering intensity" for the kneeling male and female figures.[36] Nowhere is it more clear that this is a card of ego threat than in the Renaissance card where lightning strikes a colossal head atop a citadel. From the upper corners Icarus and Phaëthon fall, reminding us of two stories of fatal pride (see **Icarus; Phaëthon**).

Unsuccessful in protecting himself from invading Saxon raiders, the fall of King Vortigern's fortress in Wales is the focus of the Legend Tarot's Arthurian card. It represents our inability to insulate ourselves from the consequences of our actions and from inevitable change.[37]

Two figures leap from a tower that has already been blown apart in the Osho "Thunderbolt" card. In the background a dark, yet ethereal figure, representing detachment and "the witnessing consciousness" meditates. The card is about "inner earthquakes" that occur so suddenly that we can no longer hold onto our previous sense of security, and are struck by enlightenment.[38]

In the RWS card the lightning-struck gray tower loses its golden crown (worldly authority, or old patterns *can* be toppled), and bursts into flames. Two figures, the female wearing a crown (perhaps it's harder to topple queens), fall toward the ground. Accompanying their fall are twenty-two *Yods* (*see* **Yod**).

Who are the two persons seen in many Tower cards? Possibly the masculine and feminine aspects of ourselves. Possibly the superior (one wears a crown) and inferior parts of our personality.

Since our defenses against anxiety begin to develop in childhood, partly in response to our relationship with our parents, we might see the two figures as the internal set of parents we carry around within. The RWS card signifies intellectual destruction. One figure represents the "literal word made void" and the other its "false interpretation."[39] It is the ruin of a "house of falsehood" or "false doctrine."[40]

The triangle at the end of the RWS flash of lightning forms the astrological glyph of Mars (the planet of conflict), which the Golden Dawn associated with this card. It also represents the fertility spear of the Roman god Mars. Three windows in the tower symbolize the "Power of the Triad" destroying the columns of darkness and establishing itself therein[41] (for another explanation, *see* **windows**).

The Robin Wood Tower, typifying the destruction of false premises, sits on faulty, crumbling ground. We are cautioned to stop acting on false assumptions and build a new operating base. Built counterclockwise, it illustrates that really important things have not been thought through.[42]

The Nigel Jackson card represents one of the most common stories associated with The Tower card, the destruction of the Tower of Babel, which the insolent Nebuchadnezzar built to reach to God. The Spiral card presents the story of King Acrisius of Argos, who built a tower to imprison his daughter Danaë, after a prophet informed him that her son would eventually destroy him and take over the kingdom (*see* **Perseus**). The top of the tower is displaced by Zeus's inseminating "shower of gold," symbolizing the awakening of consciousness.[43]

The Mythic Tarot's card associates The Tower with Poseidon's collapse of the labyrinth at Crete, where King Minos was killed, inaugurating a new era. The labyrinth's destruction represents the collapse of old, man-made forms. Past values must die, making way for a new integrity.[44]

The Tower challenges us to examine our beliefs and our defenses, to reevaluate those things we may have developed to protect us but which no longer do as good a job as they, perhaps, once did. The foundation of The Tower card is anchored in the past, rather than the present. Doubly so if it falls in a position that represents the past in a reading.

The crumbling of the Wheel of Change Tarot's Tower creates a world without order and protection. Overpowered by the forces of heaven and earth, we experience a terrible breakdown in our inner and outer worlds. More universal than personal, the Haindl Tower, created by an arrogant and greedy technology, represents the alienation of our culture from nature. The dark inside of the burning skyscraper reminds us of the dangers of not recognizing our own inner darkness (*see* **shadow**).

Keywords/phrases: reorganizing the personality; a breakthrough experience; call to sort out ideas or values, especially constricting or conditioned ones; "blasting through falseness or illusion to truth";[45] sudden change, upheaval, or disruption; loss of a sense of control; renewal through destruction; a "flash" of illumination or insight.

See **chakras**.

Tree of Life

The Tree of Life is a symbol or concept of the mystical tradition of the Kabbalah, although there are also similarly named trees associated with other traditions. Perceived as the ten emanations of energy through which God created the world, the Kabbalistic Tree of Life serves as a model of creation and a blueprint for leading a more spiritual life. It consists of three pillars along which ten spheres, called sephiroth (seph-hear-OTH), each representing an ideal necessary for human spiritual evolution, are placed and connected by twenty-two lines or paths. When so linked, the Tree represents the totality of the cosmos.[46] Each path bears one of the twenty-two Hebrew letters. Together the sephiroth and the paths comprise the "Thirty-two Paths of Wisdom."

Their arrangement is believed to have been first established around the second century in the *Sepher Yetzirah* (The Book of Creation), but it has changed over time and according to various groups who use, and modify the tree. As the Hebrew letters associated with the paths changed, different systems for making these connections or correspondences also developed.

Sometimes a flash of lightning shown moving through the ten sephiroth, or stages, represents how the Divine descends into matter, and the stages through which humans ascend toward the Divine or spiritual.

Many tarotists link the tarot cards to the Tree of Life, and through it to Kabbalistic knowledge and wisdom,[47] the twenty-two paths representing the Major Arcana and the ten sephiroth representing the numbered cards of the Minor Arcana. A diagram of the arrangement of the sephiroth appears on the RWS Ten of Pentacles card, and possibly on the veil behind the RWS High Priestess. Tiny diagrams of the Tree of Life are also superimposed on the Major Arcana cards of the Spiral Tarot. Ten chalices arranged in the form of the Tree of Life hang from a lotus plant on the Thoth Ten of Cups.

In the RWS deck, the pillars of the tree, considered to represent the pillars of King Solomon's Temple in Jerusalem, appear on either side of The High Priestess card, as they also do in the Spiral, Morgan-Greer, Alchemical, Light and Shadow, and Tarot of the Spirit Priestess cards.

All three pillars have several names. The left hand pillar is called the Left Hand of God, the pillar of form, severity, majesty, understanding, or judgement. In the RWS High Priestess card, it bears the letter B for Boaz, which means strength and also alludes to the great-grandfather of David and husband of Ruth. The right pillar is called the Right Hand of God, the pillar of force, mercy, justice, or love. In the RWS card it bears the letter J for Jachin (spelled or translated in different ways), meaning wisdom. The third or middle pillar is called the pillar of equilibrium, or mildness. In many High Priestess and Justice cards, the central figure represents the middle pillar.

See **correspondences; Kabbalah; sephiroth**.

tree(s)

Trees represent the world axis, the *axis mundi*, the cosmic source and framework of the world. They also symbolize the inexhaustible life-process.[48] Trees appear in many tarot cards, sometimes green and growing, sometimes dark (possible danger or travails overcome or to be overcome, or as an outline to suggest the type of tree), sometimes windblown, as in the trees that appear on the RWS Swords court cards, suggesting the element of air at work. Around a house or left in a small grove in the open (the RWS Page of Pentacles), they suggest the hand of civilization and manifestation at work establishing order and sanctuary.

See **forest** and specific trees.

tree, apple

The apple is the Celtic symbol for choice and a door into greater mysteries. An apple tree appears in the New Palladini Four of Cups, and on the Robin Wood Lovers card. Twigs of apple blossoms bloom on the Wheel of Change Four of Disks. Many mythic paradises contained apple trees or orchards. The apple was sacred to Aphrodite/Venus. With its five-petaled blossoms and inner pentagram (when cut), it corresponds to the five senses.

tree, beech

The queen of trees, it is a symbol of beauty and ancient wisdom,[49] prosperity, and divination.[50] Bacchus drank his wine from beechen bowls. The oracles of Zeus at Dodona, the most ancient oracular shrine in Greece, were delivered through the medium of the sacred beech and oak trees.[51] The Robin Wood Empress sits beneath a beech tree.

tree, birch

In the Celtic tree system the birch symbolizes renewal and cleansing. It also represents the cosmic tree in shamanic initiation ceremonies and healing practices,[52] linking the material and spirit worlds. In Icelandic mythology the birch was consecrated to Thor, associated with law and justice. In myths and legends, birch trees grew at the entrance to paradise. A birch forest appears in the Robin Wood Death card.

tree, cypress

Sacred to Venus and Artemis/Diana, it suggests fertility and comprises the forest (which hides the life giving essence) in the RWS Empress card. Also sacred to the gods of the underworld, namely Hades/Pluto, it can represent workings or germinations that occur in darkness, e.g., the unconscious.

tree, laurel

See **wreath, laurel**.

tree, evergreen

Evergreen trees appear in the RWS and Morgan-Greer Empress cards and suggest the continuous giving and support offered by the empress, the never-ceasing fertility of body and spirit as exemplified in the mother archetype. However, trees in The Empress cards are sometimes identified as cypress trees, partly because the empress is identified with Venus.

See **tree, cypress**.

tree, oak

The Celtic symbol for protection and strength, and the sacred tree of Heracles/Hercules and Jupiter/Zeus, an oak tree suggests "entrance to the mysteries."[53] The Greeks believed the human race sprang from the oak tree. The oak, and especially its acorns, were sacred to Thor, god of thunder and all other "thunder" gods, e.g., Allah, Jehovah (*see* **acorns**). Oak trees appear on the Robin Wood Lovers (representing strength and protection) and Strength cards. The solar king hangs from one in the Wheel of Change Hanged Man card, representing his connection with the sun, the sky, and lightning's power.[54]

tree of the knowledge of good and evil

Symbolizes the stage of consciousness in the evolution of humankind and in individual personality development. It is depicted behind the female figure in the RWS Lovers card.

See **tree, apple**.

tree, olive

The olive tree, a branch of which appears in the RWS Ace of Swords card, was a sacred tree for many cultures. The Greeks associated it with Athena; the Romans to Jupiter and Minerva. In Islamic tradition, it represents the world tree or world axis. Because its oil was used as lamp fuel in ancient times, it is associated with light and metaphors of spiritual light and enlightenment. In Judeo-Christian tradition, the dove brought back an olive branch to Noah to show him the flood was over. Symbolically it represents peace, fruitfulness, mercy, and purification.

tree, palm

Seen on the veil behind The High Priestess in the RWS deck, the palm is an esoteric symbol for the fanning of the power of the pituitary gland and ajna (third eye) chakra. Pomegranates, also decorating the veil, represent the pineal gland.[55] More simply the palm tree and its leaves signify masculine or assertive energy, the ability to create through action. It is in this sense that a palm branch hangs from the RWS Ace of Swords.

See **pomegranate**.

tree, pine

Sacred to Cybele. In Greek mythology the insatiable Dionysus (*see* his relationship to The High Priestess) often holds a pinecone in his hand, suggesting immortality, perpetuity of plant life, lordship over nature, fertility, and life force.[56]

See **Dionysus/Bacchus; pinecone.**

triangle

The triangle is inescapably related to the number three, and often represents the divine trinity when presented as an equilateral triangle. Pointing upward, a triangle refers to humanity's ascent to heaven. Pointing downward, it represents divine descent into lower realms. Combined in one figure, the two upward-downward triangles form the six-pointed Star of David or Seal of Solomon (*see* **sixes; star, six-pointed**), often seen as the glowing light in the lantern of The Hermit. The arm placement of some figures—notably, the arms of the RWS Hanged Man and the Thoth Emperor—form triangles, complete in themselves or as part of an alchemical sigil. Triangles incorporated into other designs appear on the RWS Temperance and Tower cards.

See **tattvas.**

trickster (archetype)

Trickster energy is both obvious and elusive. If it were ice cream, it would be a scoop of pistachio with a chocolate covered strawberry hidden in its core. A surprise. A delight. The unexpected for the naïve, friendly recognition by those in the know.

Every culture develops some way to personify trickster energy—actually a primitive state of consciousness—and to portray the trickster archetype in writings, mythologies, and folktales. From the cunningness of Br'er Rabbit to the nonsense of Edward Lear, from the sharply honed wit of Oscar Wilde to the coyote tales of Southwestern Native American cultures, trickster energy pervades and invades the psyches of all humankind. Trickster energy can plague you daily if you ignore it, for nothing wreaks more havoc than trickster energy gone awry. Accepted or not, it insists on being acknowledged and honored. Psychologically, it is a threshold phenomenon. Wherever and whenever we are most complacent, trickster appears, challenging us to be different, to shatter tradition,[57] to face a new alternative, which is what some think a tarot reading should provide. We are called upon to break the boundaries of rigid ego thinking.

In the tarot, trickster energy is specifically associated with The Fool and Magician cards. The Daughters of the Moon deck replaces The Fool card with two, one of which is "The Trickster." The Hanged Man as a bungee jumper from the Songs for the Journey Home is a direct expression of trickster energy.

Synchronistic events related to tarot readings, intuitive flashes, and cards that represent crossroads or threshold situations are all examples of some of the ways that we can recognize trickster energy in action in tarot work. Trickster energy is most often manifest when situations involve boundaries and change, the elements of a good tarot reading.[58]

See **synchronicity.**

trumps

In older decks, the Major Arcana were referred to as the trumps, and The Fool was not included in this category. Their ordering also varied considerably from the present-day ordering of the Major Arcana.

turtle

By carrying their shells, their homes, on their backs, turtles frequently represent independence, as well as the inherent ability to take quick refuge from attack. Turtles often play important roles in myths of primordial cosmology. A turtle, "upholder of the world," begins a journey from the sun to the moon in the

Shining Tribe Hermit card.[59] A turtle representing the earth lies inside the womb of The World mother on the Light and Shadow card. Representing the protected inner world, a turtle sits in a chalice held in the right hand of the Thoth Princess of Cups. For the meaning of the turtle on the Shining Tribe Two of Stones, *see* **Pentacles, Two of.**

twenty-one

Related to the twenty-one attributes of wisdom in the Old Testament, the number is considered a symbol of developmental cycles ($7 \times 3 = 21$) and subsequent maturity.[60] It is, of course, the number of trumps, excluding The Fool, in most tarot decks.

See **Major Arcana; numbers.**

twin motif

In dreams, when some unconscious content is attempting to make itself known, approaching the threshold of consciousness, it often appears in duplicate or doubled (two not necessarily identical items).[61] This motif is found in several RWS cards. The two identical chalices in the RWS Temperance card and the two pitchers in The Star card suggest these cards deal with material not yet fully conscious but about to emerge from the unconscious. The two acolytes at the feet of the Hierophant have their backs to us, suggesting their message is still concealed although more available inasmuch as they are human figures. They support the theme of the Hierophant's hand signal ("all is not revealed"). The double sphinxes and other double animals in various Chariot cards face us, making more obvious the world of duality into which the charioteer is entering. The two "gateway" towers, between which the "sun of immortality"[62] shines in the RWS Death card, are duplicated again in The Moon (XVIII) card, a double duplication, linking the two with the message of new or emerging awareness (beyond "civilized" knowledge) in our spiritual journey.

See **elevens.**

twos

As choices become available, action begins. Division and conflict that may challenge our self-concepts develop. The need for balance arises. We recognize that polarities exist in both outer and inner worlds, yet we have not begun to seriously consider their reconciliation. Consequently, tarot twos show the first actual experience after the expression of the basic principle or element of the suit by the ace. It may be a divisive task or one calling for careful balancing of certain elements of our lives, perhaps to create new partnerships that will help us do so. We begin to develop wisdom and insight about the complexities of the suit. Twos are associated with the sephira Chokmah (Wisdom) on the Tree of Life.

See the twos of each suit.

Typhon

The child of Hera's rage (some say of Gaia or Mother Earth), the giant Typhon was raised by the serpent Pytho and was half human, half animal, swathed with vipers. Mythologically, Typhon is considered the foe of spirit. He is the power of "aberrant instinct," which rejects sublimation and surrenders to earthly drives."[63] Typhon in his serpent form appears on the RWS Wheel of Fortune card.

See **snakes(s)**.

u

*

undines

The lower half of their body being fishlike, and the upper part
being human, water nymphs or mermaids represent the perilous
nature of water (the unconscious). As a composite creature, they
represent attempts at reconciling the conscious, tamed, or hu-
manized aspects of our psyche with the as-yet-untamed material
of the unconscious. Undines are the elemental spirits associated
with the Minor Arcana Cups suit and appear on the throne of
the RWS Queen of Cups. Her equivalent, the World Spirit Sibyl
of Cups actually is a blue-skinned mermaid sitting on a coral
throne. Undines rise from the waves in the Legend Arthurian
Judgement card, where they represent transformation.

unicorn(s)

Through the ages the mystical unicorn has symbolized various concepts including kingship, power, the sword, the word of God, sincerity, and purity or innocence. The legend that the unicorn is tireless when pursued, but falls meekly to the ground when approached by a virgin, suggests that it is also symbolic of sublimated sex.[1] In China the unicorn was a symbol of yin and yang, the rhythm of the world.[2] In ancient alchemy, it seems to have had many different meanings, sometimes representing primordial virility or sexuality and sometimes representing the *mercurius* (feminine or lunar) spirit.

Unicorns, which only obey the pure of heart, pull the Robin Wood Chariot. They are seen on the Haindl Lovers, and Wheel of Fortune (symbolizing Spirit leaping beyond the wheel) cards. The large one dominating the Haindl Moon card emphasizes the realm of imagination and fantasy; the card represents knowledge that is beyond rational explanation. A white unicorn appears on the cape of the female in the Shapeshifter Nine of Earth Element (Pentacles), representing prosperity, "Success" (the card's name), and "purely directed thought that can accomplish anything."[3]

Uranus (planet)

The seventh planet from the Sun, it co-rules Aquarius.

Uranus was the first planet discovered after the invention of the telescope, and is historically connected with the American and French revolutions and the development of modern technology and medicine, particularly electricity. Cards attributed to this planet partake of its capacity for originality, procreativity, eccentricity, and its untamable nature. Uranus is the planet of sudden changes and upheavals, but also of inventive brilliance. The meanings for a well-dignified Uranus card include: mental brilliance; inventiveness; boldness in discovery, unquenchable curiosity about the world; visionary ideas about society, economics, and politics; sudden awareness or enlightenment. An ill-dignified or reversed Uranus card may mean: unpredictability; intolerance; erratic and quirky behavior; schizophrenia; dispassionate disregard of the well-being of others; a cold, unfeeling nature; irritations, disruptions, interruptions; extreme solutions that fail to preserve worthy contributions of the past; a disregard for history or tradition.[4]

See **Aquarius; Ouranos/Uranus; Saturn** (planet).

uroboros
   See **ouroboros**.

*

veil/curtain

A veil symbolizes separation, secrets, things hidden. Veils represent the distinction between the known and the unknown, e.g., conscious versus unconscious knowledge, individual versus divine or cosmic knowledge. Veils connect the pillars in the RWS High Priestess and Justice cards. They invite the tarot querent to discover the hidden knowledge behind them and are, therefore, associated with the unveiling of one's own mysteries.

Venus (goddess)
   See **Aphrodite/Venus**.

Venus (planet)

The second planet from the Sun rules the astrological signs of Taurus and Libra.

A card attributed to Venus emphasizes the flow of love and desire, luxury items connected with comfort, beauty or adornment, music, dance, and the fine arts. Venus rules desire for pleasure of the senses, so neighboring cards will indicate whether the Venusian desires rule the senses and intellect, create a longing for relationships or artistic pursuits; or if excessive desires are at the root of problems. The qualities of a well-dignified Venus card include: sensitivity to beauty, good taste, graceful manners and social skills, the ability to attract lovers or friends, proclivities both erotic and refined, love of comfort, talents in the arts. The traits of an ill-dignified or reversed Venus card include: a demanding attitude, petulance or wrathful retaliation when thwarted, impoverishment, dishonorable or deviant forms of love and sex, illicit love affair, immodesty, lewdness, laziness, or excessive self-indulgence.[1]

See **Libra; Taurus**. For the mythic qualities associated with this planet, see **Aphrodite/Venus**.

vine
See **grapevine**.

violet (color)
See **purple**.

Virgo (astrological sign)
The sixth sign of the zodiac (August 23–September 23).

Element: Earth
Modality: Mutable
Polarity: Yin
Ruled by the planet Mercury

Cards attributed to the earthy sign of Virgo are invested with its analytic skills and perfectionism. Virgo is the sign of work and service, and exemplifies qualities of purity, modesty, and quiet dedication. It also represents mentors, teachers, aunts and uncles—adults other than parents who mold a child's development. The Sun is in Virgo during the harvesting season, and the woman depicted in the constellation holds a sheaf of wheat, representing the abundance of the fields. Virgo is associated with the Virgin Mary, and in earlier times to Demeter/Ceres, the grain goddess who taught humanity the Eleusinian mysteries. A well-dignified Virgo card's meanings include: industriousness; caution; analytical skills; patience; expertise; a focus on health and hygiene; food products derived from the earth, including domesticated animals; guidance during developmental phases. An ill-dignified or reversed Virgo card may be interpreted as: hypochondria, extremes of cleanliness or slovenliness, unbridled criticism, fanatical beliefs or opinions, sexual frigidity or excess.[2]

See **Mercury** (planet).

W

Much speculation has occurred regarding the possible meaning of the letter W embellished on the RWS Ace of Cups. It may signify Waite's name; it may stand for water, the suit's element.[1] Resembling an inverted "M," it may represent the Hebrew letter "Mem" assigned to the element of water.[2] Yet another possible explanation relates to a fifteenth century esoteric painting "The Sacred Allegory of Jesus and Mary Magdalene," by Jan Provost. Upturned hands form a reversed M, a symbol of Mary Magdalene, and in the painting, she frees the dove of the Holy Spirit.[3]

Speculation also exists about the "W" comprising the uppermost element of the RWS Hierophant's crown. One theory is that it represents the Hebrew letter *shin* (*see* **hidden letters**). Another is that it represents one of the three letters (U, V, W) that the Golden Dawn used to represent the Hebrew letter *vav*, associated with the astrological sign of Taurus, attributed to The Hierophant.[4]

Waite, Arthur Edward (1857–1942)

A member of the Golden Dawn, and influenced by its teachings, and his understanding of alchemy and the Kabbalah, he created in 1910 the most popular tarot deck ever, employing as his artist Pamela Colman Smith. In his book *The Pictorial Key to the Tarot*, Waite denounced the Egyptian origin of the tarot promulgated by tarotists before him. One of his purposes for creating a deck was to restore or correct what he considered fraudulent presentations of previous information by other tarotists, most notably Eliphas Lévi. Waite also contended that the placement of Justice as the eighth and Strength as the eleventh Major Arcana cards was a "blind," i.e., the presentation of false information, and reversed the two cards in his own deck. Since that time there has been much debate among tarotists about which is the proper placement. Without being more specific, Waite wrote that the cards, especially those of the Major Arcana, contained some parts of Secret Tradition and Secret Doctrine.

See **Smith, Pamela Colman** and Part 1, Chapter 3, for a description of Waite's deck.

wall

See **stone wall**.

wallet

This refers to the bundle or pack that the figure in many Fool cards carries, tied or fastened to his stick. The Tarot of the Spirit Fool carries a box-shaped purse over his wrist. There are as many guesses about the pack's contents as there are tarotists, determined by the kind of material out of which it is constructed, its color, and how it is decorated. The symbol that appears on the wallet in the RWS Fool card has been identified variously as a shell, a bird, and an eagle.

Most commonly, The Fool's pack is said to contain unused or unavailable knowledge. Some suggest it holds memories of past experiences, information from the unconscious, or from past lives (karma), and the life force that propels The Fool on his journey. The Robin Wood Fool wears a backpack containing all the items he needs for his life's journey, but which are not really accessible because the pack is strapped down behind him.[5]

wand(s)

Wands represent power or authority. They can indicate a high or special level of training, or special skills and abilities, as in a magic wand. In fairy tales, wands—magic objects that can transform or redeem people—are symbols of the Self. In ancient Celtic mythology, wands were the symbol of the Druids' power over the elements and other material things. Mythologically related to straight lines and sticks (one of humankind's simplest and oldest instruments), wands embody the symbology of power and intensity. Sticks appearing in fairy tales often symbolically extend a character's will power and purposiveness "beyond mere momentary impulses."[6]

A healing wand entwined with snakes, which became the caduceus in medicine, was the special attribute of Asclepias, Greek god of healing, and of Hermes/Mercury. Both wands likely relate to ancient tree cults and the serpent worship of the Aegean area and the Middle East[7] (*see* **caduceus**).

Wands are frequently seen in The Magician and World cards. In The Fool and The Hermit cards, they masquerade, respectively, as a stick to carry a bundle and a walking staff. They figure prominently in the Minor Arcana suit of Wands. They become gem- or crystal-tipped wands made of various metals in the Robin Wood suit, where they are often wrapped with other items, which change or enhance the meaning.

If the wand is held in the left hand, it likely represents information available or sought from the unconscious—what information depends on the material from which the wand is made and how it may be wrapped with other material.

See **staff.**

Wands (suit)

Also called clubs, staves, rods, or batons, Wands cards depict experiences related to creative ideas, inner vision, and the necessary passion for the development of enterprise. They are associated with Jung's intuitive function and usually with the element of fire, the most energetic and transforming of the four "energies" and a symbol of the human will or willpower.

The ancients believed the fire element or principle to be present in persons who possessed sharp, active actions or reactions. Fire energy definitely is not passive, but exists in reactions that propel or push something, or someone, forward. Wands cards often emphasize the future, although fire energy is usually what we need more of to help us get out of bed on Monday mornings. Fire reactions or activities take on a dynamic leadership role, never waiting for "the mood to strike" before getting down to creative work. They have the qualities of dramatic intensity and inspiration, which can also be unstable in situations or relationships. Wands cards speak of getting things going, of energizing and transforming, not because of logic or thinking but because our inner being tells us to.

Because of its connection with living trees, the suit of wands can be mythologically associated with the Norse world tree Yggdrasil, the world axis (*see* **world axis**), and the Buddha's Bodhi tree of enlightenment. The Renaissance Tarot associates the suit with many of the twelve trials of Heracles[8] (*see* **Heracles/Hercules**). Morgan-Greer rods are made from oak, associated with Zeus/Jupiter. The Mythic Tarot suit tells the story of Jason and the Argonauts. Haindl chose the concepts of Hinduism to express his understanding of the suit.

As a fire suit Wands connect with the myth of Prometheus, who took pity on struggling humans and stole fire (divine consciousness) from Zeus to give to mankind. Liz Greene calls him the "first cosmic social worker"[9] (*see* **Hanged Man, The (XII); Prometheus**).

Because of its relationship with intuition, Wands mythology is also associated with stories of visionaries, seers and seeresses, druids, and other "directing force" gods and goddesses. From their special or "second sight," they got the message and got it out there.

Fire energy equates with the alchemical process of *calcinatio/* calcination. Base matter is heated until all liquid has evaporated and it is reduced to ash. *Calcinatio* was the purification process for passion and ambivalence, so Wands experiences will deal with catalytic experiences, with powerful desires and passions and their inevitable frustration in order to promote the development of inner integrity and self-confidence.[10]

Many Wands in a reading suggest either too much attention or not enough (depending on where the cards lie) on developing creative ideas or enterprises, or on taking care of business issues. In the Tarot of the Spirit, the Suit of Wands becomes Fire, as in the Osho deck, where it is called the Suit of Fire: Action. In the Shining Tribe deck, it becomes the Suit of Trees.

Wands, Ace of

Like all aces, the Ace of Wands says that we are being drawn into a new energy, or that a new task is now moving into our consciousness. The card is one of excitement; aliveness; eagerness to deal with, sort out, or develop our conscious ideas and fantasies. It is a card of creativity and self-confidence. An inner creative force has been stimulated or awakened, encouraging us to be courageous in developing our ideas.

In the RWS card, a gleaming, heavenly hand emerges from the gray cloud of wisdom, holding a stick bearing ten (the potential of completion) budding leaves. Eight leaves in the shape of the Hebrew letter *yod* (creative seeds) fall or float beside the stick (*see* **yod**).

A fiery, quartz-tipped wand bearing DNA markings (endless possibilities) dominates the Robin Wood card. It crackles, glows, and burns with energy."[14] A flaming torch dominates the Thoth card. A maypole, topped with a golden globe and situated behind a triangle of flaming twigs, waits to be wrapped with flowing ribbons in the Wheel of Change's card. The central image of the Shining Tribe card is that of the umbilical cord of an infant in the earth's womb becoming the Tree of Life. In the Ancestral Path card a large ankh-topped staff is seen before the Great Sphinx.

The Legend Arthurian card carries the Grail Lance. The Mythic Tarot portrays Zeus, the moving power behind the tale of Jason and the Golden Fleece. A fruiting grapevine grows around the top of the staff/stave in the Renaissance Tarot. From its center hangs a small cameo showing Heracles strangling two snakes, which reflects the idea of success in new undertakings. The Haindl Tarot presents a dark stone (lingam, phallic stone) standing in a pool of water (yoni, feminine symbol). Before them a flaming spear represents both lust and the immortal spark. The scene refers to the union of the two fundamental energies of the universe.[12]

The Ace of Wands alerts us that it is time to pay more attention to the intuitive aspects of our lives or situations. When we turn inward and listen carefully to our inner voice, the Ace of Wands is active within. We are able to tune in to the "cosmic soup" and create a "healing intelligence," a balance between reason and intuition.[13]

Keywords/phrases: inner vision; passion for development of ideas (but not the actual work); stimulation of inner creative ideas or force; new career; a promotion; initiative.

See **aces; sunflowers.**

Wands, Two of

Activities and endeavors pertaining to developing and honoring our intuition begin. We can use our imagination at this point in our development; our ideas are grandiose (globe in RWS card) and possibly far-reaching (the distant sea and mountains, RWS). We have yet to hone them to facilitate our inner stillness and development, but we are listening.

In the RWS card, a man dressed in earth tones (fantasy made real) and a red hat (active mind) looks over sea and shore from a battlement roof. The Robin Wood figure wears red (courage) and blue (deep spirituality) colors in the elaborate pattern of his clothes. The gem on his hat indicates that he is "waiting for a gem of wisdom."[14] The well-dressed businessman in the Spiral Tarot's card looks across a river to fantastic skyscrapers (a vision?). The scene represents the balance between stillness and activity.[15] The woman in the Shining Tribe Two of Trees stands, arms upraised, between two bent trees forming the gateway to a new experience. On the rolling mountain before her are inscribed the words "Blessed is the mother who has given us shape." It is a card of awakening to a new consciousness.[16] In the Alchemical Two of Staffs, a hand emerges from a cloud and lights its staff from one already burning on the ground. The card represents growth of the spirit and a desire for the unification of opposites, which will lead to a higher level of development.[17]

In the Mythic Tarot's card, Jason stands before the cave of the Centaur Chiron before he begins his journey to reclaim his heritage as the rightful heir to the throne of Iolkos. Our future goals or projects are full of potential if we have the courage to follow the new path even though its direction or conclusion may be uncertain.[18] On the Haindl "Dominion" card, the ruins of an ancient, deserted church suggest that while we may neglect sacred power, it still exists.

When you allow yourself to imagine a number of possibilities without judgmental sorting, you are in a Two of Wands process.

Your ideas are vast and expansive, but you remain calm because you know that later you will organize or prioritize them and accomplish those you choose, being true to yourself and your vision.

Keywords/phrases: beginning of activities or endeavors that honor intuition; paying attention to grandiose and far-reaching ideas; not paying attention to what's going on; trying to balance complacency or stillness (or "remaining") and adventurousness, or activity (or "going"); waiting for an inner gem of wisdom; balance between stillness and activity.

See **twos.**

Wands, Three of

The RWS card is one of still dreaming or planning, as a richly dressed man stands on a green promontory and stares out toward a yellow sea with three tiny ships on it. A vision or insight may be about to come through. We are called up to spread our sails in "the right way" in the pursuit of more sublime aims.[19] Two flaming staffs on the Alchemical card await the arrival of a red-sailed ship with a flame atop its mast. Energy spent is returning as a reward. The Shining Tribe Three of Trees derives from a spirit image of the Ojibwa people, the Manitokan, and speaks of trusting what life gives us and opening our arms to it. Haindl "Virtue" reminds us to act in a holy way from an awareness of truth.[20] In the Renaissance deck, Heracles captures the golden hind of Cerynea after a year's chase. The card represents achievement (prize or reward) attained through effort, as well as persistence, patience, and restraint.[21]

Keywords/phrases: important message; vision; insight about to come through but still partly in the unconscious (RWS ships); awareness that occurs by attending to other cultural values or practices; moving on to new possibilities; promising prospects.

See **threes.**

Wands, Four of

In many decks (World Spirit, Mythic) this is a card of success and celebration, or commitment (Spiral, Alchemical) that will lead to celebration. People dance in the Robin Wood card. Our inner processes are in movement. As only dances can do, our mood or motivational energy will be changed or aroused. Peace and harmony, a balance of energy, have been achieved in the Haindl "Perfection" card. The Nigel Jackson card represents the satisfaction of achievement from our labors. On the Four of Flames (Daughters of the Moon), the flames of conflict and opposition are fanned, so that resolution may occur.

Keywords/phrases: preparation for cosmic dance or rhythm; mood or motivational energy about to be changed; squaring up things in one's career; forming new liaisons; networking; bringing order and structure into career; joyful, lighthearted new approach; accumulation of new experiences.

See **fours.**

Wands, Five of

In the eighteenth century, this card represented victory, bright spirits, and heritage, yet by the nineteenth century it had acquired a far more negative meaning. Likely this occurred when the Golden Dawn assigned all fives to the Tree of Life sephira representing severity. The card then represented strife and intensified opposition.[22]

The Thoth card suggests striving rather than strife. It is an ambitious, problem-solving card, and forces us to confront the situation of change (new ideas?) and our resistance to it. It represents our internal struggle between inactivity or apathy and challenge or creation. Can we let go the "known" and confront the "unknown"?

On the RWS card five youths brandish sticks in a somewhat chaotic manner, described as "mimic warfare."[23] They may be seen as coming together to organize and construct something;

hence, the card frequently refers to the simultaneous or subsequent adjustments called for due to the "initiation to new circumstances."[24] Or, it could represent a "brainstorming" session, where it is important to keep ideas coming in a free and playful manner.[25]

The five lads in the Robin Wood card move (fighting, playing, dancing?) among one another so vigorously and energetically that they raise a cloud of dust that obscures the surroundings. We can lose sight of important things we might need to attend to while enmeshed in our own struggles. By having the colors of the men's hair and clothes go round the color wheel and by hinting that the men have almost completed making a pentagram, the card symbolically suggests buried harmony waiting to reveal itself.[26]

Heracles mourns the loss of his lieutenant Hylas in the Renaissance card. He searches in vain for him, symbolizing a project abandoned or cut short because of a loss or the departure of a necessary colleague.[27]

The Five of Wands refers to times of crises when we attempt to clarify any idea with which we are working. It can represent an inner test, or reflect concerns about working with others. It calls for restructuring our priorities, or sorting out what it is we really believe compared to conflicting or provocative new beliefs, possibly suggested by influential persons in our lives.

We are in a questioning process and, as the Six of Wands shows, we will be victorious. But the trick is not to end the battle too soon; not to kill the dragon too quickly (the Mythic Tarot's card portraying Jason's battle with the dragon that guards the Golden Fleece). Wrestling with ideas is an important self-growth process, and even if we decide to retain our original ideas, the very wrestling strengthens our intellectual efforts for the next time a challenging issue comes up.

Recognize the Five of Wands at work when you or others take a stand for, or against, a particular idea or situation because you believe it to be "the right thing to do" even though others, possibly even family members, strongly oppose it.

Keywords/phrases: competition and struggle; problem-solving activity; confronting change and our resistance to it; frustration or anxiety regarding one's creative expression; initial act of construction or organization; concerns about working with others; scattered energy needing more focus; facing a challenge that requires considerable effort.

See **fives.**

Wands, Six of

In the Golden Dawn system and the Haindl deck, this card is called "Victory," and most decks portray success in some way. A victor is crowned with a wreath on the Nigel Jackson cards. The RWS card portrays a victory parade with a wreath-crowned hero surrounded by followers. He has yet to reach his destination, however,[28] so the downside of the card may be that the victory here is transient or short-lived, our brief fifteen minutes of fame. Like the dance, however, processions (serious and spiritual) and parades (fun and earthly) express the movements of the psyche, so the card actually speaks to more than brief or exterior victory. This is more fully represented by the meditating Buddhist monk on the Ancestral Path card, which represents a mental journey toward inner harmony.

Keywords/phrases: integration; harmony; equilibrium; moving or making progress toward one's destination or goal; movements and changes in the psyche; reward for success; acclaim or acknowledgment from others.

See **sixes.**

Wands, Seven of

In the RWS card, a young man stands on a hill brandishing a wand. Six wands are in a valley before and below him. The card represents having the courage and stability of our convictions in the face of opposition—those times when our ideas are pitted against the ideas of others and we have to hold our own moral ground. Although the young man's wand crosses his heart chakra, closing off the heart to new input, the impetus for change has already begun (sevens represent the seven stages of alchemical transformation).

Another view is that each of the rods represent hidden aspects of ourselves (since they are not fully revealed in the card), which we may have difficulty seeing or accepting. They now attempt to get our attention. A third view is that each of the rods represents one of the seven chakras. Their awakening or rising energies can initially result in chaotic and confusing action.

The Shining Tribe Seven of Trees shows the spinal column as the Tree of Life within our own bodies. It contains the "hidden" truth that our bodies are not separated from the "body" of the Great Cosmos.[29] The seven spears on the Haindl "Courage" symbolize humanity's upward striving.

Representing "juggling" as managing many things at once, the fiery wands of an unseen juggler fly in the air beneath carnival fireworks in the Wheel of Change's Seven of Wands card. They, and the other colorful aspects of the carnival, symbolize the varying patterns or aspects of our lives that we employ. By ignoring confusing parts of our lives and focusing instead on simpler things, we engage in deception and illusion.[30]

Keywords/phrases: significant communication; introspection; valuing one's ambition and competitive instinct; pondering what one can do better in one's career (How can I serve this career better so it can serve me better?); need for strength and determination; inner imbalance.

See **sevens.**

Wands, Eight of

The RWS "flying wands" represent "motion through the immovable."[31] A solution for our ideas, plans, inner actions is at hand. All the wands on the Robin Wood card are different, showing that there may be a wide range of things going on.

The downside of the card is that it can represent "spinning your wheels," i.e., your ideas are up in the air, not grounded, and won't work. There's no follow-through. Or, the card can express the momentum behind a rigidly held stance or set of convictions.[32] The Shining Tribe Eight of Trees refers to situations that are out of control, yet the figure leaping through the air, golden hair streaming behind, suggests our ability to free ourselves from destruction by an act of will.[33]

The Mythic Tarot's Jason, successful in obtaining the Golden Fleece, sails home, reflecting the release of creative energy that occurs after overcoming previous struggles. The Thoth card refers to sudden ideas and flashes of insight that interrupt previously held notions. The "Swiftness" with which this occurs is reflected in the Haindl card. The upward-pointing spears also suggest that the movement can be spiritual. The Wheel of Change Tarot's card shows an artist's drawing of a rainbow-colored, eight-spoked wheel (*see* **wheel**) trailing fire through a universe dotted with stars. Around it are the eight pencils and brushes that represent the various stages of the creative process.

Keywords/phrases: wrapping up some phase of one's career; get busy and get going; time for initiative and action rather than reaction; finding a new direction; implementing a plan; inability to delay intensity of some issue; movement toward new or specific goals.

See **eights.**

Wands, Nine of

The RWS card has been called "strength in opposition."[34] If attacked, the wounded person will meet the onslaught boldly. His build suggests that he may prove a formidable antagonist, going along with the Haindl's title of this card, "Power," which represents personal energy and the power of human culture over nature.

The man in the RWS card, backed by a certain orderliness in the way the other eight wands are arranged, holds firmly onto one of his ideas. And that may be his problem, the source of the woundedness expressed by this card: that he holds too securely onto that one idea or attitude. He does have a gap behind him wherein he could leave this "field of battle," and walk into the green, fertile hills behind him. Yet, he looks toward the left of the card, suggesting that his problem, attitude, or woundedness has something to do with what he's carrying from his past, some attitude that he holds onto and of which he is likely unaware. But he's getting there; he's looking and wondering.

Sometimes the RWS figure's stance is seen as defensive, suggesting that he expends too much energy waiting for an attack that never comes, since nines are a symbol of completion. Indeed, the Robin Wood card is called "Waiting," and represents the calm in the eye of the storm.

The wounded man in the Osho "Exhaustion" card lives through conscience not consciousness. His wounds result from intense efforts to keep fueling his sense of self-importance and to avoid the anxiety and mystery of the chaotic and the spontaneous. They prevent him from taking a trip into uncharted waters.[35] In the Mythic Tarot Jason's ship fights its way through turbulent seas. The scene reflects "strength in reserve" and the "power of creative imagination" evoked through the challenge of one more final test.[36]

The complicated Wheel of Change Nine of Wands displays Australian Aboriginal petroglyphs and didgeridoos (a hollow pipe that is a musical instrument), connecting it with the spirits of dreaming, and of the Dreamtime where resides the collective unconscious of the Aboriginal people and their connection with the greater universe. In part, the card represents coming to understand something that at first seems beyond, or out of, our understanding.[37]

The Shining Tribe Nine of Trees refers to the myth of Inanna and her descent to earth to take on mortal form and experience the world. Card designer Rachel Pollack says it would take a book of its own to fully explore this one card and its implications. At its simplest, it refers to grief and pain for something precious that has gone wrong. It also refers to distortions of reality and the way we limit personal power and truth when we try to see the world as *only* light and joy.[38]

Keywords/phrases: "retirement"; getting ready to do something else because a particular phase of one's career has been completed; determination; messages arriving; endurance; defiance and resistance; feeling threatened; opposition to new ideas.

See **nines.**

Wands, Ten of

Many people regard the RWS figure as unable to see where he is going. He plods along carrying his bundle of wands, obviously successful in amassing creative efforts, yet a "man oppressed by the weight" of his burden.[39] The Haindl "Oppression" card reflects the situation of becoming the victim of power or conquest, rather than living in affection and equal partnership.

As the reverse of that message, flags of different nations rising together beneath a flag of the planet Earth on the Wheel of Change Ten of Wands symbolize the embodiment of various truths. The Shining Tribe Ten of Trees bursts forth with the fulfillment and consciousness that grows from the varieties of our life experiences. The central tree stands in a series of nine concentric circles arranged around a tenth orange, sun circle. The total represents our solar system, and the "solar system of our past decisions and life events—the source of who we have become."[40]

Keywords/phrases: oppression (especially self-imposed); feeling overwhelmed; problem soon to be resolved through one's own abilities or effort; assuming too great a responsibility or burden.

See **tens.**

Wands, Page of

In the clothing of the RWS page we see the ouroboros (*see* **ouroboros**), one of the most predominant signs in the RWS Wands' court cards. This links the initiates, or royalty, of this suit with the RWS Magician, who wears the ouroboros belt around his waist. For the young page, however, his new pathway is only beginning so the serpent or lizard does not quite connect with its tail. He stands in the "act of proclamation," and his "tidings are strange."[41] Like all neophytes, his attention is single-minded.

The RWS page stands in the hot desert (fire element) in Egypt; however, the pyramids in the distance are further evidence that new territories or ideas need to be checked out.

The Wheel of Change Tarot's young Native American page has gone to the top of a mountain to receive a vision. A dark raven shows him a Haida totem pole and a long path through the mountains. He will need to make a long journey through "unfamiliar" lands to learn and grow.[42]

The Shining Tribe's Place of Trees is a sacred grove where we can feel our lives flourish. The goddess sits by her Tree of Life, across from the Tree of Knowledge. We are inspired to develop our own individuality, and to return time and again to a place or state of mind "where knowledge makes us more alive."[43]

Playing his flute, the Haindl Son/Prince of Wands is Krishna, the incarnation of Vishnu. He brings divine music into physical reality (*see* **music**), and represents the love of life, especially its sensual aspects, its tricks, and jokes. A woman dances to celebrate the joy of being alive on the Osho card. Seeing life as "A Playfulness" lifts the serious burden of fears, anxieties, and stresses we typically carry around; we begin to live life weightlessly.[44]

Likewise playful, the Spiral's Princess of Wands, dressed in a gown with a sunflower pattern, sits beside a baby dragon. Both she and the dragon are amazed at the growth potential available. A bundle of firecrackers hangs from the belt of the young female Robin Wood Page to remind us that she can be a little explosive.

The Mythic Tarot's Page of Wands is Phrixus (see **Phrixus**). He is a "stage-setter," a prelude to action before better-known characters of the story begin their own successful plot-fulfilling actions.[45]

In traditional decks, the card represents an earth/fire combination. This page is not as comfortable with himself, or as stable, as some of the other pages. When the card appears in a spread, it may indicate little stresses or annoyances that we need to stop and analyze or dissect in order to use and develop page energies creatively.

Keywords/phrases: developing new aspects of inner vision or intuition; quick, intuitive personality; restlessness; emergence of new phase of creative activity; potential or possibilities not yet realized; new idea that needs grounding.

See **court cards; pages.**

Wands, Knight of

As an air card in the fire suit, this knight is pretty comfortable with his dualities. He plunges ahead toward new challenges, not being as careful as he might because of inflated feelings that he always will be safe. The Mythic Tarot's Knight of Wands is Bellerophon, who rides Pegasus (*see* **Pegasus**). He represents the constant craving for new adventure and the expression of arrogance rather than modesty—referring to Bellerophon's defeat of the Chimaera, a fire-breathing monster.

The RWS knight is roaring to go with fiery energy, as shown in the flame-like plume from his helmet and the decoration on the arms of his armor. Like the RWS page he, too, is in the desert, suggesting hidden or unexplored emotion. His horse, like that of the Robin Wood knight, seems to show more emotion than the knight himself, suggesting that if and when this knight explodes with the energy equivalent to that expressed by his horse, the situation will be rife with anger or passion. A more deliberately focused "Intensity" is the theme of the Osho card. The figure in the card moves so swiftly that he has almost become pure energy. We are to be neither followers nor imitators, but rather find our own core and follow it.[46]

The Wheel of Change's Princess of Wands is all about rhythm. As she performs the dance of life in her small village, symbolizing incarnate life and sacred space, her wand penetrates the center of the spiral of the universe. Given the knowledge she has learned from her tribe as to the right time and the right way to perform her dances, she combines the powers of dark and light and directs her will toward creating something new.[47]

The woman on the Shining Tribe's Knower of Trees stands with arms outstretched like a tree. Vines grow over her. We are to embrace life and recognize the power we experience and incorporate when we find our own connections to nature and to the roots of our experiences.[48]

Radha, the wife of Krishna (*see* **Wands, Page of**) represents the Haindl Daughter/Princess of Wands. Like her husband, she holds a flute (*see* **music**), which blends the colors of the rainbow (*see* **rainbow**). She gives soul to the material world. The card is one of abundance, joy, and delight in sensual or sexual experience.[49]

Keywords/phrases: the dichotomy between expanding energy and the need for control in the continuing quest for developing inner vision or intuition; charisma; excess energy that needs grounding; learning to live within one's own natural rhythm.

See **court cards; knights.**

Wands, Queen of

This combination (water/fire) can spur us to action and provide great creative power. Here is a queen who knows and recognizes her personal mental power. She is "tireless versatility."[50]

The Spiral Tarot's queen wears a gown embossed with sunflowers and holds the ouroboros (*see* **ouroboros**) in her hands to symbolize her relationship with time and continuity. Although a straightforward speaker, even with her power she needs admiration and respect from others to feel complete,[51] whereas the Osho Queen of Fire "dispenses her treasures without limits." Called "Sharing," the card is one of overflowing love and compassion, enjoyment without possessiveness or attachment.[52]

Like her page and knight, the RWS queen is in the desert, but her throne sits on a gray pad of wisdom. Carved lions embellish the base of her throne, and a scrawny black cat sits at her feet (*see* **cat(s)**). The queen's posture is reminiscent of that of the King of Swords, but she is neither as forward facing, nor as emotionally forward as he. Sunflowers figures prominently on the back of her throne, and she holds one in her left hand, connecting her with Sul/Sol, the British sun goddess, worshipped at Avebury, and with the great feminine sun goddesses of antiquity.

The Robin Wood Queen of Wands stands in the desert because she has too much energy to sit. The lion embossed on the bosom of her brightly colored gown shows that she is a linear problem solver. A black cat playing at her feet implies that her characteristics are more practical and useful than those of her king, and also that she is more sensual.[53]

The Haindl Queen/Mother of Wands is the dark mother, Kali Ma, mother of the night. She represents our ability to know, or learn, how to deal with the dark energy of our desires. The Mythic Tarot's queen is Penelope, the inventive wife of Odysseus. She has great inner strength and trusts her own intuition (Penelope always knew her wandering husband would return).

The queen of music and sound plays her flute on the Wheel of Change Tarot's card. As her music appears, it bursts into flames, symbolizing her wild response to the music. She is deeply involved in a magical experience. She has become the music; hence, the card is one of the passionate transformation that can occur in creativity.[54]

In the Shining Tribe's Gift of Trees, a pair of snakes wind around an apple tree, simultaneously suggesting the caduceus of Greek myth, the famous tree in the Garden of Eden, twining kundalini energy, and the double helix of DNA. It is a card of joining knowledge with understanding for the gift of true wisdom.

Keywords/phrases: self-confidence; self-determination; equanimity; willingness to become more mature; lover of life; works easily with inner visions or fantasies; potential for deep spirituality; time to open to creating one's own life.

See **court cards; queens.**

Wands, King of

As a fire card in the fire suit, this is a king whose various aspects—for good or bad—tend to be synthesized and integrated. They act on one another and build together rather than produce discordance; however, it's not a very challenging combination.

One of the most strong-willed and self-disciplined of the court cards, the King of Wands represents self-mastery in terms of bandying ideas back and forth, and as a leader in keeping his students or workers on the appropriate path or task. He acts forcefully and decisively when necessary but, unfortunately, that does not always suit him well. He is not particularly adept at dealing with or understanding the subtle or complex issues of a situation, and does not particularly like to compromise or adjust. Although comfortable enough not to deliberately "make waves," when thwarted he can be overbearing, tyrannical, arrogant, abusive, intolerant, "showy and theatrical."[55] The Robin Wood king stands in a posture that matches the title of the card, "I Am." He is conscientious, noble, proud, certain of his place in the center, but also hasty and willful.[56]

The salamanders (representative animals of the element of fire) of earlier cards are completely joined on the RWS king's throne and his robe (*see* **ouroboros**). A live one even sits on the gray pad on which the king's throne is mounted, as well as at the feet of the Robin Wood king.

The Zen master is the subject of the Osho "Creator" card. He has harnessed the energy of fire for self-integration and teaches and expresses himself from this "inner masterpiece."[57] The Wheel of Change's king (called a Knight) is also a Buddhist monk. Sitting outdoors upon a bed of stars of the universe and beneath lightning, he meditates with a dorje, which simultaneously represents the lightning bolt of Indra (Hindu thunder god), supreme and invincible spiritual power, compassion, and union of life-giving and death-wielding powers.[58]

King Theseus of Athens occupies the golden throne on the Mythic Tarot's card (*see* **Theseus**). He is the embodiment and personification of all that is exciting and outgoing in the adventurous life and in love. His vision is that "humanity might be more than it is."[59]

Keywords/phrases: empowerment; foresight; worldliness; the creative mind at its highest and best; appreciation of life's pleasures; a consummate strategist who leaves the details to others; strong motivator; initiative; being in command of the situation.

See **court cards; kings**.

water

As an element it usually is associated with the Minor Arcana Cups suit, which has to do with underlying emotions. On individual tarot cards, it typically refers to the workings of the unconscious (instinctual emotions), and its meaning changes depending on whether it is contained, flowing and, if a body of water, what is in or on it.

In various world traditions, water has one, or simultaneously, several meanings: a source of life (associated with the womb or birth) and as a means of cleansing (as in cleansing the soul or the ego/personality, or as in ceremonial preparation or purification). When used for anointing purposes, water symbolizes regeneration or rebirth and is related to the concept of dissolution or dissolving of "what was" into something new.

The ocean as a large body of water can symbolize the divine essence of creation—connected to the belief that our primordial existence arose from oceanic waters. Rain water is typically seen as more "pure"—coming from "heaven"—than salt or sea water, although storms may signify inner turbulence. Streams and rivers, like paths and roadways, can symbolize the course or direction of humankind's collective, or one's personal, experiences—the flow of life energy and growth potential.

In the tarot, water sometimes symbolizes the formless powers of the soul (the inner Self) and its workings. Metaphysically, water symbolizes secret doctrines or esoteric teachings. The RWS High Priestess sits in front of a veil that shields a body of water, and her gown appears to be dissolving into water, suggesting hidden knowledge about to emerge into consciousness. Traditionally, all the waters on subsequent cards in the Major Arcana originate from the dissolution of the High Priestess's gown.

See **High Priestess, The (II); ocean/sea; rivers/streams.**

water lilies
See **lily/lilies.**

waterfall
Water falls in the background of several Empress cards (Aquarian, Morgan-Greer, New Palladini, RWS, Spiral, World Spirit) and represents the stream of consciousness, and the fecund creativity of the flow of the unconscious. The grain-near-a-waterfall motif was a Gnostic symbol of fertility, later adopted by Freemasonry to symbolize earth-sea fertility.[60]

waves
Associated with the symbolism of water, waves, as one of water's movements, suggest emotional movement, liveliness, and instincts that may be out of control or threatening loss of control. Rolling waves suggesting the ups and downs of our emotional life appear in the RWS Two of Cups. Rolling waves also occur on the RWS Page of Cups (insight into one's emotional life becoming available) and the King of Cups (emotional control of turbulent inner emotions, as well as the threat of losing control any moment). Wavy water lines appear in the RWS Six of

Swords (Mercury in Aquarius) and on the tent design of the RWS Seven of Swords (Moon in Aquarius), possibly to depict the Golden Dawn astrological association with Aquarius.[61]

waterway, winding
See roadway/path.

weaver/weaving
The act of weaving symbolizes creation and sometimes represents the workings of fate or the actions and motions of the greater universe. It can represent the uniting or combining of different influences. The design may give further clues as to the story or direction of the phases or possibilities of one's life.

In Greek mythology weaving is connected with Arachne (Uh-RACK-knee). She attained such skill in spinning and weaving that she angered Athena/Minerva, goddess of spinning, who turned her into a spider. The Three Fates, who wove individual destinies, were also Moon goddesses (*see* **Moon, The (XVIII)**). An old woman weaves on the Ancestral Path Moon card, while the Robin Wood Empress spins the life thread of her unborn child and, as the archetypal mother, of us all.

See **spider; spider's web; Wheel of Fortune (X)**.

well-dignified cards
Well-dignified cards are beneficial, helpful, or favorable to the cards next to them. They strengthen each other's meanings. In the most simple form of dignities, the cards of a suit are all well-dignified to the other cards in the same suit. As suits, Cups and Pentacles are well-dignified to each other; Swords and Wands are also well-dignified to each other.

There are two popular ways to consider the dignities of Major Arcana cards. The most common is that they are neutral to whatever cards they are with, neither enhancing nor negatively influencing them. A more complicated way to consider the dignities of the Major Arcana is that all even-numbered cards are well-dignified to Cups and Pentacles, while all odd-numbered Major Arcana cards are well-dignified to Wands and Swords.

See **dignities, numerological; ill-dignified cards; suit/element dignities.**

werewolf
See **Moon, The (XVIII).**

wheat
As the staff of life, wheat represents nurturing and abundance. Its more complex meaning is that of representing the entire cycle of nature and of death, rebirth, and resurrection; hence, it also expresses, and is related to, other cyclical symbols. Psychologically, sheaves of wheat (wheat tied together) represent the process of integrating inner opposites, the conscious and the unconscious. Wheat grows and seeds on the RWS Empress card, while sheaves of wheat appear on the World Spirit's Wheel of Fortune card. A field of wheat fills the background of the Thoth Hermit card, indicating Crowley's belief that the highest symbolism of The Hermit card was fertility.[62]

See **grain(s).**

Wheel of Fortune (X)
Although the wheel mythologically refers to the Roman goddess Fortuna, symbol of good or bad luck, to Urðr, Icelandic goddess of fate, and to all the gods and goddesses of other mythologies who were in charge of human destiny, the tarot card refers not so much to fate as to cyclic activity, continual change, and the core of motions and activities that produce effects. Still, in the Renaissance Tarot, a personification of Fortune stands on a high cliff before a wheel that depicts the tarot trumps on each of its panels. It represents the archetypal journey we must make in search of our destiny.

The RWS card is one of universal, cyclical, and personal

change. It represents recognition of a recurring pattern of events[63] and, therefore, is sometimes associated with the laws of karma, the cause-and-effect principle, while others link Justice to the same concept. The design of the card is adapted from Eliphas Lévi's diagram of the Wheel of Ezekiel in his *Ritual of the Sanctum Regnum.*[64]

The RWS Wheel is related visually to The World card in that in the corners of both appear simultaneous symbolic representations of the four elements, the four disciples, the four fixed zodiacal signs, the four archangels, and the four Magician's tools of the Minor Arcana.[65] Each of the four winged figures holds or studies the Book of Life (*see* **wings**). They may refer to the four "beasts" from the Book of Revelation 4:7–8, although there are a number of biblical references which could also apply.

The most common form of the wheel displayed in tarot cards, and in the RWS Wheel card, is eight-spoked, symbolically connecting it with the eight-petaled lotus (regeneration and renewal),[66] and, by association, with the crown chakra, sometimes depicted as the Hindu thousand-petaled lotus. It also links it with the eight basic trigrams of the *I Ching.*

On the right side of the RWS wheel a jackal-headed creature (Anubis, Egyptian guardian of tombs) rises. On the left Typhon, in his serpent form, descends (*see* **Typhon**). The card represents the "perpetual motion of a fluidic universe" and "the "flux of human life." The blue sphinx at the top represents equilibrium, stability amidst movement.[67] It also alludes to the mystery of all things, to "higher" or greater secrets and, possibly, therefore, to the collective unconscious (*see* **sphinx**). In the Thoth deck, these three represent the three basic alchemical substances: sulphur (sphinx), mercury (Anubis), and salt (Typhon). Sigils from the top of the RWS card, reading clockwise, represent mercury, sulphur, water (element), and salt.

Mercury represents consciousness and the source of all opposites, hence, the ego. Sulphur refers to passion, activity, will, and motivation. Salt reflects the ignorance and inertia that leads to human suffering. Water represents one of the fundamental processes of alchemy, that of dissolution. (*See* **mercury; salt; sulphur; water.**) On the Alchemical card, the double ouroboros (the scaly masculine, the winged feminine) swallow and transform each other in an unending alchemical cycle.

In the outer rim of the RWS card, the letters "TARO" (reading clockwise) or "TORA" (reading counterclockwise)—the letters on the scroll of The High Priestess—are interspersed with the Hebrew letters Yod Heh Vau Heh of the Tetragrammaton (*see* **Tetragrammaton**). When reading counterclockwise, the Arabic letters also may refer to Hathor, Athor, or Ator, the Great Mother.[68]

The Robin Wood card depicts each of us in the top segment of a roulette wheel as the star of our respective lives. Other segments show the ups and downs, the highs and the lows, we can experience as the rolling ball of fate lands in the other segments.

The Spiral Wheel of Fortune card depicts the Moirae, the triple goddesses of fate and destiny. While Clotho, goddess of birth, spins the thread of life, Lachesis, goddess of chance and luck, sits ready to measure it. Atropos, goddess of destiny, with scissors raised, awaits her opportunity.

The wheel has figured prominently in the mythologies of all cultures. It is usually associated with solar myths and those in which wheels, including spinning wheels (see the Robin Wood Empress) represent the life process. To the Hindus and the Celts, the wheel was a cosmic symbol, the hub representing the still center of the world. The Spiral of Fortune (Shining Tribe) derives from a rock carving in Nine Mile Canyon, Utah. A red spiral, symbolizing life, fits within the blue circle, the sea of existence. At the top of the circle, which is surrounded by the purple limits of the known universe, the spiral becomes the neck and head of a bird to demonstrate that we *can* break out of old, repetitive patterns.[69]

The Wheel of Fortune is also linked to The Chariot card, since the wheels of the chariots of sun gods were often as important as the chariots themselves, many possessing magical powers. The rumbling wheels on Thor's goat-drawn chariot produced the sound of thunder. In Celtic mythology the mythic druid Mag Ruith was the "Wizard of the Wheels," and in Greek mythology Jupiter was the god with the wheel. The card has been linked back to the World Mother, the primordial Mother Center-of-the-Earth.[70]

Coming as it does after The Hermit, The Wheel of Fortune calls upon us to reverse our inner focus (introversion) and to pay attention to the actions of our worldly or physical life (extroversion). Jung believed that all circular objects represented the mandala, which, in turn, represented the cosmic center and the mystic personal center. So, even in worldly oriented cards, it is difficult to separate from the internal spiritual. Although Waite reads the words as "ROTA," suggesting a clockwise spin of the wheel, some believe that because of the positions of the creatures, the wheel is, in fact, turning counterclockwise, reflecting the need to give time to oneself, one's libido, and one's "systolic needs."[71]

Of course, within each of our overall cycles, we have daily physiological cycles, monthly cycles (especially for women) and, when we become attuned to them, many other personal cycles that we can identify. So, although the card is about change, it is also about constancy in the sense of repeating cycles. The card symbolizes both stability and change, the world of becoming.

In medieval times the moon was associated with Fortuna, which links the Wheel of Fortune card with The Moon card.[72] The Wheel of Fortune card represents the establishment of order,[73] and the expression of equilibrium or balance between the dual forces of the Universe.

Keywords/phrases: balance between action and reaction; a change in circumstances; the workings of destiny; expect the unexpected; new opportunities (especially as the result of past choices and decisions); need to examine personal progress; attending to, or the ability to see, natural or personal patterns and cycles.

wheel(s)

In general, wheels represent the cycles and/or movement of life. Wheels sometimes represent the circular motion of the cosmos or the universe (*see* **zodiac**), conceived as an eternal wheel. Psychologically, wheels represent the unfolding of consciousness, the manner by which the psyche (the hub) expresses itself in the patterns or sequences of daily life.[74] Some biblical scriptures refer to wheels as unrolling divine revelation.[75]

As a circle, wheels refer to perfection or the Self. Although a longtime ancient lunar symbol (the disk in ancient Egypt), today, in many cultural traditions, the wheel is a solar symbol, likely because of the spokes radiating out from its center. Its meaning may change depending on the number of spokes. For instance, the ten-spoked wheel in the Thoth Fortune card represents the number of the ten sephiroth on the Kabbalistic Tree of Life.[76] The eight wheels on the RWS Fool's garment may represent the Golden Dawn's symbol for spirit.[77]

See **mandala; Wheel of Fortune (X)**.

white

Comprised of all the colors of the spectrum, it represents light; the process of reflection; spirit; truth; purity; pure spirit; innocence; illumination.

See **colors**.

wind

Appearing as it does in many creation myths, wind represents the creative spirit. Blowing wind is implied in tarot cards where bending trees can be seen (RWS Page and Knight of Swords). This relates partially to the fact that air is the element of RWS Swords, and also suggests that new thinking and conceptualizing is occurring. Although the trees on the RWS Queen and King of Swords are not actively bending, their shape suggests they have done so in the past. What was once new learning has been incorporated into wisdom.

window(s)

Windows represent a way in which we look out on and interpret, understand, and perceive the world.[78] When open to air and light, windows can represent receptivity, especially receptivity to spirit and, therefore, a change in consciousness. They can symbolize a way of looking in or within (as in the "window to the soul") to see the inner light or enlightenment.

Their shape—square or round—may give an indication of whether we need to be receptive to worldly information and wisdom (four-sided) or spiritual information (round). The number of panes in a window may relate to the symbology of that number. Designs or color can also add to the meaning. Black windows spurting flames mark the top ("above-it-all" position) of the RWS Tower card, where they carry out the theme of the disintegration of present consciousness, and an inflated ego that is being challenged and cleansed by the flames. The scene in the stained-glass window in the RWS Four of Swords suggests we go within for spiritual teaching and regeneration (*see* **hidden letters**). The lighted, stained glass church window on the RWS Five of Pentacles represents overseeing and available spiritual guidance that is being ignored, i.e., a state of spiritual impoverishment that results in, and maintains, the worldly crisis of the fives. Although cold without, we can become warm and enlightened within.

winged egg

Eggs, in general, have long been considered symbols of fertility and life and sometimes represent the seat of the soul.[79] It is in this sense that the winged egg on the Thoth Magus card represents the Quintessence[80] (*see* **Quintessence**). When carved over the doorways of Egyptian temples, it served as a talisman against evil.

winged disk

A circle with wings extending from either side, the winged disk represents heavenly power, sometimes heavenly healing power, the Egyptian Lord of the Upper Regions, and the sun god of any of a number of cultures. In Egyptian mythology Horus, the falcon-headed sun god, took this form to slay Seth, the god of evil. It appears on The Chariot cards of the RWS, Ancestral Path, and Robin Wood decks. It is one of the items the Thoth "Magus" juggles, and it tops the staff of The Devil card, serving on the latter as a veil for the creative energy symbolized by the card.[81]

winged horse

See **horse** (winged); **Pegasus**.

winged lion

In alchemy, the winged lion represented the transmutation of the lower self to a higher realm. It represents both the process and the result, the lapis or philosopher's stone. A winged lion appears in several Two of Cups cards (RWS, Ancestral Path, New Palladini), indicating the card really deals with one's relationship with oneself, whether that comes about through individual work or is influenced by relationship with another.

wings

Associated with angels, wings often represent heavenly (higher) qualities and liberation. They also represent motion and action. Greek gods are often winged, as is Eros in the pips cards of the Renaissance Cups suit.

wings, red

In the RWS deck, angels with red wings appear on The Lovers, Wheel of Fortune, and Judgement cards, where they possibly show that the angel is the same angel, the archangel Michael. Some do identify the angel on the Judgement card, however, as Gabriel, who blows his horn. More likely the red wings all convey the angel's passionate energy and message.

Wirth, Oswald (1860–1943)

Joseph Paul Oswald Wirth was a Swiss Mason and theosophist who lived in Paris. In 1889, he created a twenty-two card deck and, in 1927, published an accompanying book, *Les Tarot, des Imagiers du Moyen Age*. Translated and published in English in 1985, *The Tarot of the Magicians* contains detailed information about the deck's symbolism, as well as other occult information from the French tradition. In 1976 U.S. Games added Minor Arcana pip cards and published a new deck. The artistic style of Wirth's deck was similar to the Marseilles, with changes based on the writing of Eliphas Lévi. He used the Hebrew letters assigned to the Major Arcana by Lévi rather than those assigned by the Golden Dawn system.

Wise Old Man/Woman (archetype)

This is an archetypal figure who appears in stories, dreams, and images representing the spiritual factor in one's life. He/she is often portrayed as an authority figure, such as a magician (Merlin of Arthurian legend), a doctor, priest (the tarot Hierophant), teacher, professor, grandfather/grandmother, who presents good advice and insight that the younger hero seems to be lacking at the moment. Often the male is portrayed as someone with long white hair and beard. Sometimes he appears as a dwarf or hooded person (the tarot Hermit; one of the children in the RWS Six of Cups?). Jung used only the Wise Old Man archetype. The Wise Old Woman archetype has come into recent use as we begin to recognize the wisdom of the goddess within. More frequently, in regard to tarot cards, she is referred to as the crone, the third aspect of the Triple Goddess, usually associated with Moon cards.

wolf

Although the wolf can symbolize both the diabolical and the spiritual, in the tarot it seems to pertain more to humanity's wild nature. When the Icelandic wolf Fenrir battles with Óðinn and devours him, it represents the capacity of greed and aggression to destroy knowledge and inspiration.[82]

Like its cousin the dog, the wolf sometimes appears in stories as a psychopomp, a spirit guide, and the guardian of the unconscious. The Greek god Hades wore a cloak of wolf pelt, causing the wolf to be associated with the mythical underworld, or the psychological unconscious. The wolf also symbolizes two of the seven deadly/mortal sins: gluttony and avarice.[83]

Wolves frequently appear on The Moon cards of various decks and as the spirit animal of The Magician in the Legend Arthurian deck.

See **dog; Moon, The (XVIII).**

world axis

Many mythologies indicate that an axis (sometimes portrayed as a ladder) unites the three realms of the cosmic zone, i.e., the upper world, earth, and the lower world, by whatever names they are known. Also called the *axis mundi*, this archetype is considered a stabilizing force, the central point in the cosmos. It is regarded as an enduring or eternal life process or principle. The Kabbalistic Tree of Life is such a symbol (appearing on the RWS Ten of Pentacles). Likewise, the Tree of Life in the Garden of Eden is considered a symbolic *axis mundi*, as is Yggdrasil, the tree on which Óðinn hung. Eden's Tree of Life is portrayed in the RWS Lovers card and symbolically represented in the grape-like tail of the female figure in the RWS Devil card. The myth of Óðinn has been associated with The Hanged Man card.

The upright-pointing sword on tarot cards can be considered as joining spirit and matter and, thus, symbolic of the axis. Other upright natural or man-made objects can, at times, represent the world axis, such as trees, mountains, staffs, and pillars, but do not necessarily do so in each and every tarot card in which they appear.

World, The (XXI)

In the Thoth, Tarot of the Spirit, Haindl, and World Spirit decks, this card is titled "The Universe," the name of the Golden Dawn equivalent of the card. The Haindl card develops the idea of transcending our limitations through a link with the World Serpent of Scandinavian mythology (*see* **dragon(s)**). We, as the dragon, unwrap ourselves from the world, returning back into the ordinary world from our ascent into heaven, even as the spiral shape of the dragon suggests this is a continuous process.

Numerologically, twenty-one breaks down into three, further linking The World back to The Empress (the mother of the entire process), as well as The Hanged Man, the card of "giving birth to the soul."[84] We could not fully comprehend these as "cosmic life force" cards until this point in our journey. The woman in the RWS World card is our divine essence.

In many cards, (RWS, Nigel Jackson, Marseilles), a nude (spiritual freedom) female figure dances within a wreath of green leaves (*see* **mandorla**). She swirls "in a perpetual dance" because movement is the generator of all things.[85]

She holds in her hands the now balanced magic of The Magician (two wands), or the pillars of dualism now completely under control (the victory wreath in the Nigel Jackson card). She is the realization of pure truth[86]—a representation of the alchemical philosopher's stone, and of the Jungian concept of the Self.

The figure's feet (RWS, Nigel Jackson cards) are in the same position as those of The Hanged Man (XII). Twelve has been reversed to become twenty-one or 3×7, the product of the divine (3) and the mystical (7).[87]

The figures in the four corners of the RWS card duplicate those found on the Wheel of Fortune, again linking it to that card and showing us that by our work toward wholeness, we can, indeed, shape our own fortune or destiny. In the Thoth deck, the figures spit out the waters of creation. On the World Spirit card, they represent the four Minor Arcana suits (cow for earth, crow for air, lion for fire, and dolphin for water).

It is almost as if the figure on the card has become a planet within herself, which we can understand as someone who has achieved a universal or transpersonal consciousness. Based on earlier decks, some writers have defined the figure as androgynous as a means of explaining that duality is now transcended, but also linking it to the androgynous Mercury, hence back again to The Fool or The Magician. A nice ending to a long story, until we read that Waite calls this linking the figure to the Magus when he has reached his highest degree of initiation "one of the worst explanations" of the card. Waite intended the card to represent "the perfection . . . of the Cosmos, the secret . . . within it, the rapture of the universe when it understands itself in God."[88] It is a luminous realization or insight of astronomic proportions, a psychic supernova.

Yet, since the planet Mercury signifies the power to "overcome the gap between separate entities,"[89] then perhaps a full-circle ending is not so absurd as Waite said. Mercury "represents the power of symbol-making."[90] From this point on, by focusing on understanding our life experiences as symbols, we will live what Jung called the symbolic life or soulful life. By living the magic of The Magician, we are transformed; and we are transformation in action.

In Jungian terms, the card represents the "realized Self." It is the "sense of unity" we experience when, as a result of personal growth work, "the many archetypes begin to give their energy to one [the Self]."[91] We have outgrown our sense of separateness internally and externally and can now live in relationship. To use the terms of both religious and esoteric teachings, we are "awakened," "enlightened."

Mythologically the androgynous or hermaphroditic figure is

linked to the story of Hermaphroditus, son of Hermes and Aphrodite, and the card from the Mythic deck portrays him. When the nymph Salmacis fell in love with him, she prayed they would never be separated. The gods merged the two bodies into one, neither exclusively male nor female. Naturally, this myth relates to the integration of opposites, so The World card can be perceived as the ultimate tarot archetype of the resolution of opposites.

An enormous African "mother," who never runs out of milk, sits on a lotus in the Light and Shadow card. Within her body she carries a turtle (*see* **turtle**). Within the turtle, an embryo waits to be born. We live within her. She shelters all nature and makes it possible for us to thrive. Like The World cards of other decks, she represents completion and perfection (*see* **lemniscate; lotus; spiral; yin-yang**). On the Osho "Completion" card, the last piece of a jigsaw puzzle of a face is being put into place. The piece fits in the area of the third-eye, and reflects that rare moment of inner perception when we observe "the whole picture."[92]

The card in the Shining Tribe deck is, of course, "Shining Woman". Her body is "painted" with bright, colorful designs representing mythical images and psychological processes: double-headed snakes, a bird of instinct, double spirals, a fish, turtle, stone circles and tombs. Surrounded by colorful energy lines, she dances in a void that pulsates with her own light. She represents the ultimate in wholeness and personal sacredness and power.

At its simplest, The World card can suggest there is a greater world or universe out there than that which we are seeing or understanding at present. Perhaps we have too narrow a view of our present issue or situation. It is time to change or expand our life task so that we regard our life experiences in a different light.

The World card speaks to the notion that success does not mean achieving certain material goals. Rather success is learning to balance our energy, our inner aspects, in order to live through our life challenges and to comprehend them from their greatest symbolic value. The sum of our collective sacred history is shown by The World card. The sum of our personal sacred history is shown by our notebook of personal tarot readings.

Keywords/phrases: recognizing one's wholeness; fulfillment; resourcefulness; being able to dance to your own music; harmony with, or awareness of, cosmic consciousness and world spirit; living by, or ordering one's life by, higher or cosmic principles.

wounded healer
See **Hierophant, The (V)**.

wreath
The wreath is related to the same symbolism as that of the circle, the mandala, and the crown. Wreaths can be presented as tribute, and a wreath's general meaning is changed by the material from which it is constructed and where it is worn or carried. Wreaths of ivy, for instance, were said to protect their wearers from intoxication, while wreaths of oak leaves were given to those who had saved another's life.[93] Wreaths figure prominently in RWS cards, beginning with The Fool who wears a laurel wreath, symbolizing his victorious spirit, as do the wreaths comprising the base of the charioteer's and the King of Pentacles's crowns. Flowered wreaths may signal joy or celebration (*see* **wreath, flowered**). In the RWS Two of Wands, the male wears a red wreath of passion and the solar principle (*see* **circle with a dot within**); the female wears a green wreath of leaves (growth, fertility) and lunar colors. Together they symbolize the wholeness that comes from the alchemical marriage.

wreath, flowered
The meaning can change depending on the flowers used and where it is carried or worn. If worn on the head, it would symbolize that one's power or authority derives from natural awareness, i.e., from one's connection with nature in general and one's own inner nature specifically. Such a flowered wreath is worn by

the maiden in the Robin Wood Strength card and tells us that the qualities of the specific flowers in the wreath (daisies for fresh spirit, violets for sweetness, forget-me-nots for caring, spring beauties for joy, and baby's breath for childlikeness) go on forever.[94] The child in the RWS Sun card wears a sunflower wreath (six that can be seen), which may relate to an emphasis on soul development, inasmuch as sunflowers and the number six are associated with the human soul (*see* **sixes**).

wreath, laurel

Current or past accomplishments or victories. In the RWS and Spiral Tarot's Chariot cards, the charioteer wears a laurel wreath. He is able to claim victory and success via his intellect. In Greece, laurel wreaths were associated with Apollo, and in the Mythic Sun card, Apollo stands in front of a pair of laurel trees. As a fantasy desire for fame and honor, the laurel wreath appears in one of the cups on the RWS and Morgan-Greer Seven of Cups cards. Likely it is a laurel victory wreath that the rider on the RWS Six of Wands carries on his wand and wears on his head.

See **wreath**. For an explanation of how the laurel wreath came to represent Apollo and symbolize victory, *see* **Daphne**.

wreath, myrtle

Myrtle being sacred to Venus, such a wreath (worn by the RWS Empress) may suggest identification with female fertility symbols and with rulers of the forces of nature. It is also a symbol of immortality.

X

X

Related to the symbolism of crossroads and St. Andrew's cross, X refers to decisions needing to be made, chances to take, the need for communication between upper and lower worlds, between the conscious and unconscious. It can also refer to information or material seeking to emerge from the unconscious. Xs appear in the form of a St. Andrew's cross in the RWS Two of Wands and Six of Cups.

See **cross of St. Andrew; crossroads.**

Y

year cards

A process first developed by Angeles Arrien and made popular by Mary K. Greer, computing one's year card involves adding the month and day of birth to the current year and reducing the separate digits to the higher of two numbers between two and twenty-two, to associate it with a Major Arcana card (twenty-two equals The Fool). Year cards indicate lessons and opportunities for the current year,[1] and should be especially noted when appearing in a reading as they may denote important developments.

See **personality cards; reduction; soul cards.**

yellow

In the Middle Ages, yellow was associated with envy (in some early tarot cards Vice, depicted in The Lovers card, wore bright yellow clothes). It bears some of the symbolism of the color gold and, like gold, is associated with solar symbolism. In the tarot it usually represents the intellect, positive mental activity and awareness, willpower, intention, outer self-expression, change, and radiant energy. It is linked to the planet Mercury.

yin-yang symbol

A Chinese symbol showing a dark and light section separated (or combined) by a wavy, S-shaped line, with each "half" having a dot (embryo/germ) of the opposite. It is a symbol of cosmic duality and struggle, ultimate balance and totality. It depicts, or reflects, the constant interchange or action between all the complementary opposite principles in the universe. The yin (dark) side represents the feminine principle, passiveness, shadow, and earth. The yang (light) side represents the masculine principle, action, light, and the heavens. The yin-yang symbol decorates the Robin Wood Chariot. In the Light and Shadow deck, it shines as the moon on the Justice card, acts as the head of the turtle resting in the womb of the mother figure on The World card, and forms the core of The Hermit's candle. A yin-yang tray is at the heart of the Wheel of Change Tarot's Eight of Cups.

Yod ׳

Considered the primary Hebrew letter, because all other Hebrew letters are a variation on it, *yod* is associated with the astrological sign of Virgo. The first letter of God's name in the Tetragrammaton, *yods* represent divine grace and healing and can be translated to mean "open hand." The letter's placement in the Hebrew alphabet (ten) often associates it with the Wheel of Fortune card. *Yods* appear on many RWS cards, notably the Major Arcana cards of The Moon, and The Tower, where as twenty-two tiny, falling flames, they represent the twenty-two letters of the Hebrew alphabet, the twenty-two paths of the Kabbalistic Tree of Life, and the archetypes of the twenty-two Major Arcana cards. The ten above the female likely represent the ten elementary Hebrew letters and/or the ten sephiroth of the Kabbalistic Tree of Life. The twelve around the male represent the twelve zodiacal Hebrew letters/signs.

Yods also appear on the RWS aces of Cups (as "dew," or drops of water), Swords (as flames), and Wands (as falling leaves). They represent the new possibility of divine energy or intelligence coming through us and becoming manifest in the material act of creation. In a more sinister mode, nine *yod*-shaped drops of blood fall from the waning moon above in the Thoth Moon card, where they represent "impure blood" in the poisoned darkness.[2] On the RWS Moon card, they are defined as the "dew of thought."[3] Did Waite know the use of the term "divine dew" for the alchemical action of mercury or luna?

See **Tetragrammaton.**

yoni

The Sanskrit term for the womb, it is typically associated with the lingam (phallic symbol), and shown as a circle, sometimes as a pool of water. Together the two constitute the fundamental principle of duality, the feminine and the masculine, as in the yin-yang symbol. The lingam-yoni symbol appears in the shield on the front of the RWS Chariot card.

*

Zain, C. C. (1882–1951)

The pseudonym for Elbert Benjamine, founder of the Church of
Light in Los Angeles. Zain published a twenty-two-volume correspondence course of occult instruction, of which *Sacred Tarot*
was one volume. His teachings, revealed by discarnate Masters
of the Brotherhood of Light, traced the history of initiations used
with tarot images back to the civilizations of Atlantis and Mu.
His tarot deck uses a modified "Egyptian" tradition, which
evolved from an 1896 French deck by R. Falconnier, a designer
of Egyptian-style tarot decks. It employs the French system of
Hebrew letter attributions and uses astrological correspondences
from sidereal astrology.[1] The zodiac of sidereal astrology is based
on the actual position of the stars and, therefore, moves forward
one day every seventy-two years.

zero

Zero, associated with The Fool card, reflects the Zen concept of no-thing, no fixed point, "the gaps between the stages of development."[2] It represents nothing and everything. In the Daughters of the Moon deck, "The Dreamer" on the fool-equivalent card symbolizes the opening that is birth, beginnings, and *kairos*, the potential about to be born.

Zeus/Jupiter (Greek/Roman god)

The mythic qualities of Jupiter, associated with the astrological signs of Pisces and Sagittarius and the planet Jupiter, focus on his role as the allfather, king of the gods. Zeus's symbolic creature was the eagle (*see* **eagle**), his tree, the oak (*see* **tree, oak**). Constantly cheating on his wife, he often shapeshifted to pursue his lovers and elude his wife's detection. In this manner, Zeus fathered numerous love children.

Lightning is one of the attributes of Zeus, and one of the better-known myths of Zeus involves lightning (*see* **lightning**), and his affair with Princess Semele, which he carried out disguised as an old neighbor. After Zeus's jealous wife Hera persuaded Semele to request that he reveal himself in his true nature, he appeared in his chariot of lightning and thunder, hurling lightning bolts, which consumed Semele (some stories say she went mad).

As a behavioral model, Zeus/Jupiter represents the drive to manifest thought into form, to achieve immortality, to be potent in one's area of the world through extended influence and mastery. Ambition and the need to establish a "kingdom" are driving forces when the Zeus/Jupiter archetype is active. He is the quintessential "alpha male." When these qualities are taken to extremes, there is the risk of excessive force, intemperance of passions, and an overbearing compulsion to control the thoughts and beliefs of others.[3]

See **Dionysus/Bacchus; Pisces; Sagittarius.**

zodiac

One symbolic understanding of the zodiac is that all the characteristics that it contains are aspects of each of us, in greater or lesser proportion, which may be more or less expressed at any given time. In a greater sense, the myths behind the zodiac constellations relate to deeds and actions of the gods. Thus the zodiac reveals patterns, traits, tendencies, preferences, skills, and failings that can be associated with tarot cards. Zodiacal attributions differ between systems. Generally the twelve signs are assigned to the Major Arcana, along with the seven planets and the four elements. Golden Dawn zodiacal attributions are extended to also include court cards and the Minor Arcana.[4]

Apparently, in the original Golden Dawn deck, the Wheel of Fortune card contained twelve spokes and was intended to represent the zodiac in its entirety,[5] a concept lost in the ten-spoked wheel of the Thoth deck and the eight-spoked wheel of the RWS deck. Objects or pieces of jewelry presented as twelve parts or pieces, as in the twelve stars on the crown of the RWS Empress, symbolize the principles or influence of the zodiac and the figure's relationship to it (*see* **Empress, The (III)**).

See **astrological signs; zodiacal attributions**; and specific astrological signs.

zodiacal attributions

Zodiacal signs, planets, and elements are commonly attributed to the twenty-two cards of the Major Arcana. There are twelve zodiac signs, two lights (Sun and Moon), five traditional and three modern planets, and four elements. Combinations of these units are assigned in a vast variety of attribution sets, although earlier systems consistently utilize only the twelve signs and seven ancient planets. Some decks feature the zodiac or planetary glyph on the rendering.

Zodiacal and planetary attributions to tarot cards require a basic knowledge of zodiacal and elemental dignities. Planetary cards benefit in proximity to the zodiacal cards that they rule, and struggle near cards assigned to the signs of fall or detriment. Planets have affinity to the signs, and they have affinity to each other as well. Planets considered "benefic" are the Sun, Moon, Venus, and Jupiter. Mars and Saturn are considered "malefic" planets. Mercury is neutral. The three outer planets are less often used in attribution systems, but when used, symbolize the more universal and collective influences.[6]

In the Golden Dawn tradition, the thirty-six decantes of the zodiac were assigned to the Minor Arcana, the two through ten numbered pip cards in each suit. The cardinal signs corresponded to the two, three, four pip cards. Fixed signs correspond to the pip numbers five, six, seven. Mutable signs correspond to the pip cards eight, nine, and ten. It is possible that Waite took these astrological characteristics into account in creating the scenes for his Minor Arcana cards.[7]

Another astrological technique grafted into use for tarot is the twelve-house system. The reader spreads twelve cards in a circle, moving from 9:00 (card one) counterclockwise to 10:00 (card twelve) and reads the cards that appear as a view of each area of life signified by the house. Many tarot books teach a twelve-card horoscope spread where each position represents the view of life signified by one of the houses.[8]

See **archetypes; astrological signs; court cards** (astrological aspects); **Major Arcana** (elemental and astrological associations); **zodiac**; and individual astrological signs and planets.

ENDNOTES

✳

1: FLASHCARDS OF THE SELF

1. Mary K. Greer and Rachel Pollack, introduction to *New Thoughts on Tarot* (North Hollywood, Calif.: Newcastle Publishing Co., Inc., 1989), 1–7.

2. The TarotL discussion group can be accessed at http://www.egroups.com/group/TarotL. Readers interested in more historic information differentiating the many tarot myths from fact will find it at http://www.villarevak.org/misc/tarotL_1.html

3. Mary K. Greer, *Tarot for Your Self. A Workbook for Personal Transformation*, 2d ed. (Franklin Lakes, N.J.: New Page Books, 2002), 273–274.

4. Jean Houston, *A Mythic Life. Learning to Live Our Greater Story* (New York: HarperSanFrancisco, 1996), 99.

5. Jean Shinoda Bolen, M.D., *Goddesses in Older Women. Archetypes in Women Over Fifty* (New York: HarperCollins Publishers, 2001), x.

6. Christine Downing, prologue to *Mirrors of the Self. Archetypal Images that Shape Your Life* (Los Angeles: Jeremy P. Tarcher, Inc., 1991), xi–xx.

7. There are three other classic mythological themes in this movie: the wounded hero, the notion of an archetypal mentor-student relationship that serves to teach the hero how to deal with adversity, and the death/rebirth/afterlife concept.

8. Marie-Louise von Franz, *Alchemy. An Introduction to the Symbolism and the Psychology* (Toronto, Canada: Inner City Books, 1980), 66.

9. Edward C. Whitmont, *Return of the Goddess* (New York: Continuum, 1997), ix.

10. Rachel Pollack, personal communication.

11. Frank X. Barron, *Creativity and Psychological Health: Origins of Personal Vitality and Creative Freedom* (Princeton, N.J.: D. Van Nostrand Co., 1963), 199.

12. Mary Baird Carlsen, *Meaning-making: Therapeutic Processes in Adult Development* (New York: Norton, 1988).

13. von Franz, *Alchemy*, 66.

2: DELVING THE DEPTHS OF THE TAROT

1. Benjamin Sells, ed. *Working with Images. The Theoretical Base of Archetypal Psychology* (Woodstock, Conn.: Spring Publications, 2000), 20.

2. Robert Wang, *An Introduction to the Golden Dawn Tarot* (York Beach, Maine: Samuel Weiser, Inc., 1978), 30.

3. *Ibid.*, 18–19.

4. For instance, Aleister Crowley assigned The Emperor to the twenty-eighth path, while Paul Foster Case assigned it to the fifteenth path. Likewise Crowley assigned The Star to the fifteenth path, and Case assigned it to the twenty-eighth path. For a list of the variations in others' assignment of the cards to Kabbalistic pathways and the assignment of Hebrew letters, see Robert V. O'Neill, *Tarot Symbolism* (Lima, Ohio: Fairway Press, 1986), 253–254.

5. Wang, *Golden Dawn*, 19.

6. Christine Payne-Towler, *The Underground Stream* (Eugene, Oregon: Noreah Press, 1999), 16.

7. *Ibid.*

8. Frederic Lionel, *The Magic Tarot. Vehicle of Eternal Wisdom* (London: Routledge & Kegan Paul, 1982), 174.

9. Irene Gad, *Tarot and Individuation. Correspondences with Cabala and Alchemy* (York Beach, Maine: Nicolas-Hays, Inc., 1994).

10. Paul Foster Case, *The Tarot. A Key to the Wisdom of the Ages* (Richmond, Va.: Macoy Publishing Co., 1975).

11. Harriette A. Curtiss and F. Homer Curtiss, *The Key of Destiny*, 4th ed. (North Hollywood, Calif.: Newcastle Publishing Co., 1983); Harriette A. and F. Homer Curtiss, *The Key to the Universe*, 6th rev. ed. (North Hollywood, Calif.: Newcastle Publishing Co., 1983).

12. Irene Gad, *Tarot and Individuation*; Juliet Sharman-Burke, *Mastering the Tarot. An Advanced Personal Teaching Guide* (New York: St. Martin's Griffin, 2000); Rosemary Ellen Guiley and Robert M. Place, *The Alchemical Tarot* (London: Thorsons, 1995)

13. Houston, *Mythic Life*, 7.

14. C. G. Jung, *Four Archetypes: Mother, Rebirth, Spirit, Trickster*, trans. R. F. C. Hull (London: Routledge & Kegan Paul, 1972), 136.

15. Houston, *Mythic Life*, 16.

16. Marie-Louise von Franz, *Archetypal Dimensions of the Psyche* (Boston & London: Shambhala, 1999), 18–19.

17. Cynthia Giles, *The Tarot. History, Mystery and Lore* (New York: Simon & Schuster, 1992), 23.

18. *Ibid.*, 121.

19. Al Siebert, *"The Survivor Personality,"* (Paper presented at the meetings of the Western Psychological Association in San Francisco, April 1983).

20. Marie-Louise von Franz, *Archetypal Patterns in Fairy Tales* (Toronto, Ontario, Canada: Inner City Books, 1997), 182.

3: DECKS: TWENTY-FIVE TOP GATEWAYS

1. Judi Lethbridge, "The Hermit, the Hand, and the Hankie," *The ATA Newsletter* Vol. VI, No. 2 (Spring 2001): 15–16.

2. Robin Wood, *The Robin Wood Tarot: The Book* (Dearborn, Michigan: Livingtree, 1998).

3. Carl Japikse, *Exploring the Tarot* (Columbus, Ohio: Ariel Press, 1989).

4. Brian Williams and Michael Goepferd, *The Light and Shadow Tarot*, (Rochester, Va.: Destiny Books, 1997), 126.

5. Akron and Hajo Banzhaf, *The Crowley Tarot*, trans. Christine M. Grimm (Stamford, Conn.: U.S. Games Systems, Inc., 1995); Angeles Arrien, *The Tarot Handbook*, (Sonoma, Calif.: Arcus Publishing Co., 1987).

6. Rachel Pollack, *The Haindl Tarot. Volume II: The Minor Arcana* (North Hollywood, Calif.: Newcastle Publishing, Inc., 1990), 32.

7. Rachel Pollack, *The Haindl Tarot. Volume I: The Major Arcana* (North Hollywood, Calif.: Newcastle Publishing, Inc., 1990); Rachel Pollack, *Haindl*, Vol. II.

8. Nigel Jackson, *The Nigel Jackson Tarot* (St. Paul, Minn.: Llewellyn Publications, 2000), 88.

9. Brian Williams, *A Renaissance Tarot* (Stamford, Conn.: U.S. Games Systems, Inc., 1994).

10. James Wanless, *Voyager Tarot: Way of the Great Oracle* (Carmel, Calif.: Merrill-West Publishing, 1989).

11. Ffiona Morgan, *Daughters of the Moon Tarot*, rev. ed. (Novato, Calif.: Daughters of the Moon, 2000).

12. Arielle Smith, personal communication.

4: DESTINY NARRATIONS

1. Giles, *Tarot History*.

2. Stephen Walter Sterling, *Tarot Awareness: Exploring the Spiritual Path* (St. Paul, Minn.: Llewellyn Publications, 2000), 342.

3. Arthur Rosengarten, *Tarot and Psychology. Spectrums of Possibility* (St. Paul, Minn.: Paragon House, 2000), 74, 86.

4. Sylvia Abraham, *How to Use Tarot Spreads*. (St. Paul, Minn.: Llewellyn Publications, 2001).

5. Evelin Burger and Johannes Fiebig, *Complete Book of Tarot Spreads* (New York: Sterling Publishing Co., Inc., 1997).

6. Contact the association by mail at 3176 Richmond Rd., #123, Lexington, Kentucky, 40509. For Internet and Web site information see Internet Resources section.

7. Teresa Michelsen, personal communication.

8. Sandra A. Thomson, Robert E. Mueller, and Signe E. Echols, *The Heart of the Tarot* (San Francisco: HarperSanFrancisco, 2000).

9. Used with Jayne's permission.

10. Gail Fairfield, *Choice Centered Tarot*, rev. ed., (York Beach, Maine: Samuel Weiser, Inc., 1997); Donald Michael Kraig, "A New Tarot Paradigm," *The Tarot Journal*, Vol. 1, No. 1 (Spring 2001), 13–15.

11. Rosengarten, *Tarot and Psychology*, 22, 29.

12. Examples of this type of spread can be found in Gad, *Tarot and Individuation*, 1994, 412–413; Mary K. Greer, *Tarot for Your Self. A Workbook for Personal Transformation*, (North Hollywood, Calif.: Newcastle Publishing Co., Inc., 1984), 164–168; Juliet Sharman-

Burke, *Understanding the Tarot. A Personal Teaching Guide* (New York: St. Martin's Griffin, 1998), 12; Sterling, *Tarot Awareness*, 372–375.

13. Greer, *Tarot for Self*, 160–164.
14. Kraig, *Tarot Paradigm*.
15. James Ricklef, *KnightHawk's Tarot Readings* (San Jose: Writers Club Press, 2001).

A: References

1. R. J. Stewart, *The UnderWorld Initiation. A Journey Towards Psychic Transformation* (Lake Toxaway, N.C.: Mercury Publishing, Inc., 1998), 60, 63.
2. Mary K. Greer, *Tarot Mirrors. Reflections of Personal Meaning* (North Hollywood, Calif.: Newcastle Publishing Co., Inc., 1988), 58–60.
3. John Opsopaus, *Pythagorean Tarot* (St. Paul, Minn.: Llewellyn Publications, 2001), 44.
4. *See* Irene Gad, *Tarot Individuation*; Rosemary Ellen Guiley and Robert M. Place, *Alchemical Tarot*.
5. C. G. Jung, "The Child Archetype" in Christine Downing, ed., *Mirrors of Self*, 158–159.
6. Karen Hamaker-Zondag, *Tarot as a Way of Life. A Jungian Approach to the Tarot* (York Beach, Maine: Samuel Weiser, Inc., 1997), 52.
7. Oswald Wirth, *The Tarot of the Magicians* (York Beach, Maine: Samuel Weiser, Inc., 1985), 154.
8. Clarissa Pinkola Estés, *Women Who Run With the Wolves*. (New York: Ballantine Books, 1992), 311.
9. Hamaker-Zondag, *Way of Life*, 42.
10. Jean Shinoda Bolen, *Goddesses in Every Woman, A New Psychology of Women* (New York: Harper & Row, 1984), 233–262; Elizabeth M. Hazel, personal communication.
11. Charles Mills Gayley, *The Classic Myths in English Literature and in Art*, rev. ed. (Boston: Ginn & Co., 1939), 26.
12. Elizabeth M. Hazel, personal communication.
13. Alexandra Genetti, *The Wheel of Change Tarot* (Rochester, Vermont: Destiny Books, 1997), 129.
14. Contributed by Elizabeth M. Hazel.
15. Akron and Banzhaf, *Crowley Tarot*, 36.
16. Williams and Goepferd, *Light and Shadow*, 28.

17. James Hillman, "Why 'Archetypal' Psychology?" in Sells, ed., *Working with Images*, 13.

18. Benjamin Sells, "Introduction" in Sells, ed., *Working with Images*, 6.

19. Gayley, *Classic Myths*, 23–24.

20. Jean Shinoda Bolen, *Gods in Everyman. A New Psychology of Men's Lives and Loves* (New York: Harper & Row, 1989), 192–218; Elizabeth M. Hazel, personal communication.

21. Contributed by Elizabeth M. Hazel.

22. In an unpublished manuscript written several years ago, I attributed this symbolism to Oswald Wirth, but have been unable to find its source for this volume.

23. Gayley, *Classic Myths*, 29.

24. *Ibid.*, 15.

25. Gertrude Jobes and James Jobes, *Outer Space: Myths, Name Meanings, Calendars* (New York: The Scarecrow Press, Inc., 1964), 273.

26. Hajo Banzhaf and Brigitte Theler, *Keywords for the Crowley Tarot* (York Beach, Maine: Weiser Books, 2001), 70.

B: REFERENCES

1. Pollack, *Haindl*, Vol. I, 17.

2. Akron and Banzhaf, *Crowley Tarot*, 36, 39.

3. Hans Biedermann, *Dictionary of Symbolism* (New York: Meridian, 1994), 36.

4. von Franz, *Archetypal Dimensions*, 89.

5. Udo Becker, *The Continuum Encyclopedia of Symbols.* (New York/London: Continuum, 2000), 39.

6. Pollack, *Haindl*, Vol. I, 18–19.

7. Biedermann, *Dictionary*, 37–38.

8. Jean Chevalier and Alain Gheerbrant, trans. John Buchanan-Brown. *The Penguin Dictionary of Symbols* (London: Penguin Books, Ltd., 1996), 432–433.

9. Jack Tresidder, *Dictionary of Symbols* (San Francisco: Chronicle Books, 1998), 26.

10. Alexander Roob, *Alchemy and Mysticism* (Cologne: Taschen, 1997), 420.

11. Akron and Banzhaf, *Crowley Tarot*, 119.

12. Richard Prosapio, *Intuitive Tarot* (Dobbs Ferry, N.Y.: Morgan & Morgan, 1990), 49.

13. Biedermann, *Dictionary*, 49.
14. Anthony Stevens, *Ariadne's Clue. A Guide to the Symbols of Mankind* (Princeton, N.J.: Princeton University Press, 1999), 156.
15. Chevalier and Gheerbrant, *Penguin Dictionary*, 131.
16. *Ibid.*, 135.

C: REFERENCES

1. Joseph Campbell, *The Masks of God, Vol. 1, Primitive Mythology* (New York: Viking, 1959), 416.
2. Biedermann, *Dictionary*, 56.
3. Chevalier and Gheerbrant, *Penguin Dictionary*, 149.
4. Pollack, *Haindl*, Vol. I, 31–36.
5. Contributed by Elizabeth M. Hazel.
6. Case, *Tarot Key*, 2–3.
7. Marie-Louise von Franz, *Shadow and Evil in Fairy Tales* (Boston & London, Shambhala, 1995), 65.
8. *Ibid.*
9. Barbara G. Walker, *The Woman's Encyclopedia of Myths and Secrets* (San Francisco: Harper & Row, 1983), 325.
10. Marie-Louise von Franz, *The Cat. A Tale of Feminine Redemption* (Toronto, Canada: Inner City Books, 1999), 58–59.
11. D. J. Conway and Sirona Knight, *Shapeshifter Tarot* (St. Paul, Minn.: Llewellyn Publications, 1999), 69, 105.
12. Walker, *Woman's Encyclopedia*, 150–154.
13. Pollack, *Haindl*, Vol. I, 92.
14. *Ibid.*
15. For information on certification, the TCBA board can be reached at its website: http://tarotcertification.org. Mailing address: P.O. Box 6935, Albany, NY 12206-0935.
16. The Canadian Tarot Network can be reached through its Web site at www.tarotcanada.com or by e-mail to info@tarotcanada.com. Mailing address: P.O. Box 51175 Biddington RPO, Calgary, Alberta, Canada T3K 3V9.
17. To support those instructors who wish to offer CEUs with their classes, the ABTC lists on their website classes that offer CEUs. The Web site of the ABTC is www.americanboardfortarotcertification.org. Mailing address: P.O. Box 6304, Woodbridge, VA 22192.
18. Anodea Judith, *Eastern Body, Western Mind; Psychology and the Chakra*

System as a Path to the Self (Berkeley: Celestial Arts Publishing, 1996).

19. Caroline Myss, *Anatomy of the Spirit* (New York: Three Rivers Press, 1996).

20. Judith, *Eastern Body*.

21. David Allen Hulse, *The Western Mysteries: An Encyclopedic Guide to the Sacred Languages and Magickal Systems of the World: The Key of It All. Book 2* (St. Paul, Minn.: Llewellyn Publications, 2000), 429.

22. Gareth Knight, *Tarot and Magic. Images for Rituals and Pathworking* (Rochester, Vermont: Destiny Books, 1991), p. 47.

23. Payne-Towler, *Underground Stream*, 28.

24. Marie-Louise von Franz, *Individuation in Fairy Tales* (Boston & London: Shambhala, 1990), 45.

25. Paul Foster Case offers a wonderful description of the cube as having six sides, eight corners, and twelve edges or boundary lines. Their sum, twenty-six, is the sum of the values of the Hebrew letters of the Tetragrammaton. Hence the cube represents the "real presence" of the Divine, "the basis of all subconscious activity" (Case, *Tarot Key*, 53).

26. Kay Steventon, *Spiral Tarot. A Story of the Cycles of Life* (Stamford, Conn.: U.S. Games Systems, Inc., 1998), 49.

27. Arthur Edward Waite, *The Pictorial Key to the Tarot.* (Stamford, Conn.: U.S. Games Systems, Inc., 1997), 96–99.

28. Waite, *Pictorial Key*, 96–99.

29. Mary K. Greer, *Tarot Constellations. Patterns of Personal Destiny* (North Hollywood, Calif.: Newcastle Publishing Co., Inc., 1987), 108.

30. Payne-Towler, *Underground Stream*, 29.

31. Sallie Nichols, *Jung and Tarot. An Archetypal Journey* (York Beach, Maine: Samuel Weiser, Inc., 1980), 142.

32. Gad, *Tarot Individuation*, 77.

33. Georgia Lambert R., personal communication.

34. Thanks to Mary K. Greer and James Revak for much of this information.

35. Howard Sasportas, "Sun, Father, and the Emergence of the Ego: The Father's Role in Individual Development," in Liz Greene and Howard Sasportas, *The Luminaries. The Psychology of the Sun and Moon in the Horoscope* (York Beach, Maine: Samuel Weiser, Inc., 1992), 118.

36. Marie-Louise von Franz, *The Psychological Meaning of Redemption*

Motifs in Fairytales (Toronto, Canada: Inner City Books, 1980), 91; Estés, *Women Who Run*, 55.

37. J. E. Cirlot, *A Dictionary of Symbols*, trans. Jack Sage, 2d ed., (New York: Philosophical Library, 1983), 278.

38. Genetti, *Wheel of Change*, 283–284.

39. Johanna Gargiulo-Sherman, *Guide to the Sacred Rose Tarot* (Stamford, Conn.: U.S. Games Systems, Inc., 1997) 38.

40. Chevalier and Gheerbrant, *Penguin Dictionary*, 220.

41. Roob, *Alchemy*, 185.

42. This term was coined by Valerie Sim-Behi.

43. The term was coined by Valerie Sim-Behi.

44. Greer, *Tarot Constellations*, 35.

45. Gayley, *Classic Myths*, 53.

46. Brian Williams, *Renaissance Tarot*, 162.

47. Author of *Putting the Tarot to Work*, forthcoming from Llewellyn.

48. Charles Poncé, *The Game of Wizards: Roots of Consciousness & the Esoteric Arts* (Wheaton, Ill.: Quest Books, 1991), 18.

49. Many correspondences are listed in Greer, *Tarot for Self*, 245–247.

50. Contributed by Elizabeth M. Hazel.

51. I am indebted to Lynne Luerding and to the American Tarot Association for allowing me to use some of the unique material from her chapter "The Court Cards: Guidelines for 'Advanced Beginners,'" which first appeared in *The American Tarot Association Mentor's Manual*, Jan., 2000.

52. Aleister Crowley, *The Book of Thoth (Egyptian Tarot)* (York Beach, Maine: Weiser Books, 2000), 156.

53. Akron and Banzhaf, *Crowley Tarot*, 158.

54. Robert Hand, *Horoscope Symbols* (West Chester, Pa.: Whitford Press, 1981), 218.

55. Chevalier and Gheerbrant, *Penguin Dictionary*, 244.

56. Biedermann, *Dictionary*, 81.

57. Marion Woodman and Elinor Dickson, *Dancing in the Flames: The Dark Goddess in the Transformation of Consciousness* (Boston: Shambhala, 1997), 24.

58. Amber Jayanti, *Living the Tarot* (St. Paul, Minn.: Llewellyn Publications, 1993), 47.

59. R. V. O'Neill, *Death: Sources of the Waite/Smith Symbolism*. http://www.geocities.com/ninaleeb/oneill/13.htm.

60. Cirlot, *Dictionary of Symbols*, 68.

61. Rachel Pollack, *The Complete Illustrated Guide to Tarot* (Shaftesbury, Dorset, England: Element Books, LTD., 1999), 16.

62. Cirlot, *Dictionary of Symbols*, 72.

63. R. V. O'Neill, *Temperance: Sources of the Waite/Smith Symbolism.* http://www.geocities.com/ninaleeb/oneill/14.htm.

64. Cirlot, *Dictionary of Symbols*, 74.

65. Wood, *Robin Wood Tarot*, 164, 177.

66. Biedermann, *Dictionary*, 85.

67. Crowley, *Book of Thoth*, 159.

68. Williams and Goepferd, *Light and Shadow*, 6.

69. Case, *Tarot Key*, 67–69.

70. David Allen Hulse, *New Dimensions for the Cube of Space* (York Beach, Maine: Samuel Weiser, Inc., 2000).

71. Pamela Eakins, *Tarot of the Spirit* (York Beach, Maine: Samuel Weiser, Inc., 1992), 123.

72. Osho International Foundation, *Osho Zen Tarot: The Transcendental Game of Zen* (New York: St. Martin's Press, 1994), 118.

73. Rachel Pollack, *Shining Tribe Tarot: Awakening the Universal Spirit* (St. Paul, Minn.: Llewellyn Worldwide, 2001), 134.

74. Estés, *Women Who Run*, 47.

75. Osho International Foundation, *Osho Zen*, 104.

76. Christine Downing, "The Healer," in Downing, ed., *Mirrors of Self*, 248.

77. Osho International Foundation, *Osho Zen*, 106.

78. Jessica Godino and Lauren O'Leary, *The World Spirit Tarot* (St. Paul, Minn.: Llewellyn Publications, 2001), 86.

79. Dwarf gods like the Cabiri and the Dactyls were gods of invention, personifications of creative impulses.

80. Akron and Banzhaf, *Crowley Tarot*, 148.

81. Allan Combs and Mark Holland, *Synchronicity: Through the Eyes of Science, Myth, and the Trickster* (New York: Marlowe & Co., 1996), 135.

82. Arrien, *Tarot Handbook*, 170.

83. Rachel Pollack, *Seventy-eight Degrees of Wisdom. Part 2: The Minor Arcana and Readings* (Wellingborough, Northamptonshire: The Aquarian Press, 1983), 61.

84. Sharman-Burke, *Understanding Tarot*, 68.

85. Godino and O'Leary, *World Spirit*, 92.
86. Akron and Banzhaf, *Crowley Tarot*, 149.
87. From the LWB accompanying the deck, text by Tracey Hoover.
88. Myss, *Anatomy*, 197–198.
89. Godino and O'Leary, *World Spirit*, 95.
90. Pollack, *Haindl*, Vol. II, 62.
91. Eakins, *Tarot Spirit*, 148.
92. Juliet Sharman-Burke and Liz Greene, *The Mythic Tarot* (New York: A Fireside Book, 1986), 106.
93. Akron and Banzhaf, *Crowley Tarot*, 152.
94. *Ibid.*
95. Sharman-Burke and Greene, *Mythic Tarot*, 108.
96. Akron and Banzhaf, *Crowley Tarot*, 154–155.
97. Eden Gray, *A Complete Guide to the Tarot* (New York: Crown Publishers, Inc., 1970), 64.
98. Akron and Banzhaf, *Crowley Tarot*, 156.
99. Godino and O'Leary, *World Spirit*, 101.
100. Genetti, *Wheel of Change*, 264–265.
101. Sharman-Burke and Greene, *Mythic Tarot*, 112.
102. Akron and Banzhaf, *Crowley Tarot*, 158–159.

D: REFERENCES
1. Combs and Holland, *Synchronicity*, 143.
2. Thomas Moore, *Care of the Soul* (New York: HarperPerennial, 1992), 309.
3. Godino and O'Leary, *World Spirit*, 80.
4. I am indebted to Mary K. Greer and James Revak for this information.
5. Waite, *Pictorial Key*, 120.
6. Steventon, *Spiral Tarot*, 71.
7. Pollack, *Haindl*, Vol. I, 121.
8. Mircea Eliade, *Myth and Reality* (New York: Harper & Row, 1963), 114–121.
9. *Ibid.*, 129.
10. Pollack, *Shining Tribe*, 59–61.
11. Williams, *Renaissance Tarot*, 87.
12. R. V. O'Neill, *Death: Sources of the Waite/Smith Symbolism*. http://www.geocities.com/ninaleeb/oneill/13.htm

13. Waite, *Pictorial Key*, 120.
14. R. V. O'Neill, *Death: Sources of the Waite/Smith Symbolism*. http://www.geocities.com/ninaleeb/oneill/13.htm
15. Genetti, *Wheel of Change*, 78.
16. Valerie Sim-Behi, personal communication.
17. Estés, *Women Who Run*, 35.
18. Rollo May, *The Meaning of Anxiety* (New York: The Ronald Press Co., 1950), 193.
19. Wood, *Robin Wood Tarot*, 64–65.
20. Osho International Foundation, *Osho Zen*, 34.
21. I am indebted to Mary K. Greer for these ideas.
22. Ruth Ann Amberstone, The Tarot School New York, personal communication.
23. Williams, *Renaissance Tarot*, 42.
24. Ricklef, *KnightHawk*, 149.
25. von Franz, *Redemption Motifs*, 42.
26. Hand, *Horoscope Symbols*, 67–71.
27. Williams and Geopferd, *Light and Shadow*, 48.
28. Case, *Tarot Key*, 155–159.
29. Wood, *Robin Wood Tarot*, 68–69.
30. John Gilbert, personal communication.
31. Lessons on using the dignities in Tarot card readings can be obtained from the Web site of Paul Hughes-Barlow (see Internet Resources).
32. R. V. O'Neill, *The Magician: Sources of the Waite/Smith Symbolism*. http://www.geocities.com/ninaleeb/oneill/1.htm
33. Gayley, *Classic Myths*, 41.
34. Sharman-Burke and Greene, *Mythic Tarot*, 19.
35. Robert Graves, *Greek Myths*, illustrated ed. (London: Penguin Books, 1981), 17.
36. Marie-Louise von Franz, *The Interpretation of Fairy Tales*, rev. ed., (Boston & London: Shambhala, 1996), 130.
37. Sharman-Burke and Greene, *Mythic Tarot*, 128.
38. Akron and Banzhaf, *Crowley Tarot*, 152.
39. Crowley, *Book of Thoth*, 159.
40. Akron and Banzhaf, *Crowley Tarot*, 152.
41. Pollack, *Haindl*, Vol. I, 42.
42. Pollack, *Shining Tribe*, 68.

43. Roob, *Alchemy*, 131, 198.

44. Conway and Knight, *Shapeshifter*, 58.

45. Liz Greene, "The Hero with a Thousand Faces: The Sun and the Development of Consciousness" in Greene and Sasportas, *Luminaries*, 81–115.

46. Pollack, *Haindl*, Vol. I, 179.

E: REFERENCES

1. von Franz, *Alchemy*.

2. Gad, *Tarot Individuation*, 56.

3. Crowley, *Book of Thoth*, 100.

4. Wirth, *Tarot of Magicians*, 75.

5. Chevalier and Gheerbrant, *Penguin Dictionary*, 342.

6. Cirlot, *Dictionary of Symbols*, 233.

7. Curtiss and Curtiss, *Key of Destiny*, 287, 294.

8. Tom Chetwynd, *A Dictionary of Symbols* (London: Granada Publishing, 1984), 289.

9. Roob, *Alchemy*, 28.

10. *Ibid.*, 106.

11. *Ibid.*, 30.

12. Church of Light deck, Mary K. Greer, personal communication.

13. El Gran Tarot Esoterico, Mary K. Greer, personal communication.

14. Pollack, *Haindl*, Vol. II, 113–114.

15. Chevalier and Gheerbrant, *Penguin Dictionary*, 349.

16. *Ibid.*, 347.

17. Wirth, *Tarot of Magicians*, 75.

18. von Franz, *Alchemy*, 116.

19. R. V. O'Neill, *The Emperor: Sources of the Waite/Smith Tarot Symbols*. http://www.geocities.com/ninaleeb/oneill/4.htm

20. Walker, *Woman's Encyclopedia*, 841.

21. Akron and Banzhaf, *Crowley Tarot*, 40.

22. Eliade, *Myth and Reality*, 40–41.

23. *Ibid.*, 51.

24. Joseph Campbell, *The Hero with a Thousand Faces*, 2d ed. (Princeton: Princeton University Press, 1968), 303.

25. Eakins, *Tarot of Spirit*, 266.

26. Waite, *Pictorial Key*, 83.

27. Barbara G. Walker, *The Woman's Dictionary of Symbols and Sacred Objects* (San Francisco: HarperSanFrancisco, 1988), 284–288.

28. R. V. O'Neill, *The Empress: Sources of the Waite/Smith Tarot Symbols.* http://www.geocities.com/ninaleeb/oneill/3.htm.

29. Robert Wang, *An Introduction to the Golden Dawn Tarot* (York Beach, Maine: Samuel Weiser, Inc., 1978), 136.

30. Waite, *Pictorial Key*, 83.

31. Pollack, *Shining Tribe*, 25.

32. von Franz, *Cat*, 70.

33. Pollack, *Haindl*, Vol. I, 40, 43.

34. Williams and Goepferd, *Light and Shadow*, 16.

35. Payne-Towler, *Underground*, 103.

36. *Ibid.*

37. To view some of these, see the Web site page of James W. Revak at http://www.villarevak.org//td/td_3.htm

38. James W. Revak, personal communication.

F: REFERENCES

1. Conway and Knight, *Shapeshifter*, 21.

2. Beatrex Quntanna, *Tarot: A Universal Language* (Carlsbad, Calif.: Art Ala Carte Publishing, 1989), 30.

3. Genetti, *Wheel of Change*, 190.

4. Jung, *Four Archetypes*, 76.

5. Williams and Goepferd, *Light and Shadow*, 10.

6. M. Esther Harding, *Woman's Mysteries: Ancient and Modern* (Boston & Shaftesbury: Shambhala, 1990), 80, 84.

7. Marie-Louise von Franz, *Number and Time* (Evanston, Illinois: Northwestern University Press, 1974), 65.

8. Chevalier and Gheerbrant, *Penguin Dictionary*, 394–396.

9. Wood, *Robin Wood Tarot*, 43.

10. Prosapio, *Intuitive Tarot*, 16.

11. Robert Wang, *Tarot Psychology* (Germany: Urania Verlags Ag, 1988), Wang designed the Jungian Tarot deck.

12. TarotL Tarot History Information Sheet, compiled and edited by Tom Tadfor Little.

13. Hajo Banzhaf, *Tarot and the Journey of the Hero* (York Beach, Maine: Samuel Weiser, Inc., 2000), 17.

14. *Ibid.*, 12.
15. Françoise O'Kane, *Sacred Chaos. Reflections on God's Shadow and the Dark Self* (Toronto, Canada: Inner City Books, 1994), 86.

G: References

1. Contributed by Elizabeth M. Hazel.
2. Pollack, *Shining Tribe*, 29.
3. Crowley, *Book of Thoth*, 108.
4. Chevalier and Gheerbrant, *Penguin Dictionary*, 434.
5. R. V. O'Neill, *The Hierophant: Sources of the Waite/Smith Tarot Symbols*. http://www.geocities.com/ninaleeb/oneill/5.htm.
6. Roob, *Alchemy*, 294.
7. Barbara G. Walker, *The Secrets of the Tarot. Origins, History, and Symbolism* (San Francisco: Harper & Row, 1984), 71.
8. Genetti, *Wheel of Change*, 140–143.
9. Williams, *Renaissance Tarot*, 27.
10. Banzhaf and Theler, *Keywords for Crowley*, 70.
11. Pollack, *Haindl*, Vol. II, 81.
12. *The Herder Symbolic Dictionary*, trans. Boris Matthews (Wilmette, Illinois: Chiron Publications, 1986), 123.

H: References

1. Gayley, *Classic Myths*, 51.
2. Bolen, *Gods in Everyman*, 104.
3. Bolen, *Gods in Everyman*, 98–123; Elizabeth M. Hazel, personal communication.
4. Wood, *Robin Wood Tarot*, 37.
5. Waite, *Pictorial Key*, 88.
6. Eakins, *Tarot Spirit*, 280.
7. Giles, *Tarot History*, 24.
8. Williams and Goepferd, *Light and Shadow*, 40.
9. Nichols, *Jung and Tarot*, 217.
10. R.V. O'Neill, *The Hanged Man: Sources of the Waite/Smith Symbolism*. http://www.geocities.com/ninaleeb/oneill/12.htm.
11. Guiley and Place, *Alchemical Tarot*, 100.
12. Giles, *Tarot History*, 116.
13. Knight, *Tarot and Magic*, 57.

14. Gareth Knight, *The Magical World of the Tarot* (York Beach, Maine: Samuel Weiser, Inc., 1996), 11.

15. R.V. O'Neill, *The Hanged Man: Sources of the Waite/Smith Symbolism*. http://www.geocities.com/ninaleeb/oneill/12.htm

16. Pollack, *Haindl*, Vol. I, 109–114.

17. Pollack, *Shining Tribe*, 56–57.

18. Myss, *Anatomy*, 87.

19. Walter Lippman, *Public Opinion* (New York: Harcourt Brace, 1922), 10.

20. Catherine Cook and Dwariko von Sommaruga, *Songs for the Journey Home. Alchemy through Imagery: A Tarot Pathway* (Aukland, New Zealand: Alchemists & Artists, 1996), 49.

21. Bolen, *Gods in Everyman*, 169.

22. Graves, *Greek Myths*, 24.

23. Bolen, *Gods in Everyman*, 162–191; Elizabeth M. Hazel, personal communication.

24. Steventon, *Spiral Tarot*, 55–57.

25. Georgia Lambert R., personal communication.

26. Myss, *Anatomy*, 197–198.

27. Wood, *Robin Wood Tarot*, 56.

28. Kenneth D. Newman, *The Tarot. A Myth of Male Initiation* (New York: C. G. Jung Foundation for Analytical Psychology, 1983), 40.

29. Moore, *Care of Soul*, 246.

30. Lynne Luerding, personal communication.

31. Akron and Banzhaf, *Crowley Tarot*, 156.

32. Mary K. Greer, personal communication.

33. Crowley, *Book of Thoth*, 115; Hulse, *Western Mysteries*, 405.

34. Hulse, *Western Mysteries*, 405.

35. *Ibid.*, 357–409.

36. Rachel Pollack, *Seventy-eight Degrees of Wisdom. Part I: The Major Arcana* (Wellingborough, Northamptonshire: The Aquarian Press, 1980), 52.

37. *Ibid.*, 49.

38. R. V. O'Neill, *The Hierophant: Sources of the Waite/Smith Symbolism*. http://www.geocities.com/ninaleeb/oneill/5.htm.

39. *Ibid.*

40. Gad, *Tarot and Individuation*, 63.

41. Georgia Lambert R., personal communication.
42. Wood, *Robin Wood Tarot*, 46, 48.
43. Waite, *Pictorial Key*, 88.
44. Waite, *Pictorial Key*, 91.
45. Genetti, *Wheel of Change*, 49.
46. Godino and O'Leary, *World Spirit*, 14–15.
47. Crowley, *Book of Thoth*, 78.
48. The roots of the Roman Pope's title lay in the pagan Roman myths of a city-god called Petra. Assimilated into the Mithraic *pater patrum* (Father of Fathers), the title was then corrupted into the Italian *papa* and finally "pope." A stone Petra (phallic) pillar, topped with a pine-cone, remained in the Vatican well into the Middle Ages. (Walker, *Woman's Encyclopedia*, 787–788).
49. Sharman-Burke and Greene, *Mythic Tarot*, 33–35.
50. Mario Jacoby, *The Longing for Paradise: Psychological Perspectives on an Archetype*, trans. Myron B. Gubitz (Boston: Sigo Press, 1985).
51. Pollack, *Shining Tribe*, 22.
52. Williams and Goepferd, *Light and Shadow*, 13.
53. R. V. O'Neill, *The High Priestess: Sources of the Waite/Smith Tarot Symbols*. http://www.geocities.com/ninaleeb/oneill/2.htm
54. Williams, *Renaissance Tarot*, 41.
55. Newman, *Male Initiation*.
56. Crowley, *Book of Thoth*, 73.
57. Walker, *Woman's Encyclopedia*, 454.
58. Williams and Goepferd, *Light and Shadow*, 12.
59. Williams, *Renaissance Tarot*, 39.
60. Pollack, *Illustrated Guide*, 29.
61. Wood, *Robin Wood Tarot*, 43.
62. Stevens, *Ariadne's Clue*, 398.
63. Anna-Marie Ferguson, *A Keeper of Words. Legend: The Arthurian Tarot* (St. Paul, Minn.: Llewellyn, 1995), 89.
64. Tresidder, *Dictionary of Symbols*, 104.
65. Godino and O'Leary, *World Spirit*, 87.
66. Gayley, *Classic Myths*, 93–94.

I: References

1. Pollack, *Haindl*, Vol. II, 8.
2. Williams, *Renaissance Tarot*, 35.
3. Matthews, *Herder Dictionary*, 104.
4. Crowley, *Book of Thoth*, 71.
5. Graves, *Greek Myths*, 88.
6. O'Kane, *Sacred Chaos*, 19.
7. Cook and von Sommaruga, *Songs for Journey*, 49.

J: References

1. Waite, *Pictorial Key*, 151.
2. O'Neill, *Tarot Symbolism*, 286.
3. Knight, *Magical World*, 65.
4. Sharman-Burke and Greene, *Mythic Tarot*, 78–80.
5. Wood, *Robin Wood Tarot*, 79–80.
6. Jung, *Four Archetypes*, 57.
7. *Ibid.*, 54.
8. Richard Cavendish, *The Tarot* (New York: Harper & Row, 1975), 136.
9. Genetti, *Wheel of Change*, 103–105.
10. Contributed by Arielle Smith.
11. Eugene Pascal, *Jung to Live By* (New York: Warner Books, 1992), 16–24.
12. Janice Brewi and Anne Brennan, *Mid-life Spirituality and Jungian Archetypes*, rev. ed. (York Beach, Maine: Nicolas-Hays, 1999), 141.
13. Rose Gwain, *Discovering Your Self Through the Tarot: A Jungian Guide to Archetypes & Personality* (Rochester, Va.: Destiny Books, 1994), 36–37.
14. Contributed by Elizabeth M. Hazel.
15. Waite, *Pictorial Key*, 115.
16. Georgia Lambert R., personal communication.
17. One of the most poetic examples of this is given by Paul Foster Case, who writes that the arithmetical symbol for a circle (the crown and the jewel in the cape clasp) is twenty-two, while that for a square (the crown jewel and the cape clasp) is four. Together they form twenty-six, the value of the Tetragrammaton, the Divine name (Case, *Tarot Key*, 127).

18. D. Norman, *The Hero: Myth/Image/Symbol* (New York & Cleveland: World, 1969).
19. Walker, *Woman's Encyclopedia*, 562.
20. Wood, *Robin Wood Tarot*, 61.
21. Godino and O'Leary, *World Spirit*, 28.

K: REFERENCES
1. Mary K. Greer, personal communication.
2. Crowley, *Book of Thoth*, 149.
3. von Franz, *Cat*, 71.
4. Ruth Ann Amberstone, The Tarot School (New York), personal communication.

L: REFERENCES
1. Wirth, *Tarot of Magicians*, 64.
2. Eakins, *Tarot Spirit*, 215.
3. Contributed by Elizabeth M. Hazel.
4. Hulse, *Western Mysteries*, 410.
5. David Fontana, *The Secret Language of Symbols: A Visual Key to Symbols and Their Meanings*, (San Francisco: Chronicle Books, 1994), 180.
6. Chevalier and Gheerbrant, *Penguin Dictionary*, 612.
7. Liz Greene, "Mothers and Matriarchy" in Greene and Sasportas, *Luminaries*, 14–15.
8. Tracey Hoover, *The Ancestral Path Tarot* (Stamford, Conn.: U.S. Games Systems, Inc., 1996), 27.
9. Guiley and Place, *Alchemical Tarot*, 134.
10. Banzhaf and Theler, *Keywords for Crowley*, 76.
11. Akron and Banzhaf, *Crowley Tarot*, 90.
12. Steventon, *Spiral Tarot*, 87–88.
13. Sharman-Burke and Greene, *Mythic Tarot*, 36–38.
14. Payne-Towler, *Underground Stream*, 28.
15. Nichols, *Jung and Tarot*, 134.
16. Wood, *Robin Wood Tarot*, 49–51.
17. Newman, *Male Initiation*, 27.
18. *Ibid.*, 29.
19. Wang, *Golden Dawn*, 27.

M: REFERENCES

1. Poncé, *Wizard's Game*, 115.
2. Eakins, *Tarot Spirit*, 258.
3. Cook and von Sommaruga, *Songs*, 39.
4. Hoover, *Ancestral Path*, 7.
5. Williams and Goepferd, *Light and Shadow*, 9.
6. Hulse, *Western Mysteries*, 344–351.
7. Eliade, *Myth and Reality*, 25.
8. Poncé, *Wizard's Game*, 44.
9. José Argüelles and Miriam Argüelles, *Mandala* (Boulder, Colorado: Shambhala, 1972), 12.
10. Marie-Louise von Franz, *On Divination and Synchronicity. The Psychology of Meaningful Chance* (Toronto, Canada: Inner City Books, 1980), 98.
11. J. C. Cooper, *An Illustrated Encyclopaedia of Traditional Symbols* (London: Thames & Hudson, Ltd., 1978), 10.
12. Robert A. Johnson, *Owning Your Own Shadow: Understanding the Dark Side of the Psyche* (San Francisco: Harper & Row, 1991).
13. Genetti, *Wheel of Change*, 224.
14. Contributed by Elizabeth M. Hazel.
15. Howard Sasportas, "Sun, Father, and the Emergence of the Ego: The Father's Role in Individual Development" in Greene and Sasportas, *Luminaries*, 136.
16. Gargiulo-Sherman, *Sacred Rose*, 38.
17. Wang, *Golden Dawn*, 16.
18. Contributed by Elizabeth M. Hazel.
19. There is some indication that the fifteenth century Sola Busca deck used Minor Arcana illustrations, but they did not catch on. See Holly Voley's RWS page at http://home.attbi.com/~vilex/.
20. Hulse, *Western Mysteries*, 412.
21. I am indebted to Lynne Luerding and Arielle Smith for debating this issue with me and contributing their ideas.
22. Contributed by Elizabeth M. Hazel.
23. Contributed by Elizabeth M. Hazel.
24. Steventon, *Spiral Tarot*, 91.
25. Waite, *Pictorial Key*, 140.
26. Wirth, *Tarot of Magicians*, 13–140.

27. Pollack, *Haindl*, Vol. I, 153.
28. Liz Greene, "Mothers and Matriarchy: The Mythology and Psychology of the Moon" in Greene and Sasportas, *Luminaries*, 16.
29. Case, *Tarot Key*, 177.
30. Wood, *Robin Wood Tarot*, 74–76.
31. Hoover, *Ancestral Path*, 59–62.
32. Eakins, *Tarot Spirit*, 358.
33. Guiley and Place, *Alchemical Tarot*, 116–117.
34. R. V. O'Neill, *The Moon: Sources of the Waite/Smith Symbolism*. http://www.geocities.com/ninaleeb/oneill/18.htm.
35. Osho International Foundation, *Osho Zen*, 38.
36. Wood, *Robin Wood Tarot*, 66–67.
37. *Ibid.*, 43.
38. M. K. Wren, *King of the Mountain* (New York: Ballantine Books, 1994), 313.
39. Genetti, *Wheel of Change*, 142.
40. Conway and Knight, *Shapeshifter*, 69.
41. Full details on moving meditations can be found in Greer, *Tarot Mirrors*, 27–30.
42. Biedermann, *Dictionary*, 233.
43. Wood, *Robin Wood Tarot*, 74.
44. The name derives from the folk belief that fairies danced within a circle created by mushrooms, usually *Marasmius oreades* as it extends its initial growth outward in a circle.
45. Ferguson, *Keeper of Words*, 49.
46. Case, *Tarot Key*, 1975.
47. Greer, *Tarot for Self*, 246.
48. Thomas Moore, "Musical Therapy" in Sells, *Working Images*, 161.

N: REFERENCES
1. Graves, *Greek Myths*, 80–81.
2. Contributed by Elizabeth M. Hazel.
3. von Franz, *On Divination*, 22.
4. von Franz, *Number and Time*, 38.
5. *Ibid.*, 75.
6. John Gilbert, personal communication.

O: REFERENCES

1. Stevens, *Ariadne's Clue*, 113.
2. Pollack, *Haindl*, Vol. I, 22.
3. Williams, *Renaissance Tarot*, 99.
4. Wirth, *Tarot of Magicians*, 80.
5. Graves, *Greek Myths*, 44–45.
6. Contributed by Elizabeth M. Hazel.
7. von Franz, *Alchemy*, 174.
8. *Ibid.*, 129.
9. Steventon, *Spiral Tarot*, 111.
10. Conway and Knight, *Shapeshifter*, 105.

P: REFERENCES

1. Greer, *Tarot Constellations*, 182.
2. Pollack, *Shining Tribe*, 233.
3. Gayley, *Classic Myths*, 181.
4. Williams, *Renaissance Tarot*, 27.
5. James Revak, personal communication.
6. Chevalier and Gheerbrant, *Penguin Dictionary*, 741–742.
7. Crowley, *Book of Thoth*, 156.
8. Pollack, *Haindl*, Vol. I, 104–106.
9. Steventon, *Spiral Tarot*, 62.
10. Chevalier and Gheerbrant, *Penguin Dictionary*, 743.
11. Campbell, *Hero*, 116–118.
12. Gayley, *Classic Myths*, 211, 215, 518–519.
13. Chevalier and Gheerbrant, *Penguin Dictionary*, 746.
14. Eakins, *Tarot Spirit*, 211.
15. Wood, *Robin Wood Tarot*, 98.
16. Eakins, *Tarot Spirit*, 216.
17. Guiley and Place, *Alchemical Tarot*, 128.
18. Conway and Knight, *Shapeshifter*, 172.
19. *Ibid.*, 474.
20. Steventon, *Spiral Tarot*, 128.
21. von Franz, *Archetypal Patterns*, 75.
22. *Ibid.*, 142.
23. Roob, *Alchemical*, 224.
24. Gwain, *Discovering*, 163.

25. Pollack, *Seventy-eight*, Pt. 2, 107.
26. Pollack, *Haindl*, Vol. II, 112.
27. Pollack, *Shining Tribe*, 226.
28. *Ibid.*, 228–230.
29. Godino and O'Leary, *World Spirit*, 152–153.
30. Steventon, *Spiral Tarot*, 117.
31. Guiley and Place, *Alchemical Tarot*, 133.
32. Pollack, *Seventy-eight*, Pt. 2, 100.
33. Eakins, *Tarot Spirit*, 239–241.
34. Lynne Luerding, personal communication.
35. Guiley and Place, *Alchemical Tarot*, 135.
36. Graves, *Greek Myths*, 68–71.
37. Greer, *Tarot Mirrors*, 199.
38. Jung, *Four Archetypes*, 76.
39. Gayley, *Classic Myths*, 94–98; Graves, *Greek Myths*, 53–56.
40. Jung, *Four Archetypes*, 67.
41. Graves, *Greek Myths*, 65–66.
42. Wood, *Robin Wood Tarot*, 80.
43. Chevalier and Gheerbrant, *Penguin Dictionary*, 755.
44. Contributed by Elizabeth M. Hazel.
45. Gayley, *Classic Myths*, 122–123.
46. Contributed by Elizabeth M. Hazel.
47. Roob, *Alchemical*, 250.
48. Cirlot, *Dictionary of Symbols*, 261.
49. Signe E. Echols, Robert E. Mueller and Sandra A. Thomson, *Spiritual Tarot. Seventy-eight Paths to Personal Development* (New York: Avon Books, 1996), 46.
50. Williams, *Renaissance Tarot*, 45.
51. Other stories say it was Demeter the "All-Mother" goddess who gave birth to Iacchus and his sister Kore, the primordial maiden.
52. Arrien, *Tarot Handbook*, 166.
53. Pollack, *Shining Tribe*, 141.
54. Bolen, *Gods in Everyman*, 73.
55. *Ibid.*, 80.
56. Bolen, *Gods in Everyman*, 72–97; Elizabeth M. Hazel, personal communication.
57. Neil Douglas-Klotz, *The Hidden Gospel. Decoding the Spiritual Message of the Aramaic Jesus* (Wheaton, Ill.: Quest Books, 1999), 143.

58. Gayley, *Classic Myths*, 11–12.

59. Helen M. Luke, "Mothers and Daughters: A Mythological Perspective" in C. Downing, ed., *Mirrors of Self*, 80–83.

60. Mary K. Greer, personal communication.

61. Fontana, *Secret Language*, 59.

Q: References

1. von Franz, *Archetypal Patterns*, 132.

2. *Ibid.*, 129.

3. Mary K. Greer, personal communication.

4. Chevalier and Gheerbrant, *Penguin Dictionary*, 989.

5. Campbell, *Hero*, 111.

6. Estés, *Women Who Run*, 52.

7. Georgia Lambert R., personal communication.

8. Pollack, *Haindl*, Vol. II, 143.

9. Banzhaf and Theler, *Keywords for Crowley*, 28.

R: References

1. Whitmont, *Return of Goddess*, xiv.

2. Walker, *Woman's Dictionary*, 377.

3. Maria Leach, ed. and Jerome Fried, assoc. ed., *Funk & Wagnalls Standard Dictionary of Folklore, Mythology, and Legend* (San Francisco: Harper & Row, 1972), 528.

4. Susan Hansson, *Reading Tarot Cards: A Guide to The New Palladini Tarot* (Stamford, Conn.: U.S. Games Systems, Inc., 1996), 155.

5. Banzhaf and Theler, *Keywords for Crowley*, 70.

6. Eakins, *Tarot Spirit*, 346.

7. *Ibid.*, 215, 225.

8. Hansson, *Reading Tarot Cards*, 27.

9. Mary K. Greer, *The Complete Book of Tarot Reversals* (St. Paul, Minn.: Llewellyn Worldwide, 2002).

10. Rachel Pollack, personal communication.

11. Roob, *Alchemy*, 420.

12. Waite, *Pictorial Key*, 75.

13. Fontana, *Secret Language*, 71.

14. Wood, *Robin Wood Tarot*, 37.

S: REFERENCES

1. Contributed by Elizabeth M. Hazel.
2. Guiley and Place, *Alchemical Tarot*, 148.
3. Roob, *Alchemical*, 28.
4. Akron and Banzhaf, *Crowley Tarot*, 35.
5. Contributed by Elizabeth M. Hazel.
6. O'Kane, *Sacred Chaos*, 13, 29.
7. Hamaker-Zondag, *Way of Life*, 52.
8. Brewi and Brennan, *Mid-life Spirituality*, 116.
9. Gwain, *Discovering*, 139, 143.
10. Pollack, *Haindl*, Vol. I, 25.
11. Christine Jette, *Tarot Shadow Work. Using the Dark Symbols to Heal* (St. Paul, Minn.: Llewellyn Publications, 2000).
12. This is a process devised by Mary K. Greer, *Tarot Constellations*, 30.
13. Curtiss and Curtiss, *Key to Universe*, 204–210.
14. Quntanna, *Universal Language*, 68.
15. Mary K. Greer, personal communication.
16. Greer, *Tarot Mirrors*, 405–409.
17. Williams and Goepferd, *Light and Shadow*, 32–34.
18. Crowley, *Book of Thoth*, 109.
19. Akron and Banzhaf, *Crowley Tarot*, 44.
20. Pollack, *Haindl*, Vol. I, 40.
21. *Ibid.*, Vol. I, 80–87.
22. Greer, *Tarot Mirrors*, 200.
23. Genetti, *Wheel of Change*, 39.
24. *Ibid.*, 147.
25. Crowley, *Book of Thoth*, 110.
26. Chevalier and Gheerbrant, *Penguin Dictionary*, 906–909.
27. Eakins, *Tarot Spirit*, 258.
28. Chevalier and Gheerbrant, *Penguin Dictionary*, 916.
29. Crowley, *Book of Thoth*, 201.
30. R. V. O'Neill, *Justice: Sources of the Waite/Smith Symbolism.* http://www.geocities.com/ninaleeb/oneill/11.htm.
31. Stevens, *Ariadne's Clue*, 117.
32. The Tarot School, *Tarot Tips*, Nov. 8, 2001, Issue No. 161, New York.

33. Isabel Radow Kliegman, *Tarot and the Tree of Life. Finding Everyday Wisdom in the Minor Arcana* (Wheaton, Ill.: Quest Books, 1997), 46.

34. Waite, *Pictorial Key*, 136.

35. Wirth, *Tarot of Magicians*, 134.

36. Pollack, *Haindl*, Vol. I, 147.

37. Pollack, *Shining Tribe*, 77.

38. Wirth, *Tarot of Magicians*, 132.

39. Jackson, *Nigel Jackson Tarot*, 55.

40. Williams, *Renaissance Tarot*, 112.

41. O'Neill, *Tarot Symbolism*, 387.

42. Osho International Foundation, *Osho Zen*, 36.

43. Wood, *Robin Wood Tarot*, 72–73.

44. Walker, *Woman's Encyclopedia*, 429.

45. Leach and Fried, *Funk & Wagnalls Dictionary*, 529.

46. Cirlot, *Dictionary of Symbols*, 310.

47. Chevalier and Gheerbrant, *Penguin Dictionary*, 924–925.

48. Akron and Banzhaf, *Crowley Tarot*, 100–101.

49. Roob, *Alchemical*, 469.

50. Case, *Tarot Key*, 60.

51. Case, *Tarot Key*, 183.

52. Wang, *Golden Dawn*, 45.

53. *Ibid.*, 141.

54. Crowley, *Book of Thoth*, 113.

55. Nina Lee Braden, *Tarot for Self Discovery* (St. Paul, Minn.: Llewellyn Publications, 2002).

56. Diane Wilkes, personal communication.

57. Georgia Lambert R., personal communication.

58. Wood, *Robin Wood Tarot*, 54.

59. Sharman-Burke and Greene, *Mythic Tarot*, 48–50.

60. Crowley, *Book of Thoth*, 92.

61. *Ibid.*, 95.

62. Guiley and Place, *Alchemical Tarot*, 97–98.

63. Roob, *Alchemical*, 37.

64. Chevalier and Gheerbrant, *Penguin Dictionary*, 194, 944.

65. Cooper, *Illustrated Encyclopaedia*, 163.

66. Stevens, *Ariadne's Clue*, 184.

67. Guiley and Place, *Alchemical Tarot*, 110.

68. Contributed by Elizabeth M. Hazel.

69. Stevens, *Ariadne's Clue*, 187.
70. Liz Greene, "The Hero with a Thousand Faces. The Sun and the Development of Consciousness" in Greene and Sasportas, *Luminaries*, 114.
71. Case, *Tarot Key*, 186.
72. *Ibid.*, 181.
73. C. G. Jung, "The Child Archetype" in Downing, ed., *Mirrors of Self*, 156.
74. Waite, *Pictorial Key*, 144–147.
75. Paul Foster Case, in Case, *Tarot Key*, 185, quotes Waite as saying this, but I have been unable to find the exact quote in any of Waite's writings available to me.
76. Hulse, *Western Mysteries*, 404.
77. O'Neill, *Tarot Symbolism*, 286.
78. Eakins, *Tarot Spirit*, 361.
79. Waite, *Pictorial Key*, 144.
80. Case, *Tarot Key*, 182.
81. Wood, *Robin Wood Tarot*, 77–78.
82. Kathleen McCormack, *Tarot Decoder* (Hauppauge, N.Y.: Barron's, 1998), 71.
83. Akron and Banzhaf, *Crowley Tarot*, 109.
84. Gayley, *Classic Myths*, 116–117.
85. Pollack, *Haindl*, Vol. I, 17.
86. Hand, *Horoscope Symbols*, 188.
87. Wirth, *Tarot of Magicians*, 234.
88. Marie-Louise von Franz, *C. G. Jung. His Myth in Our Time* (Toronto, Canada: Inner City Books, 1998), 172.
89. Wirth, *Tarot of Magicians*, 312–313.
90. Chevalier and Gheerbrant, *Penguin Dictionary*, 746.
91. Gad, *Tarot and Individuation*, 313.
92. *Ibid.*
93. Wirth, *Tarot of Magicians*, 24.
94. Pollack, *Haindl*, Vol. II, 67.
95. Osho International Foundation, *Osho Zen*, 138.
96. Wood, *Robin Wood Tarot*, 130–131.
97. Osho International Foundation, *Osho Zen*, 124.
98. Steventon, *Spiral Tarot*, 128.
99. Georgia Lambert R., personal communication.

100. Georgia Lambert R., personal communication.

101. Pollack, *Haindl*, Vol. II, 82–84.

102. Caroline T. Stevens, "Lesbian Family, Holy Family: Experience of an Archetype" in C. Downing, ed., *Mirrors of Self*, 144–150.

103. Georgia Lambert R., personal communication.

104. E. Dale Saunders, *Mudra. A Study of Symbolic Gestures in Japanese Buddhist Sculpture* (Princeton, N.J.: Princeton University Press, 1960).

105. Gary Van Thiel, personal communication.

106. Japikse, *Exploring Tarot*, 193.

107. Genetti, *Wheel of Change*, 303–305.

108. Pollack, *Shining Tribe*, 261.

109. Mary K. Greer, personal communication.

110. Wood, *Robin Wood Tarot*, 123–124.

111. Lynne Luerding, personal communication.

112. Godino and O'Leary, *World Spirit*, 129.

113. *Ibid.*, 131.

114. Pollack, *Shining Tribe*, 272.

115. Hoover, *Ancestral Path*, 78.

T: REFERENCES

1. Case, *Tarot Key*; Pollack, *Seventy-eight*, Part I.

2. Jayanti, *Living Tarot*, 8.

3. Hamaker-Zondag, *Tarot Way*.

4. Tom Tadfor Little, comp. and ed., *The TarotL Tarot History Information Sheet*.

5. For more information on tattvas, see Hulse, *New Dimensions*; also Harish Johari, *Breath, Mind, and Consciousness* (Rochester, Va.: Destiny Books, 1990), which details the powers and uses of tattvas, employing changes in the breath as an indicator.

6. Mary K. Greer, personal communication.

7. See Hulse, *Western Mysteries*, for information on where the tattvas are encoded in Waite's and Case's decks.

8. I am indebted to Paul-Hughes Barlow (www.supertarot.co.uk) for clarifying and adding to information included in this entry.

9. Hulse, *Western Mysteries*, 408.

10. Contributed by Elizabeth M. Hazel.

11. Connie Zweig, "The Conscious Feminine: Birth of a New Archetype" in C. Downing, ed., *Mirrors of Self*, 188.

12. Georgia Lambert R., personal communication.

13. Roob, *Alchemy*, 187.

14. Steventon, *Spiral Tarot*, 74.

15. Georgia Lambert R., personal communication.

16. Israel Regardie, *The Complete Golden Dawn System of Magic*, 10 volumes in one, (Phoenix, Ariz.: Falcon Press, 1984), 17.

17. From the "Lay of Grimner," dating from the tenth century and originally an oral recitation of mythical knowledge. Retold in Kevin Crossley-Holland, *The Norse Myths* (New York: Pantheon Books, 1980), 63.

18. Case, *Tarot Key*, 147.

19. Marie-Louise von Franz, *Aurora Consurgens: A Document Attributed to Thomas Aquinas on the Problem of Opposites in Alchemy* (New York: Bollingen, 1966), 206.

20. Waite, *Pictorial Key*, 124.

21. Wood, *Robin Wood Tarot*, 66.

22. Eakins, *Tarot Spirit*, 331–336.

23. Jackson, *Nigel Jackson Tarot*, 52.

24. Gareth Knight, *On the Paths and the Tarot*, Vol. 2 of *A Practical Guide to Qabalistic Symbolism* (York Beach, Maine: Samuel Weiser, Inc., 1978), 17.

25. Myss, *Anatomy*, 238.

26. Mary K. Greer, personal communication.

27. These ideas are from John Gilbert.

28. David Aaron, *Seeing God: Ten Life-changing Lessons of the Kabbalah* (New York: Jeremy P. Tarcher/Putnam, 2001).

29. Pollack, *Haindl*, Vol. I, 29.

30. Gayley, *Classic Myths*, 250–260; Graves, *Greek Myths*, 89–110.

31. Crowley, *Book of Thoth*, 79.

32. Leach and Fried, *Funk & Wagnalls*, 1972.

33. Tresidder, *Dictionary of Symbols*, 204.

34. Roger von Oech, *A Whack on the Side of the Head* (New York: Warner, 1983).

35. Pollack, *Complete Illustrated*, 88.

36. Guiley and Place, *Alchemical Tarot*, 108–110.

37. Ferguson, *Keeper of Words*, 93.

38. Osho International Foundation, *Osho Zen*, 34.

39. Waite, *Pictorial Key*, 135.

40. *Ibid.*, 132.

41. Wang, *Golden Dawn*, 47–48.

42. Wood, *Robin Wood Tarot*, 70.

43. Steventon, *Spiral Tarot*, 83.

44. Sharman-Burke and Greene, *Mythic Tarot*, 66–68.

45. This is an idea expressed by Ellen Lorenzi-Prince on the Comparative Tarot Internet list.

46. Lionel, *Magic Tarot*, 174–178.

47. Good books to expand your knowledge of the Kabbalistic understanding of Tarot cards are Robert Wang, *The Qabalistic Tarot* (York Beach, Maine: Samuel Weiser, Inc., 1983) for Major Arcana associations, and Kliegman, *Tarot Tree*, 1997, for the Minor Arcana.

48. Cirlot, *Dictionary of Symbols*, 347.

49. Wood, *Robin Wood Tarot*, 82.

50. Cooper, *Illustrated Encyclopaedia*, 20.

51. Leach and Fried, *Funk & Wagnalls*, 130.

52. Stevens, *Ariadne's Clue*, 385.

53. Wood, *Robin Wood Tarot*, 54–55.

54. Genetti, *Wheel of Change*, 76.

55. Georgia Lambert R., personal communication.

56. Chevalier and Gheerbrant, *Penguin Dictionary*, 755.

57. William G. Doty, "The Trickster" in C. Downing, ed., *Mirrors of Self*, 240.

58. Robin Robertson, "Foreword to the Third Edition" in Combs and Holland, *Synchronicity*, xix.

59. Pollack, *Shining Tribe*, 47.

60. Chevalier and Gheerbrant, *Penguin Dictionary*, 1045.

61. von Franz, *Number and Time*, 96.

62. Waite, *Pictorial Key*, 120.

63. Chevalier and Gheerbrant, *Penguin Dictionary*, 1052.

U: REFERENCES

1. Cirlot, *Dictionary of Symbols*, 357.

2. Chevalier and Gheerbrant, *Penguin Dictionary*, 1056.

3. Conway and Knight, *Shapeshifter*, 185.
4. Contributed by Elizabeth M. Hazel.

V: REFERENCES

1. Contributed by Elizabeth M. Hazel.
2. Contributed by Elizabeth M. Hazel.

W: REFERENCES

1. Hulse, *Western Mysteries*, 410.
2. *Ibid.*
3. Laurence Gardner, *Bloodline of the Holy Grail* (Boston: Element Books, 2000), 78–80.
4. Hulse, *Western Mysteries*, 368.
5. Wood, *Robin Wood Tarot*, 35.
6. von Franz, *Archetypal Patterns*, 33.
7. Stevens, *Ariadne's Clue*, 331.
8. Williams, *Renaissance Tarot*, 149.
9. Liz Greene, "The Myth of the Individual Journey" in Stephen Arroyo and Liz Greene, eds., *New Insights in Modern Astrology* (Sebastopol, Calif.: CRCS Publications, 1991), 69.
10. Liz Greene, "Alchemical Symbolism in the Horoscope" in Liz Greene and Howard Sasportas, *Dynamics of the Unconscious. Seminars in Psychological Astrology*, Vol. 2 (York Beach, Maine: Samuel Weiser, Inc., 1989), 278.
11. Wood, *Robin Wood Tarot*, 158–159.
12. Pollack, *Haindl*, Vol. II, 13.
13. Larry Dossey, "Creativity: On Intelligence, Insight, and the Cosmic Soup." *Alternative Therapies* Vol. 6, No. 1 (Jan. 2000), 13.
14. Wood, *Robin Wood Tarot*, 160.
15. *Ibid.*, 161.
16. Pollack, *Shining Tribe*, 105.
17. Genetti, *Wheel of Change*, 176.
18. Sharman-Burke and Greene, *Mythic Tarot*, 121.
19. Pierre Teilhard de Chardin, *The Divine Milieu* (New York: Harper & Row, 1960), 71–72.
20. Pollack, *Haindl*, Vol. II, 17.
21. Williams, *Renaissance Tarot*, 152.

22. Information on this historical change was originally provided by Mary K. Greer in the Summer 1999 issue of her *Tarot Newsletter*.
23. Waite, *Pictorial Key*, 188.
24. Knight, *Tarot and Magic*, 140.
25. Mary K. Greer, personal communication.
26. Wood, *Robin Wood Tarot*, 168.
27. Williams, *Renaissance Tarot*, 152.
28. Pollack, *Seventy-eight Degrees*, Pt. 2, 40–41.
29. Pollack, *Shining Tribe*, 120.
30. Genetti, *Wheel of Change*, 189–191.
31. Waite, *Pictorial Key*, 182.
32. Hajo Banzhaf, *The Tarot Handbook*, trans. Christine M. Grimm (Stamford, Conn.: U.S. Games Systems, Inc., 1993), 76.
33. Pollack, *Haindl*, Vol. II, 123.
34. Waite, *Pictorial Key*, 180.
35. Osho International Foundation, *Osho Zen*, 94.
36. Sharman-Burke and Greene, *Mythic Tarot*, 129.
37. Genetti, *Wheel of Change*, 197–198.
38. Pollack, *Shining Tribe*, 127.
39. Waite, *Pictorial Key*, 178.
40. Pollack, *Shining Tribe*, 129.
41. Waite, *Pictorial Key*, 176.
42. Genetti, *Wheel of Change*, 205–208.
43. Pollack, *Shining Tribe*, 236–237.
44. Osho International Foundation, *Osho Zen*, 55.
45. Sharman-Burke and Greene, *Mythic Tarot*, 133.
46. Osho International Foundation, *Osho Zen*, 52–53.
47. Genetti, *Wheel of Change*, 209–211.
48. Pollack, *Shining Tribe*, 239.
49. Pollack, *Haindl*, Vol. II, 138–140.
50. Juliet Sharman-Burke, *The Complete Book of Tarot* (New York: St. Martin's Griffin, 1985), 127.
51. Steventon, *Spiral Tarot*, 111.
52. Osho International Foundation, *Osho Zen*, 50–51.
53. Wood, *Robin Wood Tarot*, 152–153.
54. Genetti, *Wheel of Change*, 216–218.
55. Mary K. Greer, personal communication.
56. Wood, *Robin Wood Tarot*, 150.

57. Osho International Foundation, *Osho Zen*, 48–49.
58. Genetti, *Wheel of Change*, 212–213.
59. Sharman-Burke and Greene, *Mythic Tarot*, 141.
60. Walker, *Secrets of Tarot*, 71.
61. Hulse, *Western Mysteries*, 430–431.
62. Crowley, *Book of Thoth*, 89.
63. Newman, *Male Initiation*, 50.
64. Case, *Tarot Key*, 121.
65. The bull represents the element of earth, the apostle Luke, the zodiac sign of Taurus, the archangel Auriel, and the Minor Arcana suit of Pentacles. The lion symbolizes fire, Mark, Leo, Michael, and Wands. The eagle stands for water, John, Scorpio, Gabriel, and Cups, while the human symbolizes air, Matthew, Aquarius, Raphael, and Swords.
66. Chevalier and Gheerbrant, *Penguin Dictionary*, 1100.
67. Waite, *Pictorial Key*, 108.
68. Wang, *Golden Dawn*, 142.
69. Pollack, *Shining Tribe*, 48–51.
70. Walker, *Secrets of Tarot*, 13.
71. Newman, *Male Initiation*, 50.
72. Liz Greene, "Mothers and Matriarchy. The Mythology and Psychology of the Moon" in Greene and Sasportas, *Luminaries*, 8.
73. Georgia Lambert R., personal communication.
74. Chetwynd, *Dictionary of Symbols*, 424.
75. Chevalier and Gheerbrant, *Penguin Dictionary*, 1102.
76. Crowley, *Book of Thoth*, 90.
77. Hulse, *Western Mysteries*, 357.
78. Fontana, *Secret Language*, 77.
79. Leach and Fried, *Funk & Wagnalls*, 341.
80. Banzhaf and Theler, *Crowley Keywords*, 72.
81. Crowley, *Book of Thoth*, 105.
82. Ralph Metzner, *The Well of Remembrance* (Boston & London: Shambhala, 1994), 258.
83. *Herder Symbolic Dictionary*, 217.
84. Greer, *Tarot Constellations*, 69.
85. Wirth, *Tarot of Magicians*, 149.
86. Jackson, *Nigel Jackson Tarot*, 62.
87. O'Neill, *Tarot Symbolism*, 391.
88. Waite, *Pictorial Key*, 156.

89. Hand, *Horoscope Symbols*, 55.
90. *Ibid.*
91. von Franz, *Alchemy*, 121.
92. Osho International Foundation, *Osho Zen*, 44.
93. Biedermann, *Dictionary of Symbolism*, 389–390.
94. Wood, *Robin Wood Tarot*, 55.

Y: REFERENCES

1. Greer, *Tarot Mirrors*, 200.
2. Crowley, *Book of Thoth*, 112.
3. Waite, *Pictorial Key*, 143.

Z: REFERENCES

1. Giles, *Tarot History*, 57–58; Mary K. Greer, personal communication.
2. Pollack, *Shining Tribe*, 6.
3. Bolen, *Gods in Everyman*, 45–71; Elizabeth M. Hazel, personal communication.
4. Elizabeth M. Hazel, personal communication.
5. Wang, *Qabalistic Tarot*, 1983, 196.
6. Elizabeth M. Hazel, personal communication.
7. Hulse, *Western Mysteries*, 412.
8. For some horoscopic or astrological spreads, see Gad, *Tarot and Individuation*, 400–411; Hamaker-Zondag, *Way of Life*, 235–260; Hoover, *Ancestral Path*, 221–222; Pollack, *Complete Illustrated Guide*, 144–145; Sharman-Burke, *Understanding Tarot*, 116–121; Sterling, *Tarot Awareness*, 376–380; Williams, *Renaissance Tarot*, 170–171.

INTERNET RESOURCES

Organizations:

1. American Tarot Association (ATA): www.ata-tarot.com
   Membership information, newsletter, conferences, links to other tarot sites
2. International Tarot Society: www.tarotsociety.org
   Membership information, newsletter, conferences
3. Tarot Certification Board of America (TCBA): www.tarotcertification.org
   Information on U.S. certification and links to certification boards in other
      countries
4. American Board of Tarot Certification (ABTC): www.americanboardfortarot
   certification.org
   A second certification group with information on U.S. certification
5. Canadian Tarot Network: www.tarotcanada.com
   Information on certification for Canadian tarotists

Courses:

1. Tarot School (New York): www.tarotschool.com
   Free newsletter; online courses; correspondence courses; directory of free read-
      ing sites
2. Paul Hughes-Barlow: www.supertarot.co.uk
   Free lessons on elemental dignities
3. Joan Bunning: www.learntarot.com
   Free tarot course

Workshops/Conferences:

1. Barbara Rapp: hrabarb@earthlink.net
   Information on Los Angeles Tarot Symposium (LATS) and annual three-day seminar with Rachel Pollack and Mary K. Greer (MARS)
2. Thalassa: airndarkness@yahoo.com
   Information on the Bay Area Tarot Symposium (BATS)

Reviews and Articles:

1. Nina Lee Braden: www.ninalee.com
   Reviews, articles, free correspondence course
2. Mary K. Greer: www.marygreer.com
   Information and events (Tools and Rites of Transformation—TAROT—site under construction)
3. K. Hill (Solandia): www.aeclectic.net/tarot/
   Articles; deck, book and software reviews; resources; Tarot Forum (www.tarot forum.net)
3. Teresa Michelsen: www.tarotmoon.com
   Articles, free classes
4. Christine Payne-Towler: www.tarot.com
   Computerized tarot readings and articles
5. Arielle Smith: www.mystikmoons.com
   Articles and deck reviews
6. Diane Wilkes: www.tarotpassages.com
   Reviews of most decks; articles; links to Internet resources

Free Tarot Readings:

1. Free Tarot Network: www.freetarot.net
   Free one-card readings by members of ATA
2. Free Reading Network:www.freereading.net
   Free three-card readings by members of ATA

Resources and History:

1. James Revak: http://www.villarevak.org//resource.htm
   Listings of books, decks, software, biographies, and links for tarot newcomers
2. Tom Tadfor Little: www.tarothermit.com
   Historical articles

e-zines:

Tapestry Magazine: www.tapestrytarot.com
   Reviews, articles, layouts, resources, links

Bookstore/Reference

The Tarot Garden: www.tarotgarden.com
   Database of tarot decks, library (articles, deck reviews and pictures, games),
    links

BIBLIOGRAPHY

✳

Aaron, David. *Seeing God: Ten Life-changing Lessons of the Kabbalah*. New York: Jeremy P. Tarcher/Putnam, 2001.

Abraham, Sylvia. *How to Use Tarot Spreads*. St. Paul, Minn.: Llewellyn Publications, 2001.

Akron and Hajo Banzhaf. *The Crowley Tarot*. Translated by Christine M. Grimm. Stamford, Conn.: U.S. Games Systems, Inc., 1995.

Argüelles, José, and Miriam Argüelles. *Mandala*. Boulder, Colorado: Shambhala, 1972.

Arrien, Angeles. *The Tarot Handbook*. Sonoma, Calif.: Arcus Publishing Co., 1987.

Arroyo, Stephen, and Liz Greene, eds. *New Insights in Modern Astrology*. Sebastopol, Calif.: CRCS Publications, 1991.

Banzhaf, Hajo. *Tarot and the Journey of the Hero*. York Beach, Maine: Samuel Weiser, Inc., 2000.

Banzhaf, Hajo. *The Tarot Handbook*. Translated by Christine M. Grimm. Stamford, Conn.: U.S. Games Systems, Inc., 1993.

Banzhaf, Hajo, and Brigitte Theler. *Keywords for the Crowley Tarot*. York Beach, Maine: Weiser Books, 2001.

Barron, Frank X. *Creativity and Psychological Health: Origins of Personal Vitality and Creative Freedom*. Princeton, N.J.: D. Van Nostrand Co., 1963.

Becker, Udo. *The Continuum Encyclopedia of Symbols*. New York/London: Continuum, 2000.

Biedermann, Hans. *Dictionary of Symbolism*. New York: Meridian, 1994.

Bolen, Jean Shinoda, M.D. *Gods in Everyman. A New Psychology of Men's Lives and Loves*. New York: Harper & Row, 1989.

Bolen, Jean Shinoda. *Goddesses in Every Woman. A New Psychology of Women*. New York: Harper & Row, 1984.

Bolen, Jean Shinoda. *Goddesses in Older Women. Archetypes in Women Over Fifty*. New York.: HarperCollins Publishers, 2001.

Braden, Nina Lee. *Tarot for Self Discovery*. St. Paul, Minn.: Llewellyn Publications, 2002.

Brewi, Janice, and Anne Brennan. *Mid-life Spirituality and Jungian Archetypes*. Rev. ed. York Beach, Maine: Nicolas-Hays, 1999.

Burger, Evelin, and Johannes Fiebig. *Complete Book of Tarot Spreads*. New York: Sterling Publishing Co., Inc., 1997.

Campbell, Joseph. *The Hero with a Thousand Faces*. 2d ed. Princeton, N.J.: Princeton University Press, 1968.

Campbell, Joseph. *The Masks of God*. Vol. 1, *Primitive Mythology*. New York: Viking, 1959.

Carlsen, Mary Baird. *Meaning-making: Therapeutic Processes in Adult Development*. New York.: Norton, 1988.

Case, Paul Foster. *The Tarot. A Key to the Wisdom of the Ages*. Richmond, Va.: Macoy Publishing Co., 1975.

Cavendish, Richard. *The Tarot*. New York.: Harper & Row, 1975.

Chetwynd, Tom. *A Dictionary of Symbols*. London: Granada Publishing, 1984.

Chevalier, Jean, and Alain Gheerbrant. *The Penguin Dictionary of Symbols*. Translated by John Buchanan-Brown. London: Penguin Books, Ltd., 1996.

Cirlot, J. E. *A Dictionary of Symbols*. Translated by Jack Sage. 2d ed. New York: Philosophical Library, 1983.

Combs, Allan, and Mark Holland. *Synchronicity: Through the Eyes of Science, Myth, and the Trickster*. New York: Marlowe & Co., 1996.

Conway, D. J., and Sirona Knight. *Shapeshifter Tarot*. St. Paul, Minn.: Llewellyn Publications, 1999.

Cook, Catherine, and Dwariko von Sommaruga. *Songs for the Journey Home. Alchemy through Imagery: A Tarot Pathway*. Aukland, New Zealand: Alchemists & Artists, 1996.

Cooper, J. C. *An Illustrated Encyclopaedia of Traditional Symbols*. London: Thames & Hudson, Ltd., 1978.

Crossley-Holland, Kevin. *The Norse Myths*. New York: Pantheon Books, 1980.

Crowley, Aleister. *The Book of Thoth (Egyptian Tarot)*. York Beach, Maine: Weiser Books, 2000.

Curtiss, Harriette A. and F. Homer Curtiss. *The Key of Destiny*. 4th ed. North Hollywood, Calif.: Newcastle Publishing Co., 1983.

Curtiss, Harriette. A., and F. Homer Curtiss. *The Key to the Universe*. 6th rev. ed. North Hollywood, Calif.: Newcastle Publishing Co., 1983.

Dossey, Larry. "Creativity: On Intelligence, Insight, and the Cosmic Soup." *Alternative Therapies* Vol. 6, No. 1. (Jan. 2000): 12–17, 108–117.

Douglas-Klotz, Neil. *The Hidden Gospel. Decoding the Spiritual Message of the Aramaic Jesus.* Wheaton, Ill.: Quest Books, 1999.

Downing, Christine, ed. *Mirrors of the Self. Archetypal Images that Shape Your Life.* Los Angeles: Jeremy P. Tarcher, Inc., 1991.

Eakins, Pamela. *Tarot of the Spirit.* York Beach, Maine: Samuel Weiser, Inc., 1992.

Echols, Signe E., Robert Mueller, and Sandra A. Thomson. *Spiritual Tarot. Seventy-eight Paths to Personal Development.* New York: Avon Books, 1996.

Eliade, Mircea. *Myth and Reality.* New York: Harper & Row, 1963.

Estés, Clarissa Pinkola. *Women Who Run With the Wolves.* New York: Ballantine Books, 1992.

Fairfield, Gail. *Choice Centered Tarot.* Rev. ed. York Beach, Maine: Samuel Weiser, Inc., 1997.

Ferguson, Anna-Marie. *A Keeper of Words. Legend: The Arthurian Tarot.* St. Paul, Minn.: Llewellyn, 1995.

Fontana, David. *The Secret Language of Symbols: A Visual Key to Symbols and Their Meanings.* San Francisco: Chronicle Books, 1994.

Gad, Irene. *Tarot and Individuation. Correspondences with Cabala and Alchemy.* York Beach, Maine: Nicolas-Hays, Inc., 1994.

Gardner, Laurence. *Bloodline of the Holy Grail.* Boston: Element Books, 2000.

Gargiulo-Sherman, Johanna. *Guide to the Sacred Rose Tarot.* Stamford, Conn.: U.S. Games Systems, Inc., 1997.

Gayley, Charles Mills. *The Classic Myths in English Literature and in Art.* Rev. ed. Boston: Ginn & Co., 1939.

Genetti, Alexandra. *The Wheel of Change Tarot.* Rochester, Vermont: Destiny Books, 1997.

Giles, Cynthia. *The Tarot. History, Mystery and Lore.* New York: Simon & Schuster, 1992.

Godino, Jessica, and Lauren O'Leary. *The World Spirit Tarot.* St. Paul, Minn.: Llewellyn Publications, 2001.

Graves, Robert. *Greek Myths.* Illustrated ed. London: Penguin Books, 1981.

Gray, Eden. *A Complete Guide to the Tarot.* New York.: Crown Publishers, Inc., 1970.

Greene, Liz, and Howard Sasportas. *Dynamics of the Unconscious. Seminars in Psychological Astrology.* Vol. 2. York Beach, Maine: Samuel Weiser, Inc., 1989.

Greene, Liz, and Howard Sasportas. *The Luminaries. The Psychology of the Sun and Moon in the Horoscope.* York Beach, Maine: Samuel Weiser, Inc., 1992.

Greer, Mary K., and Rachel Pollack, eds. *New Thoughts on Tarot.* North Hollywood, Calif.: Newcastle Publishing Co., Inc., 1989.

Greer, Mary K. *The Complete Book of Tarot Reversals.* St. Paul, Minn.: Llewellyn Worldwide, 2002.

Greer, Mary K. *Tarot Constellations. Patterns of Personal Destiny.* North Hollywood, Calif.: Newcastle Publishing Co., Inc., 1987.

Greer, Mary K. *Tarot for Your Self. A Workbook for Personal Transformation.* North Hollywood, Calif.: Newcastle Publishing Co., Inc., 1984.

Greer, Mary K. *Tarot for Your Self. A Workbook for Personal Transformation.* 2d ed. Franklin Lakes, N.J.: New Page Books, 2002.

Greer, Mary K. *Tarot Mirrors. Reflections of Personal Meaning.* North Hollywood, Calif.: Newcastle Publishing Co., Inc., 1988.

Greer, M. K. *Women of the Golden Dawn.* Rochester, Vermont: Park Street Press, 1995.

Guiley, Rosemary Ellen, and Robert M. Place. *The Alchemical Tarot.* London: Thorsons, 1995.

Gwain, Rose *Discovering Your Self Through the Tarot: A Jungian Guide to Archetypes & Personality.* Rochester, Va.: Destiny Books, 1994.

Hamaker-Zondag, Karen. *Tarot as a Way of Life. A Jungian Approach to the Tarot.* York Beach, Maine: Samuel Weiser, Inc., 1997.

Hand, Robert. *Horoscope Symbols.* West Chester, Pa.: Whitford Press, 1981.

Hansson, Susan. *Reading Tarot Cards: A Guide to The New Palladini Tarot.* Stamford, Conn.: U.S. Games Systems, Inc., 1996.

Harding, M. Esther. *Woman's Mysteries: Ancient and Modern.* Boston: Shambhala, 1990.

The Herder Symbolic Dictionary. Translated by Boris Matthews. Wilmette, Ill.: Chiron Publications, 1986.

Hoover, Tracey. *The Ancestral Path Tarot.* Stamford, Conn.: U.S. Games Systems, Inc., 1996.

Houston, Jean. *A Mythic Life. Learning to Live Our Greater Story.* New York: HarperSanFrancisco, 1996.

Hulse, David Allen. *New Dimensions for the Cube of Space.* York Beach, Maine: Samuel Weiser, Inc., 2000.

Hulse, David Allen. *The Western Mysteries: An Encyclopedic Guide to the Sacred Languages and Magickal Systems of the World: The Key of It All. Book 2.* St. Paul, Minn.: Llewellyn Publications, 2000.

Jackson, Nigel. *The Nigel Jackson Tarot.* St. Paul, Minn.: Llewellyn Publications, 2000.

Jacoby, Mario A. *Longing for Paradise: Psychological Perspectives on an Archetype.* Translated by Myron B. Gubitz. Boston: Sigo Press, 1985.

Japikse, Carl. *Exploring the Tarot.* Columbus, Ohio: Ariel Press, 1989.

Jayanti, Amber. *Living the Tarot.* St. Paul, Minn.: Llewellyn Publications, 1993.

Jette, Christine. *Tarot Shadow Work. Using the Dark Symbols to Heal.* St. Paul, Minn.: Llewellyn Publications, 2000.

Jobes, Gertrude, and James Jobes. *Outer Space: Myths, Name Meanings, Calendars.* New York: The Scarecrow Press, Inc., 1964.

Johari, Harish. *Breath, Mind, and Consciousness.* Rochester, Va.: Destiny Books, 1990.

Johnson, Robert. A. *Owning Your Own Shadow: Understanding the Dark Side of the Psyche.* San Francisco: Harper & Row, 1991.

Judith, Anodea. *Eastern Body, Western Mind; Psychology and the Chakra System as a Path to the Self.* Berkeley: Celestial Arts Publishing, 1996.

Jung, C. G. *Four Archetypes: Mother, Rebirth, Spirit, Trickster*. Translated by R. F. C. Hull. London: Routledge & Kegan Paul, 1972.

Kliegman, Isabel Radow. *Tarot and the Tree of Life. Finding Everyday Wisdom in the Minor Arcana*. Wheaton, Ill.: Quest Books, 1997.

Knight, Gareth. *A Practical Guide to Qabalistic Symbolism*. 2 vols. in one. York Beach, Maine: Samuel Weiser, Inc., 1978.

Knight, Gareth. *The Magical World of the Tarot*. York Beach, Maine: Samuel Weiser, Inc., 1996.

Knight, Gareth. *Tarot and Magic. Images for Rituals and Pathworking*. Rochester, Vermont: Destiny Books, 1991.

Kraig, Donald Michael. "A New Tarot Paradigm." *The Tarot Journal* Vol. 1, No. 1 (Spring 2001): 13–15.

Leach, Maria, ed., and Jerome Fried, assoc. ed. *Funk & Wagnalls Standard Dictionary of Folklore, Mythology, and Legend*. San Francisco: Harper & Row, 1972.

Lethbridge, Judi. "The Hermit, the Hand, and the Hankie." *The ATA Newsletter*, Vol. 6, No. 2 (Spring 2001): 15–16.

Lionel, Frederic. *The Magic Tarot. Vehicle of Eternal Wisdom*. London: Routledge & Kegan Paul, 1982.

Lippmann, Walter. *Public Opinion*. New York: Harcourt Brace, 1922.

McCormack, Kathleen. *Tarot Decoder*. Hauppauge, N.Y.: Barron's, 1998.

May, Rollo. *The Meaning of Anxiety*. New York: The Ronald Press Co., 1950.

Metzner, Ralph. *The Well of Remembrance*. Boston & London: Shambhala, 1994.

Moore, Thomas. *Care of the Soul*. New York: HarperPerennial, 1992.

Morgan, Ffiona. *Daughters of the Moon Tarot*. Rev. ed. Novato, Calif.: Daughters of the Moon, 2000.

Myss, Caroline. *Anatomy of the Spirit*. New York: Three Rivers Press, 1996.

Newman, Kenneth D. *The Tarot. A Myth of Male Initiation*. New York: C. G. Jung Foundation for Analytical Psychology, 1983.

Nichols, Sallie. *Jung and Tarot. An Archetypal Journey*. York Beach, Maine: Samuel Weiser, Inc., 1980.

Norman, D. *The Hero: Myth/Image/Symbol*. New York & Cleveland: World, 1969.

O'Kane, Françoise. *Sacred Chaos. Reflections on God's Shadow and the Dark Self*. Toronto, Canada: Inner City Books, 1994.

O'Neill, Robert V. *Tarot Symbolism*. Lima, Ohio: Fairway Press, 1986.

Opsopaus, John. *Pythagorean Tarot*. St. Paul, Minn.: Llewellyn Publications, 2001.

Osho International Foundation. *Osho Zen Tarot: The Transcendental Game of Zen*. New York: St. Martin's Press, 1994.

Pascal, Eugene. *Jung to Live By*. New York: Warner Books, 1992.

Payne-Towler, Christine. *The Underground Stream*. Eugene, Oregon: Noreah Press, 1999.

Pollack, Rachel. *The Complete Illustrated Guide to Tarot*. Shaftesbury, Dorset, England: Element Books, Ltd., 1999.

Pollack, Rachel. *The Haindl Tarot*. Vol. I, *The Major Arcana*. North Hollywood, Calif.: Newcastle Publishing, Inc., 1990.

Pollack, Rachel. *The Haindl Tarot*. Vol. II, *The Minor Arcana*. North Hollywood, Calif.: Newcastle Publishing, Inc., 1990.

Pollack, Rachel. *Seventy-eight Degrees of Wisdom*. Part I, *The Major Arcana*. Wellingborough, Northamptonshire: The Aquarian Press, 1980.

Pollack, Rachel *Seventy-eight Degrees of Wisdom*. Part 2, *The Minor Arcana and Readings*. Wellingborough, Northamptonshire: The Aquarian Press, 1983.

Pollack, Rachel. *Shining Tribe Tarot: Awakening the Universal Spirit*. St. Paul, Minn.: Llewellyn Worldwide, 2001.

Poncé, Charles. *The Game of Wizards: Roots of Consciousness & the Esoteric Arts*. Wheaton, Ill.: Quest Books, 1991.

Prosapio, Richard. *Intuitive Tarot*. Dobbs Ferry, N.Y.: Morgan & Morgan, 1990.

Quntanna, Beatrex. *Tarot: A Universal Language*. Carlsbad, Calif.: Art Ala Carte Publishing, 1989.

Regardie, Israel. *The Complete Golden Dawn System of Magic*. Ten volumes in one. Phoenix, Ariz.: Falcon Press, 1984.

Ricklef, James. *KnightHawk's Tarot Readings*. San Jose: Writers Club Press, 2001.

Roob, Alexander *Alchemy and Mysticism*. Cologne: Taschen, 1997.

Rosengarten, Arthur. *Tarot and Psychology. Spectrums of Possibility*. St. Paul, Minn.: Paragon House, 2000.

Saunders, E. Dale. *Mudra. A Study of Symbolic Gestures in Japanese Buddhist Sculpture*. Princeton, N.J.: Princeton University Press, 1960.

Sells, Benjamin, ed. *Working with Images. The Theoretical Base of Archetypal Psychology*. Woodstock, Conn.: Spring Publications, 2000.

Sharman-Burke, Juliet. *The Complete Book of Tarot*. New York: St. Martin's Griffin, 1985.

Sharman-Burke, Juliet. *Mastering the Tarot. An Advanced Personal Teaching Guide*. New York: St. Martin's Griffin, 2000.

Sharman-Burke, Juliet. *Understanding the Tarot. A Personal Teaching Guide*. New York: St. Martin's Griffin, 1998.

Sharman-Burke, Juliet and Liz Greene. *The Mythic Tarot*. New York: A Fireside Book, 1986.

Siebert, Al. "The Survivor Personality." Paper presented at the annual meeting of the Western Psychological Association, San Francisco, April 1983.

Sterling, Stephen Walter. *Tarot Awareness: Exploring the Spiritual Path*. St. Paul, Minn.: Llewellyn Publications, 2000.

Stevens, Anthony. *Ariadne's Clue. A Guide to the Symbols of Humankind*. Princeton, N.J.: Princeton University Press, 1999.

Steventon, Kay. *Spiral Tarot. A Story of the Cycles of Life*. Stamford, Conn.: U.S. Games Systems, Inc., 1998.

Stewart, R. J. *The UnderWorld Initiation. A Journey Towards Psychic Transformation*. Lake Toxaway, N.C.: Mercury Publishing, Inc., 1998.

Teilhard de Chardin, Pierre. *The Divine Milieu*. New York: Harper & Row, 1960.

Thomson, Sandra A., Robert E. Mueller, and Signe E. Echols. *The Heart of the Tarot*. San Francisco: HarperSanFrancisco, 2000.

Tresidder, Jack. *Dictionary of Symbols*. San Francisco: Chronicle Books, 1998.

von Franz, Marie-Louise. *Alchemy. An Introduction to the Symbolism and the Psychology*. Toronto, Canada: Inner City Books, 1980.

von Franz, Marie-Louise. *Archetypal Dimensions of the Psyche*. Boston & London: Shambhala, 1999.

von Franz, Marie-Louise. *Archetypal Patterns in Fairy Tales*. Toronto, Canada: Inner City Books, 1997.

von Franz, Marie-Louise. *Aurora Consurgens: A Document Attributed to Thomas Aquinas on the Problem of Opposites in Alchemy*. New York: Bollingen, 1966.

von Franz, Marie-Louise. *The Cat. A Tale of Feminine Redemption*. Toronto, Canada: Inner City Books, 1999.

von Franz, Marie-Louise. *C. G. Jung. His Myth in Our Time*. Toronto, Canada: Inner City Books, 1998.

von Franz, Marie-Louise. *Individuation in Fairy Tales*. Boston & London: Shambhala, 1990.

von Franz, Marie-Louise. *The Interpretation of Fairy Tales*. Rev. ed. Boston & London: Shambhala, 1996.

von Franz, Marie-Louise *Number and Time*. Evanston, Ill.: Northwestern University Press, 1974.

von Franz, Marie-Louise. *On Divination and Synchronicity. The Psychology of Meaningful Chance*. Toronto, Canada: Inner City Books, 1980.

von Franz, Marie-Louise. *The Psychological Meaning of Redemption Motifs in Fairytales*. Toronto, Canada: Inner City Books, 1980.

von Franz, Marie-Louise. *Shadow and Evil in Fairy Tales*. Boston & London, Shambhala, 1995.

von Oech, Roger. *A Whack on the Side of the Head*. New York: Warner, 1983.

Waite, Arthur Edward. *The Pictorial Key to the Tarot*. Stamford, Conn.: U.S. Games Systems, Inc., 1997.

Walker, Barbara G. *The Woman's Dictionary of Symbols and Sacred Objects*. San Francisco: HarperSanFrancisco, 1988.

Walker, Barbara G. *The Woman's Encyclopedia of Myths and Secrets*. San Francisco: Harper & Row, 1983.

Walker, Barbara G. *The Secrets of the Tarot. Origins, History, and Symbolism*. San Francisco: Harper & Row, 1984.

Wang, Robert. *An Introduction to the Golden Dawn Tarot*. York Beach, Maine: Samuel Weiser, Inc., 1978.

Wang, Robert. *The Qabalistic Tarot*. York Beach, Maine: Samuel Weiser, Inc., 1983.

Wang, Robert. *Tarot Psychology*. Germany: Urania Verlags Ag, 1988.

Wanless, James. *Voyager Tarot: Way of the Great Oracle*. Carmel, Calif.: Merrill-West Publishing, 1989.

Whitmont, Edward C. *Return of the Goddess*. New York: Continuum, 1997.

Whitmont, Edward C. *The Symbolic Quest. Basic Concepts of Analytical Psychology*. Princeton, New Jersey: Princeton University Press, 1991.

Williams, Brian. *A Renaissance Tarot*. Stamford, Conn.: U.S. Games Systems, Inc., 1994.

Williams, Brian and Michael Goepferd. *The Light and Shadow Tarot*. Rochester, Va.: Destiny Books, 1997.

Wirth, Oswald. *The Tarot of the Magicians*. York Beach, Maine: Samuel Weiser, Inc., 1985.

Wood, Robin. *The Robin Wood Tarot: The Book*. Dearborn, Michigan: Livingtree, 1998.

Woodman, Marion and Elinor Dickson. *Dancing in the Flames: The Dark Goddess in the Transformation of Consciousness*. Boston: Shambhala, 1997.

Wren, M. K. *King of the Mountain*. New York: Ballantine Books, 1994.